Financial Literacy for Children and Youth

SECOND EDITION

This book is part of the Peter Lang Education list.
Every volume is peer reviewed and meets
the highest quality standards for content and production.

PETER LANG
New York • Bern • Berlin
Brussels • Vienna • Oxford • Warsaw

Financial Literacy for Children and Youth

SECOND EDITION

Thomas A. Lucey &
Kathleen S. Cooter, Editors

PETER LANG
New York • Bern • Berlin
Brussels • Vienna • Oxford • Warsaw

Library of Congress Cataloging-in-Publication Data
Names: Lucey, Thomas A., editor. | Cooter, Kathleen Spencer, editor.
Title: Financial literacy for children and youth /
[edited by] Thomas Lucey & Kathleen Cooter.
Description: Second edition. | New York: Peter Lang, 2018.
Identifiers: LCCN 2017036570 | ISBN 978-1-4331-3361-9 (hardback: alk. paper)
ISBN 978-1-4331-3360-2 (paperback: alk. paper)
ISBN 978-1-4331-4504-9 (ebook pdf)
ISBN 978-1-4331-4505-6 (epub) | ISBN 978-1-4331-4506-3 (mobi)
Subjects: LCSH: Financial literacy—Study and teaching.
Finance, Personal—Study and teaching.
Education—Social aspects.
Classification: LCC HG179 .F4629 2018 | DDC 372.37/4—dc23
LC record available at https://lccn.loc.gov/2017036570
DOI 10.3726/b11307

Bibliographic information published by **Die Deutsche Nationalbibliothek**.
Die Deutsche Nationalbibliothek lists this publication in the "Deutsche
Nationalbibliografie"; detailed bibliographic data are available
on the Internet at http://dnb.d-nb.de/.

The paper in this book meets the guidelines for permanence and durability
of the Committee on Production Guidelines for Book Longevity
of the Council of Library Resources.

© 2018 Peter Lang Publishing, Inc., New York
29 Broadway, 18th floor, New York, NY 10006
www.peterlang.com

All rights reserved.
Reprint or reproduction, even partially, in all forms such as microfilm,
xerography, microfiche, microcard, and offset strictly prohibited.

Printed in the United States of America

Table of Contents

List of Excerpts, Figures, and Tables vii
Introduction 1

Part One: Definitions 5
Chapter One: The Hidden Curriculum in Financial Literacy: Economics,
    Standards, and the Teaching of Young Children 7
    Debbie Sonu and Anand R. Marri
Chapter Two: Meaning and Money Revisited 27
    Mary E. Brenner
Chapter Three: Random Acts of Financial Literacy 33
    Kathleen S. Cooter
Chapter Four: Strategies and Resources for Teaching Financial
    Literacy to Youth with Disabilities 49
    Mary Beth Henning and Sarah Johnston-Rodriguez

Part Two: Instructional Issues 67
Chapter Five: Instructional Integration of Digital Learning Games in
    Financial Literacy Education 69
    Carmela Aprea, Julia Schultheis, and Kathleen Stolle
Chapter Six: Teaching Financial Literacy through the Arts: Theoretical
    Underpinnings and Guidelines for Lesson Development 89
    James D. Laney

Chapter Seven: Students' Money Experiences and Preconceptions of
    Financial Issues—Implications for Effective Financial Education 109
    Bettina Greimel-Fuhrmann
Chapter Eight: Financial Literacy and Youths in Jail 121
    Jaime Christensen
Chapter Nine: Teaching Probability and Learning Financial Concepts:
    How to Empower Elementary School Students in Citizenship 137
    Annie Savard
Chapter Ten: The Influence of Teacher Attributes on Financial
    Education Outcomes 153
    J. Michael Collins, Elizabeth Odders-White, and Nilton Porto
Chapter Eleven: Economic Inequality and Secondary Mathematics 169
    Andrew Brantlinger
Chapter Twelve: Personal Finance Education for Young Children:
    Why Isn't It Happening? What Needs to Be Done? 189
    Bonnie T. Meszaros and Mary C. Suiter

Part Three: Socio-Historic Moral Issues 209
Chapter Thirteen: A Representation of Vulnerability in National Strategies:
    Targeting the Needs of Disadvantaged Consumers with Financial
    Education and Inclusion Efforts 211
    Floor E. Knoote and Sofia L. Ortega Tineo
Chapter Fourteen: Grasping the Foundational Roots of Economic
    Perceptions: Precolonial West Africa and the Bantu 233
    Thomas A. Lucey, Darrell P. Kruger, and Jeffrey M. Hawkins
Chapter Fifteen: Using Stories to Teach Complex Moral Concepts to
    Young Children 251
    Chiara Bacigalupa
Chapter Sixteen: Economics, Religion, Spirituality, and Education:
    Encouraging Understandings of Compassionate Dimensions 269
    Thomas A. Lucey
Chapter Seventeen: Behavioral Economics: Making High School
    Economics Personal 285
    Kathleen S. Cooter

Contributors 297

Excerpts, Figures, AND Tables

Excerpts

Excerpt 11.1: Initial Student Response to the Initial CM Writing Prompt 175
Excerpt 11.2: Critical Student Agency in Small Groups during CM 177
Excerpt 11.3: Critical Whole Class Discussion of Economic Fairness 179

Figures

Figure 6.1: Discipline-based Art Education 96
Figure 8.1: Pretest Results Percentage Scores on Lifeschool 2000
    Assessment 127
Figure 8.2: Pretest/Posttest Comparison 130
Figure 8.3: Data for Joe 131
Figure 8.4: Data for Cory 131
Figure 8.5: Data for Stuart 132
Figure 9.1: Game Board 145
Figure 9.2: The Financial Context in Relation to the Other
    Contexts Present in the Classroom 149

Tables

Table 3.1: Mean Survey Scores Contrasted by Subject Area Taught 37
Table 3.2: Means and Analysis of Variance by Preparation 37

Table 5.1: Duration, Contents, and Superordinate Competencies
of the Five Game-based Learning Modules 80
Table 9.1: Financial Literacy Concepts 140
Table 10.1: Summary Teacher Survey Responses (Average of
All Lessons Reported), N = 43 157
Table 10.2: Summary Teacher Survey Responses (Average of
All Lessons Reported), N = 43 158
Table 10.3: Teacher Self-Efficacy and Student Outcomes (Means) 160
Table 10.4: Teacher Self-Efficacy and Student Outcomes (OLS) 161
Table 10.5: Correlations 161
Table 10.6: Teacher Self-Efficacy and Other Attitudes (N = 43) 162
Table 10.7: Teacher Attitudes and Student Outcomes (OLS) 163
Table 16.1: Framework for a Fulfilling Curriculum 279

Introduction

Every book is written in a context—a period of time and place reflected in its contents and thinking. As we considered this text—*Financial Literacy for Children and Youth 2nd Edition*—we marveled at the vast differences between our first compilation in 2008 and the present context of 2018. The rumblings and fall out of the great recession had just begun then and words like junk bonds, subprime mortgage, bailouts, derivatives, and housing bubble had not yet become part of the daily vernacular of the ordinary American. At the same time, we should not ignore the economic and political interfacings that shape our global landscape. Just as educators need to acknowledge teaching as a social and political act to fully conceptualize the teaching profession, financial educators need to acknowledge the ideological lenses through which they conceptualize their teaching and learning to fully conceptualize the social nuances of financial literacies.

Thus, clearly the socioeconomic groups most affected at the time and still recovering are those who lacked wealth or skill sets or opportunities to withstand the crisis. Yet, the framework through which one construes his or her plight undergirds his or her financial literacy. The extent to which financial literacy espouses a pedagogy of merit and blame or reflection and social responsibility to a large degree shapes interpretations of these conditions. At the same time, it is important to avoid a binary us/them mind-set by recognizing the potential for error in all social participants. The recession triggered and/or reinforced a lack of trust in politicians, government in general and certainly the financial industry. While it is impolitic to place blame at any one door, society, as a community founded on principles of trust and honesty, suffered, often greatly.

Was trust misplaced? Obviously, yes. Yet, when the focus of financial literacy relates wealth accumulation rather than social welfare, one may expect such dishonesty. The human condition involves a blend of selfishness and selflessness. It requires both independence and community. Such is the case with patterns of disinformation and social illiteracy. To assume the citizenry were simply deceived diminishes them to ciphers in the views of the privileged elite. Perhaps the broader question relates to personal finances and values. To what extent do existent financial theories and applications reinforce social ideologies that maintain a hierarchical system founded on principles of resource control and objectification? To what extent may financial education acknowledge the validity of human existence as representing one of sacrifice and cooperation versus domination and superiority?

More aptly, they lacked faith in an ethical framework to make financial and life decisions founded on compassion for others. They trusted a system in which they did not fully understand the risks of an invitation to a financial quagmire that ultimately unveiled its dangers and resulted in dire consequences for the unsuspecting. Financial naiveté is a better descriptor perhaps. The painful daily actualities brought about by the great recession for many millions of Americans alerts us to the reality that a decontextualized approach to financial literacy portends critical risks for the public at large. The importance of financial literacy extends beyond political boundaries. As Bobbitt (2002) observes, our global world's evolution beyond nation state political identities to market state relationships founded on economic identities and associations. Efforts to forge international efforts in developing children's financial literacy (see https://childfinanceinternational.org/cyfi/board.html) and assemble scholarship (e.g., Aprea et al., 2016) represent important steps in fostering global discourse occur; however, founding these processes on contributions from academics representing a variety of disciplines that provide a balanced perspective that can help assuage the ill-advised policies of financial experts founded on narcissistic premises and build the trust of naïve populations who suffer from flawed decisions.

As we put this edition together, we write it with the knowledge that there is a vast chasm on this planet between the haves and the have-nots. Those individuals at the top of the business or industry have immense wealth—beyond any seen in this global history. And yet the latest statistics in the United States cite about 15 million children in the United States—21% of all children—live in families with incomes below the federal poverty threshold, a measurement that has been shown to underestimate the needs of families (www.nccp.org/topics/childpoverty.html). We also recognize the research that clearly identifies a correlational relationship between states and countries' conditions for quality of living with wealth gaps between rich and poor (e.g., Wilkinson & Pickett, 2011). Areas of high wealth disparity face greater social risk than those of low wealth disparity.

Research by the George Washington University economics professor Annamaria Lusardi, Michaud, and Mitchell (2013) has documented the gaps in financial knowledge among different demographic groups. The data on financial literacy show that financial knowledge is unequally distributed; those with the least knowledge are also the most vulnerable groups in economic terms. As a result, the lack of financial literacy exacerbates economic inequality. Lusardi's own analysis has estimated that more than one-third of wealth inequality could be accounted for by disparities in financial knowledge. At the same time, we cannot ignore the contextual meaning of financial literacy and the different life conditions that impose various applications of its meaning. What passes for a personal financial life cycle in corporate America differs from a personal financial life cycle in rural Zimbabwe.

It is in this context—an America with startling polarities and extremes in standards of living and more importantly visions for a future, that we offer this text. We feel strongly that financial literacy is far more than money and wealth accumulation; it is the ability to live a life of fulfillment and opportunity. Financial literacy is a tool and life skill assisting people to realize their potential—it is choices and opportunities for all. And yet, as Adam Smith (1759/1976) observed, a person's loss of money represents only a loss in imagination.

We think it time, as a community, to consider whether it is money that defines us or whether we need more focus on a more fluid basis for defining ourselves. To maintain a society where people cannot achieve their life goals because of their station at birth ignores the reality that people do not choose the social context of their origins. Economic status represents a privilege. We assume the readers and students of this text are in agreement; yet at the same time, we recognize the possibility that they may not and we understand and appreciate the bases of reasoning that may cause this difference of interpretation to occur.

To this end, we feel it ethically bereft to assign financial literacy to the back burner of curricula in elementary, middle or high school and certainly in preservice teacher education—thus this book and its offerings. We acknowledge that this book is but a small piece of an overall financial curriculum, but suggest that it offers a great deal of information that will assist teacher and scholars in this work.

ABOUT THE BOOK

This edition, like the first, is a pedagogical, theoretical and sociohistorical perspective of the importance of financial literacy to schools and to the life outcomes of young people. Each section reflects one of those perspectives and each chapter "fits" into the one of those perspectives. There is a set of questions at the end of each chapter for assessment and/or discussion to facilitate its use as a text in postsecondary programs.

We are very excited to present nine new chapters in this edition. In the ten years since the first edition, knowledge and interpretation of financial literacy has broadened and we anticipate these new chapters will expand the conversation in their respective areas. We also present chapters in this edition that are reprinted from the first edition but updated and revised to reflect new learnings and research findings. These chapters have been selected for the unique issues and perspectives in financial literacy that they present and with the hope that they spark further community inquiry and dialogue.

This book will appeal to teacher candidates as the chapters offer theory and pragmatic lesson planning activities that are both rigorous and real world. Common core standards as well as other state standards demand instruction in personal finance and personal economics. We believe that the ideas and concepts presented here are varied and will greatly assist the practicing teacher in implementation. Sections one and two are of particular interest to the practitioner for those reasons. Section three explores in depth the complex sociohistorical and moral connections offering to both teacher and scholar opportunities for deep analysis and challenging perspectives.

Each chapter is designed to stand alone or to be used in conjunction with other chapters. We believe that the variation in topic and presentation is both informative and lively. We welcome you to this second edition and hope it is useful in your work as well as seen as a contribution to positive societal change, particularly for those who are most vulnerable.

REFERENCES

Aprea, C., Wuttke, E., Breuer, K., Koh, N. K., Davies, P., Greimel-Fuhrmann, B., & Lopus, J. S. (Eds.). (2016). *International handbook of financial literacy.* Singapore: Springer.

Bobbitt, P. (2002). *The shield of Achilles: War, peace, and the course of history.* New York, NY: Knopf.

Lusardi, A., Michaud, P.-C., & Mitchell, O. S. (2013, January). *Optimal financial knowledge and wealth inequality.* The National Bureau of Economic Research. NBER Working Paper No. 18669.

Smith, A. (1759/1976). *The theory of moral sentiments.* D. D. Raphael & A. L. MacFee (Eds.). Oxford: Clarendon Press.

Wilkinson, R., & Pickett, K. (2011). *The spirit level: Why greater equality makes societies stronger.* New York, NY: Penguin Books.

PART ONE
Definitions

CHAPTER ONE

The Hidden Curriculum IN Financial Literacy

Economics, Standards, and the Teaching of Young Children

DEBBIE SONU

Hunter College, City University of New York

ANAND R. MARRI

Teachers College, Columbia University and Federal Reserve Bank of New York

INTRODUCTION

Public schools in the United States carry the potential to forward a conception of citizenship that cultivates democratically oriented and informed individuals (Dewey, 1927). Educating such a citizenry involves attending to the intellectual and moral dimensions of humanness and examining the economic, political, and social forces that affect lives and the lives of others. Myriad interpretations of citizenship include a pragmatic focus on civic duty and activity (NCCS, 2013; Westheimer & Kahne, 2004), those that aim for social transformation and economic justice (Freire, 1970; Macrine, McLaren, & Hill, 2011), neoliberal approaches to individualism and material security (Stern, 1998), as well as postmodern concerns over plurality, subjectivity, and existentialism (Biesta, 2011). While notions of citizenship are inflected in all subject areas, social studies in particular seeks to cultivate a kind of civic competence that promotes the content knowledge, intellectual processes, and democratic dispositions required of students to be active and engaged participants in public life (NCSS, 2013). In addition, the solidification of neoliberal school cultures has piqued interest in the adoption of economic education in the primary grades, so much so that teaching about the economy may become just as critical as teaching students reading, writing, and numeracy skills.

Economic literacy includes the capacity to rationally identify economic problems, alternatives, costs, and benefits; analyze the incentives at work; examine the consequences of change; collect and organize evidence; and weigh costs against benefits (Marri, 2014; NCREL, 2003; Salemi, 2005). It involves an understanding of the decisions that drive public policy at the macro (fiscal and monetary policy) level and the ability to make informed choices at the micro (personal finance) level of everyday life. Financial literacy, a component of economic literacy, focuses on the ability of adults and children to use knowledge and skills to manage their financial resources effectively (Dorado, 2011). Gary Stern (1998), former President of the Federal Reserve Bank of Minneapolis, described financial literacy as a curriculum aimed to ensure that teachers and students understand the economic forces that significantly impact the quality of their lives. Financial literacy, as a proposed curriculum in schools, has been supported by the U.S. Department of Labor, the U.S. Department of Education, The National Council on Economic Education, with a 1999 symposium, "The Economic Literacy Project: Seeing a Blueprint for America," attended by over 60 representatives of academia, business, labor, K–12 education, consumers, government and financial institutions.

Educators, then, are asked to incorporate economic literacy as fundamental to preparing students for active and engaged democratic citizenship (Marri, 2014). When they go to the polls or engage in civic activities, active and engaged democratic citizens should use their economic literacy skills to understand how their choices connect to their own economic well-being as the well-being of the nation as a whole. While there will always be forces beyond individual control, economic literacy can be understood as a means to increase a young person's chances of being self-reliant and independent enough to stave off difficulties during times of austerity or recession. At the elementary, or primary school level, economic literacy focuses specifically on how children make decisions about their imagined personal finances in order to increase their chances of maintaining a level of material comfort and security in the future.

In this chapter, we analyze EngageNY's new collection of social studies curricular and instructional resources that speak directly to financial literacy in each of the lower elementary grade levels kindergarten through second, ages 5–8. These resources, released in May 2015 by the New York State Education Department (NYSED), support "key aspects" as determined by the New York State Board of Regents, the governing body responsible for the general supervision of all educational activities within the state. Although the curriculum suggested on the EngageNY website is not mandated—all curriculum decisions are local decisions in New York—the instructional resources on this website were the first, and for some time, the only examples of Common Core aligned lessons available to educators who found themselves forced to make drastic changes in their previous teaching standards and pedagogies. Therefore, the publication of financial literacy materials via the EngageNY website not only reaches a wide audience of educators who have become accustomed to using the website as a place to locate approved "best practices," but also becomes a contested site through which certain values, attitudes, and political conceptions of citizenship become legitimized and forwarded.

Using the typology of social studies education developed by Barr, Barth, and Shermis (1977), we analyze this curriculum to discern the types of messages engrained within them. In doing so, we explore how the official knowledge (Apple, 1993) of financial literacy carries with it an overt and hidden curriculum that expects students to adopt certain economic beliefs and principles, specifically those that align to neoclassical economics. Neoclassical economics, the most mainstream understanding of Keynesian economics, focuses on the determination of goods, outputs, and income distributions in markets and orients individuals toward the use of rational decision-making to maximize utility and profit. Analyzing for hidden curriculum acknowledges that in addition to content and skills, curriculum is always an imbrication of cultural values, judgments, and dispositions that influence beliefs about who we are as individuals, as well as our existence within communities and as part of the national and global landscape.

To better understand how curriculum shapes various notions of citizenship, we supplement the Barr et al. (1977) typology, applied to the financial literacy units, with the work of Joel Westheimer and Joseph Kahne (2004). Westheimer and Kahne conducted a two-year study of 10 educational programs across the United States and used democratic theory to develop a framework on the types of desirable citizens promoted in schools. By doing this, we are able to read the EngageNY curriculum at the intersections of social studies and citizenship, pushing our analysis below the surface of mere representation and literal text, and at the end of each section, present suggestions for classroom practice and further thoughts on the economic education of young children in New York City public schools.

CURRICULUM BACKGROUND

The NYSED, in conjunction with the release of the curriculum, provides educators with the Social Studies Resource Tool Kit. NYSED designed the toolkit to put instructional and curriculum design tools into the hands of teachers and instructional leaders in local districts (NYSED, 2015). The Toolkit resources focus on helping teachers implement the Inquiry Arc of The College, Career, and Civic Life (C3) Framework for Social Studies State Standards through four dimensions: (1) developing questions and planning inquiries, (2) applying disciplinary concepts and tools, (3) evaluating sources and using evidence, and (4) communicating conclusions and taking informed action.

NYSED claims to have hired K–12 New York State teachers to craft inquiries, which serve as the centerpiece of the Toolkit (NYSED, 2015). Accordingly, these inquiries set a curricular and instructional course that teachers can consider in light of the NY Framework. Although the inquiries may have been intended to enable teachers to bring in their professional expertise and knowledge of successful instructional practice, rather than scripts or modules for teachers to follow, the curriculum is presented with specific directives with little to no content knowledge.

For each grade level, the tool kit provides six suggested inquiry topics that include the usual subjects of identity, maps and geography, civic ideals, government, and immigration. The kit also includes an inquiry based on an understanding of financial literacy and economics. This release marked a concerted effort to include discussions of money and exchange at the elementary grades (https://www.engageny.org/resource/new-york-state-k-12-social-studies-resource-toolkit-kindergarten-grade-4) in New York State. We present the conceptual framework used for the chapter in the section before presenting our analysis of the K–2 curricula.

CONCEPTUAL FRAMEWORK

The Barr et al. (1977) typology categorizes social studies curriculum and pedagogy into three historical traditions: citizenship transmission, social science, or reflective inquiry.

The citizenship transmission tradition works from the premise that citizenship is best promoted by instilling proper values for making decisions in civic life. For example, it relies on direct transmission and exposition of these values by the teacher; indirect transmission through student discovery of correct interpretation; and an unquestioned acceptance of current society. Teachers or other instructional leaders select curricula/content to function as the illustration of values, beliefs, and attitudes, relying on textbooks, recitation, lecture, question and answer sessions, and structured problem-solving exercises to convey content (White, 1982). Despite numerous iterations and critiques of Barr et al.'s (1977) notation of citizenship transmission, it is generally understood as a structural-functionalist approach that positions school as transmitting the social norms and values that prepare students to conform to the existing social structure.

Social studies as a social science (Barr et al., 1977) serves as the purpose, method, and content through which to acquire knowledge that is self-justifying and self-validating. Teachers have students emulate the social scientist, not only by grasping the structure of the discipline, but also in learning the mode of inquiry characterizing certain disciplines. In the social science tradition, educators promote citizenship as the mastery of social science principles, processes, and problems.

Since social scientists have their own methods for gathering and verifying knowledge, teachers can help students discover and apply appropriate methods through the structure, concepts, problems, and processes drawn from the social science disciplines (Barr et al., 1977; Misco & Hamot, 2012; White, 1982).

Finally, the reflective inquiry tradition promotes citizenship through a process of inquiry whereby citizens examine multiple sources of data and determine courses of action that resolve identified problems. In this domain, teachers engage students in a self-reflection process that analyzes the values and interests of others in a society and responds to conflicts through the testing of situational insights (Misco & Hamot, 2012; Vinson, 1998; White, 1982). How these three typologies appear in the EngageNY financial literacy curriculum is presented in the section on analysis and discussion.

Over time no single notion of citizenship and civic education has prevailed (Ross, 2006; Westheimer & Kahne, 2004). Political scientists, politicians, historians, civic educators, parents, and community organizers continue to contest varying and contrasting conceptions of citizenship and civic education (Connolly, 1983; Levine, 2007). These conceptions are by no means neutral. In fact, each promotes particular ways of knowing, relating, and acting (Parker, 2001). Unsurprisingly, long-standing debates on the meaning of "good" citizenship have resulted in significantly varying implications for curriculum and pedagogy in classrooms. In this chapter, we supplement the Barr et al. (1977) typology by using the Westheimer and Kahne (2004) framework to examine the types of economic citizenship promoted by the NYS curricula.

THREE TYPES OF CITIZENSHIP AND CIVIC EDUCATION

In an overview of the landscape of social studies and civic education, Westheimer and Kahne (2004) provide three types of citizenship promoted in schools: the personally responsible citizen, the participatory citizen, and the justice-oriented citizen. Their categorization is based on an analysis of leading social studies educators and classroom practices of teachers. We chose to use their three categories as they capture the varying and contrasting conceptions of citizenship and civic education in the field of social studies education (Barr et al., 1977; Ross, 2006; Stanley & Nelson, 1994). These categories also resonate well with the work of classroom teachers, administrators, and curriculum writers (Westheimer & Kahne, 2004). In other words, these categories capture many common classroom practices of K–12 educators by focusing on content-centered approaches from the academic disciplines and issue-centered approaches examining specific issues.

The teaching of personally responsible citizens includes forwarding such characteristics as honesty, integrity, self-discipline, and hard work (Lickona, 1993;

Westheimer & Kahne, 2004; Wynne, 1986). For example, personally responsible citizens would act responsibly in their communities by paying taxes, recycling, donating blood, volunteering at a shelter, or contributing to a food or clothing drive. This vision of citizenship assumes that an improvement of society and a resolution of social problems result from individual actions of law-abiding citizens with good character (Westheimer & Kahne, 2004). Similarly, according to Walter Parker (1996), this notion of citizenship promotes a "traditionalist" view of citizenship in which citizens vote, develop opinions on public policy, hold deep commitments to liberty and justice, and have thorough understanding of the mechanics of democratic institutions, such as governmental agencies and organizations.

Educational practices and programs that promote personally responsible citizenship seek to increase volunteer service among students. Two examples of such programs are Character Counts! and Points of Light. The *Character Counts!* program emphasizes six pillars (trustworthiness, respect, responsibility, fairness, caring, citizenship) and teaches students to "do your share to make your school and community better, cooperate, get involved in community affairs, stay informed, vote, be a good neighbor, obey laws and rules, respect authority, and protect the environment" (http://charactercounts.org/sixpillars.html, retrieved September 28, 2016). Similarly, the Points of Light program emphasizes volunteer service as "fundamental to a purposeful life and essential to a healthy world" (http://www.pointsoflight.org/, retrieved September 28, 2016).

Participatory citizens, in contrast, place emphasis on collective community-based action to improve society and resolve social problems. These citizens seek to actively participate in the civic affairs and the social life of community at the local, state, or national levels (Westheimer & Kahne, 2004). Participatory citizens fit into a "progressive" conceptualization of citizenship in which direct participation goes beyond voting and individual action (Parker, 1996, p. 112). This category values active participation through leadership roles "within established systems and community structures" (Westheimer & Kahne, 2004, p. 240). For example, they organize a food drive rather than only contributing to it through donations. Other participatory activities may include campaigning for a representative, a ballot measure, or running for an elected office. Additionally, participatory activities might include volunteering for a leadership role in government, a nongovernmental agency, a community-based organization, or working toward solutions to local problems with other like-minded citizens.

In the classroom, this vision of citizenship stresses teaching students how to actively participate in community-based and governmental organizations as well as other organized efforts to improve society. Examples of such educational programs are school-based service learning projects, such as Newmann's citizen action curriculum (1975) or Engle's decision-making model (1960). These programs emphasize deliberation on public issues, group problem-solving, and community action.

The third vision of citizenship, justice-oriented citizen, calls for "explicit attention to matters of injustice and to the importance of pursuing social justice" (Westheimer & Kahne, 2004, p. 242). Such citizens engage in structural critiques and aim to address the root causes of social problems. They improve society through action. For example, these citizens, rather than contributing to or organizing a food drive, would explore why people are hungry and act to solve the causes of hunger in the community. According to scholars such as Ira Shor (1992), these citizens engage in social critique and aim for structural change.

Educators who promote justice-oriented citizenship engage students in deliberation about social, political, and economic structures with the goal of creating active collective strategies for societal change. These educators want students to create approaches that challenge injustice and, if possible, address the root causes of problems. Such citizens, however, must be "prepared to effectively promote their goals as individuals and groups in sometimes contentious political arenas" (Westheimer & Kahne, 2004, p. 243) as their fellow citizens will hold different perspectives. As such, educators should assist students in developing their communication skills so that they are able to work collaboratively with those who may oppose their views.

ANALYZING THE CURRICULUM

In the next section, we investigate if and how the financial literacy curriculum prioritizes personally responsible, participatory citizen, and justice-oriented citizen, and in doing so, discuss the broader possible consequences for these types of economic citizenships.

INDIVIDUAL WANTS AND NEEDS IN KINDERGARTEN

Using the definition of citizenship transmission, we examine the kindergarten curriculum, "Why Can't We Ever Get Everything We Need and Want?," as one that forwards a set of beliefs, rules, and dispositions fundamental to the economic needs and wants of larger society (Giroux, 1987). One of the earliest examples of citizenship transmission is attributed to an article entitled *Southern Workman*, published in 1907 by Thomas Jesse Jones. In the expanded book that followed, Jones lamented that young African Americans and Native Americans would never be able to become integral members of broader society unless they learned the ways in which social forces operate within society and the various available responses to social power (Ross, 2006). In the context of the United States, curriculum on economic self-reliance and responsibility is inextricably linked to the historical condition of certain racial, ethnic, rural, and gendered populations. In this account,

Jones presumed their participation in the very market systems that ostensibly justified slavery—and in turn doubled as rationale for colonist ideologies—could in some way provide social mobility for a population that has been historically stripped of their autonomy to fruitfully exist.

In "Why Can't We Ever Get Everything We Need and Want?," there is a hidden curriculum at play (Apple, 1993). This curriculum directs teachers to instruct 5- to 6-year-old children on how to categorize and sort material objects into wants and needs, and then explores "basic economic principles" as markers of "good" citizenship and "good" decision-making during times of scarcity. Scarcity, austerity, and recession are framed here as a result of natural disasters, rather than relations of power, greed, or systemic discrimination. Although the authors never explicitly state the "basic economic principle" from which they claim to draw, we find that neoclassical free market capitalism serves as the unquestioned order of things.

According to Max Weber (1930), the production of capitalist ideology involves not only rational thought and behavior, but also inculcates an ethos, a spirit, and a hidden message. This message assumes in an indiscriminate way that the market not only holds primacy over our everyday experiences, but that no other alternatives exist to the economic culture we have created. This naturalization of consumptive life is not only present in this activity, but similarly so in the following explanation of goods and services: "Goods are those tangible things we can use, keep and consume; services are those things that others do for us." These two key lines of thought—needs and wants and goods and services—are threaded throughout this kindergarten curriculum and amplify the rugged individualism and self-serving ideology upon which the United States is notorious for around the globe.

Surely, the audience here is not the exceptionally elite with whom the discernment of needs and wants takes on an entirely different way of thinking, if it is a necessary thought at all. Suffice it to say that financial literacy for low-income children may possibly lead to more financially secure livelihood, more options, more things, perhaps but not inclusive of, more opportunities. Yet, it does not allow children to begin thinking of citizenship as a kind of ethno-political response-ability that regards the individual as part of a collective well-being that carries with it a complex history corrupted by economic injustice and inequality. Regardless of the flippant condescension found in the unit—children's perspectives are described as "innate," "naïve," "silly"—in our experience as educators and teacher educators both in California and New York City, we find children to be exceptionally keen to issues of fairness, equity, sharing, and redistribution. We believe that if teachers began the unit with larger, more meaningful questions such as "what do we want for each other in this world?," children will follow in tow and begin to flourish with sophistication on issues of poverty, scarcity, and the prioritization of people over material privilege. Underlying this financial literacy curriculum is the assumption that for low-income people irrationality and lack of impulse are reasons for economic hardship, deflecting attention from a history of institutional and systemic social, political, and economic disenfranchisement.

When considering the social science framework, there exists ample research that critiques neoliberal school reforms for its unrelenting obsession with the positivist learning sciences (Biesta, 2014; Taubman, 2009). In this perspective, knowledge is caught within the dualisms of right versus wrong and is considered to embody a fixed meaning that is then utilized as a form of truth, or evidence, to complete a specific aim or task. In the NYS P–12 Common Core Learning Standards, social studies has been subsumed under English Language Arts & Science in a subsection entitled, "Informational Texts," which forwards an implicit belief that social studies is the application of information, not critical inquiry, question-making, sourcing, interpretation, and releasing the imagination. This emphasis on the rational thinking subject appears in the unit when teachers are asked to evaluate learning through and as concrete developmental stages: students move from "the identification level" when they are able to identify a need from a want; into "the application level" when they are able to explain how to satisfy said needs and wants; and finally, into an "interpretation level," in which they make decisions based on a simulated condition of scarcity.

Furthermore, this kindergarten unit instructs teachers to examine with students the concept of scarcity and to explore the options people have when "not being able to have all the goods and services that a person needs or wants." With the individual self as the centerpiece of concern, the unit provides examples of what to do when an impending snowstorm causes the community to dry up supplies at a local grocery store. Courses of action include, "pay a higher price, buy something else, or wait until the supply increases." The curriculum suggests that teachers use a simple notation system (+ or -) to record the strength of student understanding as they brainstorm how to respond appropriately during times of scarcity.

The hidden assumption suggests that there are correct ways to respond during crisis situations, which in turn governs and produces particular kinds of knowledge about what constitutes acceptable forms of citizenship, as well as moral and civic responsibility. The manner in which teachers are instructed to measure correctness and distribute quantifiable points, particularly as it concerns a subject such as citizenship, is one example of what Wayne Au (2011) calls the "New Taylorism" of school. Here, we see a resurgence of the factory-like efficiency popularized by educational reformers at the turn of the 20th century. By applying concepts of scientific management, namely the systematic regulation of individuals in order to effectively produce predetermined aims and outcomes, this curriculum tightens and constrains the imagination in order to serve a neoliberal culture of auditing and evaluation, and does so in the name of capitalism and consumerism.

In the social studies methods course that Debbie teaches, preservice student teachers develop primary grade–level curricula on the unifying theme of "Creation,

Expansion, and Interaction of Economic Systems" found in the NYS Scope and Sequence Standards for Social Studies. One semester, a student designed a first grade simulation in which the school cafeteria served as a microcosm of various formal economies that differ in their role of government intervention and resource distribution. Given a fixed supply, one scenario asks students to think about how food would be distributed if students with more money were able to buy more and students with less had access to disproportionately less. Although the vocabulary of capitalism, socialism, egalitarianism, etc. was determined developmentally inappropriate, the underlying premise demonstrated to children that classes exist based on their relationship to economic theories, capita and its distribution. In the second scenario, children consider what would happen if the principal decided to collect school monies then distribute food equally to all members of the class. Here, the teacher intended for children to begin contemplating ideas of fairness and asks them to compare and contrast the two situations with the aim of analyzing conditions of scarcity and the possibility of more equitable futurities. In the third case, children are asked to consider yet another situation in which a baseline minimum is established such that those with more money are able to buy more, only after all students have been sufficiently fed and provided for.

In this lesson, students not only considered the role of government in matters of the economy and the challenges of meeting wants and needs in a situational context that is relevant and accessible, but also did so through a reflective inquiry lens that centered on interdependence and invited possibilities outside free market fundamentalism. If we admit that our current neo-liberalist system perpetuates an increasing divide between the few wealthy and the majority middle class and poor, and that this leads to heartbreaking narratives of poverty, incarceration, desperation, and tragedy, then we must teach our children to imagine the future otherwise and to assist them in creating new systems of economic justice that are premised on notions of fairness, not materialism and self-over-others. This lesson should not be taught exclusively to the children of the poor, as curriculum on financial literacy tends to aim. It should not stem from deficit constructions of certain populations and their apparent lack of impulse control and rational choice-making. Instead, we should enact this curriculum for all kindergarten classrooms since participation by all is necessary to reconstruct a society that engages with social issues and institutions that promote a more just and equitable distribution of society's benefits.

FAMILIES AND CHOICE-MAKING IN THE FIRST GRADE

In alignment with the NYC Scope and Sequence Standards for Social Studies, this first grade unit builds off the previous year by focusing on the child as part of a family unit. Whereas in kindergarten, the teacher explores various criteria for determining an object as an individual want or a need, this unit asks the children: "How do families gain money? What do families choose to spend their money on? Why do families choose to save money?" As written into the curriculum, the foundational concept for this unit is based on the economic principal of cost-benefit analyses, or CBA. Generally known, CBA is a methodological technique used to calculate and compare the strengths and weaknesses of alternative costs, such as labor, time, and capital, in order to maximize benefits for a private sector business or governmental policy or project. By applying an assessment of a business to the decision-making process of a family, this unit approaches financial literacy through the personification of corporations as human beings, or human beings as corporations, a highly contested debate that reached the floor of the U.S. Supreme Court no more than five years ago.

By establishing an artificial legal persona, the U.S. Supreme Court passed the 5-4 First Amendment decision entitled Citizen United which expanded the rights of corporations to act as individuals and deregulated their monetary spending in candidate elections. Four years later in 2014, another 5-4 decision supported a craft store chain Hobby Lobby and its claim that companies do have the right to exercise their religious freedom, like individual citizens, and therein, were permitted to deny their 16,000 employees access to certain kinds of contraceptives that the owners considered abortifacients. This personification not only extends certain constitutional rights and responsibilities to private enterprises, but ensures protection of their economic development by, for example, protecting shareholders from being sued as individuals, or protecting them from warrantless search and seizure. Although the teacher in this unit is not instructed to use such language, the underpinning ideology is to treat the family as a unit of business.

In regard to the notion of citizenship transmission, there is a clear inculcation, both hidden and overt, of the child via teacher into the economic agenda set forth by the private sector. It is delineated in the first paragraph of the unit that 6- to 7-year-old children should be able to examine the "costs and benefits associated with decisions about spending and saving money" and be able to demonstrate this in the development of "an argument supported with evidence that addresses the question of how families make economic choices." Therefore, the unit implicitly promotes the idea that children and their families should be commodified, evaluated, and advised through the language of the market in order for them to ensure fiscal security in the future, and that children should be able to argue for this through evidence, which points them toward "a list of ways students can help their families save money."

Whether this is an appropriate discussion to pursue with children of this age is a matter of how teachers assume responsibility for the world in which children are about to enter. According to Hannah Arendt (1954), the crisis in education falls from the *fiat accompli* established through the dictatorial intervention of the adult, who instead of producing new futures and conditions, inculcates them into a world in which the new already exists. This is what Barr et al. (1977) call citizen transmission. About this Arendt (1954) writes, "education is the point at which we decide whether we love the world enough to assume responsibility for it" and by that token it is the adult who must carry the dual responsibility of changing the world while protecting children from it. Education, she continues, is "where we decide whether we love our children enough not to expel them from our world and leave them to their own devices ... but to prepare them in advance for the task of renewing a common world" (p. 193). This may signify that the education of a personally responsible citizen (Westheimer & Kahne, 2004), in which teachers ask children to assume responsibility for others, in this case, the fiscal decision-making of their family members, may not be appropriate at the age of 7–8, a time of discovery and play that may need to be safely harbored from the political world, and most certainly from the financial.

Historically, the field of education has tended to adopt and explode certain terms, acronyms, concepts, and practices. One such word has become that of "choice." Throughout this first grade unit there is ample mention of "choice" as rational decision-making, an interpretation that aligns with the personally responsible citizen who must have "good character, be honest, responsible, and law-abiding" (Westheimer & Kahne, 2004, p. 242). Yet, the most popular use of the term "choice" in the field of education today is in reference to "school choice" wherein students and their families are provided alternatives to their publicly funded schools. School choice programs are scholarship tax credit programs, which allow individuals or corporations to receive credits toward their state taxes in exchange for donations made to nonprofit organizations that grant private school funding. Framed as the positives of venture philanthropy, school choice has been highly publicized as an opportunity for poor, predominantly families of color, to escape the failures of the public system by enrolling their children in schools that are semi-controlled by private and corporate interests, multimillionaires, and their government and political apparatchiks. Choice, interchangeably viewed as freedom, is defined in a capitalist democracy as the right each individual has to determine their course of destiny, to reap the fruits of creative autonomy, and to actualize the possibility for self-development. Unfortunately, such freedoms are granted more to some than others. In a Foucauldian sense, we can examine the use of choice here, not as representative, but rather as producing a discourse in which the knowledge of choice governs and inscribes a false sense of independence; failure arising not from structural exploitation, but rather from a lack of civilized control and intellectual thought.

In the unit, children are provided a series of images, such as a medical doctor examining an X-ray or a family jogging in the park, and asked to categorize them as either a means to obtain money or an example of leisure or spending. As a supplement, there is a source reading, entitled "What is a Budget?" with statements such as, "Companies and countries have budgets to manage their spending. Putting together a budget can help you, too." Throughout, it is taught that people have choices that can either enrich or impair them. The second task asks students to consider the economic choices families make by watching a 3-minute video created by PrudentialCorpAsia, a life insurance, asset management, and consumer finance operation involved in the development and dissemination of Common Core Learning Standards. This animated video shows a money mint printing notes and shipping them to banks from which "a world of possibility" can be accessed. Thinking about money helps us understand that we can earn, spend, save, or donate that which we secure with hard work, a throwback to the Protestant work ethic that, according to Weber (1930), buttressed modern-day capitalism. The third supporting task includes the use of an online PowerPoint about short-term and long-term saving goals and an excerpt on how to use savings appropriately. "The idea," it reads "is not to SPEND money but to be money smart and learn how to HANDLE IT. Here is how smart people use the money they have" [original capitalization]. Northwestern Mutual, another life insurance and financial planning firm, produced this supplementary material.

Similar to our critique of kindergarten, we have grave concerns over the consequence of decontextualizing economic hardship through the reinscription of the mythical meritocracy. The hidden message pervasive in this unit is that hard work and rational "smart" decision-making is the panacea to poverty and struggle. The rugged individualism here is clear and as individuals help themselves out, there becomes no need for government intervention, welfare programming, or an analysis of history, discrimination, and the status quo. The danger is not only a miseducation—Carter Woodson's (1933) concern for the neglect of history particularly for the African American community—but an anti-education, in that there is no need to study; no need for inquiry, investigation, or reflection into the plight of others. Financial literacy in this way—and this is not the literacy dreamt by philosopher Paulo Freire (1970) or those of new literacy studies (for an overview, see Gee, 1996; Street, 1995)—renders elementary school teaching to logical empiricism and pragmatic skill-building, one that positions a child to judge and evaluate their own family and the decisions made by their beloved parents and guardians.

Finally, the culminating project asks children to survey the spending decisions of their family members and to then create posters that promote money-saving strategies. In an effort to include a social action component into the curriculum, children are being used as capitalist advocates in the world, a turn that does not bode well to the democratic principles foundational to this country. One possible residue of this project is an attitude of contempt toward self, family, and a child's own people, as they are taught to admire those with capital and judge those without. From our experience, children are keenly aware and sensitive to matters of money, not necessarily in terms of financial responsibility, but in their affective engagement with other children from differential and referentially classed backgrounds. An implicit hidden education bent at the intersections of poverty and individualism, capitalism and choice, and the false illusions of merit and deservedness, produces a scenario within which individuals are noticed and praised for their material prowess.

Children from low-income communities hear of summer trips to Paris told by classmates and peek into backpacks that are either glimmering with new materiality or punctured by the worn down, recycled, and renewed. They experience feelings of envy, anger, and shame, as well as pride, happiness, and contentment. However, this shame, tied to the appearances of oneself in the presence of others, is shaped both by how the subject perceives itself and also by the way in which others will judge, evaluate, and find the child either desirable or insufficient. Shame is the failure to live up to the ideal image we hold of ourselves (Taubman, 2009). The most profound lesson learned by students may be a deficit construction of themselves and their adult counterparts for making poor choices with money. Many teachers, particularly at the childhood level, are profoundly concerned with the manifestation of class disparity in their room. They redistribute classroom materials in egalitarian ways and structure communal sharing experiences. An appropriate revision could perhaps teach the child that they are more than their economic identity; that one should not be judged or evaluated based on wealth; and to love their families unconditionally despite the hardships and challenges they may face.

INTERDEPENDENCE AND COMMUNITY ECONOMICS IN THE SECOND GRADE

In the second grade, the curriculum expands into the domain of community, defined as a dynamic assemblage of individuals, desires, and interdependent relationships that move, shift, and contract as a collective "we." The unit challenges students "to understand that through businesses, town organizations, and local governments, a community meets the needs and wants of its people, finding strength in collective efforts to address problems." In contrast to the previous grades, this unit disperses responsibility from the individual into the interstitial relations that constitute our interdependence. The first segment returns to the idea of wants and needs as children brainstorm categories of workers, businesses, and organizations. The second asks students to complete a graphic organizer describing the challenges of scarcity, particularly the quality of healthy and fresh foods in poor neighborhoods and the impact of California droughts on crop yield. Both of these excerpts discuss related careers, such as farmer advocates, professors, and food scientists, which invite students to think about important kinds of work not typically visible or recognized. The third segment speaks to a sense of collaboration and highlights people's attempts "to rise above economic and geographic challenges via the use of tools and technology, new ideas, recycling, and sheer determination." News stories include Breanne, a woman who started a community garden for a charity called Su Casa; an economical solution to building a playground out of recycled materials; and the work of Alexandra Flynn Scott, an 8-year-old girl with neuroblastoma who sold lemonade as a way to raise money for pediatric cancer research.

The concept of interdependence is described as "a diverse, mutually supportive web" among material matter, forms of exchange, human beings, and situational conditions and resolutions. The emergent field of new materialisms in curriculum studies (Snaza, Sonu, Truman, & Zaliwska, 2016) represents a range of theorists who are turning attention back to the nature of matter and the place of embodied humans within the material world. New materialist thought begins by entangling the human in a horizontal relationship with a whole host of other human and nonhuman entities such that spaces become emerging sites in which entities are created, rather than separated things that merely come together. For example, the first source text, entitled "Farmers Grow Corn," does not actually position the farmer as the subject, as implied in the title, but traces the movement of the corn and the ways in which its contact with humans created subjects of farming both through culture as exemplified by American Indian innovation and those that sell crops to companies for retail or animal fodder. We believe this approach to interdependence can resonate with what Rosi Braidotti (2013) calls the web of interrelations, a concept drawn heavily from Gilles Deleuze and Felix Guattari's construction of assemblages. Here, there is a blurring of boundaries such that entities do not exist as stable and bounded things but are "intra-active" and emerging from their relationality.

In his poignant argument for a new materialist inflection in the teaching of social studies, Mark Helmsing (2016) writes, "With a focus on life and the living world, the kinds of thinking that social studies education could make possible would resonate with an unending array of unfolding material encounters to study" (p. 138). The hidden curriculum being forward here, more than in the previous grade levels, is the notion of connectivity, transaction, intra-action, mutual constitutiveness, terms that describe not only the significance of relationships over individual development, but that our very subjectivities are dependent on our relation with the other, an ethical response that acknowledges *that* which is outside the self whether *that* be human or nonhuman. For Diane Coole and Samantha Frost, "materiality is always something more than 'mere' matter: an excess, force, vitality, relationality, or difference that renders matter active, self-creative, productive, unpredictable" (2010, p. 9). The second excerpt describes a New York City schoolteacher and puts her in relation to a newly purchased home. Being the first in her family, she describes the affective experience of pride that accompanied her new acquisition and although the story still carries the narrative of individualized hard work and de-historicized success, it does present an emotional narrative that stands in stark contrast to the flattened out categorizing activities of kindergarten and first grade.

Aside from citizenship transmission and social science (Barr et al., 1977), this unit incorporates comparably more elements of reflective inquiry particularly as reading passages include the description of careers and professions that respond to environmental problems of scarcity. Again, there is no mention anywhere that scarcity impacts differentially, nor is there discussion of how certain economic systems, such as capitalism, function precisely on the production of haves and have-nots. Richard Howitt, who teaches at the University of California, is said to help farmers overcome drought conditions, and Breanne works with Su Casa, a charity that harvests healthy fruits and vegetables for poor women and children. In sourcing these texts, it is found that they are written, translated, or adapted from organizations such as Habitat for Humanity, or a group called Newsela that employs teachers to modify current events into grade-level appropriate text. While insurance companies created the online videos suggested in the previous grades, this second grade unit is decidedly infused with materials from nonprofit organizations and educators. The tone is markedly different; now, as a pedagogical affect, there is a feeling of care, not material accumulation; there is a sense of responsibility and participation, not one of judgment and definitive reasoning.

As opposed to the character-based or personally responsible approach to citizenship, this unit pushes students just beyond the limits into what Westheimer and Kahne (2004) delineate as participatory. Here, students do not contribute time to a cause, but work to actively organize and strategize community efforts. Although the students do not necessarily enact these moves, they are exposed through the readings to various models of people who commit their lives to such causes. However, an exploration of why such problems exist, what they call justice-oriented citizenship, is not present at all. Students are not asked to critically assess the social, political, and economic structures that work below the surface, nor do they examine social movements, as a collective of individuals who have historically fought for social change. This absence is most clearly seen in "Poor People Cannot Find Fresh and Healthy Food," an article featured in the Philadelphia Inquirer and adapted by Newsela. In this piece, it is clear that "poor" people—a word that must be interrogated for its pathologizing history and its inscription of a deficit characteristic onto human rather than system—do not have access to markets that stock quality food and that these same individuals have been found to digest rotten produce only to get sick. The solution, as proposed, is to promote frozen, dried, or canned goods since fresh produce tends to spoil quickly. Benjamin Chapman, described in the text as a food safety officer, contends that "poor" people eat spoiled food for one reason, because "it is better than eating nothing at all."

CONCLUSION

In *The Beautiful Risk of Education,* Gert Biesta (2014) argues that during these neoliberal times the inescapability of evidence and competency makes critical conversations on the purpose of education more difficult. The treatment of knowledge as contained, deliverable, and measured has reduced education to the development of skills at the expense of a focus on the values of and hopes for the greater good: the question of why we teach has been interred by directions on how to teach. Moreover, with increasingly more weight being placed on the production of standardized curriculum, best practices, assessments and evaluations, corporations have seized the opportunity to profit off the booming business of telling teachers what to do. What becomes compromised, he claims, is the very central tenet of teaching: the ability to exercise our judgment as teachers. By examining the recently released EngageNY curriculum on financial literacy, we have attempted to raise questions about the kinds of values and beliefs teachers are being asked to forward to young elementary-age children. Throughout, we found a general emphasis on the teaching of proper decision-making behaviors, but a suspicious disregard for a deeper analysis into the ways that the economy impacts the lives of people. This is not to say that we are against the idea of discussing the role of judgment in economic life. We believe that the pervasiveness of the free market, including its aggressive media presence and the material inequality seen by all around the world, makes financial and economic literacy an important area of study for teachers and children. What we contend here is that a critical education, one that cultivates compassion, solidarity, and justice, cannot begin from a condition that thrives on the economic disequilibrium of its people, and that this curriculum could be strengthened in two major ways: first, greater transparency of its contributors and content, including the participation of corporate benefactors, its economic platform, and general background information from which teachers are able to make judgments; and second, a move away from the presupposition of capitalism to an analysis of various forms of economies and exchanges.

The discipline of social studies is about deep investigations into how and why events occur both in the past and present contexts. It inquires, explores, and critiques traditional conventions and canonical texts in the area of history, geography, sociology, psychology, and economics with the aim of forwarding democratic values, global citizenry, and intellectual curiosity and pursuit. This means that social studies educators are charged with providing their students a kind of learning experience that not only prepares them to take up certain roles as citizens in the United States (Gutmann, 1999), but also positions them to resist, reconceptualize, and act when structures and systems express discriminatory beliefs and values. This brings to bear one very fundamental issue in the writing of this chapter—if we pay attention to the question of purpose in education, what comes to pass as we discover a difference of opinion that is insurmountable and weary of compromise. It may be very true that the authors of these financial literacy units are not interested in criticality in the way that we are. The authors of this curriculum may instead believe in the sanctity of the market and its potential to save individuals from poverty and struggle. While we consider these tenets to be problematic, overly simplified and even dangerous, what happens then to classroom teaching when the contents of a curriculum come into direct opposition with those charged to enact it? In the end, the teachers will have to make their own judgments. We hope this chapter raises some important questions that assist them in doing so.

QUESTIONS FOR DISCUSSION

1. What do you consider to be the social ideology that drives conventional approaches to financial education? To what extent does this represent a socially just ideology?
2. This article begs the question—Do teachers routinely critically analyze curriculum? Do they consider the implicit and often explicit beliefs put forth as dogma?
3. Sonu and Marri echo the writings of other researchers (e.g., Chris Arthur and Laura Pinto), who claim the presence of a hidden curriculum in existing financial literacy curricula. Locate a financial education lesson with which you are familiar. To what extent does it infer a hidden effort to maintain the social status quo? What modifications would you employ to challenge its assumptions?
4. Reconsider the solution provided to the problem of food access described before the conclusion. What would a justice-oriented solution to the situation look like?
5. What might "greater transparency" look like for curriculum contributors? How do you think having this information would affect curriculum purchasing?

REFERENCES

Apple, M. (1993). *Official knowledge: Democratic education in a conservative age*. New York, NY: Routledge.
Arendt, H. (1954). *Between past and futures*. New York, NY: Penguin Group.
Au, W. (2011). Teaching under the new Taylorism: High-stakes testing and the standardization of the 21st century curriculum. *Journal of Curriculum Studies, 43*(1), 25–45.
Barr, R., Barth, J., & Shermis, S. (1977). *Defining the social studies*. Bulletin No. 51. Washington, DC: National Council for the Social Studies.

Biesta, G. (2011). *Learning democracy in school and society: Education, lifelong learning, and the politics of citizenship*. Rotterdam: Sense Publishers.
Biesta, G. (2014). *The beautiful risk of education*. New York, NY: Paradigm Publishers.
Braidotti, R. (2013). *The posthuman*. Malden, MA: Polity.
Connolly, W. (1983). *The terms of political discourse* (2nd ed.). Princeton, NJ: Princeton University Press.
Coole, D., & Frost, S. (2010). *New materialisms: Ontology, agency and politics*. Durham, NC: Duke University Press.
Dewey, J. (1927). *The public and its problems*. Athens, OH: Swallow Press.
Dorado, G. (2011). *Financial literacy: The federal government's role in empowering American to make sound financial choices*. Washington, DC: Government Accountability Office (GAO). Retrieved from http://www.gao.gov/assets/130/125996.pdf
Freire, P. (1970). *Pedagogy of the oppressed*. New York, NY: Continuum.
Gee, J. (1996). *Social linguistics and literacies: Ideology in discourses*. London: Taylor & Francis.
Giroux, H. (1987). Citizenship, public philosophy, and the struggle for democracy, *Educational Theory, 37*(2), 103–120.
Guatarri, F. (2015). *Machinic eros: Writings on Japan*. Minneapolis, MN: Univocal.
Gutmann, A. (1999). *Democratic eEducation*. Princeton, NJ: Princeton University Press.
Helmsing, M. (2016). Life at large: New materialisms for a (re)new(ing) curriculum of social studies education. In N. Snaza, D. Sonu, S. Truman, & Z. Zoliwska (Eds.), *Pedagogical matters: New materialisms and curriculum studies* (pp. 137–152). New York, NY: Peter Lang.
Levine, P. (2007). *The future of democracy: Developing the next generation of American citizens*. Hanover, NH: Tufts University Press.
Lickona, T. (1993). The return of character education. *Educational Leadership, 51* (3), 6–11.
Macrine, S., McLaren, P., & Hill, D. (2011). *Revolutionizing pedagogy: Education for social justice within and beyond global neoliberalism*. New York, NY: Palgrave Macmillan.
Marri, A. (2014, April 11). Promoting economic literacy in K–12 schools. *Teachers College Record*. Retrieved from http://www.tcrecord.org/Content.asp?ContentId=17499
Misco, T., & Hamot, G. (2012). "He was the opposite of what we learned a teacher should be": A study of preservice social studies students' cooperating teachers, *The Journal of Social Studies Research, 36*(4), 305–328.
National Council for the Social Studies. (2013). *The College, Career, and Civic Life (C3) Framework for Social Studies State Standards: Guidance for enhancing the rigor of K–12 Civics, Economics, Geography, and History*. Silver Springs, MD: National Council for the Social Studies.
New York State Education Department (2015). *Social Studies Resource Tool Kit*. University of the State of New York, Albany
North Central Regional Educational Laboratory (NCREL). (2003). *21st Century Skills: Literacy in the digital age*. Naperville, IL: North Central Regional Educational Laboratory.
Parker, W. (1996). "Advanced" ideas about democracy: Toward a pluralistic conception of citizen education. *Teachers College Record, 98*(1), 104–125.
Parker, W. (2001). Educating democratic citizens: A broad view. *Theory into Practice, 40*(1), 6–13.
Ross, W. (2006). *The social studies curriculum: Purposes, problems, and possibilities*. Albany, NY: State University of New York Press.
Salemi, M. (2005). Teaching economic literacy: Why, what, and how. *International Review of Economics Education, 4*(2), 46–57.
Shor, I. (1992). *Empowering education: Critical teaching for social change*. Chicago, IL: University of Chicago Press.

Snaza, N., Sonu, D., Truman, S., & Zaliwska, Z. (2016). *Pedagogical matters: New materialisms and curriculum studies.* New York, NY: Peter Lang.

Stanley, W., & Nelson, J. (1994). The foundations of social education in historical context. In R. Martusewicz & W. Reynolds (Eds.), *Inside/out: Contemporary critical perspectives in education* (pp. 266–284). New York, NY: St. Martin's Publishers.

Stern, G. (1998). Do we know enough about economics? *The Region: Banking and Policy Issues Magazine, 11*(3). Retrieved from http://minneapolisfed.org/publications_papers/pub_display.cfm?id=3578

Street, B. (1995). *Social literacies: Critical approaches to literacy in development, ethnography, and education.* London: Longman.

Taubman, P. (2009). *Teaching by numbers: Deconstructing the discourse of standards and accountability in education.* New York, NY: Routledge.

Vinson, K. (1998). The "traditions" revisited: Instructional approach and high school social studies teachers. *Theory and Research in Social Education, 26*(1), 50–82.

Weber, M. (1930). *The Protestant ethics and the spirit of capitalism.* London: Routledge.

Westheimer, J., & Kahne, J. (2004). What kind of citizen? The politics of educating for democracy. *American Educational Research Journal, 41*(2), 237–269.

White, C. (1982). A validation study of the Barth-Shermis social studies preference scale. *Theory and Research in Social Education, 10*(2), 1–20.

Woodson, C. G. (1933). *The mis-education of the Negro.* Drewryville, VA: Khalifah's Booksellers.

Wynne, E. (1986). The great tradition in education: Transmitting moral values. *Educational Leadership, 43*(4), 4–9.

CHAPTER TWO

Meaning AND Money Revisited

MARY E. BRENNER
University of California, Santa Barbara

The chapter published in the first edition consisted of a reprint from a 1998 article from the journal *Educational Studies in Mathematics*. This work described the results of a study that used interview data to interpret how Hawaiian children learned mathematics at home and compared the findings to their experiences at school.

Since the original publication of the chapter, the research base about the relation between everyday activity and children's mathematical knowledge has grown substantially. While the early studies were often done in countries where children had limited exposure to Western-style schooling, the relevance of nonschool activity in the lives of American children has been increasingly the focus of researchers who seek to improve the educational achievement of diverse populations in the United States. In a review of the literature on mathematics learning, Nasir, Hand, and Taylor (2008) framed the connection between everyday learning and school achievement as an issue of social justice because schools have traditionally privileged the knowledge and cultural practices of some groups over others. They wrote that incorporating students' cultural knowledge and identities into the mathematics classroom has powerful potential for educational reform. "In this way, the teaching and learning of mathematics becomes a vehicle for shifting current power relations, to use mathematics for the purposes of empowerment at both the individual and community levels" (p. 220).

A number of studies have demonstrated the power of everyday cultural knowledge to improve how mathematics is taught with corresponding gains in the achievement of children from groups that have traditionally underachieved in American schools. A powerful and well-documented example is the curriculum developed and evaluated by Jerry Likpa and his colleagues in the Math in a Cultural Context project. This project, which spanned two decades, incorporated the cultural knowledge of the Yup'ik Native Alaskan people into 10 supplemental math modules designed for grades 2 to 7 (https://www.uaf.edu/mcc/). Rigorous evaluations of this project with thousands of students and hundreds of teachers, using quasi-experimental and experimental designs, have demonstrated the effectiveness of this approach in enhancing the academic learning of Native Alaskan children (Kisker et al., 2012; Lipka, Yanez, Andrew-Ihrke, & Adam, 2009).

Within the research into everyday mathematics, the domain of money knowledge remains a fertile area for investigating the everyday knowledge of children, with implications for educational practice in both mathematics and financial literacy. It continues to be a route to improving mathematics learning for diverse children in the United States. This short and selective review of the research done since my original study begins by highlighting research about how money experiences in everyday contexts are related to mathematical learning. It then addresses efforts to build from such research through work with teachers who wish to improve their teaching. It finishes by noting some of the challenges posed when money is incorporated into educational contexts.

RESEARCH ON CHILDREN'S EXPERIENCES WITH MONEY

As in my research, subsequent research has demonstrated the large variety of ways in which children interact with money and the complex links to their mathematical knowledge. Guberman (2004) examined the money experiences of Latin American and Korean children from the same neighborhood in Los Angeles and how it impacted their mathematical skills. The data about children's activities were obtained through interviews with parents and the children's mathematical knowledge was assessed through the administration of tasks to children individually. Latin American children were reported to engage in monetary activities about twice as much as Korean American children, and the complexity of their arithmetical calculations was higher in those contexts. The Latin American children's activities with money were instrumental; in other words, they were engaged in activities that had nonacademic goals such as shopping or playing games. In contrast, the Korean American children had more academic experiences at home such as tutoring or doing worksheets.

In order to understand the implications for school mathematics, the children were given arithmetic problems using either chips or money, with the same arithmetical demands. As expected, "Children with greater participation in commercial transactions found problems with money easier to solve, and children with greater involvement in academic activities found problems with chips easier to solve" (Guberman, 2004, p. 143). These differences tended to fall along ethnic lines, with the Latin American children doing better on the money tasks, although the out-of-school activities in which children engaged were more predictive of their performance than ethnicity. As in my study, this demonstrates that children often possess competencies that are not revealed with school-like activities such as the chip tasks and that these competencies derive from what they do in their everyday lives.

Taylor (2009, 2012, 2013) has also had a research agenda documenting how children learn about money in various contexts, and how this type of research can be profitably used in the training and development of teachers. His first study (2009) was based on very detailed observations of low-income African American children shopping in a store. As in my study, he describes the routines different children used, the mathematical complexity of the transactions, how children were supported by others when shopping, and strategies children used to deal with the complexities. He then further probed children's mathematical understandings by having them shop in a mock store with predetermined shopping lists. He found that children's success was mediated by both numerical understanding and understanding of the conventions of money. As in Guberman's study, some children lacked the shopping experience to be successful despite good numerical knowledge while children with shopping experience could not always apply it to new contexts.

Another empirical study by Taylor (2013) examined how children learn about percentages and other rational numbers through the religious practice of tithing. As in his prior research, he used intensive observation and individual interviews with children to examine their related mathematical skills. He also interviewed parents and other members of the church community to understand how adults support children's learning about tithing. Again he documented the variety of ways that children deal with mathematical tasks in context. He also found that the children tended to be more successful with problems that were posed within the context of tithing rather than identical numerical problems. This research was promising because it addressed a different and more complex mathematical domain than most of the other research into money and mathematics.

BRINGING EVERYDAY PRACTICES INTO THE CLASSROOM

Two recent articles (Taylor, 2012; Wager, 2012) document efforts to support teachers in incorporating everyday mathematics in the classroom, building in part from the empirical studies of children's everyday engagement with money. The goals of both authors were to provide meaningful and equitable learning experiences for diverse children. Taylor described a yearlong professional development project with 14 elementary teachers, based upon his Multi-approach Engagement Framework. Wager worked with 17 elementary teachers in a semester long seminar focused on culturally relevant pedagogy. In both studies, the teachers designed lessons that were either recorded or observed by the researcher and other teachers, and they engaged in a cycle of reflection and improvement.

Although the two projects differed in important ways, a striking similarity was the difficulty the teachers had with creating lessons that had authentic embedded mathematics. The teachers in both projects were able to create rich cultural contexts for mathematics lessons but it was much more difficult for them to discern and build from the informal mathematics that children already knew. Wager (2012) noted that teachers did not have the time or opportunity to study children's practices in the way that researchers do. Taylor (2011) delineated a variety of ways that teachers can bring mathematics into contextualized activities and how to move them to a more authentic Mathematics in Practice approach.

OTHER CHALLENGES

Other studies have used other methodologies to examine how prior experience impacts performance on mathematical tasks, particularly those involving money. Solano-Flores and Li (2009) examined the psychometric properties of cognitive interviews with Caucasian, African American and American Indian children when children did a lunch-money problem. They also questioned children about their interpretations of the contexts in which they used lunch money. They found that the children from the different cultural groups made sense of the problem differently based on their experiences, and this impacted how well the raters scored each group. Thus it was demonstrated that mathematical assessments are sensitive to both children's cultural backgrounds and their prior experiences, which makes fair and valid assessments difficult.

McNeil, Uttal, Jarvin, and Sternberg (2009) compared children's problem-solving on word problems with real money, which they characterized as "rich" concrete objects, fake money that was printed in black and white ("bland" objects), and no objects at all. Although the children who had real money made more errors overall, they made fewer conceptual errors. Thus money knowledge seems to tap into some important mathematical knowledge but is not easily linked to other valued academic skills. Taken together, these two studies demonstrate both the challenges that children's prior knowledge presents when trying to use it for educational purposes, but also the potential advantages for at least some children in activating everyday knowledge in context.

Although money seems to be a topic of universal relevance in the United States, simply adding it to the mathematics curriculum or mathematical tests may not benefit children who are at risk with more traditional mathematical instruction. Research needs to continue about what children know, how they use this knowledge, and how it can be leveraged in educational settings.

QUESTIONS FOR DISCUSSION

1. Visit the website of the National Council of Teachers of Mathematics, http://standards.nctm.org. How specifically do the standards relate to the patterns of child development that Brenner observes?
2. Think back on your own mathematical training. At what times did you "connect" mathematics to your daily life? When did this connection occur? What were the conditions prompting this connection? What were the teacher's roles in these environments?
3. The Kamehameha schools (http://www.ksbe.edu/) were created in an attempt to create cultural connections to all curricula. Research this Hawaiian school system and particularly its mission statement, vision, etc. How does it relate to Brenner's thinking about "every day common sense" experiences?
4. Take some time to observe children make small purchases at a local store. How may their behaviors convey cultural similarities and differences that relate the patterns Brenner describes? How does the environment of the purchase relate to your findings?
5. How do you define culture? How does your definition of culture shape the patterns of financial practice that you normalize? How does it influence your perceptions of the different ways that people learn about money and its use?

REFERENCES

Guberman, S. R. (2004). A comparative study of children's out-of-school activities and arithmetical achievements. *Journal for Research in Mathematics Education, 35*, 117–150.
Kisker, E. E., Lipka, J., Adams, B. L., Rickard, A., Andrew-Ihrke, D., Yanez, E. E., & Millard, A. (2012). The potential of a culturally based supplemental mathematics curriculum to improve the mathematics performance of Alaska Native and other students. *Journal for Research in Mathematics Education, 43*, 75–113.
Lipka, J., Yanez, E., Andrew-Ihrke, D., & Adam, S. (2009). A two-way process for developing culturally based mathematics: Examples from math in a cultural context. In B. Greer, S. Mukhopadhyay, A. B. Powell, & S. Nelson-Barber (Eds.), *Culturally responsive mathematics education* (pp. 257–280). New York, NY: Routledge.
McNeil, N. M., Uttal, D. H., Jarvin, L., & Sternberg, R. J. (2009). Should you show me the money? Concrete objects both hurt and help performance on mathematics problems. *Learning and Instruction, 19*, 171–184.

Nasir, N. S., Hand, V., & Taylor, E. V. (2008). Culture and mathematics in school: Boundaries between "cultural" and "domain" knowledge in the mathematics classroom and beyond. *Review of Educational Research, 32*, 187–240.

Solano-Flores, G., & Li, M. (2009). Generalizability of cognitive interview-based measures across cultural groups. *Educational Measurement: Issues and Practice, 28*, 9–18.

Taylor, E. V. (2009). The purchasing practice of low-income students: The relationship to mathematical development. *Journal of the Learning Sciences, 18*, 370–415.

Taylor, E. V. (2011). Supporting children's mathematical understanding: Professional development focused on out-of-school practices. *Journal of Mathematics Teacher Education.* doi:10.1007/s10857-011-9187-7.

Taylor, E. V. (2012). Supporting children's mathematical understanding: Professional development focused on out-of-school practices. *Journal of Mathematics Teacher Education, 15*, 271–291.

Taylor, E. V. (2013). The mathematics of tithing: A study of religious giving and mathematical development. *Mind, Culture and Activity: An International Journal, 20*, 132–149.

Wager, A. A. (2012). Incorporating out-of-school mathematics: From cultural context to embedded practice. *Journal of Mathematics Teacher Education, 15*, 9–23.

CHAPTER THREE

Random Acts OF Financial Literacy

KATHLEEN S. COOTER
Bellarmine University[1]

INTRODUCTION

One could generally define financial literacy as the literacy skills required to operate efficiently and successfully in a market economy. Chairman of the Federal Reserve Board Ben S. Bernanke testified in 2006 before the Committee on Banking, Housing, and Urban Affairs of the United States Senate. The following research findings were included in his words about financial literacy and the commitment of the Federal Reserve:

> … research has looked at the link between financial knowledge and broader financial management skills. For example, one study examined the relationship between financial knowledge and financial behavior such as cash flow management, savings, and investing. Overall, the study found a significant correlation between the level of financial knowledge and good financial management practices. Individuals who were familiar with financial concepts and products were found to be more likely to balance their checkbook every month, budget for savings, and hold investment accounts. Similarly, another study on consumer creditworthiness and consumer literacy determined that financial knowledge is the single best predictor of behaviors, such as budgeting, saving, and shopping responsibly, that translated into positive outcomes on credit bureau reports. This study also found that the main sources of knowledge were bad experiences, school instruction, and other education. (p. 1)

If school instruction is one of the primary sources of financial and consumer literacy for the populace, the teaching profession has a significant role in the long-term economic well-being of their students. What do beginning teachers know and value about financial literacy? Do they address financial literacy in their respective subject areas? Does their teacher preparation program affect their understanding and value of financial literacy in their classrooms?

To look at these questions, this study analyzed the understanding and practice of financial literacy in the classrooms of 55 secondary beginning teachers. These teachers received training from a wide number of universities from across the country or were currently receiving training for certification. The teachers are teaching in three subject areas—social studies, mathematics, and science in an urban area in the south. The researcher expected that there will be a relationship between subject area teaching assignment and financial literacy as a pertinent curricular topic and that a background of traditional teacher preparation would be related to a greater value for financial literacy in the secondary curriculum.

METHOD INSTRUMENTATION

The researcher developed a 10-item survey instrument to examine the perceptions and knowledge of beginning practitioners regarding financial literacy. The items derived from a data gathered using focus groups and a review of the literature (Gillin, 2002; Hogarth & Hilgert, 2002; Joo, Grable, & Bagwell, 2003; Murphy, 2005). There were three focus groups consisting of several curriculum specialists and subsequently several small group interviews from which the majority of the survey was developed. This initial survey was analyzed by a set of four secondary teachers and two education professors for readability using the Fleisch readability formula index and matched to the existing language of the Tennessee state secondary curricula. The researcher slightly revised the instrument with the teachers' and professors' feedback and the final draft field-tested with 14 secondary teachers who had taught five years or more for readability and language familiarity. The focus group teachers felt that the survey was clear and precise in language and made no modifications to the final product.

The survey contained ten Likert-type response items with a scale of 1 (strongly disagree) to 5 (strongly agree). The researcher constructed nine items to interpret the beginning teachers' perceived value and the curricular inclusion of financial literacy topics. One question intended to measure the pertinence of financial literacy to the teacher's individual classroom practice.

SUBJECTS

The researcher recruited survey participants from a large urban school district in the Midsouth. According to National Center for Education Statistics data (http://

nces.ed.gov/), the district served more than 120,000 students during the 2005–2006 school year, with 74% African American student population. Nearly one-half of the schools have 10% of students who can afford their own lunches (Board of Education Memphis City Schools, 2007). The teacher participants consisted of 27 males and 28 females, ranging in age from 23 to 46 years. None had more than one year of teaching experience. In terms of preparation, 31 respondents had completed a traditional teacher education program and were licensed in their teaching assignment, while 24 respondents were gaining certification through graduate level coursework. These 24 participants had various undergraduate degrees in arts or sciences and liberal arts, and the school district considered them as two year emergency certificated teachers during their completion of the necessary university coursework for licensure.

In terms of ethnicity 70% of the participants identified themselves African American with 30% European American. They had undergraduate degrees from eleven different universities located throughout the United States. All were teaching grades 7–12 in mathematics, social studies, or science in urban schools. The study excluded English and foreign language teachers.

Respondents split almost evenly in gender and there was at least one respondent from every secondary campus surveyed. Charter, vocational, or special purpose schools were not included in the study as they were unavailable for classroom level research. Except one, every site represents a Title I school. More than half (57%) of the respondents worked with junior high, and 43% worked with high school students. Eighteen respondents were certified or seeking certification in mathematics, 12 were certified or seeking certification in science, and 25 were certified or seeking certification in social studies. Each had a variety of teaching and nonteaching duties and six taught their content area only two class periods a day. The district asked respondents to consider themselves as content area teachers in the content area in which they were already certified or in which they were seeking certification.

PROCEDURES

The author distributed surveys to every beginning secondary teacher assigned to teach any type of social studies, mathematics, or science classes at 36 junior high and high school locations. The researcher sent the survey via intradistrict campus mail and made available at every school site through posting in the mailroom. The surveys were also available at the door after an announcement at two mandatory professional trainings for the beginning teachers. The survey was also distributed in university classrooms where many were attending to complete their certification.

The participation at every site was voluntary and confidential. To avoid duplication, the author asked each participant to give his or her personal campus ID number with the understanding that the researcher would not share the data collected and that the researcher would destroy personally identifiable information. They were urged to phone or email the researcher if they had questions about the survey and its results and seven participants did so. Their queries were about the procedures involved in the return of the survey and who had access to its contents.

At the conclusion of the survey, the researcher also asked the participants to write a brief description of their training in and understanding of financial literacy and a personal belief statement regarding financial literacy in their roles as secondary teachers. The complete survey is shown in Appendix 1 of this chapter.

The researcher then asked the participants to participate in informal taped conversations about the experience, share their thoughts and perspectives about financial literacy, its place in teaching and give general feedback about their participation in the research. Of the 55 participants, 16 individuals engaged in these post research conversations.

ANALYSIS

The researcher screened returned surveys for inappropriate understanding, survey non-completion or illegibility and, as a result, two surveys were omitted. These surveys were inaccurately completed, i.e., one participant circled every number on the Likert-type scale. Another circled all the 1s in one large all-encompassing circle. These two were not included in the data analysis. Thus, the overall response rate was approximately 50%—112 surveys distributed, 57 returned with 55 usable for the study. The researcher analyzed the mean score of each survey. A higher mean indicates greater awareness of financial literacy, and its importance and use in a secondary school curriculum.

RESULTS

Specifically, two questions guided this research: (a) Does content subject taught by the respondent influence interest in and perceived value of financial literacy in the curriculum? (b) Does traditional teacher preparation lead to a greater knowledge of the importance of financial literacy than other degree backgrounds?

The first research question concerned the relationship between subject area taught and interest in and perceived value of financial literacy. Table 3.1 provides statistics indicating that teachers of social studies had statistically significantly lower survey means than their mathematics or science counterparts.

Table 3.1: Mean Survey Scores Contrasted by Subject Area Taught.

Subject Taught	N	μ	S.D.	Post Hoc
1. Social Studies	18	3.56	0.28	1<2*
				1<3*
2. Mathematics	19	4.07	0.18	2<3
3. Science	18	3.96	0.34	.

*p<0.001.

Social studies teachers had a lower level of awareness of the importance of financial literacy in their curriculum as measured in the survey than did their teaching peers in mathematics and science.

The second research question considered the role of undergraduate preparation in understanding and value of financial literacy. Table 3.2 presents statistics indicating that participants who received traditional teacher preparation had a lower mean score than participants who had either arts and sciences or liberal arts background. This difference was statistically significant. The author utilized ANOVA to discern basic differences between each of the independent variables and the financial literacy mean scores.

Table 3.2: Means and Analysis of Variance by Preparation.

Educational Preparation	N	μ	S.D.	t
Traditional Teaching Prep	31	3.70	0.36	4.91*
No University Teaching Prep	24	4.09	0.16	

*p<0.001.

The teachers trained in traditional teacher preparation programs had a statistically significant lower mean average on the survey. The mean for traditionally trained teachers was 3.69 (S.D. = 0.36). The mean financial literacy value/awareness of teachers lacking this preparation was 4.0875 (S.D. = 0.16). The differences between the means are statistically significant at the 0.01 level DF(1, 53) = 24.11. The effect size using Cohen's d is considered large—1.36. The data strongly suggest that teachers enrolled in a variety of alternative certification programs were more aware of financial literacy and its value in their teaching than their peers who had received a traditional educational preparatory program at a college or university.

This was not a random sample. It was a voluntary exercise for the participants for which they received no compensation of any type. After analyzing the initial data, the researcher reanalyzed data to interpret whether race, gender, or grade level taught affected the mean scores. These factors did not affect the findings—the variances of each of these subgroups were not statistically significant.

PERSONAL STATEMENTS

The teachers' responses to the open-ended query at the end of the survey varied from one-sentence replies to several paragraphs. There were two questions asked in one paragraph as an addendum to the survey document.
The queries were:

1. What is your training and understanding of financial literacy?
2. Given more training and thinking of your own classroom, do you see the possibility of incorporating financial literacy topics routinely in your area of study? What would be an example of an activity you might use?

Respondents' replies were analyzed for similarities and thematic commonalities, with three general themes noted as common to the majority (greater than 50% of the replies).

First, most teachers, despite differences in preparation, believed they had little training about financial literacy in their former or current training programs. Three respondents remarked that the survey itself was their first introduction to the vocabulary or concept. Over 90% who answered the question stated that they had no previous formal training in any coursework or professional development specifically on the topic of financial literacy. Only three respondents stated that their training programs or professional development had "mentioned" financial literacy, but did not offer elaboration about this prior training or exposure. This result is not unlike Murphy's findings (2005). That research indicated that students did not receive appreciable instruction in financial literacy or its applications in their university training programs.

Second, most teachers do believe financial literacy is important (95%) but do not feel that it can reasonably be included in their daily practice due to many competing curricular demands. More than four-fifths (85%) of the respondents felt that although financial literacy might be important, too many other curricular demands take precedence due to, in great part, the state-mandated testing requirements. This resonates with Guilfoyle's (2007) assertion that the testing requirements of No Child Left Behind narrow curricula and drive curricula decisions.

Finally, there was a tendency in 66% of the responses to focus on bankruptcy as the prime issue of financial literacy, perhaps due to the local media coverage. Teachers considered bankruptcy the defining issue of financial literacy. Sixteen respondents said that bankruptcy was unrelated to their curricula, and eleven referred in their writing to predatory lending practices.

When writing about what activities could be incorporated in their personal classroom most activities cited as possible for the classroom involved check writing, computation of interest, credit card use or fraud, and bankruptcy. One participant wrote extensively about student loan and credit card debts and their influences on her employment and lifestyle choices. The teacher wrote that if she had possessed previous financial literacy knowledge, she could have prevented some of her own "costly" mistakes.

POSTSURVEY CONVERSATIONS

Sixteen teachers joined in three voluntary postsurvey conversations held at school sites after school hours about the survey and the topic of financial literacy in their teaching lives. The researcher asked the participants to reflect generally on the topic of financial literacy, their attitudes after participating in the research, and to provide feedback to the researcher. These conversations lasted from 65 to 85 minutes. The researcher taped the conversations with the permission of the participants.

Several teachers remarked that they were glad to have this topic brought to their attention and that they had simply never thought about financial literacy in terms of a teaching responsibility. It was, as one teacher put it, an "Aha!" moment. Another said that the survey brought financial literacy to her attention for the first time and she wondered why her teacher preparation classes had not brought the topic to her attention. How was she to know it was important if no one told her?

The researcher asked all three groups what financial literacy could look like in their teaching. Many felt that simple awareness and information would help them blend the data into their already existing lesson structures. Others felt that they had no "room" for it unless they dropped something else. They did not want another add-on. One teacher said she had "46 objectives to teach in 46 days" and there simply were no spontaneous learning moments in her curriculum. Several wanted materials to start the "ball rolling" as they did not feel that they had the time themselves.

When asked to give an example of a financial literacy lesson they could design which might "fit" their curriculum, only three participants had examples. These ideas were about creating interest problems, looking at creating graphs about economic activity, and evaluating car purchase versus lease. It is interesting to note that these lessons were essentially mechanical representations and reflected little dynamic or reflective activities. The researcher gave the participants a list of available web-based and curricular financial literacy resources which are already available in the school district as well as a copy of the Jump$tart survey results (Jump$tart Coalition, 2006) for their thinking and planning.

All felt that simple participation in the survey had influenced at least their thoughts about their role in financial literacy for their students. Almost half felt that at home modeling or training was a missing piece and that parents had the responsibility to present "good money models."

LIMITATIONS

Several limitations exist in the interpretation of the data presented. First, although there was identifiable information on each participant, the researcher was unable to match subject area respondent numbers and course loads. Often a teacher responder was certified in one area but teaching in another subject area for the majority of the instructional day. For example, it was unclear if the respondent was a math teacher due to certification or a science teacher due to practice. The researcher chose to label them by certification area that was reflective of their training but perhaps not of their daily practice. It may have been more difficult to envision the inclusion of financial literacy in a curriculum in which the teacher had less background knowledge. Future efforts should revise the survey and reanalyze the data, as well to look at the influence of this assignment mismatch.

Second, it is noteworthy that the timing of the survey occurred immediately after some local publicity regarding bankruptcy and the fate of the local "near poor" in the media. Many respondents (85%) referred to the almost concurrent media attention in their written remarks. The city has a history of bankruptcy issues that are often in the headlines. At this time, the nightly evening news featured bankruptcy data on almost every broadcast. There was a weeklong news series about the process of bankruptcy protection, local bankruptcy lawyers, bankruptcy effects on long-term financial health, bankruptcy and the poor, predatory lenders, and city/state resources for low-cost or free financial counseling about debt to avoid bankruptcy as a first financial option.

Additionally, the local newspaper also had a short series of written reports about how bankruptcy and level of poverty in the area was affecting community commerce, business relocation, and overall public financial health. It is unknown exactly how many survey participants read the paper or viewed the local news station that aired the reports, but certainly the media spotlighted the topic of financial literacy as it related in particular to bankruptcy and predatory lenders.

The media coverage that was coincident with the survey clearly affected the respondents' definition of financial literacy and their feelings of inclusion in their curriculum. Overall, the media depiction was dire and the respondents clearly reacted in that vein suggesting the main topic of financial literacy was bankruptcy.

Predatory lending was another topic reflected in their writing. One respondent wrote that this was a "societal issue not a school issue." The extensive media coverage did not feature any educational or curricular responses to the problem as it focused on the ramifications of bankruptcy and predatory lending in the economic life of the city and the consumers.

Third, self-report activities can be suspect. Research into self-report does however indicate that when respondents clearly understand what information is being requested, that accuracy increases (Armstrong, Jensen, McCaffrey, & Reynolds, 1976; Laing, 1988). While the reiteration and field test of the survey to refine its readability addressed this issue to some degree, collection of observational data could confirm or refute findings.

Fourth, the researcher administered the survey immediately after the Christmas holiday season and many of the campuses began their second semester "push" for state testing preparation. There have been more respondents or differing responses during another time of the year. One respondent wrote it was "the most stressful time" and she could not "add another thing." Perhaps distributing the survey at a less stressful curricular time would have affected both the survey response rate and responses themselves.

Defining university preparation is also a variable that is difficult to study. These participants came from several college settings; thus, coursework for each may have been markedly different. Overall, there can be assumptions of preparatory similarities, but one cannot quantify these similarities easily. Overall, traditional teachers with traditional teaching training do differ from their nontraditionally prepared peers but this training and its relationship to financial literacy knowledge and value warrants further study.

The other variable not considered or studied in this research was participant age. Generally, the teachers who were in the process of alternative certification are older than the traditionally prepared teachers who participated. It would be instructive to study whether older teachers with the probability of more adult financial interactions, e.g., buying a home, longer credit history, etc., might have a greater awareness, than their younger more traditionally trained peers, of the value of financial literacy.

Finally, the researcher was surprised at the level of naiveté regarding financial literacy in the respondents. Arguably, they do not yet have enough knowledge about financial literacy to recognize its importance in their curriculum. Repeatedly in conversation and in writings, they reduced financial literacy to bankruptcy, predatory lending, or savings. For a few, the topic was clearly a completely novel one for which they had no real opinion nor felt any curricular responsibility. Certainly, the lack of mention of financial literacy topics in their published curricular materials had some impact on this finding. To learn their personal knowledge of finances would have been instructive as it may influence their value of financial literacy in their classrooms.

SUGGESTIONS FOR FUTURE RESEARCH/IMPLICATIONS

Additional research needs to confirm or deny findings with larger samples collected through random processes. Nevertheless, this study provides a basis for conversation about teacher preparations, teaching expectations, and financial literacy connections.

There has been tremendous pressure placed on teachers due to state-mandated tests and No Child Left Behind legislation. As Guilfoyle (2007) writes, "In a NCLB-driven world, the list of what's not measured far exceeds any list of what is measured" (p. 12). She also writes that the old query, "Will this be on the test?" seems to have been transferred from student to teacher (p. 9). The beginning teachers repeatedly referred to the state test and its mandates in their responses, their anxiety about performance comparisons against a state-defined standard, and the overall pressure put on them by principals and peers about test performance.

In casual interviews with college faculty it is the same litany—no room in the curriculum for another topic. The universities fall into the same "test and be rated" mode as public schools.

This is an area requiring further research. Do college faculty members value financial literacy as a curricular topic? This question pertains particularly to those who train teachers for urban teaching. If they do value this area, what do these experiences look like? What materials and media do they use?

The state employing these teachers has not adopted financial literacy curriculum or standards specific to financial literacy or personal finance. In a survey of state education practices related to financial education released in July 2007 by the National Council on Economic Education, only 17 states require a course in economics as a graduation requirement and only seven states require students to take a personal finance course prior to graduation. Thus, as in many states, financial literacy as a separate curricular entity is a relatively short training often provided by outside consultants and enrollment is voluntary. Beginning teachers have a myriad of trainings to attend which are mandatory; hence, it is unlikely even if they were offered financial literacy training that they would attend. It appears that a significant disconnect occurs between current economic and social realities and the curricula of the schools. This disconnect threatens the lives of students, particularly those in communities of poverty.

Traditional teacher training did not positively affect the awareness of financial literacy in this research. This fact and the realities are that many people entering the profession are entering via nontraditional routes; alternative certification, certification through testing, emergency certification depending on the state of licensure and practice are indeed troubling for new teachers in high poverty areas. Those teachers in particular are in need of financial literacy awareness training.

Without it, the students in those classrooms, many from poverty, have little chance to learn or inculcate financial literacy practices in any environment—family, school, or community.

Financial literacy—despite being a focus of many national and state summits, grants, and programs—has yet to make its mark on public schooling in an organized and sustainable fashion. This research suggests that in many instances teacher preparation programs are not even acquainting students with the concepts of financial literacy. Practicing teachers, if they do anything at all related to financial literacy, have reduced the topic to very basic savings or bankruptcy terms. It would seem that the current environment does not provide beginning teachers sustained or meaningful training in any setting about financial literacy and its importance in the lives of students—at the university or in the workplace. Training, if it exists at all, is random and happenstance.

The exemplars given by beginning teachers in their responses to the open-ended queries were random, simplistic, and activity centered—such as check writing, opening a savings account, etc. There was little evidence in this research that beginning teachers of any educational background would initiate an activity that involved higher order thinking or discussion with a social justice or societal impact focus. Lucey (2007) reports a similar finding among mass-produced curriculum materials. Although there is some evidence of materials that prompt higher order thinking among students (e.g., http://www.publicdebt.treas.gov/mar/marmmath.pdf), educators need to employ stronger efforts in this area.

It may well be that the message of the need for financial literacy instruction is not getting to these publics in a manner which seems amenable to action. It could be that those who speak of the importance of financial literacy have not given the schools or universities the tools (or the mandates with which to infuse this needed life literacy into their daily practice.) In preparing educators and practitioners, researchers should consider studying successful university or school models that are sustainable and actionable. Until the states or nation responds to the matter of financial literacy as necessary to a long-term healthy economy, it seems clear that we will continue to have random acts of financial literacy scattered without coherence or sustainability across universities and schools.

CHAPTER UPDATE

According to the Council on Education's 2016 Survey of the States, efforts to implement financial literacy in classrooms has not changed appreciably, with only 17 states requiring high school students to take a course in personal finance,

20 states requiring students to take a course in economics, and 16 requiring testing in economics. Wendy Way and Karen Holden's (2009) seminal survey of over 500 teachers in eight states found respondents generally agree that financial literacy represents important curriculum content for K–12 education; however, they feel largely unprepared to teach the tenets of such content. Henning and Lucey (2017) observe a similar pattern of beliefs and behaviors among teacher educators.

QUESTIONS FOR DISCUSSION

1. To what extent do you observe implementation of financial literacy education in your school or institution? To what degree do the factors discussed in this chapter relate to the conditions that you observe?
2. Complete the survey in the chapter and compare your answers with classmates or colleagues. What are some classroom activities in your content area that you could have used to engage students in financial literacy? Would you consider these to be higher order thinking? Develop one question for each level of Bloom's taxonomy that you could ask the students during the activity. What activities could you devise based on the higher level thinking questions?
3. The website http://www.publicdebt.treas.gov/mar/marmmath.pdf presents four completely developed activities that could be adapted to classroom practice. In partners or small groups, choose one activity and present it to your classmates in a mini-lesson. After presenting the activity, discuss how you might modify the activity to emphasize aspects of financial literacy that relate to other content areas (e.g., social studies).
4. The current educational testing and accountability emphases/requirements have had a marked effect on what teachers teach and what teachers do not teach. This is a subject of much controversy and highly politicized debate. How does financial literacy "fit" in this environment? What subjects do you envision it most closely aligned with? How do your responses inform you about the simplicity or complexity of relating financial literacy to existing curricula?
5. Cooter mentions "communities of poverty" in the article. What similarities and differences might exist among financial literacy training needed by students coming from communities of poverty and those of students from communities that may be more affluent? How does the poverty or class of the learner change what we as teachers "expect" to teach in financial behaviors? Do children of poverty require a curriculum reflecting an awareness of that poverty?

APPENDIX 1

Please circle the number of the response that matches your understanding or current teaching practice.

1. Financial literacy is a topic of importance in the secondary curriculum in our country.

1	2	3	4	5
Strongly disagree	Somewhat disagree	No opinion/ neutral	Somewhat agree	Strongly agree

2. Financial literacy is a topic of importance in the secondary curriculum in our state.

1	2	3	4	5
Strongly disagree	Somewhat disagree	No opinion/ neutral	Somewhat agree	Strongly agree

3. Financial literacy is a topic that is addressed throughout my school district.

1	2	3	4	5
Strongly disagree	Somewhat disagree	No opinion/ neutral	Somewhat agree	Strongly agree

4. Financial literacy is a topic that is addressed in my grade/school.

1	2	3	4	5
Strongly disagree	Somewhat disagree	No opinion/ neutral	Somewhat agree	Strongly agree

5. Financial literacy is a life skill that should be taught in secondary schools.

1	2	3	4	5
Strongly disagree	Somewhat disagree	No opinion/ neutral	Somewhat agree	Strongly agree

6. If asked, I could define and explain financial literacy.

1	2	3	4	5
Strongly disagree	Somewhat disagree	No opinion/ neutral	Somewhat agree	Strongly agree

7. Financial literacy could be addressed in my current teaching assignment.

1	2	3	4	5
Strongly disagree	Somewhat disagree	No opinion/ neutral	Somewhat agree	Strongly agree

8. I have had some training or exposure to financial literacy as a curriculum topic.

1	2	3	4	5
Strongly disagree	Somewhat disagree	No opinion/ neutral	Somewhat agree	Strongly agree

9. I feel that I need training in financial literacy to better address it in my classroom.

1	2	3	4	5
Strongly disagree	Somewhat disagree	No opinion/ neutral	Somewhat agree	Strongly agree

10. Overall, I feel that financial literacy is important to the lives and futures of students.

1	2	3	4	5
Strongly disagree	Somewhat disagree	No opinion/ neutral	Somewhat agree	Strongly agree

Please answer the following open-ended questions as completely as you can. Feel free to write on both sides of this paper:

1. What is your training and understanding of financial literacy?

2. Given more training and thinking of your own classroom, do you see the possibility of incorporating financial literacy topics routinely in your area of study? What would be an example of an activity you might use?

Thank you for your participation.

NOTE

1. Dr. Cooter was affiliated with The University of Memphis at the time of the chapter's original publication.

REFERENCES

Armstrong, R. J., Jensen, J. A., McCaffrey, R. E., & Reynolds, C. H. (1976). The accuracy of self-reported class rank. *National ACAC Journal, 21*, 37–42.

Bernanke, B. S. (2006). *Financial literacy*. Testimony of Chairman Ben S. Bernanke before the Committee on Banking, Housing, and Urban Affairs of the United States Senate May 23, 2006, Washington, DC. Retrieved from http://www.federalreserve.gov/boarddocs/testimony/2006/20060523/default.htm

Board of Education, Memphis City Schools. (2007). *Regular meeting of the Board of Education of the Memphis City Schools*, April 23, 2007. Retrieved from http://www.memphis-schools.k12.tn.us/special.announcements/pdf/4-23-2007.Board.Minutes.pdf

Council on Economic Education. (2007). *Survey of the states: Economic and personal finance education in our nation's schools in 2007*. Retrieved from http://councilforeconed.org/wp/wp-content/uploads/2011/11/2007-Survey-of-the-States.pdf

Council on Economic Education. (2016). *Survey of the states: Economic and personal finance education in our nation's schools in 2016*. Retrieved from http://councilforeconed.org/wp/wp-content/uploads/2016/02/sos-16-final.pdf

Gillin, E. (2002). *Generation y flunks finance 101*. Retrieved from http://www.thestreet.com/markets/ericgillin/10007059.html

Guilfoyle, C. (2007). NCLB: Is there life beyond testing? *Educational Leadership, 64*(3), 8–13.

Henning, M. B., & Lucey, T. A. (2017). Elementary preservice teachers' and teacher educators' perceptions of financial literacy education. *The Social Studies*. Retrieved from http://tandfonline.com/doi/abs/10.1080/00377996.2017.1343792?journalCode=vtss20

Hogarth, J. M., & Hilgert, M. (2002). Financial knowledge, experience and learning preferences: Preliminary results from a new survey on financial literacy. *Consumer Interest Annual, 48*, 1–7.

Joo, S., Grable, J. E., & Bagwell, D. C. (2003). Credit card attitudes and behaviors of college students. *College Student Journal, 37*(4), 405–419.

Jump$tart Coalition for Personal Financial Literacy. (2006). *2006 survey of financial literacy among high school students*. Retrieved from http://www.jumpstartcoalition.com/upload/2006SurveyWithAnswers.doc

Laing, J. (1988). Self-report: Can it be of value as an assessment technique? *Journal of Counseling and Development, 67*, 60–61.

Lucey, T. A. (2007). The art of relating moral education to financial education: An equity imperative. *Social Studies Research and Practice, 2*(3), 486–500.

Murphy, A. J. (2005). Money, money, money: An exploratory study on the financial literacy of Black college students. *College Student Journal, 39*(3), 478–488.

National Center for Education Statistics. (2003). *School district demographic profile*. Retrieved from http://ncee.ed.gov

Way, W. L., & Holden, K. C. (2009). Teachers' background and capacity to teach personal finance: Results of a national study. *Journal of Financial Counseling and Planning, 20*(2), 64–78.

CHAPTER FOUR

Strategies AND Resources FOR Teaching Financial Literacy TO Youth WITH Disabilities

MARY BETH HENNING AND SARAH JOHNSTON-RODRIGUEZ
Northern Illinois University

Much of the standard financial literacy curriculum available to young adults fails to address students with special needs. A search of the JumpStart Clearinghouse using the search term "special education" provides only two resources (one of which, *Practical Money Skills for Life* (Visa, 2000–2016), will be recommended later in this book chapter) targeted to students with special needs.

Systemic issues such as segregated education, dropping out of school, unemployment, poverty, and lack of postsecondary training serve as barriers to financial literacy for students with disabilities (Wagner, Newman, Cameto, Garza, & Levine, 2005). Such obstacles should be recognized in implementing any curriculum and instruction for financial literacy. All students do not face an equal playing field, but if provided specific financial literacy education, all are enabled and competent to carry out financial choices (Pinto & Coulson, 2011; Roithmayr, 2014). Approaching financial education for students with disabilities from a social justice viewpoint, it is important to be "concerned with equity in all aspects of social and economic life and cultural recognition" (Pinto & Chan, 2010, p. 61). For all students to enjoy equity in relation to financial literacy, teachers need to be aware of the multiple issues that students, including those with disabilities, may be facing.

Although there are many health impairments and different physical special needs, we focus this chapter on the four categories which are most common among students receiving special education services: those who have specific learning disabilities (LD), speech and language impairments (SLI), intellectual disabilities (ID), and emotional and behavioral disabilities (EBD) (Minarik & Lintner,

2016). Because these are the most common disabilities among young adults, it is most important that financial literacy instruction address the unique needs of those with LD, ID, EBD, and SLI. While we recognize that financial literacy can and should be taught throughout the life span, the focus of this chapter is on curriculum and instruction for secondary students. The transition from school to work is most crucial and timely for financial education, thus our concern is for youth with disabilities who are of transition-age: 14–21 years old by federal definition (IDEA, 2004).

THE IMPORTANCE OF SELF-DETERMINATION

Due to the poverty circumstances experienced by many youth with disabilities and their need to develop strategies for economic self-sufficiency (Gargia-Iriarte, Balcazar, & Taylor-Ritzler, 2007; Leydorf & Kaplan, 2001; Mittapalli, Belson, & Ahmadi, 2009), this chapter is grounded in theories of self-determination. At its core, self-determination centers on personal choice and an individual's ability to make decisions and to take action centered on those decisions (Wehmeyer, 1996; Wehmeyer, Shogren, & Palmer, 2012). Self-determined individuals make choices and decisions regarding their own quality of life, free from undue external influence or interference (Wehmeyer, 1996). Individuals who can establish personal goals, engage in decision-making, participate in problem-solving, show self-awareness, and advocate for themselves are behaving in a self-determined manner (Martin & Marshall, 1995; Wehmeyer, 2015; Wehmeyer & Palmer, 2003). Clearly, self-determination is a goal for all students, but it may be more difficult for some students with disabilities to achieve. As one of the first to address the concept of self-determination for people with disabilities, Wehmeyer (1998) highlighted its importance in successful transition from school to work, career, and independent living.

Self-determination principles are integral aspects of Individual Education Plans (IEPs) and the Individuals with Disabilities Education Act (IDEA) because they are key to employment, education/training, and independent living (Mittapalli et al., 2009). Higher levels of self-determination among students with disabilities is connected to higher academic achievement (Konrad, Fowler, Walker, Test, & Wood, 2007), enhanced transition outcomes (Wehmeyer & Palmer, 2003), and higher quality of life (Shogren, Lopez, Wehmeyer, Little, & Pressgrove, 2006). Recent analyses of evidence-based transition practices indicate that self-determination is a key predictor of positive postgraduation outcomes for students with disabilities (Test, Fowler, & Kohler, 2013; Wehmeyer, Palmer, Lee, Williams-Diehm, & Shogren, 2011).

A student's ability to develop self-determination skills is shaped by access to knowledge and opportunities for wielding that knowledge through meaningful choice-making. Specific to financial education, access to curriculum and acquisition of financial skills allows students to make important financial decisions and control personal finances (Mittapalli et al., 2009).

The dearth of self-determination skills in transition curriculum (curriculum geared to preparing youth to transition from school to independence and paid employment) is viewed as a persistent impediment for students in pursuit of successful post-school outcomes (Carter, Trainor, Cakiroglu, Swedeen, & Owens, 2010; Izzo & Lamb, 2003; Stodden, 2000; Wehmeyer, 2015). However, financial literacy offers a natural curriculum area for developing self-determination. Financial literacy curriculum reflects self-determination skills by focusing on (a) individual budgets, (b) personal agency, and (c) financial management services (Ambsbaugh, 2007). As youth with disabilities enter adulthood, it is vital that they join the labor force with the necessary financial skills to assist them in achieving independence. Youth with special needs must learn the tools to advocate for themselves and make prudent financial decisions (Mittapalli et al., 2009).

From a sociocultural view of disability, barriers to conventional financial literacy for people with disabilities come from systems, policies, and legal regulations. While it is critical that youth with disabilities join the labor force with the requisite financial skills to assist them in achieving independence, it is also important that, given their unique circumstances, they also have the tools to advocate for themselves and make sound financial decisions (Mittapalli et al., 2009). Given the existing differences between employment, poverty, and postsecondary education rates between students with and without disabilities, it is urgent that youth with disabilities have access to financial education (Wagner et al., 2005).

Underlying principles of self-determination theory rest on aspects of intrinsic motivation that propel an individual to grow, learn new skills, and engage with the social environment. The same internal motivation to strive toward self-fulfillment and social engagement can be impeded by conditions or factors in the individual's social surroundings (Benita, Roth & Deci, 2014; Narvaez, 2006; Narvaez Gleason, Schorc, & Panksepp, 2013; Ryan & Deci, 2000). In other words, while a person may be motivated to act in an autonomous manner and strive toward self-growth and actualization, factors in the immediate social environment can diminish and undermine such drive. For example, a student with a disability who aspires to pursue a career in science, yet is lacking financial resources, skills, role models, or college preparation guidance, may find it difficult to overcome these obstacles. Conversely, conditions supportive of autonomy, acquisition of new skills, and engagement will promote personal growth, competence, and connectedness (Steele, 2010). In this instance, the student with a disability who receives financial literacy instruction, summer job opportunities, mentoring, and participates in a money management support group may find the path to postsecondary education achievable. Given the capacity of external factors to influence an individual's self-determination, it follows that factors such as financial literacy and financial competence could serve to either diminish or promote a sense of personal agency (Ryan & Deci, 2000, 2008).

KEY FINANCIAL LITERACY CURRICULUM CONCEPTS FOR YOUTH WITH DISABILITIES

The *National Standards for Financial Literacy* (CEE, 2013) identify fundamental concepts and skills that all students should learn for basic financial literacy. We believe earning income, budgeting, saving, banking, and insuring are most relevant to promoting self-determination: these concepts all provide context for students to develop personal goals, engage in decision-making, participate in problem-solving, and take actions that will serve their best interests. The remaining key concepts in the *National Standards for Financial Literacy* are using credit and financial investing. While credit and investment are important concepts for everyone to master, we believe that they are not the top priority for individuals with special needs whose needs, at least initially, are more basic. A rationale for these five key skills to teach in financial literacy is provided below, along with explanations of how they specifically apply to students with the most common special needs.

EARNING INCOME

While the employment rate of young adults with disabilities has increased over the past few years, income levels for most young adults with disabilities are still low. According to The National Transitional Longitudinal Study (NLTS2, 2011), 75% of young adults with disabilities report an annual income of $25,000 or less while 20% report annual earnings of less than $5,000. According to Gargia-Iriarte et al. (2007), economic and employment problems are of great concern to case managers supporting youth with disabilities. The first priority in financial literacy should be helping students understand what earning income means and how to do it. Not only does paid work give individuals with disabilities opportunities for integration into the community, but it allows them more options for budgeting, saving, banking, and insuring. Low employment expectations, and confusing government programs with conflicting eligibility criteria have prevented many young people with disabilities from making successful transitions from school to employment (National Collaborative on Workforce and Disability, 2012). In order to be more self-determined and financially literate, youth with disabilities need opportunities to set employment goals and advocate for themselves when seeking paid work. Youth with disabilities are more likely to be fired than those without disabilities, so employment supports are key (Cook, 2006; Gargia-Iriarte et al., 2007). We will recommend curriculum and instructional strategies for how to teach earning income at the end of this chapter.

BUDGETING

Youth with disabilities need ample practice budgeting, after they understand the concept that a spending plan is made for money earned. Parents in one study reported that the large majority (84%) of youth with disabilities receives an allowance or other personal spending money (Cameto, Levine, Wagner, & Marder, 200). Thus, how to make a plan for spending their money is relevant to most students with disabilities. Mittapalli (2015) describes one approach, developed by Tom Nerney of the Center for Self-Determination, to incorporate budging into Individual Education Plans (IEPs) when a

> … highly personalized individual budget [is] integrated within a student and family directed Individual Education Program (IEP). The youth with a disability or disabilities and his or her family get together with supportive people in their community to develop a vision for the youth's future. This vision becomes the basis for an implementation plan and budget for achieving the goals. This implementation plan and budget are then incorporated into the IEP to reflect the transition plans. (p. 110)

Financial literacy education should offer students practice making a budget and considering ways of changing the budget to meet different goals and circumstances. College students with disabilities have identified lack of knowledge of budgeting as a key barrier to college success (Lehmann, Davies, & Laurin, 2000). Budgeting helps students develop self-awareness, problem-solve, and make autonomous decisions: all goals of self-determination.

SAVING

Saving for emergency expenses like a car repair or medical bill strains many American budgets (Bell, 2015; Board of Governors of the Federal Reserve System, 2015). Managing government benefits makes saving and developing assets especially challenging for many students with disabilities (Mittapalli et al., 2009). National surveys indicate that eight years postgraduation, 59% of young adults with disabilities have a savings account while only 41% have a checking account (NLTS2, 2011). Undoubtedly, there is greater need for education about savings.

One strategy that promotes asset accumulation for people with disabilities is the Individual Development Account (IDA) (Leydorf & Kaplan, 2001; Lombe, Huang, Putnam, & Cooney, 2008). IDAs allow lower-income families and persons with disabilities who receive financial assistance such as Supplemental Security Income to save a portion of their earned income without losing benefits. These savings must be earmarked for specific purposes such as education (AFI, 2016; Center for Self-Determination, 2005). But one study has suggested that individuals with disabilities save less than their counterparts without disabilities (Lombe et al., 2008). Financial literacy instruction should introduce students with disabilities to savings options such as IDAs. Learning to save is a topic for which there is need for more self-determination and financial literacy.

BANKING

Due to a prevalence of low income, youth with disabilities are more likely to be in families that use alternative banking services (such as Walmart MoneyCards), so financial literacy curriculum should introduce youth to the benefits and accessibility of banks and credit unions (FDIC, 2014). Not only do teachers need specific resources to teach about banks to youth with disabilities, they must have the local contextual knowledge to share with students which financial institutions will be accessible to them (Johnson & Sherraden, 2007). Financial literacy education should introduce how to use check registers and debit cards. While some students with disabilities may have personal agents (either a family member, guardian, or appointed agent) who act on their behalf in terms of making purchases, banking or other transactions, most students with disabilities can learn to bank. With differentiation and systematic instruction, the goal should be for all young adults to understand the role of credit unions and banks in their lives.

Financial literacy education should promote self-determination by empowering youth to make informed choices about where they do their banking. One study reported that over 60% of families of people with disabilities were asking their physicians about financial planning, instead of a financial professional (Harnett, 2006). Youth with special needs can be taught to advocate for themselves in financial institutions by developing trusting relationships with financial service providers.

INSURING

Students with disabilities need to understand the importance of insuring their health, place of residence, and vehicle (if applicable). While earning income allows more flexibility in budgeting and saving, it also offers the opportunity for different kinds of health and life insurance. Understanding the relative merits of Medicaid, the Health Insurance Exchange of the Affordable Medical Care Act, and private insurance is crucial for all students with disabilities.

As many youth with disabilities may come from families with fewer resources, the need to have insurance seems contraindicated. However, health insurance provides an individual with autonomy and opportunities for decision-making in terms of selecting health care and health care providers. Additionally, insurance provides protection for assets and against liability claims.

UNIVERSAL DESIGN FOR MAKING INSTRUCTION RELEVANT TO STUDENTS WITH SPECIAL NEEDS

Access to high quality education for all students, inclusive of those with disabilities, is a right embedded in educational law and mandates, specifically No Child Left Behind and IDEA (2004). However, for many students with disabilities, legal mandates are not enough to unlock the doors to understanding what is being taught in a classroom. While the majority of students with disabilities spend much of their day in the general education classroom, the presence of inflexible curriculum and instruction contributes to ongoing difficulties in their learning (NCUDL, 2014). Inflexible curriculum was not created for use with diverse groups of students and does not provide instruction for students at various levels of understanding by modeling or scaffolding information (Fowler, Test, Cease-Cook, Toms, & Bartholomew, 2014: NCUDL, 2014).

Universal Design for Learning (UDL) is a research-based framework for designing curriculum and instruction that allows diverse students to understand and engage in the learning process (CAST, 2011; Fowler et al., 2014; NCUDL, 2014). In UDL,

> students are provided with scaffolds and supports to deeply understand and engage with standards-based material. They not only have access to content and facts, but they learn to ask questions, find information, and use that information effectively. They learn how to learn. (CAST, 2011)

Essentially, UDL serves as a blueprint for generating teaching objectives, strategies, materials, and assessments while simultaneously creating abundant supports and minimizing obstacles. UDL makes it possible for students with wide differences in their abilities, such as speaking, reading, writing, understanding English, paying attention, organizing, engaging, or remembering, to more fully participate in inclusive settings (Burgstahler & Cory, 2008; Casper & Leuichovius, 2005). An example of UDL that helps everyone (disabled and nondisabled alike) would be offering menus with pictures. Allowing all learners to see photos along with text improves understanding for almost everyone. Just as a fast-food menu with photos is helpful for making informed choices, financial literacy curriculum that offers pictures along with text can help everyone access the curriculum. The goal of UDL is to minimize the difference between the requirements of the curriculum and a student's lack of ability by enriching and modifying the learning context (Wehmeyer, 2015). Thus, integrating UDL into curriculum and teaching allows financial literacy educators to address diverse learning needs with an array of instructional methods and materials.

As outlined by the Center for Applied Special Technology (CAST), UDL incorporates three primary learning principles: multiple means of representation, multiple means of expression, and multiple means of engagement (Rose & Meyer, 2006). All of these principles are recommended by the National Collaborative on Workforce and Disability for Youth (NCWD, 2012). They are essential to high quality curriculum for all subject areas, including the topic addressed here—financial literacy.

MULTIPLE MEANS OF REPRESENTATION

Financial literacy can be quite demanding if the content is unclear to the student and requires undue effort for the student to comprehend. Only offering worksheets about budgets or printed material would not meet the UDL criterion of multiple means of representation. UDL recognizes that it is critical to make important curricular content perceptible to all learners. This requires that key information is offered in a more malleable and customized manner through various modalities that let the learner adapt (e.g., enlarge the text or focus on pictures). Examples could include a call-out box of background information displayed on the side, or enlarged or colored text presented digitally. Or, key ideas can be presented through video, pictures, graphs, or charts instead of text. This UDL principle suggests that educators offer multiple ways of teaching any financial literacy concept.

For example, when learning how to earn income, students could access information through a variety of pathways. Earning income could be demonstrated via a field trip to different job sites, listening to different stories about work, or by interviewing a guest in the classroom. A student with a cognitive disability could view pictures or video clips that help explain earning income, as opposed to struggling to decipher content by reading text. In short, students should not just read about financial literacy or hear about it, they should see multiple examples of the concept shown in myriad ways.

MULTIPLE MEANS OF EXPRESSION

There is no method of expression that matches every student need. Using multiple means of expression provides students with different avenues to demonstrate or display their knowledge. Students with speech disabilities can communicate their learning using alternative communication or assistive technologies. A student with a LD such as dyslexia may succeed at telling stories; however, the same student may do poorly in efforts to convey the same information in an essay. UDL would provide the opportunity for the student to convey financial concepts orally or visually. This illustrates the need to offer alternative means for expression, to provide a level playing field, and to facilitate opportunities for a student with a disability to successfully convey learning and ideas in the classroom setting.

This UDL principle is that students must be offered different ways of exhibiting their learning. Besides methods that rely primarily on writing, such as typical paper and pencil tests or essays, students could demonstrate knowledge about saving by designing a savings plan, creating a savings plan online using a template or interactive simulation, or by developing a video to teach others money saving tips. By using the principles of UDL, students with disabilities should have various ways to demonstrate their mastery of financial literacy concepts.

MULTIPLE MEANS OF ENGAGEMENT

Students vary significantly in how they can be motivated or involved in learning. For some students with emotional or LD, offering choices during lessons can increase motivation for learning. Providing opportunities for choice in tasks, tools, sequence, or timing of the lesson can promote self-determination, satisfaction in completion, and enhance students' feelings of connectedness to learning (CAST, 2011; Courey, Tappe, Siker, & LePage, 2013; NCUDL, 2014).

UDL suggests engaging students in learning centers to stimulate their curiosity and enthusiasm via creative, authentic, and hands-on activities (CAST, 2011; Fowler et al., 2014; NCUDL, 2014). By offering various means of engagement, financial educators capture learners' attention and maintain their interaction with the curriculum (Courey et al., 2013). While some students with disabilities may respond positively to innovative or spontaneous approaches, others, such as some students with autism, may react negatively to changes in routine or to the unfamiliar. Thus, a combination of routines, careful attention to preparation and directions, as well as flexibility, is necessary in financial literacy education for students with special needs.

Financial literacy educators should offer options related to student interests and promote student collaboration. UDL principles suggest that financial literacy education should optimize relevance and authenticity as a means of connecting students to the materials. Given that many students with disabilities live below or at poverty level, background knowledge and experience with financial matters may be less than positive. Such students may face difficulty in reading articles or completing worksheets on topics that they perceive as having little relevance to their life. Instead, many students with disabilities may be more engaged in financial activities related to insurance when allowed to connect insurance needs to their families, cultural backgrounds, and community context.

RECOMMENDED FINANCIAL LITERACY CURRICULUM AND STRATEGIES FOR STUDENTS WITH SPECIAL NEEDS

We recommend specific lessons and resources from five financial literacy curricula that are web-based and/or easily available to teachers and students. These curricula are *Financial Fitness for Life* (Gellman & Laux, 2011), *Practical Money Skills* (Visa, 2000–2016), *Finance in the Classroom* (Utah, n.d.), *Money Talks 4 Teens* (University of California Cooperative Extension, 2008), and *Money Smart for Young Adults* (FDIC, 2011). They were selected based on principles of universal design (CAST, 2011), self-determination theory (Wehmeyer, 2015), and the recommendations of Caniglia and Courtney (2013). These five curricula are further reviewed by Henning and Johnston-Rodriguez (in press).

All of the curricula recommended in this chapter, with the exception of *Financial Fitness for Life* (Gellman & Laux, 2011), are available at no monetary cost to all. The visuals from the teachers' guides for *Financial Fitness for Life* are available at no cost on the Council for Economic Education website (http://councilforeconed.org/resource/financial-fitness-for-life-grades-9-12/), but *Financial Fitness for Life* is sold for a moderate cost from the online store at the Council for Economic Education website (http://store.councilforeconed.org/t/categories/financial-fitness-for-life/s/ascend_by_name). Teachers may be able to receive all the *Financial Fitness for Life* materials without financial cost, if they register for a professional development workshop offered by the Council for Economic Education (CEE) or one of the state or regional centers of economic education affiliated with the CEE.

EARNING INCOME

Financial Fitness for Life (Gellman & Laux, 2011) includes four different lesson plans on earning income. Financial educators will find the *Financial Fitness for Life* curriculum contains many different kinds of representations, engagement, and opportunities for students' expression of their learning. The first lesson, "Looking for a Job," specifically discusses the Americans with Disabilities Act when preparing the students for practice job interviews and résumé writing. The second lesson plan, "Making Your Own Job," encourages entrepreneurship and taps into students' creativity to develop commercials. These two lessons, in particular, encourage students' development of self-determination as they promote choice-making, empowerment, self-awareness, and self-advocacy.

An entire section of the *Practical Money Skills* (Visa, 2000–2016) website (https://www.practicalmoneyskills.com/foreducators/lesson_plans/special.php) is devoted to lesson plans that are approved by the Council for Exceptional Children targeted for young adults with LD. The scripted lesson plan "Making Money" includes worksheets, quizzes, presentation slides, and an interview guide. Students who would appreciate their financial literacy represented by superheroes, may like *Guardian of the Galaxy*, a comic created in 2016. *Practical Money Skills* offers several full-color, quickly downloadable comics in seven different languages. This comic format may appeal to and engage students interested in comics, while teaching key concepts of earning income, saving, and budgeting.

Money Talks 4 Teens (University of California Cooperative Extension, 2008) provides links to pdfs for teen guides: magazine-like newsletters that can be used to teach about earning income, budgeting, and banking. There are four full-color magazines that can be printed out or projected to teach about working. Students who enjoy easy-to-read magazines will appreciate this medium for learning about earning income.

Many worksheets related to earning income can be found on the *Finance in the Classroom* (Utah, n.d.) website. Especially relevant to students with special needs were the lesson plans entitled "Career Short Stories" and "Wages and Me" on the *Finance in the Classroom* website. "Career Short Stories" asks students to write their own fictional short story about a specific career. "Wages and Me" guides students to use the Federal Bureau of Labor Statistics online to investigate particular jobs of interest to them.

BUDGETING

Financial Fitness for Life (Gellman & Laux, 2011) features a lesson plan to teach budgeting with a script for a call-in radio show. Students are invited to take roles in the radio show as well as problem-solve different budgeting dilemmas. *Financial Fitness for Life* offers exemplary opportunities for students to engage in budgeting and express their learning in multiple ways.

One of the lesson plans, approved by the Council for Exceptional Children, on the *Practical Money Skills* (Visa, 2000–2016) website is called "Budgeting your Money." Besides worksheets, quizzes, and presentation slides, it includes a budgeting game with manipulatives. *Avengers Saving the Day* teaches budgeting (and banking) through a story featuring Spider-Man, Iron Man, Black Widow, and Thor. The comic book can be found on the *Practical Money Skills* (2000–2016) website. From a UDL perspective, *Practical Money Skills* offers a variety of different forms of representation of the concept of budgeting.

Many lesson plans and videos can be found on budgeting on the *Finance in the Classroom* (Utah, n.d.) website. The practical resources for students to use in planning low-cost dates are particularly relevant to promoting self-determination as they promote making choices, empowerment, and self-awareness.

Money Talks 4 Teens (University of California Cooperative Extension, 2008) features online games for students needing to make healthy inexpensive grocery store purchases within a budget. The Expense Station game allows players to create a budget, based on diverse and realistic expenses. Students can choose to play the game with the status of single parent with a child, which includes variables like receiving welfare, food stamps, earned income credit, and a childcare subsidy while taking General Educational Development (GED) classes. Considering the prevalence of poverty among students with special needs, this is a notable approach to budgeting.

The *Money Smart for Young Adults* (FDIC, 2011) module "Setting Financial Goals" offers students an opportunity to practice self-efficacy and explicitly practice goal-setting and budgeting skills. Financial educators wanting scripted instruction, as well as cooperative learning activities and different multiple-choice assessments, will appreciate the 40-page instructor guide and 29-page student guide offered by the FDIC.

SAVING

Finance in the Classroom (Utah, n.d.) offers many online videos, songs, PowerPoints, and lesson plans about saving. Some of the videos are accessed more easily by Utah educators, but many are freely available online. The savings lesson plans in *Finance in the Classroom* are correlated with standards in social studies, language arts, or mathematics at the 9th grade level. Many online calculators (to calculate insurance, benefits, retirement, and savings goals) and printables under student resources may be especially applicable to students with special needs.

Money Talks 4 Teens (University of California Cooperative Extension, 2008) provides links to three different magazines about saving. A video entitled "Making Your Dreams Come True" offers an introduction to saving from the perspective of multicultural teens. Goal-setting and self-awareness tie closely to saving and self-determination.

The *Money Smart for Young Adults* (FDIC, 2011) "Pay Yourself First" module on saving includes a pretest, posttest, and PowerPoint slides within its 60-page instructor guide. The 43-page participant guide explains about IDAs and 529 savings plans, both very relevant to students with special needs. *Practical Money Skills* (Visa, 2000–2016) also features a lesson plan on "Saving and Investing" that is traditional in its direct instruction and worksheets to assess knowledge of different interest rates. Charts and case studies of two different savers make *Financial Fitness for Life* (Gellman & Laux, 2011) more engaging on the topic of saving than *Money Smart for Young Adults* or *Practical Money Skills*.

BANKING

The "Banking Basics" lesson plan in *Financial Fitness for Life* (Gellman & Laux, 2011) includes numerous worksheets to analyze online banking compared to traditional checking accounts. An interview guide suggests students survey different financial service institutions in their community about services relevant to them. By teaching students how to make decisions about different banks, *Financial Fitness for Life* offers opportunities for youth with special needs to improve their self-determination.

Money Talks 4 Teens (University of California Cooperative Extension, 2008) has three full-color magazines about banking. *Money Talks 4 Teens* also offers online games for students needing to learn how to select an ATM or just review banking skills. These multiple forms of representation and engagement will appeal to students who prefer using more technology in their learning and financial life.

Money Smart for Young Adults (FDIC, 2011) provides a participant guide and scripted teacher guide to teach directly about topics such as using a check book, protecting against identity theft, and selecting a bank. The modules are very explicit, and abundant current material allows teachers to pick and choose from the banking resources that best serve their students. Multiple-choice assessments, PowerPoint slides, role plays, and other activities are reflective of UDL principles for representation, engagement, and expression. Worksheets to compare banks and practice using a check register are notable. *Practical Money Skills* (Visa, 2000–2016) offers a shorter lesson plan entitled "Using Banking Services," which is more basic.

INSURING

Insurance is the topic that seems to have the least-developed curriculum and resources available within the curriculum we recommend. *Financial Fitness for Life* (Gellman & Laux, 2011) provides a well-developed lesson plan entitled "Managing Risk" which asks students to choose among different assets to insure. A card game simulating chances of loss is included to help students understand the need for multiple types of insurance.

Several good videos on life insurance can be found on the *Finance in the Classroom* (Utah, n.d.) website. *Finance in the Classroom* also offers several lesson plans aimed at 10th graders regarding car and renters' insurance. But many times, insurance is embedded or hidden within other topics. For example, *Money Talks 4 Teens* (University of California Cooperative Extension, 2008) provides a "How to Buy a Car" video, in which the teen hosts briefly discuss car insurance costs. Hopefully, the more that students can see that making goals and decisions to protect and meet their goals, the more self-determination they will develop. Insurance is an area ripe for more development of self-awareness among youth with special needs.

CONCLUSION

As students with disabilities make the transition from school to adult life, the responsibilities facing them can be overwhelming. Given that many students with disabilities face issues of poverty, lack of opportunity, and high unemployment, becoming proficient in essential financial skills can play a vital role in their development as self-determined adults. While the need for financial education is compelling, the demand for accessible curriculum is critical. Understanding the unique needs and learning challenges that students with disabilities present and how to provide comprehensible materials is a timely and essential task facing financial educators.

No single financial literacy curriculum, that we reviewed, meets every goal of universal design and self-determination. Yet, we were able to find many lessons and compelling resources for an individualized approach for financial education for students with disabilities. A targeted approach to the four websites we recommend, as well as selections from *Financial Fitness for Life* (Gellman & Laux, 2011), can provide a strong foundation for accessible lessons and assessments about earning income, budgeting, saving, banking, and insuring. Educators can use published online budgeting games, team-based savings games, interviews of bankers, songs, videos, magazines, and comic books to engage learners with special needs in meeting transition goals and developing requisite skills for adult life.

In all financial literacy curricula, teachers need to be aware of biases and relevance of the resources that they use (Willis, 2008). Some financial literacy concepts will be more difficult or more important for certain students, based on individual situations and learning needs. A customized approach that makes as much financial literacy accessible to all should benefit all members of our society.

QUESTIONS FOR DISCUSSION

1. This article asserts that self-determination and targeted financial literacy skills will assist individuals with disabilities to achieve life goals. Since many live at home for extended periods into adulthood, how would you suggest their families be involved in this work?

2. How does poverty as a life circumstance make financial literacy training not only more necessary but also more difficult?
3. Have you personally considered UDL in your work? What accommodations or changes have you made or might you make in your teaching and classroom?
4. The authors remark that a "customized approach" is necessary for students with disabilities. How might that be a challenge for a regular classroom teacher?
5. What training/resources would you recommend as a critical first step for teachers' knowledge in their financial literacy work with students with disabilities?

REFERENCES

Ambshaugh, T. (2007). *Smart start. Enhancing access, equity, and opportunity for youth with disabilities.* Retrieved from http://wid.org
Assets for Independence. (2016). *Understanding asset development for individuals with disabilities.* Retrieved from http://idaresources.acf.hhs.gov
Bell, C. (2015). *Budgets can crumble in times of trouble.* Retrieved from http://www.bankrate.com/finance/smart-spending/money-pulse-0115.aspx
Benita, M., Roth, G., & Deci, E. L. (2014). When are mastery goals more adaptive? It depends on experiences of autonomy support and autonomy. *Journal of Educational Psychology, 106*(1), 258.
Board of Governors of the Federal Reserve System. (2015). *Report on the economic well-being of U.S. Households in 2014.* Retrieved from www.federalreserve.gov/econresdata/2014-report-economic-well-being-us-households-201505.pdf
Burgstahler, S., & Cory, R. (2008). Moving in from the margins: From accommodation to universal design. In S. L. Gabel & S. Danforth (Eds.), *Disability and the politics of education: An international reader* (pp. 561–582). New York, NY: Peter Lang.
Cameto, R., Levine, P., Wagner, M., & Marder, C. (2004). *Transition planning for students with disabilities.* Menlo Park, CA. SRI International. Retrieved from http://www.nlts2.org/reports/2004_11/index.html.
Caniglia, J., & Courtney, S. (2013). A review of financial literacy programs for K-12 students with intellectual disabilities: Utilizing the principles of universal design for learning. *The Practical Teacher.* Retrieved from http://www.naset.org/3738.0.html
Carter, E.W., Trainor, A. A., Cakiroglu, O., Swedeen, B., & Owens, L. (2010). Availability of and access to career development activities for transition-age youth with disabilities. *Career Development for Exceptional Individuals, 33*(1), 13–24.
Casper, B., & Leuichovius, D. (2005). *Universal design for learning and the transition to a more challenging academic curriculum: Making it in middle school and beyond* (NCSET Report). Retrieved from http://eric.ed.gov/ERICWebPortal/detail?accno=ED495873
CAST (2011). *Universal design for learning guidelines.* Retrieved from http://www.udlcenter.org/sites/udlcenter.org/files/updateguidelines2_0.pdf
Center for Self-Determination. (2005). *Individual development accounts support financial goals.* Retrieved from http://www.centerforself-determination.com/docs/Archive/2% 203.pdf

Cook, J. A. (2006). Employment barriers for persons with psychiatric disabilities: Update of a report for the president's commission. *Psychiatric Services, 57*(10), 1391–1405.

Council for Economic Education. (2013). *National standards for financial literacy.* New York, NY: Author.

Courey, S. J., Tappe, P., Siker, J., & LePage, P. (2013). Improved lesson planning with universal design for learning (UDL). *Teacher Education and Special Education: The Journal of the Teacher Education Division of the Council for Exceptional Children, 36*(1), 7–27.

Federal Deposit Insurance Corporation. (2011). *Money Smart—A financial education program.* Retrieved from https://www.fdic.gov/consumers/consumer/moneysmart/young.html

Federal Deposit Insurance Corporation. (2014). *2013 FDIC National Survey of Unbanked and Underbanked Households.* Retrieved from https://www.fdic.gov/householdsurvey/2013report.pdf

Fowler, C. H., Test, D. W., Cease-Cook, J., Toms, O., & Bartholomew, A. (2014). Policy implications of high school reform on college and career readiness of youth with disabilities. *Journal of Disability Policy Studies, 25*(1), 19–29.

Gargia-Iriarte, E., Balcazar, F., & Taylor-Ritzler, R. (2007). Analysis of case managers' support of youth with disabilities transitioning from school to work. *Journal of Vocational Rehabilitation, 26*(3), 129–140.

Gellman, S., & Laux, S. (2011). *Financial fitness for life (Grades 9–12).* New York, NY: Council for Economic Education.

Harnett, J. (2006). New century workers with disabilities: Why financial education matters for Americans with disabilities. *World Institute on Disability.* Retrieved from http://wid.org/center-on-economic-growth/programs-of-the-center-on-economic-growth/access-to-assets/equity/equity-e-newsletter-summer-2006/new-century-workers-with-disabilities-why-financial-education-matters-for-americans-with-disabilities/

Henning, M. B., & Johnston-Rodriguez, S. (in press). Evaluating financial literacy curriculum for young adults with special needs: A review of content, universal design for learning, and culturally responsive curriculum principles. *Journal of Social Studies Research.*

Individuals with Disabilities Education Improvement Act. (2004). Pub.L. No. 108–446, 20 U.S.C. §§1400 et.seq.

Izzo, M., & Lamb, M. P. (2003). Developing self-determination through career development activities: Implications for vocational rehabilitation counselors. *Career Development for Exceptional Individuals, 19*, 71–78.

Johnson, E., & Sherraden, M. S. (2007). From financial literacy to financial capability among youth. *Journal of Sociology & Social Welfare, 34*(3), 119–146.

Konrad, M., Fowler, C. H., Walker, A. R., Test, D. W., & Wood, W. M. (2007). Effects of self-determination interventions on the academic skills of students with learning disabilities. *Learning Disability Quarterly, 30*(2), 89–113.

Lehmann, J. P., Davies, T. G., & Laurin, K. M. (2000). Listening to student voices about postsecondary education. *Teaching Exceptional Children, 32*(5), 60–65.

Leydorf, D., & Kaplan, D. (2001). *Use of individual development accounts by people with disabilities: Barriers and solutions.* Policy Brief. Oakland, CA: World Institute on Disability.

Lombe, M., Huang, J., Putnam, M., & Cooney, K. (2008). Exploring saving performance in an IDA for people with disabilities: Some preliminary findings. CSD Working Papers No. 08–27.

Martin, J. E., & Marshall, L. H. (1995). ChoiceMaker: A comprehensive self-determination transition program. *Intervention in School and Clinic, 30*(3), 147–156.

Minarik, D., & Lintner, T. (2016). *Social studies & exceptional learners.* Silver Springs, MD: National Council for the Social Studies.

Mittapalli, K. M. (2015). Financial literacy for youth with disabilities: Issue paper. In G. Lowry (Ed.), *Financial literacy for youth with disabilities* (pp. 85–181). New York, NY: Nova.

Mittapalli, K. M., Belson, S. I., & Ahmadi, H. (2009). *Financial literacy for youth with disabilities.* Gaithersburg, MD: Social Dynamics.

Narvaez, D. (2006). Integrative ethical education. In M. Killen & J. G. Smetana (Eds.), *Handbook of moral development* (pp. 703–733). Mahwah, NJ: Lawrence Erlbaum.

Narvaez, D., Gleason, T., Schore, A., & Panksepp, J. (2013). The value of using an evolutionary framework for gauging children's well-being. In D. Narvaez, J. Panksepp, A. Schore, & T. Gleason (Eds.), *Evolution, early experience and human development: From research to practice and policy.* New York, NY: Oxford University Press. doi:10.1093/acprof:oso/9780199755059.003.0001

National Center on Universal Design for Learning. (2014). *UDL guidelines: Theory to practice.* Retrieved from http://www.udlcenter.org/

National Collaborative on Workforce and Disability for Youth. (2012). *Using Universal Design for Learning: Successful transition models for educators working with youth with learning disabilities.* InfoBrief, 33.

National Longitudinal Transition Study 2. (2011) *The post-high school outcome of young adults with disabilities up to 8 years after high school.* Retrieved from http://www.nlts2.org/reports/2011_09_02/index.html

Pinto, L. E., & Chan, H. (2010). Social justice and financial literacy: Are gender and socio-cultural equity missing from the discussion? *Our Schools, Our Selves, 19*(2), 61–77.

Pinto, L. E., & Coulson, E. (2011). Social justice and the gender politics of financial literacy education. *Journal of the Canadian Association for Curriculum Studies, 9*(2), 54–84.

Roithmayr, D. (2014). *Reproducing racism: How everyday choices lock in white advantage.* New York, NY: New York University Press.

Rose, D. H., & Meyer, A. (2006). *A practical reader in universal design for learning.* Cambridge, MA: Harvard Education Press.

Ryan, R. M., & Deci, E. L. (2000). Self-determination theory and the facilitation of intrinsic motivation, social development and well-being. *American Psychologist, 55*(1), 66–78.

Ryan, R. M., & Deci, E. L. (2008). Self-determination theory: A macrotheory of human motivation, development, and health. *Canadian Psychology, 49*(3), 182–185.

Shogren, K. A., Lopez, S. J., Wehmeyer, M. L., Little, T. D., & Pressgrove, C. J. (2006). The role of positive psychology constructs in predicting life satisfaction in adolescents with and without cognitive disabilities: An exploratory study. *The Journal of Positive Psychology, 1*(1), 37–52.

Steele, C. M. (2010). *Whistling Vivaldi and other clues to how stereotypes affect us.* New York, NY: W.W. Norton.

Stodden, R. A. (2000). The study of postsecondary educational supports: A formative approach to an emerging area of study. *National Review Forum Briefing Materials,* March 9–10. University of Hawaii at Manoa, Center for the study of Postsecondary Education Support, Rehabilitation Research Training Center.

Test, D., Fowler, C., & Kohler, P. (2013). *Evidence-based practices and predictors in secondary transition: What we know and what we still need to know.* Retrieved from http://transitionta.org/sites/default/files/effectivepractices/Execsummary_PPs 2013.pdf

University of California Cooperative Extension. (2008). *Money talks 4 teens.* Retrieved from http://moneytalks4teens.ucanr.edu/index.cfm

Utah State Board of Education. (n.d.). *Finance in the classroom.* Retrieved from http://financeintheclassroom.org/

Visa. (2000–2016). *Practical money skills for life.* Retrieved from http://www.practicalmoneyskills.com/

Wagner, M., Newman, L., Cameto, R., Garza, N., & Levine, P. (2005). *After high school: A first look at the postschool experiences of youth with disabilities*. A Report from the National Longitudinal Transition Study-2 (NLTS2). Online submission. Retrieved from http://files.eric.ed.gov/fulltext/ED494935.pdf

Wehmeyer, M. L. (1996). Student self-report measure of self-determination for students with cognitive disabilities. *Education and Training in Mental Retardation and Developmental Disabilities, 31*(4), 282–293.

Wehmeyer, M. L. (1998). Self-determination and individuals with significant disabilities: Examining meanings and misinterpretations. *Journal of the Association for Persons with Severe Handicaps, 23*(1), 5–16.

Wehmeyer, M. L. (2015). Framing the future self-determination. *Remedial and Special Education, 36*(1), 20–23.

Wehmeyer, M. L., & Palmer, S. B. (2003). Adult outcomes for students with cognitive disabilities three years after high school: The impact of self-determination. *Education and Training in Developmental Disabilities, 38*(2), 131–144.

Wehmeyer, M. L., Palmer, S. B., Lee, Y., Williams-Diehm, K., & Shogren, K. A. (2011). randomized-trial evaluation of the effect of *Whose Future is it Anyway?* On self-determination. *Career Development for Exceptional Individuals, 34*(1), 45–56.

Wehmeyer, M. L., Shogren, K., & Palmer, S. B. (2012). The impact of the self-determined learning model of instruction on student self-determination. *Exceptional Children, 78*(2), 135–153.

Willis, L. E. (2008). *Against financial literacy education*. Faculty Scholarship, Paper 199. Retrieved from http://scholarship.law.upenn.edu/faculty_scholarship/1999

PART TWO

Instructional Issues

CHAPTER FIVE

Instructional Integration of Digital Learning Games in Financial Literacy Education

CARMELA APREA, JULIA SCHULTHEIS, AND KATHLEEN STOLLE
Friedrich Schiller University Jena, Germany

INTRODUCTION

Due to recent trends in society and economy (e.g., shrinking public support systems, shifting demographic profiles, changes in financial markets), financial literacy can be considered as a key skill in the 21st century, especially for underprivileged target groups (e.g., Aprea, Wuttke, & Stock, 2015). Under these conditions, financial literacy represents a complex issue requiring interpretations of scholars from various disciplines including (but not limited to) finance, psychology, sociology, philosophy, and education. In addition, financial literacy education is expected to fulfill a wide range of expectations, e.g., fostering individual and collective economic well-being as well as providing possibilities for participation (cf. Lucey & Laney, 2012). These challenges cannot be adequately addressed only by family socialization but require institutionalized learning processes. The financial education community has begun to recognize the depth and difficulty of its mission. On the political level, many countries have developed national strategies, and/or have submitted surveys and tests to measure financial literacy of their populations, especially the young (e.g., OECD, 2014). On the practical level, financial literacy education programs have been implemented. Moreover, research efforts have been fostered in this field (for a comprehensive overview of the activities at the different levels, see Aprea et al., 2016).

However, despite these efforts, recent empirical evidence by meta-analyses (e.g., Fernandes, Lynch, & Netemeyer, 2014; Miller, Reichelstein, Salas, & Zia,

2014) indicates that traditional financial literacy education programs very often do not reach the goals they aim at (i.e., deepen understanding of financial issues, enhance reasonable financial behavior, support participation) and are thus not as effective as they should and probably could be. This finding might be attributed to the fact that these programs are usually knowledge-centered, whereas financial decision-making and behavior are mostly omitted. An additional problem is that they often do not sufficiently consider students' motivation and socio-emotional needs as well as their social practices. These needs have changed drastically for the generation of the so-called digital natives and their propensity toward virtuality, immediate payoff, fantasy, play and technology (e.g., Lonka, 2012; Prensky, 2001; Wagner, 2008).

In this chapter, we argue that game-based learning can offer one possibility to overcome these obstacles, and thus to make financial literacy programs more appealing and effective. More specifically, our aim is to demonstrate how digital learning games (also known as educational or serious games) could be embedded into classroom instruction in order to support learning, motivation, and transfer in the context of financial literacy education. For the purpose of this chapter, we define "digital learning games" in accordance with Wouters, van Nimwegen, van Oostendorp, and van der Spek (2013) as

> being *interactive*, based on a set of *agreed rules and constraints*, and directed toward a clear *goal* that is often set by a *challenge*. In addition, games constantly provide *feedback*, either as a score or as changes in the game world, to enable players to monitor their progress toward the goal. (p. 250; emphasis in the original)

As these authors further contend, computer games may also involve a competitive activity (against the computer, another player, or oneself). In addition, a narrative or the development of a story can be very important in a computer game (e.g., in adventure games), but both of these characteristics are not indispensable for being a computer game (e.g., action games do not necessarily require a narrative). The supplement "serious" indicates that the primary purpose of the computer game is not to entertain the player, which would be an added value, but to use the entertaining quality for training, education, or other mental and/or behavioral change objectives (Zyda, 2005).

The structure of the chapter is as follows: First we will sketch the potential benefits of learning with digital games and then briefly outline the available empirical research regarding the effects and conditions of game-based learning. Next we will describe an effort to develop, implement, and evaluate a set of game-based learning arrangements in a secondary school financial literacy program in Switzerland. On this basis, we will provide preliminary instructional guidelines, summarize the main issues of the chapter, and make suggestions for future research and development activities.

POTENTIAL BENEFITS OF LEARNING WITH DIGITAL GAMES

Over the last 40 years, digital games—also known as computer or video games—have increasingly replaced more traditional games as leisure activities and have had a transformational impact on how people spend their leisure time (e.g., Connolly, Boyle, Hainey, McArthur, & Boyle, 2012). This seems to be especially true for the young: For example, in the United States, more than 90% of children between the ages of 2 and 17 play video games (cf. NPD Group, 2011). In addition, video games brought in over $25 billion in 2010, more than doubling Hollywood's 2010 box office sales of $10.8 billion in the United States and Canada (cf. Motion Picture Association of America, 2011). However, despite the enormous popularity of digital games, much of the earlier public and scientific discussion has been primarily focused on their possible detrimental effects such as aggression, isolation, addiction, and depression (e.g., Gentile & Gentile, 2008; Schmierbach, 2010), and it is only more recently that popular media (e.g., Hagel & Brown, 2009; Johnson, 2006) as well as academic educational research (e.g., Gee, 2003; Prensky, 2001; Squire, 2006) are concentrating their attention on the potential benefits that digital games may have for human development and learning. As Granic, Lobel, and Engels (2013, p. 66) state, "[c]onsidering these potential benefits is important, in part, because the nature of these games has changed dramatically in the last decade, becoming increasingly complex, diverse, realistic and social in nature." The potential benefits of digital games become particularly evident from the perspective of contemporary learning theories, notably constructivist, situated, and experiential approaches (e.g., Collins, Brown, & Newman, 1989; Greeno, 1998; Lave & Wenger, 1991; Moon, 2004). These theories, in turn, are inspired by tenets from pragmatism (e.g., Dewey, 1963), sociocultural and cultural-historical psychology (e.g., Vygotsky, 1978) as well as fundamental findings in cognitive and motivational psychology (e.g., Malone & Lepper, 1987; Suchman, 1987). In particular, they view learning as an active, contextually bounded and socially mediated process of making meaning out of individual experiences. This process aims at the formation of a multidimensional and, first and foremost, transferable set of competencies. Teaching, in turn, is conceived as the provision of adequate learning opportunities, i.e., the design of learning arrangements which stimulate students' active participation and guide their experiences. Within the frame of contemporary approaches, the following (non-exhaustive) advantages of digital learning games could be emphasized:

(1) *Digital games may support domain-related knowledge construction and higher order cognitive skills.* In digital games, learning is at its essence a kind of performance, as students learn by doing within the affordances and constraints of information-rich virtual worlds, instantiated through software

and social systems. The primacy of game-based learning is on experience, constantly inviting the learner to understand and manipulate complex situations, learn through failure and related feedback, and develop identities as expert problem solvers (Squire, 2008). Thus, game-based learning provides what Barab, Gresalfi, and Ingram-Goble (2010, p. 525) call "consequential engagement," and is particularly expected to foster the acquisition of different forms of domain-related higher order knowledge and skills, such as conceptual understanding, strategic decision-making, and/or problem-solving.

(2) *Digital games can promote enjoyment, intrinsic motivation, and positive attitudes.* Due to their entertaining qualities, digital games are believed to be personally enjoyable and thus much more attractive for learners, especially the ones from the digital native generation. This may lead to more affective involvement as well as to sustained intrinsic motivation. As already proposed by Malone (1981) and confirmed by more recent developments in motivational research (for an overview, see Elliot & Dweck, 2005), the primary factors that make an activity intrinsically motivating are challenge, curiosity, control, and fantasy. Digital games incorporate these factors, for example through the need to attain goals, through sensory and cognitive activation, or with the help of narratives. In addition, their immersive nature may also enable the experience of flow (e.g., Csíkszentmihályi, 2008). In sum, these characteristics may positively influence attitudes toward learning both, in general and in specific domains.

(3) *Digital games may foster generic abilities as well as psycho-motoric skills.* As for example, Granic et al. (2013) assume, digital games may also foster more generic, often meta-cognitive abilities such as handling of complexity, or information processing under the condition of risk and uncertainty as well as persistence, ambiguity tolerance, and self-efficacy. Depending on the specific game condition, they are moreover expected to support psycho-motoric skills such as speed of reaction or eye–hand coordination.

However, as especially researchers from media psychology and instructional design (e.g., Kerres, Bormann, & Vervenne, 2009; Myers & Reigeluth, 2016; Petko, 2008) point out, it is quite improbable that these beneficial effects of digital games come naturally. It is rather expected that, in order to develop its full potential, game-based learning requires two key prerequisites, notably high quality game design and adequate instructional integration, i.e., learning arrangement design. With regard to the first key prerequisite, scholars in the field of game design (e.g., Adams, 2014; Bopp, 2005; Dondlinger, 2007; Mayer, 2011) highlight that a good game design should guide the learner through the game world and help him or her to understand its logic and rules. This should be preferably done as easy and immersive as possible, for example by designing game situations which afford learners to actively manipulate objects in an intended way, or by sequencing the game play according to increasing levels of difficulty. With regard to the second prerequisite, instructional integration, it is particularly emphasized that simply playing a game might not be enough for effective and sustainable learning to occur, but that these gaming experiences need to be complemented with adequate preparation, elaboration, practice, debriefing/reflection, and transfer of what has been learned during the game play (e.g., Leemkuil & de Jong, 2011; Paras & Bizzocchi, 2005). As we will elaborate in the second following section, a powerful instructional remedy for guiding these processes is the design of learning tasks, mainly because of their impact on regulating students' learning processes. In addition to highlighting the importance of these design issues, scholars in the field of game-based learning also underscore the need for empirically investigating the effects and conditions of using games for educational purposes. This aspect will be addressed next.

GAME-BASED LEARNING: SUMMARY OF THE AVAILABLE EMPIRICAL RESEARCH

In the last decade, a steadily growing number of individual research studies concerning the effects and conditions of game-based learning have begun to emerge. In addition to the individual studies, around a dozen literature reviews (e.g., Boyle et al., 2015; Connolly et al., 2012; Donovan, 2012; Granic et al., 2013; Hamari, Koivisto, & Sarsa, 2014), both narrative and systematic, as well as a handful of meta-analyses (e.g., Clark, Tanner-Smith, & Killingsworth, 2016; Sitzmann, 2011; Vogel et al., 2006; Wouters et al., 2013) exist, which are of particular interest for our concern. Even though far from being conclusive—and, most importantly, at least to our knowledge completely omitting the domain of financial literacy education—the existing research offers important indications with regard to the questions of whether and under which circumstances digital games could be effectively used to support human learning and development. Three types of results should be highlighted here:

(1) In terms of cognitive learning outcomes, the available empirical evidence basically seems to confirm the expected beneficial effects of digital learning games. This is corroborated by all quantitative meta-analyses, including the most recent one by Clark et al. (2016), with 69 studies from 2000 to 2012, spanning K–16 students, the one by Vogel et al. (2006) with 32 studies from 1986 to 2003 covering all age groups as well as the one by Wouters et al. (2013) with 39 studies from 1990 to 2012,

also encompassing a wide range of age groups. All of these meta-analyses covered various types of games (e.g., adventure games, online quizzes, simulation games) and content areas (e.g., science, math, and psychology). As Ke (2009) states in her qualitative meta-analysis, the expected benefits seem to be particularly salient with regard to higher order thinking skills such as planning or reasoning. These results were also confirmed in an additional meta-analysis by Sitzmann (2011) who specifically addressed simulation games for adult workforce trainees, synthesizing results from 65 studies from 1976 to 2009. This author moreover could demonstrate the positive effects of serious games on self-efficacy, i.e., a more generative ability.

(2) However, differently than expected, the available empirical research is rather inconsistent concerning motivational and attitudinal effects. In this respect, Vogel et al. (2006) reported positive effects of serious games whereas such effects could not be found in the meta-analysis by Wouters et al. (2013), who offer three plausible reasons for this lack of evidence. The first reason pertains to the methods that are commonly used for the measurement of motivation. In this regard, it can be questioned whether it makes sense to measure affective states such as motivation and enjoyment with questionnaires and surveys after game play, when the player's motivation may be attenuated. In contrast, measures which can be collected during game play (e.g., observation, eye tracking, and skin conductance) might be more valid but are yet very rarely used. This suggestion is corroborated by one exceptional study by Annetta, Minogue, Holmes, and Chen (2009) that employed the rating of observed engagement during game play as motivation measurement, and found that the game was more motivating than the instructional treatment of the comparison group that received practice and group discussion. As a second reason, the case might be that serious games are not more motivating because in instructional contexts learners do experience them as obligatory as other instructional methods. This might limit their sense of autonomy and control which, in turn, are important conditions for motivation (e.g., Ryan, Rigby, & Przybylski, 2006). Lastly, it is also possible that the lack of motivational appeal is—at least partly—a reflection of poor game design and poor instructional integration. This interpretation is supported by the moderator analyses from the research syntheses, which are addressed next.

(3) In particular, the moderator analyses demonstrate that games with an active involvement of the player and high control (Vogel et al., 2006; Wouters et al., 2013) as well as games with unlimited access (Sitzmann, 2011) do not only lead to significantly better learning outcomes relative to the comparison group but are also perceived as more motivating. With

regard to instructional integration, the moderator analyses also reveal that games were more effective and motivating when supplemented with other instruction, when multiple training sessions were involved, and when players worked together in groups (Vogel et al., 2006; Wouters et al., 2013). In contrast to these game and instructional design characteristics, no significant differences were reported in terms of learner characteristics (e.g., age group or gender). As Vogel et al. (2006) notice,

[t]his finding is somewhat counterintuitive since it is a common assumption that children, due to shorter attention-spans, higher interest in play activities, and lower intrinsic motivation to learn, enjoy and thus learn better using computer games and interactive simulations compared to adults. (p. 237)

However, this rather surprising finding might, in our view, indicate a generalizable positive effect of digital learning games—even though this interpretation must be treated with caution because many important research questions, and especially those regarding learner-related prerequisite (e.g., prior knowledge) of effective game use, have not yet been considered. Taken together, the results of the current empirical studies thus seem to stress the affordances of games for learning as well as the key role of design beyond medium.

DEVELOPMENT, IMPLEMENTATION, AND EVALUATION OF GAME-BASED LEARNING ARRANGEMENTS IN A SECONDARY SCHOOL FINANCIAL LITERACY PROGRAM IN SWITZERLAND

In this section we will illustrate how the previously depicted theoretical considerations and empirical findings were used to design, implement, and evaluate a set of game-based learning arrangements in a secondary school financial literacy program in Switzerland. To this end, we will (1) briefly delineate the background of the program, (2) describe the process of development of the game-based learning arrangements, and (3) report on an effort to implement and formatively evaluate them within the scope of a field testing.

Background of the Program

The activities described in this section are part of a larger development project which has been initiated as a joint venture of two Swiss Teacher Associations (LCH Dachverband Lehrer und Lehrerinnen Schweiz and SER Syndicat des Enseignants Romands) and the Association of Swiss Cantonal Banks (VSKB Verband Schweizerischer Kantonalbanken)[1] as response to a recent reform in

Swiss basic education curricula, the so-called Lehrplan 21 initiative. This reform involved a shift from knowledge-oriented to competence-oriented curricula, and besides other issues also encompassed for the first time the inclusion of competencies related to financial literacy, especially in grades 7 to 9. Given that this subject was completely new for this age group, and teachers in this kind of school usually have no formal training in finance or economics, there was an urgent need for a sound instructional approach, including instructional resources fitting to the new curriculum requirements. In order to cope with these requirements and encouraged by the above described theoretical considerations and empirical findings, the decision was made in favor of combining game and nongame instruction within an integrative approach. This approach included the development of a digital learning game and its instructional integration within game-related learning modules. Together, these instructional incidents (i.e., learning game and learning modules) form what we subsequently call "game-based learning arrangements."

Development of the Game-based Learning Arrangements

Due to the innovative character of including financial education in the Swiss secondary school context, the project activities have been inspired by a design-based research approach (e.g., DBRC, 2003), and encompassed the close collaboration of a team of interdisciplinary experts (notably researchers *from* media psychology, business and economics education, economics, behavioral and household finance, and business ethics), game designers, media designers, and secondary school teachers. In addition, students, parents, and other relevant stakeholders were involved, and an accompanying steering committee was constituted. In accordance with the design-based research approach, different but interrelated cycles of analysis, design, testing, and redesign were carried out. More specifically, the following steps were conducted:

(1) Needs Analysis

In order to be able to respond to the needs and concerns of the persons directly or indirectly affected by the game-based learning arrangements, a pre-study was accomplished, including four preparatory focus group workshops with (i) students, (ii) teachers, (iii) parents, and (iv) professionals from the fields of credit counseling, consumer protection, youth work, and the finance sector, respectively. In these workshops, participants were first invited to express what they spontaneously associate with the notion of financial literacy education for secondary school students. Then, they were asked (a) to describe typical and critical situations in which, in their experience, young people get in touch with money and finance issues; and (b) to specify which competencies they consider important to successfully deal with these situations. The workshops were complemented with semi-structured interviews with further representatives of the Swiss educational field (e.g., the president of the parents association or the head of the secondary school section within the teacher association). All workshops and interviews were held in summer and autumn 2014. Moreover, in-depth content analyses of the new curriculum documents and additional reviews of the literature on financial literacy education in other age groups and countries were conducted. These activities led to (i) a detailed description of situations, tasks, and contents which could possibly be focused by the game-based learning arrangements, and (ii) a first list of requirements for the game and the related modules. This list included issues such as compatibility with the new curriculum and with the technical possibilities in schools, or avoidance of violence to humans or animals. The results of the pre-study were discussed in the team of experts and the steering committee. It was then decided to focus on budgeting (including avoidance of excessive indebtedness), and a model of related contents was built. Moreover, additional content-related, technical and organizational requirements were identified. All these information were merged into a tender specification.

(2) Development of the Digital Learning Game

Based on the tender specification, a dedicated team of game designers was selected in December 2014 and commissioned with the development of a corresponding digital learning game.[2] The game was developed as a rogue-like action-adventure game, and has a classical superhero plot with ten levels of increasing difficulty. It is located in a fictive town where the local bank has been hacked by hostile robots. For this reason, the savings of all inhabitants and even the class kitty are in danger. Players are invited to step into the shoes of a game character which can be customized in terms of visual style, and whose mission is to rescue the savings by overcoming the robots. The robot scenario was chosen in order to satisfy the demand of minimizing violence or damage, especially to living beings. The game incorporates an immersive approach, i.e., it is designed in a way that makes planning of money and time obligatory. Moreover, it provides ample opportunities for autonomous choices and control: Money can be earned either by conquering the robots and/or by pursuing a part-time job.[3] Thus, at the beginning of every mission, the player has to decide how much time to spend with each of these activities. In this context, he or she has also to plan enough time for learning in order to avoid a decline of school grades. To prepare for the mission, the player can then buy equipment in a shop, such as special clothing to inhibit losing energy, drinks to improve attacking skills, and various "weapons" such as a frypan or a swab. With regard to these weapons, a humoristic approach was chosen, again to prevent glorification of violent behavior to humans or animals. Besides the money that the player spends for buying the equipment, he or she may also lose it by being defeated during the game. At the end of each round, a detailed account of incomes and expenses is provided, together with some advice on how to optimize financial decision-making. Besides these design elements, the game also includes a tutorial device which is supposed to familiarize students with the game world and mission. The game contains no in-app purchases, and can be downloaded for free. Unlimited access is thus guaranteed.

During the game development process, various consultative meetings were held with the game designers on the one hand, and the experts and the steering committee on the other. In order to optimize the communication flow and ensure appropriateness for the application context, a group of four secondary school teachers as well as one faculty staff from a teacher education college were occasionally involved. These were the same persons as those who collaborated in the development of the accompanying learning modules (see next bullet point). In addition, previous versions of the game were tested with selected samples of secondary school students with regard to usability, appeal, etc.

(3) Development of the Game-related Learning Modules

Parallel to the game development activities, a total of five learning modules were created in close cooperation between experts, designers, and practitioners. In particular, three researchers from economics education, two professional media designers, and the already mentioned group of four secondary school teachers as well as the teacher educator were mainly involved in this part of the project. In addition, one person from the game designer team was regularly consulted in order to support reciprocal update and feedback between the two design teams (i.e., game designers and learning module designers). The activities for developing the game-related learning modules encompassed a two-hour kick-off meeting and two half-day face-to-face workshops with all the abovementioned participants and several Skype meetings between some of them, especially between the media designers and the economics education researchers. In the kick-off meeting, which was held in June 2015, the background of the project as well as the basic idea of the game was explained, and organizational issues of the workshops were elaborated. The first workshop then took place in September 2015. In this workshop, a beta-version of the game was presented, and relevant theoretical considerations and empirical findings (see previous sections of this chapter) were briefly summarized in order to provide a conceptual background for developing the game-based learning arrangements. Moreover, key objectives (so-called superordinate competencies) and learning goals were specified according to the new curriculum requirements, and discussed with the teachers.

Given the pivotal role of learning tasks for guiding students' learning processes, it was decided that the accompanying learning modules should be focused on the provision of game-related task assignments. To support teachers to create such assignments, six different types of learning tasks with different instructional functions[4] were also presented during the first workshop. These tasks included: (1) introduction tasks which intend to familiarize students with a situation or problem, (2) elaboration tasks which support students to develop the knowledge and skills relevant for coping with the situation or problem, (3) exploration tasks which invite students to try out different approaches and solutions, (4) practice tasks which are designed to deepen knowledge or automatize skills, (5) reflection tasks which are expected to stimulate students' critical thinking, and (6) transfer tasks which should encourage processes of decontextualizing and recontextualizing knowledge and skills in different application settings. The teachers were asked to develop learning arrangements which are centered on the game and include the different task types. Their suggestions were supposed to be brought to the second workshop in October 2015, discussed with the colleagues, the researchers and the media designers, and then reviewed according to the feedbacks, which resulted from these discussions. Initially the teachers were not at ease with their task, and tended to propose rather detached task assignments that had nothing to do with the learning game. So this further opportunity for reciprocal exchange and feedback was indispensable. In addition to this, the second workshop addressed questions regarding the implementation and evaluation of the game-based learning arrangements. The products which resulted from this process (i.e., sequences of learning tasks and respective worksheets) were then submitted to a field testing, and subsequently revised and fine-tuned according to the evaluation results (cf. next section). Revision and fine-tuning were done by the media designers in close cooperation with the economics education experts. As depicted in Table 5.1, in the final version (i.e., after the evaluation results have been incorporated), the learning modules comprise between two and four lessons, with one lesson corresponding to 45 minutes. Basically, they are offered as best practice models which have to be adapted by any given teacher who uses them to meet the circumstances of a specific class. The modules include a description of learning goals and contents, activity outlines, and worksheets with concrete task assignments. In addition, some suggestions regarding the implementation of the respective module are given. Two out of the five modules are most suitable for use in grade 7 or at the beginning of grade 8, respectively, whereas the other three were constructed for older students (i.e., end of grade 8 or grade 9). Each of the modules can be used individually or be combined with one another. Table 5.1 also summarizes the contents and the superordinate competencies of the five game-based learning modules.

Table 5.1: Duration, Contents, and Superordinate Competencies of the Five Game-based Learning Modules.

	Grade 7–8 Module 1	Grade 7–8 Module 2	Grade 8–9 Module 1	Grade 8–9 Module 2	Grade 8–9 Module 3
Contents	(3 lessons) - Incomes/expenses - Functions of a budget - Goods and costs	(2 lessons) - Personal buying behavior - Purchase and financing decisions	(4 lessons) - Durable and nondurable consumer goods, luxury goods - Purchasing and follow-up costs - Functions of a budget	(3 lessons) - Consumer behavior and financial decisions - Risk and safety - Borrowing - Costs, return, interest	(4 lessons) - Financial strategies - Probability of success and risk - Impact of purchasing decisions on budget
Superordinate competencies	Learners are able to draw up a budget and to consider it when making purchase decisions.	Learners are able to critically reflect their purchase and financial decisions.	Learners are able to estimate purchasing and follow-up costs of different durable and nondurable consumer goods. They are able to draw up a budget and to consider it when making purchase decisions.	Learners are able to critically reflect their purchase and financial decisions.	Learners are able to choose proper financial strategies for specific purchases.

Implementation and Formative Evaluation of the Game-based Learning Arrangements

In order to optimize the game-based learning arrangements and to locate possible shortcomings, a field testing with a total of 60 secondary school students was conducted between January and February 2016. All students came from the classes of the four participating teachers. Therefore, they might be considered as "convenience" sample. In the field testing, the three game-based learning modules for grade 8–9 and one of the grade 7–8 modules were implemented and evaluated with 36 and 24 students, respectively. Module 1 in grade 7/8 could not be tested due to illness of the respective teacher.

Given the formative intent of the evaluation, we were especially interested in gathering information on the practicability of the game-based learning modules in general, and of the usability of the learning tasks in particular, both in terms of temporal feasibility and perceived difficulty by teachers and students. In addition, we wanted to get some first impressions concerning the motivational appeal of the game-based learning arrangements as well as their perceived effectiveness for supporting learning and transfer. For this purpose, the following evaluation instruments were used: Teachers were asked to observe students during the accomplishment of the tasks, to take notes of their observations, and to use these notes to fill out a questionnaire. This questionnaire included general questions concerning the learning arrangement. Teachers were asked to judge how easy or difficult they found (i) to handle the learning module, both in terms of content and time; and (ii) to explain the game and the game-related learning tasks to the students. Additionally, the teachers should state (iii) to what extent they think that students have enjoyed the lessons, and have learned what is specified in the learning goals. Besides these general questions, specific questions regarding the learning tasks were included. To get an accurate picture on what needs to be enhanced, these questions were customized for the single learning modules. All questions (i.e., the general and specific ones) were open-ended and explicitly invited the respondents to make suggestions for improvements in case of inconsistencies or problems. At the end of the questionnaire, they were also asked if they had any other kind of observation, proposal, or advice. The utterances of the teachers were analyzed qualitatively by collecting themes that emerged in their answers. All answers were read, interpreted, and discussed by at least two researchers. Then, the interpretations were cross-checked by the teachers and corrections were made where necessary.

To minimize disruptions of the learning processes, but nevertheless obtain informative statements from the students, their worksheets were prepared with a traffic light for every learning task, so that they just had to tick if they fully understood (green), partially understood (yellow), or not understood (red) what the task assignment asked them to do. Additionally, they had to answer a few questions which asked them if and to what extent they enjoyed playing the game and completing the tasks, and if and to what extent these instructional resources helped them to understand the respective financial literacy contents in such a way that they could explain them to a friend. With regard to these questions, students were asked to indicate whether they totally agree, agree to some extent, or do not agree, and to provide a brief explanation of their respective judgment. Finally, they were also invited to express further concerns or ideas regarding the experienced game-based learning arrangements. Note that in order to avoid students to answer in a socially desirable manner, all of their data were collected anonymously. In addition to analyzing the students' perceptions, we also conducted a first analysis of their solutions of the learning tasks. Students' ratings and number of correct task solutions were then submitted to frequency analysis. In case of open-ended questions, again, emerging themes were distilled.

With respect to the practicability of the learning arrangements, time pressure was the main concern expressed by the teachers, and according to them, the possible reasons for this concern are twofold. One reason was the fact that at the date of the field testing the game was not yet accessible to the public, so all preparatory activities to familiarize students with the game had to be done during class hours, which was quite time consuming. A second reason they mentioned had to do with the temporal feasibility, and partially also the difficulty of the learning tasks. In this regard, it could be stated that introduction tasks—unsurprisingly—were implemented in all modules. Even though they caused no particular problems in terms of difficulty, two of the four introduction tasks took longer than planned. Thus, the time specifications had to be adapted in the module descriptions. The elaboration tasks led to more problems. In two of the four learning arrangements the teachers articulated that these tasks were too difficult, and that students needed more support. They suggested explaining the respective task assignments orally because this is easier for students to understand. The exploration tasks, the reflection tasks, and the transfer tasks posed the greatest challenge in all four tested learning arrangements. The reflection tasks were realized in three of the four cases. However, additional help from the teacher was needed in each case. Exploration tasks were employed in two classes, but worked out properly only in one of them. A transfer task was put into practice only once and also required further assistance from the teacher.

In the main, the teachers' evaluations of task difficulty were also mirrored by the task-related judgments from the students as well as by the first analysis of the task solutions which they proposed. As this analysis shows, only about half of the tasks were executed correctly. However, despite these problems, the ratings regarding the motivational appeal and the effectiveness of the game-based learning arrangements were very positive. Here, the evaluation results indicate that in three of four learning arrangements students unequivocally stated that they have enjoyed playing the game, and also have liked to process the learning tasks. This conviction was largely confirmed by the observations of the teachers. In case of the fourth arrangement, it happened that the respective topic had already been treated in class. Thus, those students found the lessons somewhat repetitive and boring, but nonetheless appreciated the game approach. In addition to their perceptions regarding the motivational appeal of the game-based learning arrangements, most of the students stated that they had understood the financial literacy content treated in the respective learning module, and that they would be able to explain it to a friend. This seems to be in some contradiction with the analysis of students' solutions to the learning tasks, and interestingly enough those who answered all questions correctly rated their knowledge lower than the ones who answered only half of the questions correctly. However, such inconsistencies in the objective and subjective ratings of competencies are quite common in financial literacy assessments (e.g., Aprea & Wuttke, 2016), and may point to a nontrivial lack of proficiency in adequately judging one's own abilities in this domain. All suggestions for improvements derived from the field testing were incorporated into the revised version of the game-based learning modules, or reported to the game designers, if they concerned the game, respectively.

PRELIMINARY GUIDELINES FOR INTEGRATING LEARNING GAMES INTO FINANCIAL LITERACY EDUCATION

The results from the evaluation, together with our experiences in the process of developing the game and the learning modules, offer a potential for suggesting some preliminary guidelines concerning the integration of digital games into financial literacy education. First, there seems to be no indication that the expected beneficial effects of game-based learning do not apply to the domain of financial literacy, which, so far, has been neglected. In addition, the results also support the pivotal role of adequate design, both in terms of game design and instructional design. Relating to the former, it can be assumed that an immersive approach, with high autonomy and control to the player is a recommended design strategy also for digital games in financial literacy education. With regard to instructional design, we would like to underline the need to integrate the game with the nongame instruction as well as the need to guide students' game-related activities with the help of respective learning tasks in the classroom setting. Both, the alternation between game and nongame instruction, have to be carefully planned, and teachers as well as students need sufficient time to familiarize themselves with the respective requirements. However, as our experiences also reveal, such planning is not achieved automatically, but needs to be supported through appropriate measures of teacher education and/or teachers' professional development (for a similar concern, see Luccy, 2016). This is especially required if teachers have to react to new curriculum demands and/or if they have no formal education in the related field, as is very often the case in financial literacy education. Finally, we would like to stress an organizational aspect which is concerned with the way in which the game and the learning modules were developed. Concerning this matter, we would conclude that the close collaboration with the teachers as well as the exchange between the design teams and the contact with all stakeholders can be considered a key element for ensuring the effectiveness of the process and supporting the acceptance of the resulting products.

SUMMARY AND OUTLOOK

Given the importance of financial literacy as a key 21st-century skill, in this chapter, we argued that game-based learning can offer one possibility to overcome the shortcomings of currently available financial literacy programs. This approach makes financial education more effective with regard to the demands of financial decision-making and more appealing with regard to the needs and preferences of the target group. More specifically, our aim was to demonstrate how digital learning games could be instructionally embedded in order to support learning, motivation, and transfer in the context of financial education. For that purpose, we sketched the potential benefits of learning with digital learning games, summarized the available empirical research regarding the effects and conditions of game-based learning, and described an effort to develop, implement, and evaluate a set of game-based learning arrangements in a secondary school financial literacy program in Switzerland within the scope of a field testing. On the basis of the results and experiences from this field testing, we finally provided suggestions for guidelines concerning the integration of digital games into financial literacy education.

Our study was a first attempt to formatively evaluate the practicability and usability as well as the perceived motivational appeal and learning effectiveness of game-based learning arrangements in a financial education program in Switzerland. This attempt showed that well designed digital games could be productively used in secondary school financial literacy education. It additionally showed the value of integrating game and nongame instructions. However, of course, we are aware that this attempt has its limitations, particularly with regard to methodological issues such as the convenience sample, the limited number of participants, and the instrumentation. Given these limitations, further research and development activities are warranted. These activities should, among others, specifically address the following aspects: (1) additional formative evaluation studies to further optimize game-based learning arrangements (e.g., with regard to the sequencing and the assignments of the game-related learning tasks), possibly with a more systematic sample of teachers and students; (2) implementation studies to locate the organizational conditions for an effective use of the game-based learning arrangements; and (3) summative evaluation studies with randomized field trials to determine the comparative effectiveness of game-based learning arrangements in financial literacy education as well as the generalizability of the results.

QUESTIONS FOR DISCUSSION

1. The study findings indicate that the video game motivated students, but did not seem to affect their knowledge of personal finance. The authors suggest many plausible options to further this research in their last paragraphs: which do you believe would be most helpful to informing about this mode of learning about personal finance?
2. There is some literature that associates addiction to electronic devices with socialization difficulties. To what extent may one associate this relationship with skills in personal finance?
3. With what video games that focus on personal finance are you familiar? How might they be similar to, or different from, that described in this chapter?
4. What are the different ways that a teacher may facilitate a learning experience based on a video game? How might those different ways shape student outcomes?
5. If you were to design a video game that taught youth about money, what would it entail? Justify your reasoning on the information provided in this chapter.

NOTES

1. It is important to note that in May 2016, the abovementioned associations have funded the umbrella organization "Finance Mission Association" which serves as contact platform for schools and teachers interested in using the various instructional resources presented in this part of the chapter. For further information, see also http://financemission.ch/ueber-financemission/.
2. Selection criteria included, among others: Originality and appeal of the game concept, fidelity to the contents that should be covered, experience and references of the design team, feasibility in terms of available budget and technical requirements.
3. Incurring debts is also possible, but only at higher levels of difficulty.
4. This differentiation of task types is inspired by and adapted from a classification scheme proposed by Luthiger, Wilhelm, and Wespi (2014).

REFERENCES

Adams, E. (2014). *Fundamentals of game design* (3rd ed.). New York, NY: Pearson.

Annetta, L. A., Minogue, J., Holmes, S. Y., & Chen, M.-T. (2009). Investigating the impact of video games on high school students' engagement and learning about genetics. *Computers & Education, 53*(1), 74–85.

Aprea, C., & Wuttke, E. (2016). Financial literacy of adolescent and young adults: Setting the course for a competence-oriented assessment approach. In C. Aprea, E. Wuttke, K. Breuer, N. K. Keng,

P. Davies, B. Fuhrmann, & J. Lopus (Eds.), *International handbook of financial literacy* (pp. 397–414). Singapore: Springer.

Aprea, C., Wuttke, E., Breuer, K., Keng, N. K., Davies, P., Greimel-Fuhrmann, B., & Lopus, J. (Eds.). (2016). *International handbook of financial literacy*. Singapore: Springer.

Aprea, C., Wuttke, E., & Stock, M. (2015). Exploring the possibilities for a bildungs-oriented conceptualisation of financial literacy. In S. Hillen & C. Aprea (Eds.), *Instrumentalism in education—Where is bildung left?* (pp. 89–104). Münster: Waxmann.

Barab, S. A., Gresalfi, M., & Ingram-Goble, A. (2010). Transformational play: Using games to position person, content, and context. *Educational Researcher, 39*(7), 525–536.

Bopp, M. (2005). Immersive Didaktik: Verdeckte Lernhilfen und Framingprozesse in Computerspielen. *kommunikation@gesellschaft, 6*(2). Retrieved from http://www.soz.uni-frankfurt.de/K.G/B2_2005_Bopp.pdf

Boyle, E. A., Hainey, T., Connolly, T. M., Gray, G., Earp, J., Ott, M., ... Pereira, J. (2015). An update to the systematic literature review of empirical evidence of the impacts and outcomes of computer games and serious games. *Computers & Education, 94*, 178–192.

Clark, D., Tanner-Smith, E., Killingsworth, S. (2014). *Digital Games, Design and Learning: A Systematic Review and Meta- Analysis (Executive Summary)*. Menlo Park, CA: SRI International.

Collins, A., Brown, J. S., & Newman, S. E. (1989). Cognitive apprenticeship: Teaching the crafts of reading, writing, and mathematics. In L. B. Resnick (Ed.), *Knowing, learning, and instruction: Essays in honor of Robert Glaser* (pp. 453–494). Hillsdale, NJ: Lawrence Erlbaum Associates.

Connolly, T. C., Boyle, E. A., Hainey, T., McArthur, E., & Boyle, J. M. (2012). A systematic literature review of empirical evidence on computer games and serious games. *Computers & Education, 59*(2), 661–686.

Csíkszentmihályi, M. (2008). *Flow: The psychology of optimal experience*. New York, NY: Harper Collins Publisher.

Design-Based Research Collective (DBRC). (2003). Design-based research: An emerging paradigm for educational inquiry. *Educational Researcher, 32*(1), 5–8, 35–37.

Dewey, J. (1963). *Experience and education*. New York, NY: Collier Macmillan. (Original work published 1938).

Dondlinger, M. J. (2007). Educational video *game* design: A review of the literature. *Journal of Applied Educational Technology, 4*(1), 21–31.

Donovan, L. (2012). *The use of serious games in the corporate sector: A state of the art report*. Retrieved from http://www.learnovatecentre.org/research-report-the-use-of-serious-games-in-the-corporate-sector/

Elliot, A. J., & Dweck, C. S. (Eds.). (2005). *Handbook of competence and motivation*. New York, NY: Guilford Press.

Fernandes, D., Lynch, J. G., Jr., & Netemeyer, R. G. (2014). Financial literacy, financial education, and downstream financial behaviors. *Management Science, 60*(8), 1861–1883.

Gee, J. P. (2003). *What video games have to teach us about learning and literacy*. New York, NY: Palgrave/St. Martin's.

Gentile, D. A., & Gentile, J. R. (2008). Pathological video-game use among youth ages 8–18: A national study. *Psychological Science, 20*(5), 594–602.

Granic, I., Lobel, A., & Engels, R. C. M. E. (2013). The benefits of playing video games. *American Psychologist, 69*(1), 66–78.

Greeno, J. (1998). The situativity of knowing, learning, and research. *American Psychologist, 53*(1), 5–26.

Hagel, J., & Brown, J. S. (2009, January 14). How World of Warcraft Promotes Innovation. *Business Week: Innovation*. Retrieved from http://www.businessweek.com/innovate/content/jan2009/id20090114_362962_page_2.htm

Hamari, J., Koivisto, J., & Sarsa, H. (2014). Does gamification work?—A literature review of empirical studies on gamification. *Proceedings of the 47th Hawaii International Conference on System Sciences, Hawaii, USA*, January 6–9. Retrieved from http://www.hiit.fi/u/hamari/2014-hamari_et_al-does_gamification_work.pdf

Johnson, S. (2006). *Everything bad is good for you: How today's popular culture is making us smarter*. London: Penguin.

Ke, F. (2009). A qualitative meta-analysis of computer games as learning tools. In R. E. Ferdig (Ed.), *Handbook of research on effective electronic gaming in education* (pp. 1–32). New York, NY: IGI Global.

Kerres, M., Bormann, M., & Vervenne, M. (2009). *Didaktische Konzeption von Serious Games: Zur Verknüpfung von Spiel- und Lernangeboten*. Retrieved from http://mediendidaktik.uni-due.de/sites/default/files/kerres0908_0.pdf

Lave, J., & Wenger, E. (1991). *Situated learning: Legitimate peripheral participation*. New York, NY: Cambridge University Press.

Leemkuil, H., & de Jong, T. (2011). Instructional support in games. In S. Tobias & J. D. Fletcher (Eds.), *Computer games and instruction* (pp. 353–369). Charlotte, NC: Information Age.

Lonka, K. (2012). Engaging learning environments for the future The 2012 Elizabeth Stone Lecture. In R. Gwyer, R. Stubbings, & G. Walton (Eds.), *The road to information literacy: Librarians as facilitators of learning* (pp. 15–30). Berlin: De Gruyter Saur.

Lucey, T. A. (2016). Preparing preservice elementary teachers to teach about financial literacy: Towards a broader conception. In C. Aprea, E. Wuttke, K. Breuer, N. K. Keng, P. Davies, B. Fuhrmann, & J. Lopus (Eds.), *International handbook of financial literacy* (pp. 655–673). Singapore: Springer.

Lucey, T. A., & Laney, J. D. (Eds.). (2012). *Re-framing financial literacy: Exploring the value of social currency*. Charlotte, NC: Information Age Publishing.

Luthiger, H., Wilhelm, M., & Wespi, C. (2014). Entwicklung von kompetenzorientierten Aufgabensets—Prozessmodell und Kategoriensystem. *Journal für LehrerInnenbildung, 3*, 56–66.

Malone, T. W. (1981). What makes computer games fun? *Byte, 6*(12), 258–277.

Malone, T. W., & Lepper, M. R. (1987). Making learning fun: A taxonomy of intrinsic motivations for learning. In R. E. Snow & M. J. Farr (Eds.), *Aptitude, learning and instruction III: Conative and affective process analyses* (pp. 223–253). Hillsdale, NJ: Erlbaum.

Mayer, R. E. (2011). Multimedia learning and games. In S. Tobias & J. D. Fletcher (Eds.), *Computer games and instruction* (pp. 281–305). Charlotte, NC: Information Age.

Miller, M., Reichelstein, J., Salas, C., & Zia, B. (2014). *Can you help someone become financially capable? A meta-analysis of the literature*. Policy Research Working Paper WPS 6745. Washington, DC: World Bank Group. Retrieved from http://documents.worldbank.org/curated/en/2014/01/1880/418/can-help-someone-financially-capable-meta-analysis-literature

Moon, J. (2004). *A handbook of reflective and experiential learning: Theory and practice*. London: Routledge Falmer.

Motion Picture Association of America. (2011). *Theatrical market statistics 2011*. Retrieved from www.mpaa.org/resources/5bec4ac9-a95e-443b-987b-bff6fb5455a9.pdf

Myers, R. D., & Reigeluth, C. M. (2016). Designing games for learning. In C. M. Reigeluth, B. J. Beatty, & R. D. Myers (Eds.), *Instructional-design theories and models, Vol. IV: The learner-centered paradigm of education* (pp. 205–242). New York, NY: Routledge.

NPD Group. (2011). *The video game industry is adding 2–17-year-old gamers at a rate higher than that age group's population growth*. Retrieved from https://www.npd.com/wps/portal/npd/us/news/pressreleases/pr_111011

OECD. (2014). *PISA 2012 results: Students and money: Financial literacy skills for the 21st century* (Vol. VI), PISA, OECD Publishing. Retrieved from http://dx.doi.org/10.1787/9789264208094-en

Paras, B., & Bizzocchi, J. (2005). Game, motivation and effective learning: An integrated model for educational game design. *Changing Views: Worlds in Play, Conference of the Digital Games Research Association*, June 16–20, 2005, Vancouver, BC.

Petko, D. (2008). Unterrichten mit Computerspielen. Didaktische Potenziale und Ansätze für den gezielten Einsatz in Schule und Ausbildung. *MedienPädagogik: Zeitschrift für Theorie und Praxis der Medienbildung, 15*, 1–15. Retrieved from http://www.medienpaed.com/globalassets/medienpaed/15-16/petko0811.pdf

Prensky, M. (2001). *Digital game-based learning*. St. Paul, MN: Paragon House.

Ryan, R. M., Rigby, C. S., & Przybylski, A. (2006). The motivational pull of video games: A self-determination theory approach. *Motivation and Emotion, 30*, 347–365.

Schmierbach, M. (2010). "Killing spree": Exploring the connection between competitive game play and aggressive cognition. *Communication Research, 37*(2), 256–274.

Sitzmann, T. (2011). A meta-analytic examination of the instructional effectiveness of computer-based simulation games. *Personnel Psychology, 64*(2), 489–528.

Squire, K. D. (2006). From content to context: Videogames as designed experience. *Educational Researcher, 35*(8), 19–29.

Squire, K. D. (2008). Video games and education: Designing learning systems for an interactive age. *Educational Technology, March/April*, 17–26.

Suchman, L. (1987). *Plans and situated actions: The Problem of Human-Machine Communication*. New York, NY: Cambridge University Press.

Vogel, J. J., Vogel, D. S., Cannon-Bowers, J., Bowers, C. A., Muse, K., & Wright, M. (2006). Computer gaming and interactive simulations for learning: A meta-analysis. *Journal of Educational Computing Research, 34*(3), 229–243.

Vygotsky, L. (1978). *Mind in society: The development of higher psychological functions*. Cambridge, MA: Harvard University Press.

Wagner, M. G. (2008). Serious Games: Spielerische Lernumgebungen und deren Design. In L. J. Issing & P. Klimsa (Eds.), *Online-Lernen—Handbuch für das Lernen mit Internet* (pp. 297–306). München: Oldenbourg.

Wouters, P., van Nimwegen, C., van Oostendorp, H., & van der Spek, E. D. (2013). A meta-analysis of the cognitive and motivational effects of serious games. *Journal of Educational Psychology, 105*(2), 249–265.

Zyda, M. (2005). From visual simulation to virtual reality to games. *Computer, 38*(9), 25–32.

CHAPTER SIX

Teaching Financial Literacy THROUGH THE Arts

Theoretical Underpinnings and Guidelines for Lesson Development

JAMES D. LANEY
University of North Texas

Most educators probably would agree that teaching is an art as well as a science. Numerous theory- and research-based instructional elements and principles have been identified that enhance initial learning, retention of learning, and transfer of learning to new contexts, but it is the way that a teacher puts these elements and principles together that constitute the art of teaching. It is my contention that by teaching with, about, in, and through the arts (Cornett, 2007), a master teacher achieves both scientific and artful instruction.

In Laney, Moseley, and Pak (1996), my colleagues and I demonstrated that an integrated arts-economics unit could be effective in teaching both economic concepts and arts-related concepts. Visual works of art were employed as the organizing centers for instruction, resulting in full integration and allowing "teaching through the arts" (Cornett, 2007, p. 13). The artworks served as much more than mere illustrations of the economic ideas being studied, for a symbiotic relationship emerged. By studying the economic content, the students better understood the art content, and by studying the art content, the students better understood the economic content.

Lucey (2007) extends my arts-economics integration ideas to the subdiscipline of personal finance, providing a moral framework for financial education, and suggests that the arts hold promise as an underutilized means of introducing students to human ethical dilemmas related to financial literacy. He lists sample activities in visual arts, music, drama, and dance that can be used to promote students' learning about income, money management, savings and investments, spending and credit, and general economic concepts.

The connections between the arts and economics in general, and the arts and financial literacy in particular, may not be readily apparent to many readers. What is the underlying rationale for this kind of curriculum integration? How is curriculum of this type developed? And what would a model lesson look like? The purpose of this chapter is to answer these three questions.

WHAT IS THE RATIONALE FOR TEACHING FINANCIAL LITERACY THROUGH THE ARTS?

The integration of financial literacy and arts education can be justified based on content utilization theory, multiple intelligences theory, generative teaching/learning theory, and the inherent nature of the art domains themselves. Each of these four rationale-building sources is addressed separately below.

As noted by Welton (2005), many individuals have the misconception that subject matter content is something that "teachers teach and students are expected to know" (p. 13), but content can also be seen as a vehicle or tool used by teachers and students to reach a destination—i.e., a predetermined educational purpose or goal. Even unconventional, mundane content, such as a can of corn, can be an effective content vehicle for social studies and other subject areas as well. For example, in social studies, students can learn about the productive resources that go into producing a can of corn, and they can study the various occupations involved in getting corn from the producer to the consumers. Whether a particular content vehicle is appropriate or not depends on one's specific goals/purposes.

The ultimate goal/purpose of social studies education (and schooling in grades K–12 in general) is to foster in the nation's young the skills, dispositions, and knowledge for effective participation in our social and political democracy (Goodlad, Soder, & Sirotnik, 1990; Soder, Goodlad, & McMannon, 2001; Welton, 2005). Far from being mundane in nature, works of art (in all art domains—visual arts, music, dance, drama, and literature) seem to constitute ideal content vehicles for promoting citizenship education.

Welton (2005) describes three approaches to citizenship education, including (1) teaching the cultural heritage (i.e., our literary, scientific/technological, and social/political/economic heritages), (2) teaching the social science disciplines (including both social science content and process skills for adding new knowledge to each discipline), and (3) teaching children how to think (e.g., through rational decision-making, creative problem-solving, values analysis/clarification, and moral reasoning). The arts fit neatly into each of the three approaches mentioned above, for they are part of our cultural heritage and thus reflect our diverse society. Arts knowledge contributes to the wisdom of a culturally literate citizenry and promotes different ways of knowing (i.e., more intuitive, impressionistic, emotional paths to truth). Finally, the arts provide avenues through which students can develop decision-making and problem-solving skills as applied through the art disciplines of art history, art criticism, aesthetics, and art production.

Howard Gardner's (1993a, 1993b) theory of multiple intelligences can also be used to help build a case for teaching financial literacy through the arts. According to Gardner, there are eight separate intelligences—verbal/linguistic, visual/spatial, musical, interpersonal, intrapersonal, logical/mathematical, bodily/kinesthetic, and naturalistic. Intelligence is defined as the capacity to solve problems and create products that are valued by a given cultural group/society. Each individual has all eight intelligences, but s/he may be stronger in some intelligences than others. One's capacity in each intelligence can improve with instruction. Unfortunately, school-based instruction often emphasizes verbal/linguistic and logical/mathematical intelligences to the exclusion of the other six intelligences.

Cornett (2007) notes that four of the eight intelligences parallel domains in the arts. Specifically, visual/spatial intelligence corresponds with the visual arts; musical intelligence suggests music; bodily/kinesthetic intelligence evokes dance and drama; and verbal/linguistic intelligence denotes literature. In turn, three of the remaining intelligences also have connections to the various art domains. Problem-solving in all arts areas requires logical intelligence. Interpersonal intelligence is needed when one works with groups of people in the arts, and intrapersonal intelligence is essential when engaged in self-examination/introspection in the arts.

In order to develop the whole person and maximize human intellectual capacities, schooling should address all eight intelligences. Gardner (1993a, 1993b) argues that deep information processing and true understanding depends on a person's transforming ideas/skills from one domain/intelligence to another. In other words, the intelligences operate jointly, not in isolation from each other. Works of art provide us with content vehicles for translating ideas and feelings/emotions using both verbal and nonverbal teaching/learning modalities. Through the employment of multiple modalities (or different ways of processing information), initial learning and retention of learning are enhanced.

Similarly, Merlin Wittrock's (1992, 1977) generative teaching/learning theory supports arts integration and learning through the arts. According to this theory, learning occurs as connections are made—new learning to old learning; new learning to prior knowledge/experience; and parts of a new learning to other parts of that same new learning. Three teaching-learning principles emerge from the theory as follows: (1) the more connections that are made, the greater the learning/retention; (2) the more learning modalities used, the greater the learning/retention; and (3) moving from teacher-generated connections (known as "elaborations") to student-generated connections (known as "generations") enhances learning/retention. Because the arts represent different modalities of teaching/learning through which new learning connections are made, students learn *through* the arts, with works of art employed as vehicles or organizing centers for instruction. In effect, the arts serve as meaning-makers for new learning (Cornett, 2007).

Finally, if a major goal of financial education should include increasing students' awareness of human, value-laden issues related to financial literacy as Lucey (2007) suggests, then artworks are definitely appropriate content vehicles for this purpose. The inherent nature of the art domains themselves provide a convincing rationale for relating financial, moral, and arts education. Cornett (2007) refers to the arts as the primary source of human communication—past, present, and future. By nature, the arts are emotional and passionate. Thoughts and feelings that are difficult to express in words alone can be expressed through the arts, leading to a better understanding of self and others. With respect to the visual arts, a picture "paints a thousand words," for images stimulate sensory-rich, higher-order thinking. Music, on the other hand, is a communication symbol system, mnemonic device, and learning tool that teaches through storytelling and song. Drama develops empathy and causes reflection on moral issues and values, while dance uses the body as a language, increasing our sensitivity to different points of view and satisfying our aesthetic need for beauty. In short, the arts are integral to real life and can be applied easily to any social science area, including financial education.

WHAT ARE SOME PROCEDURAL GUIDELINES FOR DEVELOPING FINANCIAL LITERACY LESSONS THAT USE WORKS OF ART AS CONTENT VEHICLES?

I have previously written two articles (i.e., Laney, 1996, 2005) that suggest seven steps for developing integrated arts-social studies lesson plans. This seven-step process can be simplified and collapsed into three main phases—(1) identifying appropriate works of art for use as organizing centers or content vehicles; (2) providing for discipline-based arts education; and (3) providing for comprehensive arts education.

In the first phase (i.e., identifying appropriate works of art for use as instructional content vehicles), I find it easiest to start with the visual arts by brainstorming topics/ideas related to financial education that can be represented pictorially—either directly or indirectly. Several examples come quickly to mind—images of class/income disparity; blue-collar vs. white-collar workers; the unemployed/homeless; Depression-era breadlines; money; banks; the stock market; marketplaces; and product advertisements. Internet search engines, such as Google (and its image-finding function), can also aid in the location of works of art. On Google, I had success in using search terms such as "art and income," "art and money/money management," "art and credit card debt," "art and capitalism," "art and advertising," etc. Finally, I am always on the lookout for promising art posters and art postcards, available online or in museum shops/stores, to give me inspiration. When possible, for quality control purposes, I use well-known works of art and/or well-known (or at least established) artists as my organizing centers for instruction. The *Encyclopedia of World Art* (1959–present) and the *Illustrated Dictionary of Art and Artists* (Piper, 1984) are great resources for background information on artists and their creations.

Below, for illustrative purposes, I have listed some artists and artworks with possible links to financial literacy topics. The entries are grouped under five guiding questions that cut across the various content areas in financial education, including income, money management, savings and investments, spending and credit, and general economic concepts. These questions seem to have value in bringing out the ethical/moral and values-related aspects of financial literacy. As suggested by Jacobs (1989), guiding questions such as these can be used to provide a scope and sequence of lessons/activities for an integrated unit of study.

WHAT IS MONEY? HOW AND WHY DO PEOPLE USE IT?

- JSG Boggs' "Boggs Notes" (http://pennylicious.com/2006/08/22/jsg-boggs-art-money/ and Obadiah Eclcut's "noney" (http://noney.com). Visual/performance art functioning as real-world complementary currencies.
- Carmen Lomas Garza's *The Fair at Reynosa*. Provides a visual representation of "market economy," "market opportunity," "goods and services," "producers and consumers," and "entrepreneurship" (Laney & Moseley, 1997).

HOW/WHY DO SOME PEOPLE HAVE/MAKE MORE MONEY THAN OTHERS?

- Dorothea Lange's *Toward Los Angeles, California*. Migrant hitchhikers walk past a roadside billboard that suggests, "NEXT TIME TRY THE TRAIN … RELAX."
- George Segal's *The Breadline*. One of three sculptural ensembles depicting the era of The Great Depression; part of the Franklin Delano Roosevelt Memorial in Washington, D.C.

HOW/WHY DO PEOPLE MAKE/GROW MONEY?

- Diego Rivera's *The Making of a Fresco, Showing the Building of a City*. Blue-collar workers, white-collar workers, and artists labor collaboratively,

combining their individual knowledge and skills to construct a modern industrial city in the United States (Laney & Moseley, 1995).
- Anthony White's money series (http://www.anthonywhite.net). The U.S. Series begins with an image of a dollar sign and the numeral one. The series then goes up in one-unit increments, with each painting selling for the dollar amount pictured on the canvas. Because the artist claims no one has ever lost money on his artwork, the series humorously reflects the investment value of art.
- James Rosenquist's *World's Fair Mural and Nomad.* The artist, who formerly made a living as a billboard painter, uses the language of advertising and pop culture to create montages of images that stimulate viewers' associative responses.
- Caravaggio's *The Cardsharks*. Sixteenth-century gentlemen cheat as they gamble for money in a game of cards. The work presents interesting analogies to playing the stock market, economic risk-taking, and insider trading.

HOW/WHY DO PEOPLE SPEND MONEY?

- Saint Clair Cemin's Monument to Credit Card Debt (http://www.chelseaartmuseum.org/exhibits/2005/bogeyman). A humorous offering to (or not-so-funny commentary on) the credit card god of consumption.
- Andy Warhol's paintings of cans of Campbell's Soup. Pop Art commentary on American consumerism, American market culture, and what constitutes art.

WHAT ARE THE ETHICS AND/OR VALUES-RELATED ASPECTS OF MONEY?

- George Segal's *Rush Hour*. Sculpture that serves as an allegory of the fate of the individual in modern society and as a tribute to the sacrifice of middle-class workers. Commuters, caught up in their routine, seem to move mindlessly and wearily forward.
- George Tooker's *Market*. Portrays the isolation/alienation of individuals in a competitive market economy (Laney & Moseley, 1997).
- Paul Strand's *Wall Street*. One of the most critically acclaimed photographs of the 20th century, this image of rush-hour pedestrians and the bleak windows of the Morgan bank speaks to the power of Wall Street and its impact on humanity.

- Christopher (or C.K.) Wilde's currency collages (http://www.artichokey-inkpress.com/new.php). Made with shapes cut from paper currencies from around the world, these images convey strong economic and political messages.

The second phase in lesson development involves providing for discipline-based art education (DBAE). According to the tenets of DBAE, art education should no longer be limited to art production (i.e., making art; expressing ideas and feelings through some art form). Instead, educators should expand art education curricula to include the following topics/processes: (a) art history (i.e., knowledge about the contributions artists and art make to culture and society); (b) art criticism (i.e., responding to and making judgments about properties and qualities that exist in works of art; interpreting meaning and making critical judgments about individual, contemporary works of art); and (c) aesthetics (i.e., discovering and understanding the varieties of meanings and values of art; questioning the nature, significance, and purposes of art in general) (North Texas Institute for Educators on the Visual Arts, 1993). Graphically, this approach can be visually represented with four overlapping rectangles—each representing one of the four art disciplines. These four overlapping rectangles form a pinwheel around the organizing center (or content vehicle) for instruction—one or more works of art (see Figure 6.1).

The challenge is for teachers to generate inquiry-oriented questions and/or learning tasks/activities for each of the four art disciplines. Some very general questions and tasks, which can be used by teachers to develop more specific questions/tasks to go with a particular work of art, are described below. Again, based on personal preference, I begin by focusing on one or more visual works of art, although it would be possible to start with songs, dramatic readings, dances, and/or poems.

ART HISTORY

- What is the content/context of the image?
- What is the sequence/chronology of the image (in relationship to other works of art)?
- What concepts/ideas from history (and/or other social science disciplines) are directly depicted and/or implied by the image?

ART CRITICISM

- What is your interpretation of the image? What inferences can you make about the artist's intent/message?

```
                    ┌─────────────────────────┐
                    │ ART PRODUCTION          │
                    │                         │
                    │ Making art.             │
                    │                         │
                    │                         │
                    │            ┌────────────┼──────────────────────┐
                    │            │            │   ART HISTORY        │
┌───────────────────┼────────────┼────────────┤                      │
│ AESTHETICS        │            │            │  Acquiring knowledge │
│                   │   ┌────────┼────┐       │  about the contributions │
│ Discovering and   │   │  WORK  │    │       │  artists and art make to │
│ understanding     │   │        │    │       │  culture and society.│
│ varieties of      │   │   OF   │    │       │                      │
│ meanings and      │   │        │    │       │                      │
│ values of art.    │   │  ART   │    │       │                      │
│                   │   └────────┼────┘       │                      │
└───────────────────┼────────────┼────────────┘                      │
                    │            │   ART CRITICISM                   │
                    │            │                                   │
                    │            │   Responding to and               │
                    │            │   making   judgments              │
                    │            │   about the properties            │
                    │            │   and  qualities  that            │
                    │            │   exist in works of art.          │
                    │            │                                   │
                    └────────────┴───────────────────────────────────┘
```

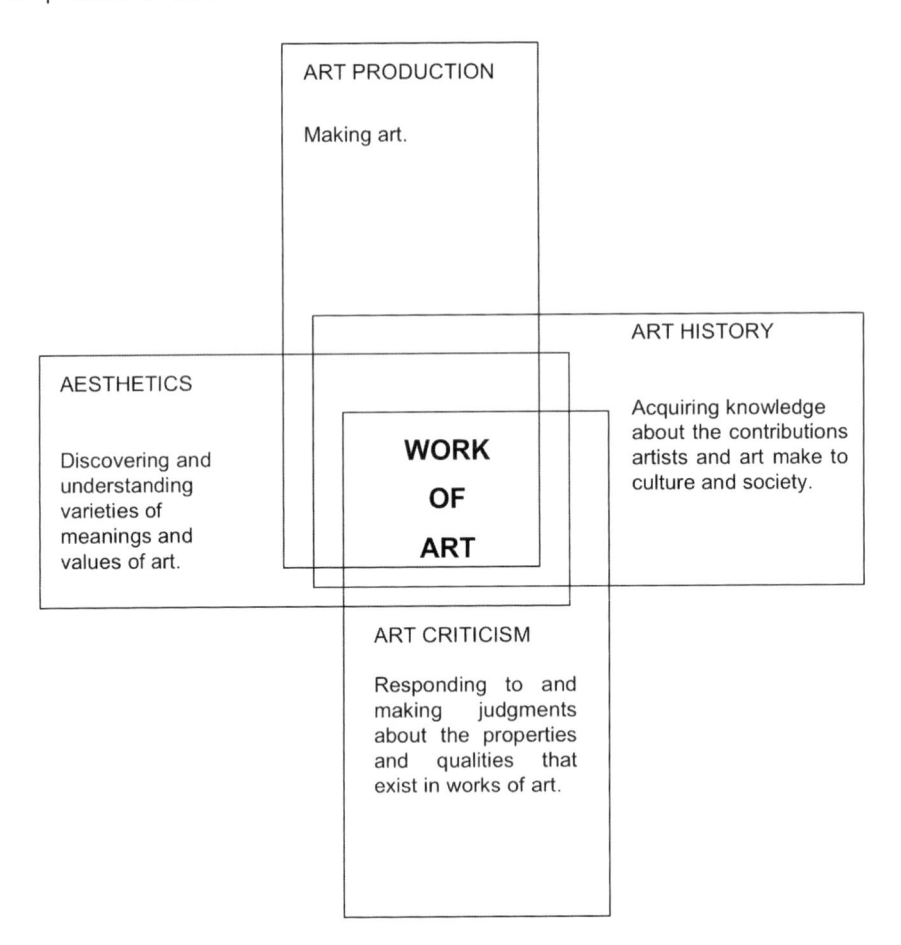

Figure 6.1: Discipline-based Art Education.
©North Texas Institute for Educators on the Visual Arts.

- How are various art elements (e.g., line, color, texture, values, forms, design structures, unity, emphasis, balance, variety, pattern, and proportion) used by the artist to communicate with his/her audience?

AESTHETICS

- Did the artist effectively apply art elements and principles?
- Did the artist effectively communicate his/her message?
- What is the worth/value of the work of art—aesthetically, ethically, and monetarily? Is it beautiful?

ART PRODUCTION

- Create an original work of art using the same art elements/principles emphasized in the work of art being studied.
- Create an original work of art, based on one's own knowledge base and experiences, with a similar topic/theme/message as the work of art being studied.

In the third and final lesson-development phase, the teacher should build in comprehensive arts education. The art disciplines listed above still serve as focal points of study, but this comprehensive approach to arts education pulls in the other art domains—music, drama/storytelling, dance, and literature.

As an advocate for comprehensive arts education, Cornett (2007) describes "seed strategies" for use in conjunction with each art domain. In effect, these seed strategies constitute activity ideas for teachers to use in their integrated lesson planning. Some of my own adaptations of these activity ideas, reflecting my personal preference of starting with a visual work of art and branching out to other art domains, are briefly outlined below.

VISUAL ARTS SEED STRATEGIES

- Brainstorm descriptive words (or force-fit random, unrelated adjectives and adverbs) to create a descriptive paragraph about a visual work of art.
- Compare/contrast works of art and/or artists using a Venn diagram.
- Create frozen tableaus of a visual work of art.

MUSIC SEED STRATEGIES

- Choose a piece of music to "go with" a visual work of art and justify the choice, analyze its theme(s) and other musical elements (i.e., tempo, rhythm, beat and accent, meter, notes, syncopation, pitch, timbre, dynamics, texture, melody, harmony, form, and ostinato).
- Create an original song or rap to "go with" a visual work of art—i.e., same subject matter, theme, and/or mood/feeling.

DRAMA AND STORYTELLING SEED STRATEGIES

- Make a visual work of art come to life through the use of pantomime and/or role play. Pantomime and/or role play before, during, and after the "snapshot" of time captured by the visual work of art.

- Create a reader's theater presentation based on a book scene/chapter, a poem, or song lyrics; self-critique the use of drama elements (i.e., characters, conflict, plot, setting, and mood).

DANCE SEED STRATEGIES

- Based on a visual work of art, isolate several objects and/or identifiable actions that are shown or implied, creating a dance movement for each; then link the dance movements based on a pattern (e.g., AABCAABC …).
- Critique the original dance based on how well it "goes with" the visual work of art and on its use of dance elements (i.e., body, energy, space, time, and choreographic principles).

LITERATURE SEED STRATEGIES

- Choose a piece of literature to "go with" a visual work of art and justify your choice; analyze its theme(s) and other literary elements (i.e., plot, character, setting, point of view, and stylistic/poetic elements).
- Use an art-based work of children's literature for a class read aloud (Cornett, 2007; Laney, 2005).

Seed activities such as those listed above constitute meaningful, mindful integration. Through such activities, teachers begin to teach with the arts and about the arts. Students, in turn, are involved in the arts, with arts experiences prompting strong emotions/feelings and evoking high-level thinking. Ultimately, teachers achieve complete integration when they teach through the arts. Students are immersed in an aesthetically-rich classroom environment in which the arts are used as learning tools/vehicles and organizing centers for interdisciplinary units that can potentially encompass all art disciplines, art domains, and other academic subject areas (i.e., social studies, science, mathematics, and reading/language arts) (Cornett, 2007).

WHAT DOES A MODEL ARTS-FINANCIAL LITERACY LESSON LOOK LIKE?

Sample lessons, developed using the three lesson-planning phases described above, are available in the professional literature. I have published articles and curriculum materials (i.e., Laney, 1996; Laney & Moseley, 1994, 1995; Laney et al., 1996) that demonstrate how to teach basic economic concepts through the application of arts-related content vehicles, DBAE, and comprehensive arts education.

As an addendum to this chapter, I have created an original lesson plan to illustrate a model arts-financial literacy lesson. The lesson "Art Money and Money Art: The Ethics and Aesthetics of Complementary and Conventional Currencies" uses some contemporary works of art (in visual arts and music) and inquiry-oriented guided discussion questions and tasks/activities based on the four art disciplines (i.e., art history, art criticism, aesthetics, and art production) and three art domains (i.e., visual arts, music, and drama/storytelling).

CHAPTER UPDATE

There has been some research regarding using the arts for teaching economic concepts notably from the Federal Reserve Bank of Atlanta (2014) and Watts and Chineze in 2012. This growing interest in approaching economics and economic concepts in ways appealing to learners is evident. The work by Vidagan and Arriba in 2016 expands the notion of the use of the arts to movies, music, and photography to the teaching of economics in higher education as well perhaps with a possibility of use in teacher education programs.

QUESTIONS FOR DISCUSSION

1. To what extent have you been invited to create or study artworks as part of a course in economics or personal finance? What do you perceive as being the strengths or weakness of such activities?
2. Laney describes how various art forms act differently to stimulate affective responses. What emotions do you associate with financial literacy and what art form would best represent them?
3. A matter of personal finance is that one should take the emotion out of one's decision. To what extent is this a valid principle? How might discipline-based art education relate to your reasoning?
4. Review the four elements contained within a work of art, as depicted in Figure 6.1. Locate a painting with which you are familiar and try to map out the four components. How do your findings affect your understanding of the artwork?
5. Laney's chapter does not appear to emphasize language arts activities (e.g., poetry) to describe money and characteristics. What do you think differentiates language arts from the other art forms described?

REFERENCES

Cornett, C. (2007). *Creating meaning through literature and the arts: An integration resource for classroom teachers* (3rd ed.) Upper Saddle River, NJ: Pearson Merrill Prentice Hall.

Encyclopedia of World Art. (1959–present). New York, NY: McGraw-Hill.

Federal Reserve Bank of Atlanta. (2014). *Commerce on the Canvas: Discovering Economics through Art*. Retrieved September 12, 2016 from https://frbatlanta.org/education/publications/extra-credit/2014/spring/commerce-on-canvas-discovering-economics-through-art

Gardner, H. (1993a). *Frames of mind: The theory of multiple intelligences*. New York, NY: Basic Books.

Gardner, H. (1993b). *Multiple intelligences: The theory into practice*. New York, NY: Basic Books.

Goodlad, J., Soder, R., & Sirotnik, K. (Eds.). (1990). *The moral dimensions of teaching*. San Francisco, CA: Jossey-Bass Publishers.

Jacobs, H. (1989). The interdisciplinary concept model: A step-by-step approach for developing integrated units of study. In H. Jacobs (Ed.), *Integrated curriculum: Design and implementation* (pp. 53–65). Alexandria, VA: Association for Supervision and Curriculum Development.

Laney, J. (1996). Developing your own integrated art-social studies lessons using the discipline-based art education model. *Children's Social and Economics Education, 1*(1), 89–91.

Laney, J. (2005). The art of teaching social studies. *The Social Studies Texan, 21*(1), 70–72.

Laney, J., & Moseley, P. (1994). Images of American business: Integrating art and economics. *The Social Studies, 85*(6), 245–249.

Laney, J., & Moseley, P. (1995). Integrating art and social studies using the DBAE model: A sample lesson. *The Social Studies Texan, 10*(3), 54–56.

Laney, J., & Moseley, P. (1997). *Interdisciplinary connections: Art and social studies*. Teacher's Guide, Take 5 Series. Glenview, IL: Crystal Productions.

Laney, J., Moseley, P., & Pak, L. (1996). Children's ideas about selected art and economic concepts before and after an integrated unit of instruction. *Children's Social and Economics Education, 1*(1), 61–78.

Lucey, T. A. (2007). The art of relating moral education to financial education: An equity imperative. *Social Studies Research and Practice, 2*(3), 486–500.

North Texas Institute for Educators on the Visual Arts (NTIEVA). (1993, Winter). Picturing DBAE. *North Texas Institute for Educators on the Visual Arts Newsletter, 4*(1), 1–3.

Piper, D. (Ed.). (1984). *Illustrated dictionary of art and artists*. New York, NY: Random House.

Soder, R, Goodlad, J., & McMannon, T. (Eds.). (2001). *Developing democratic character in the young*. San Francisco, CA: Jossey-Bass Publishers.

Vidagan, M., & Arriba, R. (2016). When economics meets arts … in the classroom. In *Procedia—Social and Behavioral Sciences, 228*, 20 July 2016, pp. 323–328.

Watts, M., & Chineze, C. (2012). Using art (Paintings, Drawings, and Engravings) to teach economics. *The Journal of Economic Education, 43*(4), 408–442.

Welton, D. (2005). *Children and their world: Strategies for teaching social studies* (8th ed.). Boston, MA: Houghton Mifflin Company.

Wittrock, M. (1977). Learning as a generative process. In M. Wittrock (Ed.), *Learning and instruction* (pp. 621–631). American Educational Research Association, Readings in Educational Research. Berkeley, CA: McCutchan Publishing Corporation.

Wittrock, M. (1992). Generative learning processes of the brain. *Educational Psychologist, 27*(4), 531–541.

TEACHING FINANCIAL LITERACY THROUGH THE ARTS: A SAMPLE LESSON

Topic/Title: Art Money and Money Art: The Ethics and Aesthetics of Complementary and Conventional Currencies

Guiding Question(s): What is money? How/why is it used? What are the ethics and/or values-related aspects of money?

Related Financial Education Theme(s): Money Management, Economics

Suggested Grade Level(s): Upper Elementary and Middle School

Background Information in Financial Education:

According to Kourilsky (1996a), many children (and adults) incorrectly believe that money has some kind of inherent value. Or they believe money has value because a government has proclaimed that it has value or that it is backed by some valuable scarce resource such as gold or silver (Kourilsky, 1996b). Simply put, money has value because people have faith that it will be accepted by others in exchange for goods and services; it has value in terms of what it can buy. When people lose faith in money or when no money system exists, people resort to a barter system (the exchange of goods and services for other goods and services, such as citizens bartering for scarce goods/services with rationing coupons during World War II and soldiers in prisoner-of-war camps exchanging cigarettes for other things they wanted).

Among monetary innovations today is the increasing use of complementary currencies. Bernard Lietaer, as interviewed in Dykema (2003), defines money as an agreement between community members to use something as a medium of exchange within their community. He describes complementary currencies as private, nonconventional, non-national currencies that are often used to solve social, environmental, and educational problems in a noncompetitive, cooperative, and community-building way; these alternative currencies operate in parallel with conventional currency systems, bringing together unmet needs with unused resources. For example, airlines issue currency in the form of frequent flyer miles, a kind of commercial loyalty currency. In Great Britain, customers of a British airline can use their earned frequent flyer miles to purchase goods from the largest supermarket chain in the country.

There are hundreds of private currency systems in Japan that help pay for health care needs of the elderly not covered by the Japanese national health care insurance system. By helping take care of others, Japanese citizens earn "caring relationship tickets" or credits, which can be deposited in a savings account and used for their own care when sick or the care of other family members who need some health-related service (Dykema, 2003).

Hundreds of "time dollar" operational systems are currently being used within U.S. communities where conventional money is a scarce resource—i.e., in ghettos, low-income/low-employment areas, retirement communities, and student communities. In a time dollar system, the unit of currency is the hour, and people exchange hours of service with one another. For example, one U.S. community established a time dollar system to fund a neighborhood watch system aimed at reducing gang and drug-related activities (Dykema, 2003).

BACKGROUND INFORMATION IN ART EDUCATION

According to *Pennylicious* (http://www.pennylicious.com/2006/09/09/noney/), a "funny money" blog on the Internet, "noney" is the creation of artist Obadiah Eelcut (9/9/06). It has the dimensions and feel of government-issued money, but that is where the similarity ends.

The illustrations appearing on noney are hand-drawn and then hand-screened onto tough, acid-free paper. There are ten different faces, showing portraits of everyday people of Rhode Island (e.g., a painter, photographer, musicians, community advocate, librarian, waiter), each with his/her favorite bird and vegetable. The noney notes are also hand-editioned and hand-signed by the artist, with only 10,000 notes (1,000 of each face) printed. The denomination of each noney note is zero, and the value of the note lies in the aesthetic value of the artwork itself. The artist's website (Eelcut, n.d., http://www.noney.net) states that noney is available from the artist in exchange for goods and services. Website visitors are encouraged to send transaction proposals based on a trade wish list provided by the artist. Visitors to the website can see how and where the notes have traveled by reading stories from people who have already used or come across noney notes.

Similarly, as described in **Pennylicious** (8/22/06, http://www.pennylicious.com/2006/08/22/jsg- boggs-art-money/), JSG Boggs' "Boggs Notes" constitute economic art and a form of complementary currency. The artist created his own funny-money versions of U.S. banknotes and banknotes from other countries. At first glance, they look like real, government-issued currency, but there are obvious differences (e.g., one bill created for a Florida United Numismatist convention features the motto "IN FUN WE TRUST"). Because of the high-quality of Boggs' illustrations, Boggs Notes were in great demand by art collectors. Prior to most of Boggs' artwork being confiscated by the U.S. Secret Service, Boggs refused to sell his creations directly to collectors. Instead, he used the notes in face-value exchanges for various goods and services (e.g., a ten dollar bill was drawn and exchanged for ten dollars worth of goods/services), and then he told interested collectors where they might search for the notes. The artist considered his exchanges/transactions to be a kind of performance art. Boggs was arrested multiple times abroad for counterfeiting but was acquitted. Although the U.S. Secret Service never charged Boggs with counterfeiting, they never returned his artwork.

OBJECTIVE(S)

- The student will be able to define "money."
- The student will be able to compare/contrast conventional vs. complementary currencies.
- The student will be able to compare/contrast the value of money vs. the value of art.
- The student will be able to provide an ethics-based rationale for complementary currencies and an aesthetics-based rationale for art money/money art.
- Collectively, the students will be able to resolve a classroom problem using a complementary currency system.

MATERIALS

- Images of "noney" and "Boggs Notes" from the Internet or other sources.
- Teacher and/or student resources (e.g., books, articles, Internet sites) related to money, complementary currencies, conventional currencies, the Federal Reserve System (FED), the International Monetary Fund (IMF), the art of money (history/design of paper currency and coins around the world), Obadiah Eelcut, JSG Boggs, the U.S. mint, etc.
- Art materials/media for use in designing banknotes or coins.

PROCEDURES

- The teacher shows students images of "Boggs Notes." She asks: What is pictured here? What, if anything, do you notice that is unusual? (e.g., "IN FUN WE TRUST" instead of "IN GOD WE TRUST;" "Florida United Numismatists" instead of "United States of America;" the acronym "FUN" instead of the denomination wording, etc.)
- The teacher shows students images of "noney." She asks: What is pictured here? What, if anything, do you notice that is unusual? (e.g., portraits of

everyday people/citizens rather than U.S. Presidents or famous Americans; images of vegetables and birds rather than the White House, national monuments, U.S. government buildings)
- The teacher asks students to write and share descriptive paragraphs and/or two word poems (with each line consisting of two words) about the Boggs Notes and noney they observed.
- The teacher presents background information on or has students conduct and share independent Internet/library research on the following: artist JSG Boggs and Boggs Notes; artist Obadiah Eelcut and noney; definitions/descriptions/examples of money, bartering, conventional/national currencies, complementary currencies, the Federal Reserve System (FED), the IMF, etc.
- Based on the information above, students are asked to construct Venn diagrams on the following: Boggs Notes vs. U.S. banknotes; noney vs. U.S. banknotes; Boggs Notes vs. noney; money/currency systems vs. barter systems; complementary currencies vs. conventional/national currencies; and the Federal Reserve System vs. the International Monetary Fund.
- The teacher conducts a guided discussion with the class using the following questions:
  o Why did artist JSG Boggs create Boggs Notes that so closely resemble U.S. and other world currencies? Why did artist Obadiah Eelcut choose to put images of everyday people/citizens and their favorite birds and vegetables on the noney he created? What are the messages behind the artworks of these two artists? Are their illustrations artful? Why/why not? What creative choices did they make—in terms of color, media, content/subject matter, and humor? Do you think their artwork is entertaining/humorous? Why/why not? Should Boggs and/or Eelcut be found guilty of counterfeiting? Why/why not?
  o Boggs Notes and noney are sought after by art collectors, who pay much more than the face/denominational value in order to obtain them. Why do you think these art collectors are willing to pay more? Would you pay more? Why/why not?
  o Performance art can be defined as a dramatic presentation by a visual artist (rather than a theater/dance artist) in front of an audience (usually in a nontraditional, non-theater setting). Some consider Boggs Notes and noney as examples of performance art. Do you think Boggs Notes and noney fit the definition for performance art? Why/why not?
  o Do Boggs Notes and noney constitute money? Why/why not? Are they examples of a conventional/national currency or complementary currency? Why?

- What is the difference between monetary value and aesthetic value? Do Boggs Notes and noney have monetary and aesthetic value? Why/why not?
  - What are ethics? (standards of conduct; values related to right/wrong behaviors) Most conventional (national and world) currency systems are based on competition. As a result, some people/countries have more money than others. Is this ethical/fair? Why/why not?
  - Proponents say that complementary currencies can help solve social, environmental, and educational problems where conventional/national money and resources are scarce. Instead of promoting competition, complementary currencies are said to promote cooperation and community. Based on what you have learned in this lesson, do you think complementary currencies are really needed in the United States and in the world today? Why/why not? Will they be needed in the future? Why/why not?
  - Is money value neutral (i.e., devoid of ethical considerations and emotional connections)? What emotions do we have concerning money? Does money affect the kinds of transactions we make and the kind of relationships we establish during these exchanges? If you were an older adult in Japan, would you prefer to have services provided by people that you paid in "caring relationship tickets" (a complementary currency) or by people that you paid in yen (the national/conventional currency)? Why? If you had a friend who had helped you (to paint a house or move to a new home), would it "feel right" to pay him/her in national/conventional currency? Would if feel better to pay him/her in complementary currency? Why/why not?
- In order to bring in drama and storytelling, the teacher has students pantomime and/or role play hypothetical (a) bartering situations, (b) exchanges using Boggs Notes and noney, (c) exchanges using a conventional/national currency, and (d) exchanges using a complementary currency. In addition, students can pantomime and/or role play a social problem situation—before and after the implementation of a complementary currency system to help deal with the problem.
- As an extension activity in music, the teacher has students analyze the lyrics to the Beatles' "Can't Buy Me Love" (available at http://www.fab4lyrics.stonegauge.com). In the line, "I don't care too much for money, money can't buy me love," what are the songwriters saying about the worth/value of conventional currency? Or the teacher has the students analyze the lyrics to Pink Floyd's "Money" (available at http://www.pink-floyd-lyrics.com). What messages are conveyed about the ethics and value/worth of conventional currency?

SUMMARY/ASSESSMENT

As a culminating project, the teacher has students (a) design their own paper currency and implement their own complementary currency system for use in the classroom, with the purpose of resolving an identified classroom problem (e.g., scarcity of resources in providing homework assistance) and (b) write a short essay on how their newly designed currency has aesthetic, ethical, and monetary value. As an extension activity, in preparation for creating their own original complementary currency designs, students can research U.S. national/conventional currency design, including the history of (a) the artworks appearing on U.S. bills and coins and (b) the artists who created them.

Students' Venn diagrams and answers to guided discussion questions can be graded based on accuracy, logic, and completeness/thoroughness. The role play activities can be evaluated on student participation and the successful application of financial education and arts-related content. Finally, the success of the culminating project can be assessed based on whether the students achieve a positive social change in the classroom.

REFERENCES

Dykema, R. (2003, July/August). Complementary currencies for social change: An interview with Bernard Lietaer. *Nexus: Colorado's Holistic Journal.* Retrieved from http://www.nexuspub.com/articles/2003/july2003/interview.htm

Eelcut, O. (n.d.). *The people's currency.* Retrieved from http://www.noney.net

Pennylicious. (2006, August 22). *JSG Boggs art money.* Retrieved from http://www.pennylicious.com/2006/08/22/jsg-boggs-art-money/

Pennylicious. (2006, September 9). *Noney.* Retrieved from http://www.pennylicious.com/2006/09/09/noney/

Bibliography of Related Teacher Resources

Kourilsky, M. (1996a). *Entrepreneurship: Debriefing teachable moments.* Kansas City, MO: Center for Entrepreneurial Leadership Inc., Ewing Marion Kauffman Foundation.

Kourilsky, M. (1996b). *Law, government, & ethics: Debriefing teachable moments.* Kansas City, MO: Center for Entrepreneurial Leadership Inc., Ewing Marion Kauffman Foundation.

Lietaer, B (2000). *The mystery of money.* Munich: Riemann Verlag.

Lietaer, B. (2001). *The future of money.* New York: Random House.

Lietaer, B. (2003). *Access to human wealth: Money beyond greed and scarcity.* Munich: Access Books.

Olav, V. (2002). In Boggs we trust. *Tout-fait: The Marcel Duchamp Studies Online Journal, 2*(4), 1–2. Retrieved from http://www.toutfait.com/issues/volume2/issue_4/articles/velthuis/velthuis2.html

Standish, D. (2000). *The art of money: The history and design of paper currency around the world.* San Francisco: Chronicle Books.

Internet Resources

http://www.fab4lyrics.stonegauge.com
http://www.noney.net
http://www.pennylicious.com
http://www.pink-floydlyrics.com

CHAPTER SEVEN

Students' Money Experiences AND Preconceptions OF Financial Issues— Implications FOR Effective Financial Education

BETTINA GREIMEL-FUHRMANN
Vienna University of Economics and Business

PROBLEM STATEMENT AND OBJECTIVES OF THIS CHAPTER

There is a large number of empirical studies on financial literacy from countries all around the world (Atkinson & Messy, 2012; Lusardi & Mitchell, 2011, 2014). They have consistently shown that for large portions of the population, the level of financial literacy (mostly an assessment of their financial knowledge) is rather low (Atkinson & Messy, 2012; OECD, 2014). Not only do most people lack understanding of sophisticated financial concepts but also of very basic ones like interest and inflation. Especially women, elderly people as well as young people often show particularly low levels of financial literacy (e.g. Atkinson & Messy, 2012; Lusardi & Mitchell, 2011, 2014; OECD, 2014; Silgoner, Greimel-Fuhrmann, & Weber, 2015).

It has long been known that dealing with money is not only a task to be fulfilled by adults but also by children and very young people as soon as they make their own purchases and decide whether to save or to spend money. Hence, financial literacy—as a combination of financial knowledge, skills, attitudes and behaviors as defined in the second section of this chapter—is initially shaped at a very early stage in our lives (Kirchler, 2011; Whitebread & Bingham, 2013). Nevertheless, a large portion of recent studies on financial literacy focus on adults (Atkinson & Messy, 2012; Lusardi & Mitchell, 2011, 2014), and most studies—even those which research financial literacy of young children—mainly comprise information on the respondents' levels of financial knowledge, but rarely explore other aspects of financial literacy and their development (OECD, 2014). Although children's development of understanding the economy has been researched, little is known about the sort of experiences that influence young people's money attitudes and financial behaviors as well as their preconceived ideas of various financial issues (Kirchler, 2011). In particular, it would seem desirable to learn more about the situations in young people's lives that make them think about dealing with money that shape their attitudes and values and influence their financial behavior. Such information could contribute to better understand young people's (mis)conceptions about money and financial issues and improve financial education measures.

This chapter conveys findings from two research studies to close this knowledge gap. The studies comprise 65 interviews with Austrian students at the secondary school level (for an analysis of financial education in the Austrian education system, please refer to Greimel-Fuhrmann, Silgoner, Weber, and Taborsky 2016). Both studies aimed at identifying critical incidents in the respondents' lives that they think have helped them gain experience with money matters and influenced their money management. They also give deep insight into the students' money attitudes, behaviors, and their preconceived ideas of various financial concepts.

In the next section of this chapter the terms financial literacy and financial education will be defined. The research designs of the interview studies are described in the third section with presentation and discussion of findings and their implications for the enhancement of financial education for the young in the following sections.

DEFINING FINANCIAL LITERACY AND FINANCIAL EDUCATION

Though there is no single universally accepted definition of the term financial literacy (Hung, Parker, & Yoong, 2009), most authors refer to the definition that has been established by the OECD for their *Measuring Financial Literacy* project. It defines financial literacy to be "a combination of financial awareness, knowledge, skills, attitude and behaviours necessary to make sound financial decisions and ultimately achieve financial wellbeing" (Atkinson & Messy, 2012, p. 14). Hence, according to the OECD, financial literacy is much more than just knowledge of financial concepts, it also comprises skills, attitudes, values, and behaviors that enable people to make sound financial decisions and tackle their financial problems. These abilities contribute to their financial well-being because sound financial decisions usually reduce the risks of over indebtedness and are conducive to achieving financial stability in life. Financial education is sometimes used as a synonym for financial literacy, but usually refers to the educational process that enables people to become financially literate (Atkinson & Messy, 2012; Kaminski & Friebel, 2012; Reifner, 2011).

Personal finance is at the heart of the aforementioned OECD definition as well as of most definitions of financial literacy because they focus on people's individual money management, financial behaviors and decisions and consequently the financial well-being of individuals. Some definitions choose a broader perspective as they additionally comprise a person's ability to understand the whole financial system and the influence of the system on individual choices and vice versa (e.g. Aprea, Breuer, Davies, & Wuttke, 2012). According to the concept of Retzmann and Seeber (2016), financially literate persons are able to do much more than just manage their own finances; they can see and understand the interrelationships between their own financial actions and the whole economic system, and they are able to reflect on their behaviors and their effects on the economy and on society. From a societal and educational view, this is a very important enhancement of the definition because people do not only focus on their own finances but also take other individuals and the whole society in consideration.

RESEARCH DESIGN OF THE INTERVIEW STUDIES

In both studies, semi-structured qualitative interviews were used to learn more about the students' experiences with money, the way they deal with their money, how they think they have learned about money matters, and how they understand financial concepts like debt or inflation. All these issues are likely to influence the effectiveness of financial education but have rarely been researched before. Hence, the focus of the empirical studies was also on personal finance, the core element of financial literacy, and how it has been shaped, but will be shifted to a broader understanding of financial literacy in future work (e.g., Greimel-Fuhrmann, 2015).

Both interview studies were based on a questionnaire with open-ended questions that served as a guideline for the interviewers. Some of the questions were (almost) identical for both studies so that the answers of both groups of respondents can be compared and summarized. Some respondents were very talkative at the beginning of the interview and provided a valuable insight into their money management and how it was shaped. Unfortunately, in these cases there was little time left for a few questions at the end of the interview. All interviewers were trained to focus on the most important questions in the interview and make sure they could be posed in all interviews. All respondents seemed to be happy to participate in the studies, talking freely without any apparent hesitations or inhibitions. The interview transcripts were analyzed by conducting a summarizing content analysis that aims at inductively developing categories that reflect the respondents' answers (Mayring, 2010).

The first study was carried out at the higher secondary level (corresponding to the level ISCED 4a according to the International Standard Classification of Education of the UNESCO). 33 students (24 female and nine male, aged between 16 and 20 years, coded I1-I33) were interviewed for this study. They all attended the third year of a business school or business college in Vienna. The interviews were conducted by Melber and Schachenhofer (2015) who made the first analysis of the interview data. The author of this chapter conducted an additional summarizing content analysis (Mayring, 2010) in order to study the following questions in depth: How do the respondents describe their money management? Which experiences have the respondents made that potentially influenced their money management and other aspects of financial literacy? How well are the respondents able to explain selected financial terms like "debt" and "inflation"? Would the respondents like to have more financial education?

The second study focused on students at the end of the lower secondary level (correspondent to the level ISCED 2). There were 32 students (19 female and 13 male, coded i1-i32), most of them aged 13 or 14, who attended the eighth year of schooling who were interviewed. They were selected from different types of lower secondary schools in four different federal states of Austria (Greimel-Fuhrmann, Grohs, & Rumpold, 2016). The content analyses presented in this chapter focus on similar aspects as the first interview study, mainly on the respondents' money management, their learning experiences, and their preconceived ideas of some financial terms.

The results of both studies are presented and discussed in the following sections of this chapter. They are based on the content analyses conducted by three different researchers who first analyzed the data independently and later compared and aggregated their findings. The results are illustrated by some selected citations from the interview material that have been translated into English as the original material is in German. The results do not only answer the research questions, they also allow to learn more about why students who are taught business studies still think that they lack financial education. Important implications for more effective financial education can be derived from these results.

SELECTED RESULTS OF THE CONTENT ANALYSIS OF THE INTERVIEWS ASSOCIATIONS WITH MONEY AND MONEY MANAGEMENT

Much can be learned about the students' money management and their attitudes and behaviors by asking them about their immediate associations with money.

This is how all interviews were started after introducing the interviewer(s) and explaining the aim of the study. Asking about first associations usually is an easy open-ended question that enables interviewers to introduce the respondents to the topic of the interview and encourage them to speak freely.

The responses show very clearly that there mainly are two different groups of "money managers" among both target groups of respondents. One half of the respondents tend to economize, plan their income and their expenses very carefully and always try to spend only small amounts of money. Some can tell the exact amounts of money they get and they spend:

> *"I know that I have 200 euros in my savings account. So I will be able to buy a new skiing helmet, I have it all figured out already."* (I2)
>
> *"You really need to be careful with your money, because I—for example—I only have 150 euros per month at my disposal, so I need to plan my expenses"* (I17) and
>
> *"I almost do not spend any money—it is like I am sitting on my money."* (I32)

The other half of the respondents admit that they have difficulties dealing with their money and making ends meet. They typically spend more than they have and need to ask their parents for more money to cover all their expenses. Many of them realize that this is the reason why they cannot stick to their budget—they know that there is more money available if they ask for it:

> *"And I see that as soon as I spend my money ... I mean I spend it quickly. I do not really have a knack for money, it is gone quickly. And then I go back to my parents and beg for more and most of the time I get more"* (I22) and
>
> *"I lavish money, and most of the time I do not even know what I buy."* (I5)

Some respondents criticize this policy of "money on demand" that some parents have established for their children. They may mean well but in many cases their children get used to not having to plan their expenses and to economize and might have serious financial problems later in their lives.

LEARNING EXPERIENCES

In the context of the first question on the students' associations with money and money management some respondents have already mentioned situations they have experienced and that have influenced their financial behavior (like spending too much money and having none left when they need it). But there was an additional question in the interview guideline that addressed such situations that have made students think about how they deal (or how they think they should deal) with money.

Many students mentioned situations in which they just had **a limited amount of money to cover their expenses** and there was no simple chance to get more. Excursions and school trips very often are such occasions:

"... When we went to Venice I really had to be careful to get along with little money. Everything was expensive so I could only buy one pizza, not maybe three or four." (I4)

"I was in England during the summer all by myself. And towards the end of my stay I had almost no money left and so I had thought that I should have taken more care." (I32)

Going shopping—especially impulse buying that they will regret later—makes a lot of students think. The following statements illustrate this category:

"Each time I buy something I realize how important it is to deal carefully with your money" (I20) and

"If you buy something and some days later you realize that this purchase was a mistake, but you cannot return it" (i30)

"... For example, if I buy way too much and then one week later I regret my purchases. And I think that I should have spent my money more wisely." (I7)

Earning their first salary has been a special occasion for many students. And some spent the money more quickly than they had thought. They realize that a certain amount of money like 100 euros is not just the amount that you need to have to buy something that costs 100 euros. It also represents an amount of money that they had to earn before being able to spend it.

Watching other people's financial behavior and talking about financial affairs have proved influential too. Family members and friends are potential role models. Usually, young people tend to copy the behavior of role models (Kirchler, 2011). But if they dislike the observed behavior and/or experience its negative consequences, they choose not to follow the example.

"All my friends spend their money. And so I spent it too, I did this for some time, but then nothing was left when I needed some money. So I chose to change my behavior" (i1)

"Well when I go out I see a lot of other young people. And they spend so much money, it doesn't make any sense. But their parents give it to them and they just spend it without thinking, although the parents need to work for that the whole year round." (I6)

A few students talk about the influence of their parents, the conversations that they have with them, and how they profit from these conversations. Others admit that they would like to learn from their parents, but they have the impression that their parents are unable to cope with their financial problems and do not have a lot of explanations and advice to offer.

"I closely watch my earnings and my expenses. And how much money I have left. My father told me to do so because he is an accountant, and watching over money is what he does in his job" (I27)

"My father tells me about the expenses he has to cover. 1,200 euros are just the fixed costs. And the variable costs ... he doesn't even mention" (I17) and

> *"I like watching the news, and whenever they mention something about money that I am interested in, my father explains the news to me."* (i3)
>
> *"I got my very first stock at the age of six. And since then I have got some more and every evening, my father and I sit together and talk about the stocks we have. That is our thing."* (I32)

These statements reveal that learning about money and money management usually takes place at home within the families and close friends. It does not seem to be a topic discussed in schools although it is part of the curricula of secondary schools in Austria.

PRECONCEIVED IDEAS OF FINANCIAL ISSUES

Questions around the students' understanding of the financial concepts of "debt" and "time value of money" revealed that a large number of students have misconceptions of these—and most likely also of other—financial terms.

The first question addressed the students' understanding of the term "debt." Most students were able to give definitions like "borrowing money" or "spending more money than you have." Most interestingly, some students added some further details to this definition. One of the most common was that debt constitutes money that you have borrowed and probably will not be able to pay back.

> *"If you borrow money that you will not able to pay back. That means that you have no money left"* (i2). Or in a similar way i4, *"You have borrowed money and it really takes you a very long time to pay it back."*

Some other students mentioned that debt is a considerable high amount of money and that smaller amounts cannot be considered a debt. An 18-year-old student (I11) even said that you can only have debts at the age of 40+. These perceptions are highly surprising as all respondents from business schools have already had three years of business studies and accounting at school and there is no doubt that they must have come across the concept of debt in many contexts. And in none of them debt was defined as a high amount of money that you were not able to pay back.

A follow-up question was intended to study this misconception in depth. Students were asked whether they think that money they have borrowed from a friend constitutes debt. Half of the respondents clearly said yes. And many of them added that they would not like borrowing money from friends because that situation made them feel uneasy. But the remaining half of the respondents did not consider money borrowed from a friend to be a debt. They explained that they only borrowed small amounts of money and that they would be willing to pay it back as quickly as possible. Some also argued that they knew their friend personally whereas a debtor usually does not know the creditor. So in addition to the misconceptions that have already been detected, some students obviously think that usually creditors and debtors do not know each other. Even if this is the case, however, it is completely irrelevant for the definition of debt.

The second concept that has been addressed was inflation. Students most probably have already heard of this concept when being taught economics or business studies at school. But less than half of the respondents were able to give an answer. And most answers were not very precise; students knew inflation had something to do with increasing prices or a decreasing value of money but were not able to explain the concept. Some of the younger students mentioned that their teachers had explained them that a higher amount of money in the world would not help the poor but just decrease the value of money for everybody. This is how they have heard about the concept but not gone into the details. Therefore, an additional question was posed in order to see if students have recognized the importance of inflation for everybody's life. They were asked if they thought that they are affected by inflation. Most students answered that they simply had no idea; some students said that they thought that inflation only would become more important later in life. Being asked to explain their reasoning, they said that they did not spend a lot of money anyway and that they always spent the same amount of money regardless of the price level (!). These answers reveal that the students have not really understood the concept of inflation.

WISHING MORE FINANCIAL EDUCATION

Finally, students were asked if they would like to have more financial education. An overwhelming majority of the respondents in both studies clearly answered yes. Their answers reveal that they feel poorly prepared for tackling the financial problems that lie ahead. On the one hand, many of them argue that money is not an issue that is thoroughly discussed at home. So, most of the students do not seem to have any chance to learn about money (management) from their parents. "I would really like to know how money can be saved and how it should be spent. (...) And I would like to learn more about the stock exchange" (i20).

On the other hand, they also do not consider their education at school as helpful for their own money management, and this applies to the students who attend business schools as well. 19-year-old student I1 for example thinks that more financial education is extremely important. "Soon I will be 20 and I need to learn about paying the rent and so." This is astounding because students learn about paying bills, bank accounts, making money transfers and similar topics in their business subjects. Maybe they have the impression that what they have learnt at school is not applicable to their everyday financial tasks. 17-year-old student I2 also argues that more financial education at school "would be good, because we are in a business school. And if you start a business you need to know about dealing with money. Not just business studies and accounting ... what is that good for if you do not know anything about dealing with money." There are several possible interpretations for this finding. Firstly, financial education might not be sufficiently integrated into business studies so students feel poorly prepared for money management, not only in a private, but also in a business context. Findings from interviews with teachers support this assumption. Most teachers feel that dealing competently with money should be learned at home and not be integrated into their lessons at school (Melber & Schachenhofer, 2015). Secondly, students might have problems realizing that what they have learnt at school applies very well to solving problems outside the classroom, so their learning transfer might be weak. Anyway, both interpretations have important implications for improving the effectiveness of financial education, as discussed in the following section of the chapter.

SUMMARY AND IMPLICATIONS OF THE RESULTS FOR EFFECTIVE FINANCIAL EDUCATION

Both interview studies revealed very clearly that students at all ages like talking about money and had no difficulties to open up to the interviewers. Conversations about money and financial issues seem to be rare occasions in their lives. An overwhelming majority of the respondents mentioned in the interviews that money matters are hardly discussed at home and their parents usually do not involve them in their everyday financial decisions. Given the fact that socialization within the families plays a crucial role for developing financial skills of children and adolescents (Grohmann & Menkoff, 2015), it becomes clear that for some students an important contribution to their financial education is missing.

Nevertheless, many students described in the interviews that they observe the financial behaviors of their parents and peers. Unfortunately, in many cases it seems that they do not find convincingly positive role models in their social environment.

This makes effective financial education at schools even more important. Schools also can make an important contribution to the students' financial education (Grohmann & Menkoff, 2015). However, the respondents in our studies only talked about learning incidents in the private context (like saving for an intended purchase, shopping, and going out with friends). They did not mention any situation that relates to what they learn at their (business) schools. This is surprising as they are supposed to learn about business and money at the secondary level. Some students have (business) projects at their schools that require planning of scarce resources; others have already run virtual enterprises at school. But when it comes to reflecting on how they think they have learnt how to deal with money, they do not mention a single incident from school.

As argued above, financial education at schools needs to complement (or even substitute) financial education within the students' families. But meta-analyses of studies on the effectiveness of financial education measures have shown that they differ in effectiveness and many effects tend to fade over time (Miller, Reichelstein, Salas, & Zia, 2013). In order to be effective, financial education needs to be "hands on" and problem-oriented so that students are able to connect their knowledge and skills to the challenges outside the classrooms and to apply their skills in their everyday financial situations. Additionally, parents also need to be continuously supported by comprehensive and impartial information campaigns about money matters targeted at adults in their roles as investors, savers, creditors, debtors, and many more, ready and available when they need it (Grohmann & Menkoff, 2015).

Many of the respondents admit that they struggle with their money management: some of them spend too much money (and sometimes cannot even recall on what they have spent it), the others have difficulties spending any money because they feel they need to hoard it. Both groups would benefit from lessons on financial planning, budgeting, and saving. After learning the basic principles, they should be encouraged to plan their own financial resources and develop their own (weekly, monthly) budgets and savings plans. This can also be done by using Apps for mobile phones and tablet PCs that most young people have at their disposal and love using. All kinds of school projects in which students are involved need planning of resources and budgeting as well as monitoring the expenses and earnings. So students could (and should) be put in charge of controlling the financial aspects of schools projects, supported by their teachers. Setting up a (virtual) business for the duration of one school year is one of several options to provide challenging tasks for students that help them develop their financial skills.

It was an unexpected finding that even students at business schools seem to lack financial education and feel unsecure about tackling financial problems in their everyday lives. Being taught business and accounting at school obviously is no guarantee that students also learn how to deal with money. Additionally, the students' preconceived ideas of financial issues such as debt may interfere with conventional financial education and make it difficult to use financial information effectively and make sensible financial decisions. The interviews have shown that not only on the lower secondary level, but also in business schools at the higher secondary level students still stick to their subjective, preconceived meaning of (financial) terms although they most probably have learnt something different at school. It is important to know about these misconceptions and explicitly address them in order to help students realize the true meaning and scope of (financial) terms and support their transfer of learning. Students need to understand that money they borrow—regardless of the amount, the duration, the creditor, and their ability to pay it back—constitutes debt, and having debts does not necessarily mean that you are overindebted. As most of the students are likely to have some sort of debt later in their lives and/or will be confronted with numerous offers of financing by way of credit, they should be well aware of the nature and consequences of debt.

As teachers might consider financial topics to be difficult to teach and highly sensitive, case studies should be prepared that can be used to illustrate the different financial situations of people and the various financial challenges that they face in their lives. Students could work on these case studies, try to find financial solutions by researching financial products, then compare their solutions to some recommended "good practices" and enhance their financial knowledge, awareness, and skills. Not only is this important for their later lives (OECD, 2014), but they also wish to learn more about financial issues at school (Melber & Schachenhofer, 2015).

QUESTIONS FOR DISCUSSION

1. Under what circumstances do you talk about money? How do you decide when and to whom you converse?
2. To what extent would you say that your knowledge of finance was influenced by a critical moment and habits brought about by environmental experiences?
3. Respondents differed in their interpretations of debt from a friend. Why do you think these differences occurred?
4. These young consumers had already developed concepts of spending and debt. Their preconceived ideas were not necessarily accurate. How might you challenge these ideas respectfully in a classroom?
5. The author suggests guided financial literacy experiences in school—for instance, school project budget planning. Would this be feasible in schools in your context? What could be some of these projects?

REFERENCES

Aprea, C., Breuer, K., Davies, P., & Wuttke, E. (2012, September). *Exploring multiple conceptions of financial literacy*. Roundtable presentation at the European Conference on Educational Research (ECER), Cadiz, Spain.

Atkinson, A., & Messy, F.-A. (2012). *Measuring financial literacy: Results of the OECD/International Network on Financial Education (INFE) Pilot Study*. OECD Working Papers on Finance, Insurance and Private Pensions, No. 15, OECD Publishing.

Greimel-Fuhrmann, B. (2015, September). *Ökonomische Bildung von Jugendlichen in Österreich— eine empirische Analyse der economic literacy von Schüler/inne/n in der achten Schulstufe*. Presentation held at the European Forum Alpbach, Breakout Session on Economic and Financial Literacy, Alpbach (Austria).

Greimel-Fuhrmann, B., Grohs, St., & Rumpold, H. (2016). Die Vorstellungen von Jugendlichen zu Wirtschaft und Geld—Implikationen für die Entrepreneurship-Erziehung. In B. Greimel-Fuhrmann & R. Fortmüller (Eds.), *Facetten der Entrepreneurship Education* (pp. 37–52). Vienna: Manz.

Greimel-Fuhrmann, B., Silgoner, M., Weber, R., & Taborsky, M. (2016). Financial literacy in Austria. In C. Aprea, E. Wuttke, K. Breuer, N. K. Koh, P. Davies, B. Greimel-Fuhrmann, & J. S. Lopus (Eds.), *International handbook of financial literacy* (pp. 251–262). Singapore: Springer.

Grohmann, A., & Menkhoff, L. (2015). Schule, Eltern und finanzielle Bildung bestimmen das Finanzverhalten. In *DIW Wochenbericht, 28/2015* (pp. 655–661). Berlin.

Hung, A., Parker, A., & Yoong, J. K. (2009). *Defining and measuring financial literacy*. RAND Working Paper WR 709. Retrieved from https://www.rand.org/content/dam/rand/pubs/working_papers/2009/RAND_WR708.pdf

Kaminski, H., & Friebel, St. (2012). *Finanzielle Allgemeinbildung als Bestandteil der ökonomischen Bildung*. Working Paper of the Institute for Economic Education, Oldenburg, Germany.

Kirchler, E. (2011). *Wirtschaftspsychologie. Individuen, Gruppen, Märkte, Staat.* Göttingen: Hogrefe.

Lusardi, A., & Mitchell, O. (2011). *Financial literacy around the world: An overview.* National Bureau of Economic Research, Cambridge, Working Paper 17107. Retrieved from http://www.nber.org/papers/w17107

Lusardi, A., & Mitchell, O. (2014). The economic importance of financial literacy: Theory and evidence. *Journal of Economic Literature, 52*, 5–44.

Mayring, P. (2010). *Qualitative Inhaltsanalyse: Grundlagen und Techniken.* Weinheim: Beltz.

Melber, C., & Schachenhofer, S. (2015). *Wie gehen Schüler/innen mit ihrem Geld um?* Master thesis at Vienna University of Economics and Business.

Miller, M., Reichelstein, J., Salas, C., & Zia, B. (2013). *Can you help someone become financially capable? A meta-analysis of the literature.* Working Paper No. 6745, The World Bank.

OECD. (2014). *PISA 2012 Results: Students and money: Financial literacy skills for the 21st century* (Vol. VI). PISA, OECD Publishing.

Reifner, U. (2011). Finanzielle Allgemeinbildung und ökonomische Bildung. In Th. Retzmann (Ed.), *Finanzielle Bildung in der Schule* (pp. 9–39). Schwalbach: Wochenschau Wissenschaft.

Retzmann, T., & Seeber, G. (2016). Financial education in general education schools: A competence model. In C. Aprea, E. Wuttke, K. Breuer, N. K. Koh, P. Davies, B. Greimel-Fuhrmann, & J. S. Lopus (Eds.), *International handbook of financial literacy* (pp. 9–23). Singapore: Springer.

Silgoner, M., Greimel-Fuhrmann, B., & Weber, R. (2015). Financial literacy gaps of the Austrian population. *Monetary Policy & the Economy, 2*, 35–51.

Whitebread, D., & Bingham, S. (2013). *Habit formation and learning in young children.* Research Report for the Money Advice Service. London.

CHAPTER EIGHT

Financial Literacy AND Youths IN Jail

JAIME CHRISTENSEN

Spectrum Charter School, Pleasant Grove, Utah[1]

It is a bare room with only two chairs and a small round table. Across from the teacher/researcher sat "Joe," a nineteen-year-old African-American male inmate. The purpose of the meeting with Joe on this particular day was to administer informal reading, math, and spelling tests in order to assess his current academic functioning level. Joe seemed capable in math and reading; however, when conversation turned to his plans for the future, it was quite evident that he had none. He was sure that he did not need a job, but was positive that he would get a car "somehow," and find a place to live "somewhere." When asked how much money he thought he would need to live on, he shrugged.

BACKGROUND

The United States touts the education of its citizens as an issue of national priority and importance. It is expected, even demanded, that children receive education at least through high school. Despite these expectations and No Child Left Behind federal mandates, education for incarcerated youth has traditionally been left behind, or included on the journey (Hudson River Center for Program Development, 2001; US Department of Education, 2001).

The number of incarcerated youth ages under age 18 is disheartening. According to Collier and Thomas (2001), the number of incarcerated youth under 18 is approximately 100,000. Due to their incarceration, these youth do not have access to the range of educational opportunities of their non-incarcerated peers. Alarmingly, several studies have found that a large percentage (up to 70% in some places) of incarcerated youth have disabilities (Hudson River Center for Program Development, 2001). These dismal figures point to the critical need for intervention programs for this population. Many special educators, parents, and advocates are concerned that these youth receive state and federally mandated educational and related services while they are incarcerated (Quinn, Rutherford, & Leone, 2001).

Bullis, Yovanoff, Mueller, and Havel (2002) described a review of 20 publications on the academic characteristics of incarcerated youth that found that most function between the fifth and ninth grade levels. Those who perform lower than these levels are more likely to recidivate. Interestingly, in a recent study, Langan and Levin (2002) found that released prisoners with the highest rearrest rates were robbers. They further assert that what high-rate offenders have in common is that they were in prison for crimes that were thought to bring financial gain. By contrast, many of those with the lowest rearrest rates were in prison for crimes not generally linked with desire for monetary gain. This suggests that problems related to financial literacy may play a role in recidivism.

Petersilia (2000) adds further evidence to a recidivism link by suggesting that released prisoners who have no income are unlikely to be able to meet financial demands, including massive court costs and fees accrued while incarcerated, which leads them to recidivate. Researchers have indicated that a contributing factor of delinquency is a "failure of life skills maturation" (Kadish, Glaser, Calhoun, & Ginter, 2001, p. 85). The inability to develop life skills in one or more human development areas can be the result of many factors including having a learning disability or lack of good role models. Developing necessary life skills such as money management is crucial to students' chances for productive lives and the avoidance of recidivism (Collier & Thomas, 2001).

According to Coffey and Knoll (1998), life skills are "all of those skills and knowledge prerequisite to development of skills, in addition to academic skills, that are necessary for effective living" (p. 22). In order to achieve successful reentry into communities, families, and work environments, released inmates need a variety of life skills in addition to basic skills in reading, writing, and arithmetic. However, these are not the only skills needed to be able to effectively transition back into the community. Life skills consist of multiple components of the following four areas: work (filling out applications, writing resumes, interviewing, work ethic, and job keeping skills), practical living skills (money management, housing, transportation, parenting, and health), personal management (goal setting, responsibility, moral reasoning, and anger control), and social skills (getting along with people, conflict resolution, and mediation). Skills such as completing an application, writing a résumé, and appropriate interview conduct are critical to obtaining employment. Many also need other skills such as relating to others, avoiding confrontation, dealing with authority figures, and acting responsibly in their day-to-day actions on a job site. In addition, these youth often have the added burden of providing for a family and the financial pressures that entail (Coffey & Knoll, 1998). In 1993, the U.S. Department of Education recognized this need and sponsored nineteen separate grants for implementation of programs designed to "reduce recidivism through the development and improvement of life skills necessary for the integration of adult, state and local prisoners into the community" (Coffey & Knoll, 1998, p. 2). Harer (1994), in a study on recidivism, found that the more education an inmate had upon entry into the criminal justice system, the lower the recidivism rate. The highest recidivism rate for individuals with some high school was 54.60% and the lowest rate was 5.40% for those with college degrees. The study also found a decrease in the rate of recidivism, with inmates who received education during incarceration. Inmates who received no instruction while incarcerated recidivated at 44.10%, while inmates who completed at least one course while incarcerated recidivated at 35.50%. The challenge is to help these inmates realize that education can make a difference for them like the student from Keweenaw Academy in Michigan who earned his welding certificate and enumerated all of the things he had to learn in order to accomplish this goal. When a staff member told him that he had reason to be very proud, he replied, "Oh, I learned how to do that, too!" (White, 2002, p. 180).

A review of the literature indicates that there is little research about effective approaches to teaching life skills to delinquent youth. A program designed by competent individuals to accommodate special education students would allow correctional institutions to meet the required educational, social, and behavioral needs of this population (Glick & Sturgeon, 1999). Adventure programs have become an increasingly popular intervention approach to working with youth on life skills issues such as communication, group problem-solving, interpersonal skills, and group cooperation. The adventure-based model is based on the principles of Outward Bound and its physical, outdoor methods of reaching troubled youth (Moote & Wodarski, 1997). This type of program is, however, rarely available for the juvenile incarcerated population.

Morgenthau and Roberts (2002) described another type of life skills program in Florida designed for youths between 16 and 18 who had been incarcerated for various crimes. These youth were taken to Avon Park Academy to live in groups of six or eight in one of fifteen residential duplexes each with a house manager and several additional workers for supervision. The program includes homes, a clinic, a school, a police force, a store, an employment office, and a bowling alley that the inmates were required to run themselves under the guidance of staff. This program is based on work and inmates advance through levels based on their performance. The higher the level they attain, the greater the privileges they were allowed. At a certain level of attainment, the prison allowed inmates to have jobs with local business in order to be able to pay restitution and expenses such as rent and utilities. Eighty percent of youths released from this program held gainful employment, were attending school, or actively seeking employment (Morgenthau & Roberts, 2002). This model seems to be an extraordinary success.

Coffey and Knoll (1998) list 19 different publishers of life skills curriculums. The variety of curriculums ranges from a single life skills subject to a comprehensive, multiple-subject program. *Life Centered Career Education* and *Lifeschool 2000* are two programs that offer a wide array of life skills curriculum for in-class instruction. Both curriculum choices include daily living skills that consist of personal financial management, personal-social skills, and occupational guidance and preparation. These programs include knowledge and performance batteries, day-to-day lesson plans, and transition and portfolio management sections.

Brolin (1997) identified six skills that educators should teach students in order to manage their personal finances more effectively. These skills include counting money and making change, making responsible expenditures, keeping basic financial records, calculating and paying taxes, using credit responsibly, and using banking services. Researchers (Hudson River Center for Program Development, 2001) assert that many incarcerated youths come from dysfunctional settings that at the very core involve financial problems. These youths often feel pressure to provide for themselves or their families and, as a result, often resort to illegal activities to achieve immediate financial gain. Youths must learn the very rudiments of managing finances to meet basic needs without resorting to crime.

PROGRAM DESCRIPTION

The study and program described in this chapter were conducted within a federally mandated educational program which required delivery of instruction to special education eligible incarcerated youth ages 18–22 years. The teacher traveled between five different buildings at the Shelby County Department of Corrections in Memphis, Tennessee, in order to hold classes for various inmates for approximately two to three hours of instruction time per week. As in most special education settings, the students had a wide range of literacy competencies.

The Tennessee Department of Corrections provides some life skills training as part of their educational program. Their efforts focus on skills such as job readiness and character development but there was a noted absence of training about personal financial management. The teacher/researcher believed that the students would unquestionably benefit from the typical academic instruction they would receive, but felt it would be more useful during the time they were incarcerated to learn how to calculate income from a job, open a checking account, figure a budget, and understand rudimentary credit. With the understanding that these skills were not currently being addressed at the correctional facilities, the researcher/teacher decided to dedicate instructional time and effort to increase her students' understanding of personal financial management. The teacher/researcher chose to use a combination of materials from *Life Centered Career Education, Lifeschool 2000, Skills for Independent Living*, and *Checkbook Math*.

RESEARCH ENVIRONMENT AND PARTICIPANTS

Three special education students incarcerated for nonviolent crimes participated in this study/educational experience because they all had a security level clearance that would allow them to meet for class together, and because they expressed interest in this area of education. Joe was a 19-year-old African-American male, incarcerated since he was 14 years old. His last psychological examination indicated a diagnosis of mild mental retardation. Joe came from a single-parent, low socioeconomic background; his now incarcerated mother had been his only caregiver. Cory was a 20-year-old African-American male, incarcerated for one year. The last grade he had successfully completed was the 11th. From a single-parent home with his mother being the caregiver, Cory left home at age 12 and lived with a variety of relatives and friends. Special education records documented that he was learning disabled. Stuart was a 20-year-old African-American male, who had been incarcerated for 2 years. The last grade he attended in school was the eighth. Stuart came from a single-parent, mother-only, household at the poverty level. His special education records indicate a diagnosis of learning disabled.

The researcher conducted this study at the education building of the Shelby County Correctional Center in Memphis, Tennessee. The facility housed participants for this project in separate buildings in the facility and brought them together in one classroom for instruction.

INTERVENTION

Instruction took place once per week for two hours per session. The students were given instructional workbooks that were compiled from sources selected by the teacher/researcher: *Checkbook Math* (Remedia, 2001), *Life Centered Career Education* (Council for Exceptional Children, 2002), *Lifeschool 2000* (1994), and *Skills for Independent Living* (1997). These sources were chosen because they used life examples and case situations that these students would be likely to encounter or had already encountered in their lives. Thus, the researcher felt that the students would be more likely to have prior knowledge of some aspects of the content. In addition, these sources were rated as high interest for middle and high school age students, yet were at low enough reading level to accommodate the well below grade level literacy of these learners. Lessons were presented through direct instruction, modeling, and hands-on group participation and discussion. For each lesson, the workbook included tips on the topic, learning objectives, important words to know, and practice exercises with examples.

INSTRUMENTATION

Prior to beginning instruction in each topic, the researcher obtained quantitative data through administration of a pretest as prescribed in *LifeSchool 2000*. This assessment included short, written responses to questions about the topic. At the conclusion of the instruction each week, the researcher gave students a posttest. The researcher also collected data on attendance and participation. At the end of the study, the researcher gave students a comprehensive posttest measure using the *Lifeschool 2000*.

Prior to instruction, the researcher gathered qualitative data in the form of individual interviews with students. The students described any exposure they might have had to personal financial management, its relevance to their lives, and personal goals for attending the class. Through this discussion process, the researcher was also able to come to an understanding of the students' individual needs and the adaptations needed in order to make this instruction meaningful to all three students. Although these adaptations veered somewhat from the research plan, they were necessary due to the differential diagnoses and skills of the students. For instance, it was necessary to read instructions aloud to Joe due to his limited cognitive skills.

THE INTERVIEWS

Joe

The first interviewee was Joe. His demeanor was sullen and withdrawn. The teacher explained to Joe that she was interested in teaching a class on personal financial management and further explained what that class might entail. He received the option of attending a six-week class and he agreed. Joe maintained that he thought he saw a check once in the office at the school he used to go to, but was unsure what it was. Incarcerated since 14 years of age, Joe had heard of a paycheck but had never received one. He indicated that family members had not discussed or taught him these things. Joe's interview revealed that he had virtually no exposure to or experience with personal financial management. Joe's *Lifeschool 2000*

FINANCIAL LITERACY AND YOUTHS IN JAIL | 127

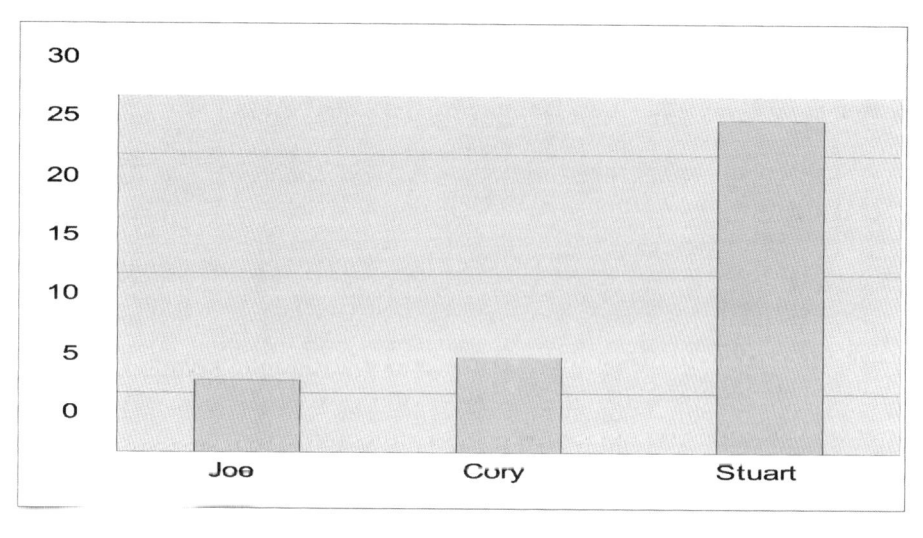

Figure 8.1: Pretest Results Percentage Scores on Lifeschool 2000 Assessment.

personal financial management pretest results indicated he had very poor skills. He received 6 out of 100 possible points, or 6% (see Figure 8.1).

Cory

Cory was very upbeat and ready to participate. When the class agenda was discussed Cory seemed interested and wanted to enroll. Cory indicated that he had had a checking account but that he didn't know how to use it. He said his sister helped him to open the account and she did all the transactions for him. Cory wanted to learn to rely on his own money skills. He had never had a savings account or owned a credit card and indicated that he was unsure about what a budget was. He had held odd jobs from the age of 14; however, he received payments "under the table" and never had to "deal" with a paycheck. Cory scored 9 out of 100 possible points, or 9% on the *Lifeschool 2000* pretest (see Figure 8.1).

Stuart

Stuart was amiable and willing to talk. After revealing the plans for the class on personal financial management, Stuart said he would be happy to participate and thought the skills might help in his upcoming parole. Stuart related he was not instructed on financial matters in his home, or at school. He indicated that what little he had learned was from friends and acquaintances "on the street" because he had never had a checking or savings account or owned a credit card. Stuart had held a few jobs, and he had received an actual paycheck but said he was unsure what the information on the stub meant. Stuart received 28 out of 100 possible points, or 28% on his *Lifeschool 2000* pretest (see Figure 8.1).

THE CLASSES

Week One

The learning objectives for lesson one included students gaining the ability to describe a checking account and explain how to open and use one. *Skills for Independent Living* (1997) recommended these objectives. With all the lessons presented, vocabulary words were included and discussed in order for the students to understand written materials and verbal instruction. The vocabulary words for this lesson included: insufficient funds, checking account, check, minimum deposit, interest, fee, signature card, and receipt. The researcher provided students with a copy of the words along with their corresponding definitions. Discussion ensued about checking accounts, their nature, and proper usage. The introduction of the differing kinds checking accounts that many banks offer, such as minimum balance checking accounts, regular checking accounts, free checking accounts, and NOW (simple checking accounts with a low minimum balance for fee reduction) checking accounts clearly confused them and the researcher instructed them to attend to the two types of accounts that they would be most likely to use: regular and free checking accounts. The students role-played opening an account and writing checks with explanations regarding information printed on a check provided.

The students had great difficulty spelling the number words for the check amount. The researcher did not anticipate this, but remedied the situation by writing out all the number words to one thousand on the white board and providing students with a small cheat sheet for their "checkbooks." The lesson was completed by giving students a "Checks and Checking Account Worksheet" as recommended by Brolin (1992). On this graded 100-point assignment, Joe received a score of 40, Cory 70, and Stuart 90. To assist in managing on task behavior, the researcher created participation points. Joe earned 7.5 of 15 possible participation points. Cory and Stuart each earned 15 of 15 participation points.

Week Two

The learning objectives for lesson two were to fill out a deposit slip and check register, and know the procedure for opening and using a savings account. The vocabulary words for this lesson included deposit, deposit slip, check register, savings account, withdrawal slip, and bank statement. The researcher provided students a detailed, example of a completed deposit slip. The researcher discussed and explained each line of information included on the deposit slip. The students completed a blank deposit slip as a group and everyone had difficulty with listing cash separately from checks. The deposit slip read "Currency." This did not translate conceptually to them as meaning "cash" despite repeated explanations. The researcher provided students with a sample check made out to them and required them to endorse it and fill out a related deposit slip. Their graded assignment was a "Deposit Worksheet" that was worth 100 points; Joe received a score of 45, Cory 80, and Stuart 70. Joe earned 7.5 of 15 participation points. Cory and Stuart earned 15 of 15 participation points.

Week Three

The learning objectives for week three included knowing what information is shown on a paycheck and describing how to cash a paycheck. Vocabulary words included paycheck, paycheck stub, gross pay, deduction, net pay, and cash a check.

The researcher provided students with a sample paycheck and paycheck stub. The students were surprised to learn that employees do not get to keep all the money they earn and were distressed with taxes and other deductions. This led to a short discussion about why citizens pay taxes and other types of possible paycheck deductions such as insurance or garnishments. They completed an "Understanding a Paycheck Stub Worksheet." Joe earned a score of 50, Cory 85, and Stuart 100. Joe and Cory earned 10 of 15 participation points and Stuart earned 15 of 15.

Week Four

The learning objectives for week four included describing how to set up a budget, explaining the difference between a want and a need, and managing your money. The researcher discussed the definition of income. All three students confused wants and needs at first. Together the class completed an income and expense worksheet, and developed a sample budget using an overhead projector. The students were then required to plan and write their own budgets based on what they thought they would be doing upon their releases. The students completed a "Plan and Write a Budget Worksheet." Joe earned a score of 60, Cory 80, and Stuart 100. Joe earned 7.5 of 15 participation points and Cory and Stuart earned 15 of 15.

Week Five

Learning objectives for week five included revisiting the difference between a want and a need, describing ways that media influence purchasing, and listing indicators of wise consumption. The researcher introduced vocabulary words such as impulse, unit pricing, refund, exchange, and warranty. Discussion ensued regarding advertisements and their influence. The class viewed several ads from various print media and discussed them. There was also discussion about tips for smart shoppers, particularly at the grocery store including unit pricing. The two students present completed their graded posttest on wants and needs. Both students received a score of 100 and earned 15 of 15 participation points.

Week Six

Learning objectives for week six were explaining the importance of paying bills on time, describing how credit cards work, and explaining minimum payment and interest as they relate to credit. Vocabulary words introduced were consumer, due date, late fee, credit, loan, interest, credit card, minimum payment, and credit report. Lesson instruction included advantages and disadvantages of using credit card, late versus timely bill payment, and the calculation of simple interest. Stuart and Cory each earned 25 of 25 possible participation points for this session. Joe earned 10 of 25 participation points.

POSTTEST

The day immediately following the last class period the *Lifeschool 2000* Post-Test (see Figure 8.2) was administered, as recommended by the publisher with the following results.

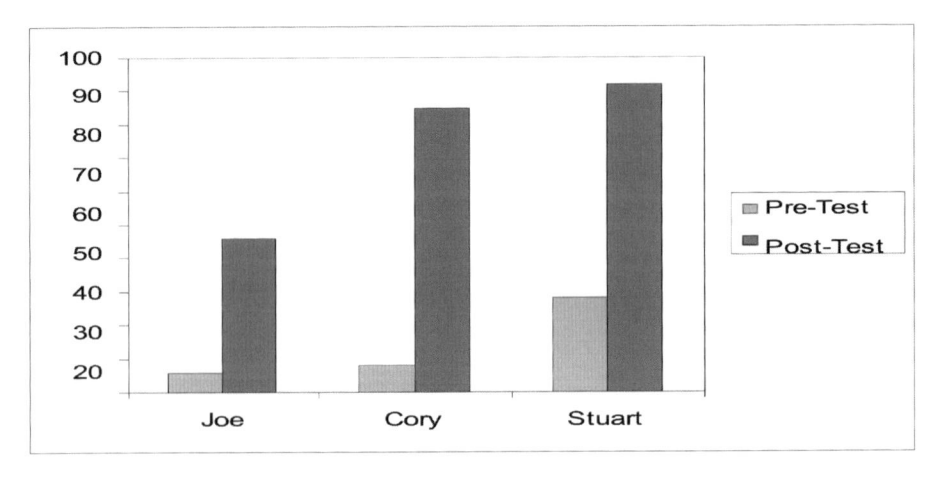

Figure 8.2: Pretest/Posttest Comparison.

FINANCIAL LITERACY AND YOUTHS IN JAIL | 131

Individual results are shown in Figures 8.3 through 8.5. Joe scored 46 out of 100 or 46% on the test, received 41 of 100 participation points, had an average of 40.1% on assignments, and attended 5 of 6 class sessions (see Figure 8.3).

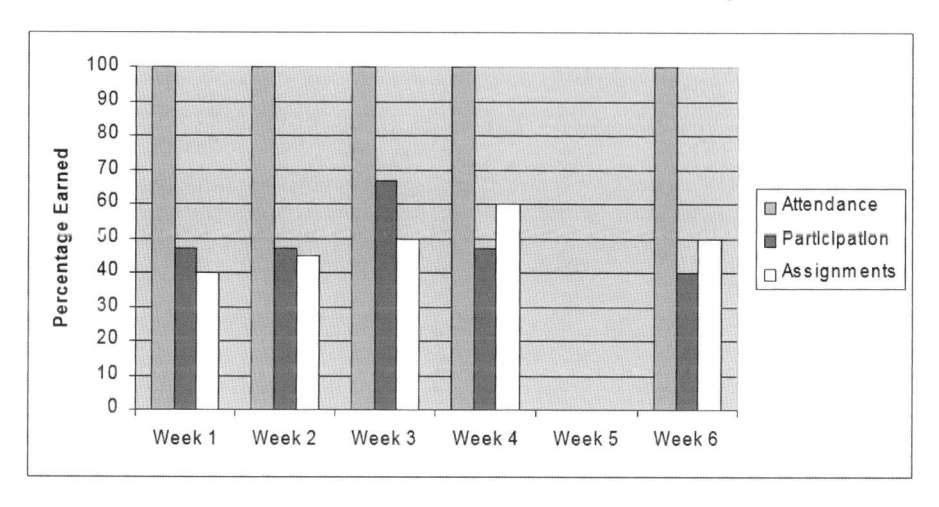

Figure 8.3: Data for Joe.

Cory scored 85 out of 100 or 85% on the test, received 95 of 100 participation points, had an average of 85.80% on assignments, and attended all si classes (see Figure 8.4).

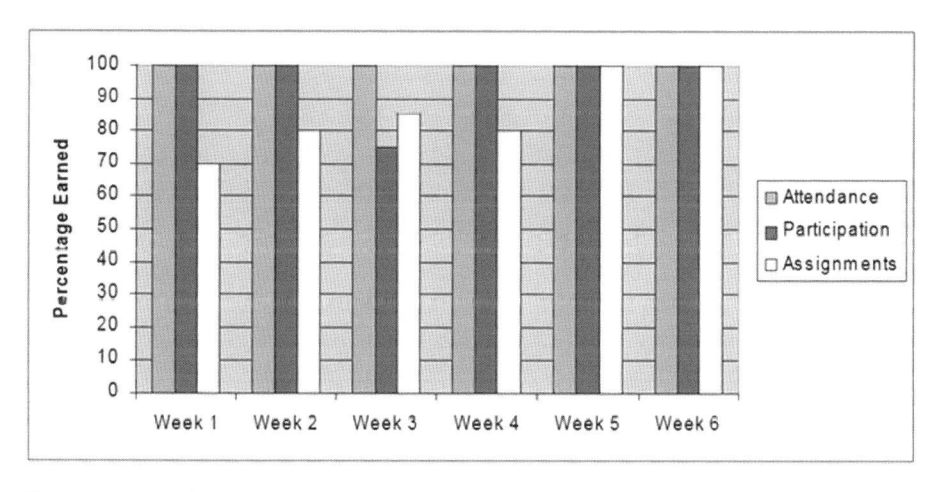

Figure 8.4: Data for Cory.

Stuart scored 92 of 100 or 92.00% on the test, received 100 of 100 participation points, had an average of 93.30% on assignments, and attended all six classes (see Figure 8.5).

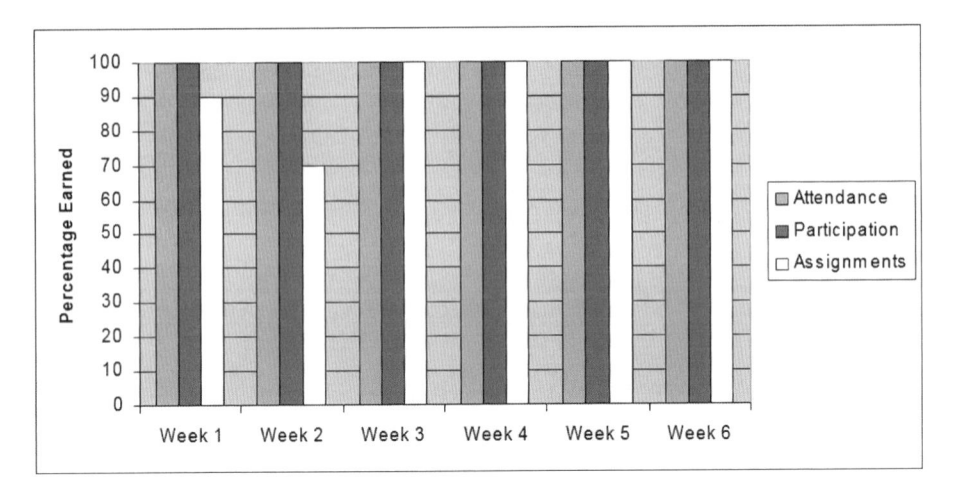

Figure 8.5: Data for Stuart.

DISCUSSION

During the course of this study, the researcher attempted to understand how to better increase her students' knowledge of personal financial management. To accomplish this, she used curricular materials and assessment tools recommended by *Lifeschool 2000* (1994), *Life Centered Career Education* (2000), *Skills for Independent Living* (1997), assignment scores, attendance, participation, and qualitative data gathered throughout this study. Evaluation took place for the group as a whole and individually.

As a group, the students' pretest score average was 14.3% and their posttest score average was 77.7%. Overall, the students raised their test scores immensely. Results showed that attendance, assignment scores, and participation correlated with higher posttest scores for all individuals.

The researcher's overall impression of the students' perception of their success was that they had a sense of accomplishment and gained the confidence necessary to take increasing responsibility for actions now and in the future. This is consistent with White's (2002) view on assessing success with a life skills program. Students' self-reports verified this perception.

IMPLICATIONS

During the course of this research, as recommended by *Lifeschool 2000* (1994), the researcher relied on pretest data, interviews, attendance, assignment scores, participation, and finally, posttest data as a means of determining improvement in her students' understanding of personal financial management. All three students demonstrated an increased knowledge of financial life skills; however, Joe made the least gain. It is noteworthy that he had more limited cognitive skills compounded by a much lengthier incarceration period than his peers.

A few questions have surfaced because of this work. Follow-up studies about the ability of inmates to translate the learned material to their out of prison lives would be of interest. At the time of this writing, none of these three young men are incarcerated in Tennessee, which may in and of itself be a rationale to continue some form of instruction. Whether or not this specific training correlates with that or with their current financial practices is unknown. A larger question is whether financial education could prevent incarceration if many crimes of youth are money related.

Looking carefully at the population of inmates is also instructive. The students involved in this work varied considerably in their learning abilities. The outlier in overall outcomes, Joe, had a more limited vocabulary, cognitive ability, and overall literacy skill set than his peers and this undoubtedly had a negative influence on his ability to benefit equally from the financial literacy instruction. Clearly, then, some incarcerated youth may benefit from this type of training more than others. Alternatively, instruction would have to be differentiated to accommodate different types and levels of learners for training to be successful.

It seems beyond argument that the crime rate of this country, particularly in poor urban areas, is a social blight destroying families and lives. The place of financial literacy as a critical part of an overall life skill preparation experience is worthy of further study and implementation, particularly in those areas of the nation that experience large concentrations of poor youth.

CHAPTER UPDATE

Since the original publication of this chapter, there remains a dearth of rigorous research regarding incarcerated population and financial literacy (Davis, Bozick, Steele, Saunders, & Miles, 2013). Still, experts say financial literacy is one of the most important skills for incarcerated individuals. In her online article, Hill (2014) provides observations from various experts on this topic.

Many times people come in without having learned even basic financial literacy," says Carl Takei, "a staff attorney at the ACLU's National Prison Project; then, when they get into prison, many don't deal with financial transactions at all except at the commissary (and, even then, they don't touch the cash)." Judi Lewen, the executive director of the Prison University Project at San Quentin State Prison in California, says that some prisoners have been in for so long they don't know how to use a computer or a credit or debit card; others have never had a bank account or written or deposited a check. Those are skills they'll need in the outside world, to do everything from rent an apartment to lease a car to pay bills. "In terms of the person living a normal life and not ending up back in jail, financial literacy is a big part of the equation," says Lee Gimpel, a spokesperson for Money Habitudes, a financial literacy organization. (p. 1)

According to the Sentencing Project (http://www.sentencingproject.org/issues/incarceration/), the United States boasts the highest incarceration rate of any industrialized country. In this environment, corrections represent an increasingly corporate process in which profit maximization seems to take priority over youth welfare (Hedges, 2015). Providing incarcerated youth with hope of navigating the economic system in the new era of civil rights requires ideologies of courage and compassion (Alexander, 2012; Pollock, 2008).

QUESTIONS FOR DISCUSSION

1. To what extent do you think that financial illiteracy represents a cause or a symptom for youth who are incarcerated? Explain your response.
2. How would you describe the curricular approach employed by Christianson? Would you employ it in your classroom? Why or Why Not?
3. Look at the bar graph that displays the results for Joe. What do you think would happen if he were not absent during the third week? Explain your response.
4. Christensen taught the students on a weekly basis. Do you think results would change if lesson were taught daily?
5. The chapter contains information that describes the low academic achievement of those incarcerated. To what extent do those who are not incarcerated possess the same degree of academic achievement?

NOTE

1. The data for this study were collected while Dr. Christensen was at the University of Memphis.

REFERENCES

Alexander, M. (2012). *The new Jim Crow: Mass incarceration in the age of colorblindness*. New York, NY: The New Press.
Brolin, D. E. (1992). *Life centered career education*. Reston, VA: The Council for Exceptional Children.
Brolin, D. E. (1997). *Life centered career education: A Competency-Based Approach* (5th ed.). Reston, VA: The Council for Exceptional Children. [ERIC Document Reproduction Service No. ED 407 757]

Bullis, M., Yovanoff, P., Mueller, G., & Havel, E. (2002). Life on the "outs"—examination of the facility-to-community transition of incarcerated youth. *Exceptional Children, 69*(1), 7–22.

Coffey, O. D., & Knoll, J. F. (1998). *Choosing life skills: A guide for selecting life skills programs for adult and juvenile offenders.* Richmond, KY: Life Skills Reintegration Program. Eastern Kentucky University.

Collier, V. P., & Thomas, W. P. (2001). *Educating linguistically and culturally diverse students in correctional settings.* Retrieved from http://www.nwlincs.org/correctional_education/articles/educating-linguist-collier.pdf

Council for Exceptional Children (CEC). (2002). *Life Centered Career Education.* Arlington, VA.

Davis, L. M., Bozick, R., Steele, J. L., Saunders, J., & Miles, J. (2013). *Evaluating the effectiveness of correctional education: A meta-analysis of programs that provide education to incarcerated adults.* Santa Monica, CA: RAND Corporation.

Glick, B., & Sturgeon, W. (1999). Rising to the challenge: Identifying and meeting the needs of juvenile offenders with special needs. *Corrections Today, 61,* 106–110, 166.

Harer, M. D. (1994). *Recidivism among federal prison releases in 1987: A preliminary report.* Federal Bureau of Prisons, Washington, DC. Retrieved from http://www.ed.gov/offices/OVAE/AdultEd/OCE/19abstracts.html

Hedges, C. (2015). *Wages of rebellion: The moral imperative of revolt.* New York, NY: Nationbooks.

Hill, C. (2014). *How prison inmates learn about money.* Retrieved from http://www.marketwatch.com/story/how-prison-inmates-learn-about-money-2014-07-10

Hudson River Center for Program Development. (2001). *From incarceration to productive lifestyle-making the transition: An instructional guide.* Retrieved from http://www.nald.ca/fulltext/hudson/iytrans/cover.htm

Kadish, T. E., Glaser, B. A., Calhoun, G. B., & Ginter, E. J. (2001). Identifying the developmental strengths of juvenile offenders: Assessing four life-skills dimensions. *Journal of Addictions & Offender Counseling, 21*(2), 85–95.

Langan, P. A., & Levin, D. J. (2002). *Recidivism of prisoners released in 1994.* U.S. Department of Justice, Office of Justice Programs, Bureau of Justice Statistics, Special Report. Retrieved from http://www.ojp.usdoj.gov/bjs/pub/ascii/rpr94.txt

Life Centered Career Education. (2000). Upper Saddle River, NJ: Globe Fearon Educational Publisher.

Lifeschool 2000, Consumer Economics. (1994). Belmont, CA: Simon and Schuster Educational Group.

Moote, G. T., & Wodarski, J. S. (1997). The acquisition of life skills through adventure-based activities and programs: A review of the literature. *Adolescence, 32*(125), 143–167.

Morgenthau, J., & Roberts, K. (2002). A hammer and nail approach to rebuilding young lives: Florida's Avon Park Youth Academy and STREET Smart. *Corrections Today, 64*(3), 98–101.

Petersilia, J. (2000). *When prisoners return to the community: Political, economic, and social consequences.* National Institute of Justice. Retrieved from http://www.ncjrs.org/txtfiles1/nij/184253.txt

Pollock, M. (2008). *Because of race: How Americans debate harm and opportunity in our schools.* Princeton, NJ: Princeton University Press.

Quinn, M. M., Rutherford, R. B., Jr., & Leone, P. E. (2001). *Students with disabilities in correctional facilities.* Retrieved from http://www.ericdigests.org/2002-4/correctional.html

Remedia. (2001). *Checkbook math.* Scottsdale, AZ: Remedia Publications.

Skills for Independent Living. (1997). Upper Saddle River, NJ: Globe Fearon Educational Publisher.

US Department of Education. (2001). *Program requirements for correctional facilities receiving funds under this section.* The No Child Left Behind Act. Part D, subpart 2, Section 1425. Retrieved from http://www.ed.gov/policy/elsec/leg/esea02/pg11.html#sec1426

White, C. (2002). Reclaiming incarcerated youths through education. *Corrections Today, 64*(2), 174–188.

CHAPTER NINE

Teaching Probability AND Learning Financial Concepts

How to Empower Elementary School Students in Citizenship

ANNIE SAVARD
McGill University

FINANCIAL LITERACY EDUCATION FOR YOUNG STUDENTS

Concerns about financial literacy education (FLE) for youth and adults are increasing worldwide (OECD, 2016). Since the financial crash in 2008 and the subsequent global recession, it seems impossible to ignore the urgent needs of the population in terms of knowledge, capability, and competency in regard to managing personal finances. In many countries, different programs have become available for diverse audiences as well as changes in official school curricula. For instance, in many countries including Canada, FLE is taught in a specific course at the high school level. As for elementary schools, some countries such as Australia and Canada (Ontario) have developed an integrated curriculum about finance. The Australian curriculum about finance is embedded in the curriculum of Mathematics and named "Money and Financial Mathematics."

As teaching FLE gets more attention, the Organization for Economic Cooperation and Development (OECD) has administered a financial literacy assessment via their triennial Program for International Student Assessment (PISA) in 2012 and 2015. These assessments examined the financial knowledge of 15-year-olds from 18 member countries of the OECD in 2012 and more countries in 2015 (the results are not yet release). OECD (2016) defines financial literacy as:

... knowledge and understanding of financial concepts and risks, and the skills, motivation and confidence to apply such knowledge and understanding in order to make effective decisions across a range of financial contexts, to improve the financial well-being of individuals and society, and to enable participation in economic life. (p. 85)

The content to be assessed has four areas of student knowledge and understanding:

1. Money and transaction: aware of the different forms and purposes of money; confident and capable of handling and monitoring transactions;
2. Planning and managing finances: monitor and control income and expenses; use income and other available resources in the short and long term to enhance financial well-being;
3. Risk and reward: recognize that certain financial products, including insurance, and processes, such as saving, can be used to manage and offset various risks, depending on different needs and circumstances; understand the benefits of contingency planning, diversification and the dangers of default on payment of bills and credit agreements; know about and can manage risks and rewards associated with life events, the economy and other external factors; know about the risks and rewards associated with substitutes for financial products; know that there may be unidentified risks and rewards associated with new financial products;
4. Financial landscape: are aware of the role of regulation and consumer protection; know about rights and responsibilities; know and understand the financial environment; know and understand the impact of their own financial decisions on themselves and others; understand that individuals have choices in spending and saving, and each action can have consequences for the individual and for society; understand the influence of economic and external factors (OECD, 2016).

The knowledge processes identified by OECD (2016) are as follows: (1) identify financial information; (2) analyze information in a financial context; (3) evaluate financial issues; (4) apply financial knowledge and understanding. These processes should be mobilized in different contexts: (1) education and work; (2) home and family; (3) individual; (4) societal. Thus, PISA's aim is to assess students' competency in regard to personal, societal, and global financial knowledge. Financial literacy is far more than counting money in a mathematics textbook word problem. It implies making a decision in complex situations, where specific knowledge is needed to generate alternatives (Halpern, 2003).

The specific knowledge about financial content has been studied over the years. Huston's (2010) review of the literature over 10 years identified four distinct content areas: money basics (time value of money, purchasing power, personal finances accounting concepts), borrowing (credit cards, consumer loans or mortgages), investing (saving accounts, stocks, bonds or mutual funds), and protecting resources (insurance or risk management). There is support for these categories in the research literature and thus these topics are part of many curricula and programs (Davies, 2015).

As noted previously, FLE might be taught in school using official curricula or programs developed by public or private organizations. Those programs exposed their own content and processes to be taught.

In the United States, two major programs are available: the National Standards from the Council for Economic Education and the Jump$tart Coalition. Launched in 2013, the National Standards present standard statements to be achieved in schools by grades four, eight, and twelve. The standards are composed of "benchmarks" that explain content to be taught, including information and insight for lifetime usefulness (Bosshardt & Walstad, 2014). Those standards are set up into six important areas: earning incomes, buying goods and services, saving, using credit, financial investing, and protecting and insuring (Council for Economic Education, 2013).

The Jump$tart Coalition for personal financial literacy launched a fourth version of an educational program in 2015, which also presents six standards to be taught from kindergarten to grade 12. Those standards are comprised of six major categories of personal finance instruction: spending and saving, credit and debt, employment and income, investing, risk management and insurance, and financial decision-making.

When looking at the standards as content areas to be taught, it is possible to see consistency among them. For example, spending, saving and managing risk are concepts that are present in all of the four frameworks or programs. In addition to that, some financial concepts embedded into the content areas are, somehow, implicit. For instance, talking about spending and saving is related to the concept of consumerism. The four categories identified by OECD (2016) are the big ideas where the financial concepts could be associated. Table 9.1 summarizes the content areas of financial literacy presented above and organized with the strands of the OECD framework.

Some content areas refer to many different concepts, thus are placed in more than one concept. For instance, the standard Spending & Saving from Jump$tart could also be seen as Money and Transaction and Planning and Managing Finances of OECD.

Clarifying the financial concepts to be taught is a first step in helping teachers to teach them. It is thus possible to find or develop learning situations beyond adding and subtracting money. This chapter presents some lesson plans on integrating financial concepts with teaching practices.

Table 9.1: Financial Literacy Concepts.

OECD	Houston (2010)	Jump$tart	National Standards
1-Money and transaction	1-Money basics	1-Spending & Saving	2-Buying goods and services
2-Planning and managing finance	1-Money basics 2-Borrowing 3-Investing	1-Spending & Saving 2-Credit and debt 3-Employment and income 6-Financial decision-making	1-Earning income 2-Buying goods and services 3-Saving 4-Using credit
3-Risk and reward	4-Protecting resources	4-Investing 5-Risk management and insurance	5-Financial investing 6-Protecting and insuring
4-Financial landscape		6-Financial services	

GAMBLING AS A RISKY ACTIVITY

Gambling can be perceived as a financial concept or practice, because gambling is betting or wagering—money, object, or action. It is not possible to predict the outcome with certitude, and it is an irreversible stake (Arseneault, Ladouceur, & Vitaro, 2001). Thus, gambling can be seen as consumerism (buying goods and services; money and transaction), because the participant has to "buy" participation by betting money. In the case of betting objects or actions, gambling is still consumerism as it can be considered a form of economical exchanges like barter. Gambling can also be seen as a path to earn money or attain wealth (planning and managing finance). Conversely, gambling is also a financial risk (risk and reward); very few win or get rewarded, and many more lose. As opposed to buying goods or services, the participant might get nothing more than the participation in the activity as well as risking serious mental health issues.

Gambling can be perceived as a financial concept, because gambling is about betting or wagering money, object, or action. It also involves elements of risks and rewards, as do financial decisions. It is not possible to predict the outcome with certitude, and it is an irreversible stake (Arseneault et al., 2001). The participant may receive a temporary stimulus of an emotional rush, or nothing more than the participation in the activity, while risking serious mental health issues through addiction. Thus, buying lottery or raffle tickets, betting money on horse races or sport pools, gambling at casinos or playing poker online, all of these represent activities that carry risks of losing money and contributing to the development of gambling addiction. Similarly, the stock market is considered a gambling activity, with people buying shares and not considering the substantial nature of their changes in value. To some, the stock market may be considered as an entertainment activity. Nevertheless, the chances of winning are low and a long-term participation costs more to the gambler than the possible gain. It is ironic to think that one of the main motivations to gamble is to easily make a lot of money to get wealthy. Gambling is still perceived as a social and non-risky form of entertainment: gambling opportunities continue to grow and are even more widely available, especially online (Derevensky & Gilbeau, 2015).

Gambling addiction is very difficult to successfully treat, because gamblers are convinced that they can win and they experience dissociative reactions. Thus, they think they have control over the outcomes of the activities. This illusion of control (Langer, 1975) leads them to think that an external power, such as luck, faith, or God might help them to win. There is a consensus among the researchers: prevention should start in elementary school (Crites, 2003). How to make gambling prevention relevant for youth is an issue.

A significant amount of literature on youth gambling provides information about gambling activities, youth addiction, and the effect of this addiction on lives, including schooling. Youth gambling is not a new phenomenon and has been studied over the last 25 years (Derevensky & Gilbeau, 2015). Despite strict laws regarding the legal age of participants in those activities in many countries, youth still do gamble (Campbell, Derevensky, Meerkamper, & Cutajar, 2011).

A FRAMEWORK TO CREATE MATHEMATICAL LESSON PLANS AND FINANCIAL CONCEPTS

Children perceive complex tasks presented in a classroom through different experiential lenses. Those contexts are important to recognize, because they provide the lens through which student interpretations are made. There are many opportunities to observe this phenomenon in a classroom. For example, this question was asked in a grade two classroom in Djibouti: "At recess time, you go to the store with your grade 1 younger brother in order to buy him a snack. Your brother has 150 Francs Djiboutien. What can you propose to him?"[1] On the black board, different snacks were presented with their price. As the teacher was walking into the classroom, a little boy stopped him and said: "I do not have a little brother." He was engaged only in the sociocultural context of the query. The teacher said to him: "You will help the little brother of your friend then." The little boy was then able to do the task and move into a mathematical context, where he modeled the problem.

Thus, a learning situation should propose at first to study an object or phenomenon coming from the sociocultural context of the students. Discussion about this context should help students understand the mathematical aspects present.

The mathematical model present in the situation, as well as the results coming from calculations, allow students to make sense of the object or the phenomenon studied in the sociocultural context (Savard, 2015).

In the case of the previous example, a financial context overlaps with the sociocultural and the mathematics skills required. At the launch of the task and after, the teacher talked about going to the store to buy snacks. He also referred to the pieces of money used. At the end, he came back to the notion of money by having students present the snacks purchased. A financial concept is introduced and discussed in the sociocultural context.

The implications of this model can also be interpreted in the financial context and then in the sociocultural context. The mathematical context is a subset of the sociocultural context, which is itself a subset of a citizenship context (Savard, 2008). Citizenship context presents sociopolitical aspects, which goes beyond the topic of personal finance. This context allows individuals to make a higher interpretation of the studied phenomenon by looking at the nature of the process of modeling, which depends on the goals and the resources available (Mukhopadhyay & Greer, 2001). In the case of the example, the teacher might ask students why they choose these snacks and not the other ones. He might also bring their attention on health, environment, and economy of the country (local products versus importations).

Arthur (2012) stated that financial literacy is more than creating better consumers; it is about citizenship and the development of civic disposition. Civic disposition includes going beyond self-determination by being critical toward choices made. A democratic participation in debates and social issues encourages members of society to contribute to it by making personal and collective choices (ten Dam & Volman, 2004). Specifically, it is about making choices using critical thinking: why this choice was made between all alternatives generated and evaluated by the citizen (Halpern, 2003; Paul & Elder, 2001; Swartz & Perkins, 1990). It also takes the context into consideration, as well as the issue and outcomes of the decision (Lipman, 2003). Thus critical thinking and decision-making might be considered as citizenship competencies, because they are articulated into the capacity to act as a citizen (ten Dam & Volman, 2004).

CREATION OF THE LESSON PLANS

My task was to create lesson plans in order to prevent gambling addiction among youth. I also wanted students to develop critical thinking skills in regard to gambling activities in order to assist them to make decisions about their personal finances. I designed a teaching experiment (Menchinskaya, 1969; Steffe & D'Ambrosio, 1996) that involved using the concept of probability. Thus, three facets of probability might be explored through the study of the gambling activities: theoretical, frequentist, and subjective (Briand, 2005; Konold, 1991). Theoretical probability can be defined using an object such as a dice or a coin; frequentist probability is defined by experimentation or simulation; and subjective probability by using information such as statistics in a race.

Each lesson plan has three steps: launching the task, performing the task, discussion and synthesis. The lesson plans created were designed in a particular order, because I wanted to use students' prior knowledge in regard to gambling and chances, especially for research purposes on addressing alternative conceptions (Savard, 2014). I designed a sequence of teaching, which can be varied in presentation. Here are the six lesson plans created, or, in other words, the topics of the learning situations:

1. The lucky charm experiment (subjective probability)
2. The library search and the game board on lucky numbers (theoretical probability)
3. Card game (theoretical probability)
4. Spins (frequentist probability)
5. Heads or Tails (frequentist probability)
6. Horoscope (subjective probability)

THE LESSON PLANS

In each learning situation, students will be explicitly told that they will have to share their thinking and their processes. As a group, they will experiment like a scientific community: discuss problems, make hypothesis, test some of the hypotheses, and arrive at conclusions developed within their community. Each contribution is valid and worthwhile.

Establishing norms for students' participations in terms of behavior and learning expectations is presented in the lesson launch and is reinforced while students perform the task as well as in the synthesis discussion. The teacher should have this scientific community in mind, because the learning situations are in fact simulation of some gambling activities and not an initiation to them.

THE LUCKY CHARM EXPERIMENT

Students will explore subjective probability. They will develop critical thinking toward the means to estimate probability to win.

A day before performing the task, the teacher asks students if they have lucky charms. The teacher facilitates a short discussion on the kind of lucky charms before concluding by asking students to bring them in class for tomorrow. In teams of six, create and execute an experiment that will allow you to check the effects of your lucky charms in a drawing.

The discussion aims to highlight the limits of their lucky charms and the methodologies employed by students. The concepts of uncertainty, randomness, and skills are supposed to emerge. The discussion questions are: "What do you notice? Is your lucky charm lucky? How can you be sure? According to you, how this might work? Why can you say that? Can you explain to me your method? In which way your method is more valid than other teams? What is the difference between randomness and skills?"

THE LIBRARY SEARCH AND THE GAME BOARD ON LUCKY NUMBERS

The Library Search

Students will develop an understanding on how playing with dice over time assists in developing a mathematical theory (probability). Students will explore probabilistic vocabulary words such as possible, impossible, and certain. Students will study some gambling activities and the role of money in such activities. They will critically think about money and gambling activities.

The teacher asks students what they know about gambling activities. Using game boards, students will make a distinction with gambling and gaming, and about false and real money. Next, the discussion will consider dice in game use.

The students will be asked to do a library search, or an inquiry about the history of dice. In teams of two, students should select a historical aspect of dice they want to investigate and share on a poster. The posters will be presented as a mini scientific colloquium in the classroom.

The teacher records the questions being investigated by students to avoid redundancy. Students collect information and create a poster. The poster includes a title and some representations on it (pictures or drawings). The teacher guides students about important points to be presented on the poster: some information about time and context (century, country, people) and how the dice were used at that time as well as citing sources.

The teacher should carefully select the order of the poster presentations. The chronological order should be considered, as well as the idea presented. Thus, the uses of dice as a popular game for betting money lead mathematicians from the past to create mathematical models (Fermat, Pascal). Each team of students presents their poster and answers classmate questions about it. All students are invited to comment; the teacher assists to make linkages between the presentations. The following day, the teacher proposes to explore further some ideas being presented by students: some gambling activities, board games, and dice.

The Board Game on Lucky Numbers

Students will explore frequentist and theoretical probabilities. They will construct sample space and develop a meaning of when and why order matters. They will develop critical thinking toward magical thinking using lucky number seven and the theoretical probability to get it using two 6-facets dice. Students will explore how some gambling activities work: fees to participate, prizes to win, and magical thinking.

Students are going to play a dice game in teams of four. Each team will receive two 6-facets dice and one board game.

Select a number and play. Each team member should throw the dice. Add the numbers on the dice and the team member who has that number can move his token one step on the board (Figure 9.1). The aim of the game is to move your token at the end of the game section. The first team member who has his or her token in the end of the game section wins.

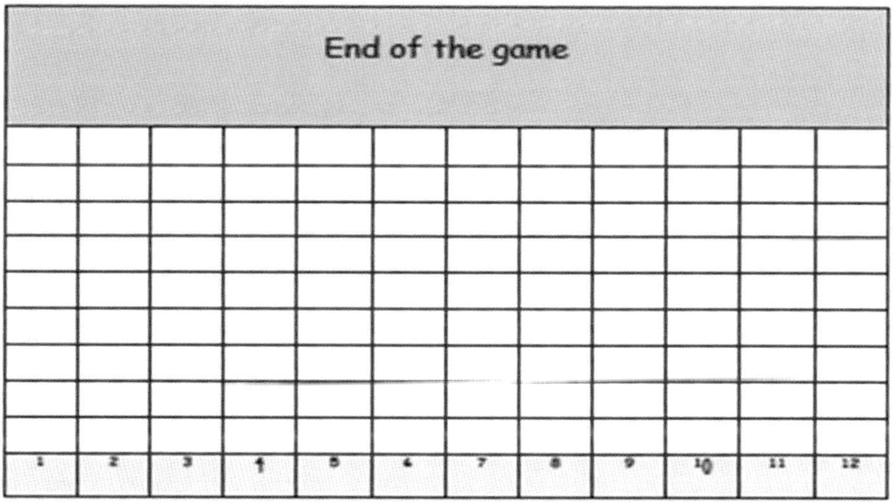

Figure 9.1: Game Board.

After students played one or two games, the teacher asks these questions: "Who won? Which number did you pick?" The teacher records the numbers on the board.

In order to guide students to think about why some numbers might be perceived as lucky, the teacher asks: "Do you think that a number is luckier than other? Why?" Numbers 6, 7, and 8 should be more popular. The teacher might then ask: "Which one could be the luckiest?" Depending on the results and the discussion, the teacher might ask: "My friend Nathan thinks there is a lucky number when playing dice, but he doesn't know which one. What do you think this number might be? Why do you think it is the luckiest one?" The teacher then invites students to write down all possible cases to get the sum using the two dice. The concluding discussion on comparing processes used should lead students to construct the probability: the probability to get 7 is 6/36, which is one of the reasons why this number is perceived as lucky.

CARD GAMES

Students will explore making predictions using theoretical probabilities. They will develop critical thinking toward some gambling activities such as poker and blackjack.

The teacher will ask students if they know or they play card games. He will provide a deck of card for each team of four students. Students will look at the cards and describe them. The teacher will show a deck of cards and ask: "Can you tell me without cheating which card will be the third one?" Students will discuss and experiment in teams how to make a prediction.

The teacher will facilitate a discussion on how to predict using a deck of cards. Each card should be recorded as presented. The teacher asks some questions on the probability to get, for example: a diamond card, a card with a spade, a red card, and a queen of heart. Then, the discussion can move toward the complexity to predict cards when playing poker or blackjack.

SPINS

Students will explore frequentist probability, using spins. They will develop their reasoning under uncertainty, such as the independence between trials. They will also develop an understanding on skills versus uncertainty. They will reflect on television shows using spinners. They will develop critical thinking toward making money using gambling.

The teacher will facilitate a short discussion on spinners: "Have you heard about spinners? What do you know about them? Where can we find them? (Circus, casino, fun fair, and television shows). How could we participate? (Paying fees). Here are some spins (small spinners with five segments in different colors. In teams of two, spin your spinners 100 times and record your results each time. You will decide on how to proceed and we will discuss your method and your results after. You might want to compare your processes and results with another team prior to the whole class discussion."

In teams of two, students will decide on a method and then make the simulation. They will record their results. The teacher will ask first about processes used to conduct the simulation and the results gotten by students. Then, the teacher will record on the blackboard all the results, on a table showing all the colors on the spins. The teacher will facilitate a discussion on the differences in the results (frequency and variability) and press on independence (between each trials) and uncertainty (we can't really know which color we will get). The teacher will direct students' attention to the contrast between the theoretical probability (20% for each color) and the results gotten (close to 20% for each color).

HEADS OR TAILS

Students will explore frequentist probability in relation to the sequence of the outcomes. They will develop critical thinking toward gambling and its impact on their personal finances.

The teacher asks students which means they use when they want to share an object that they and a friend want. The teacher wants to press on students by saying that this object can't be separated in two parts, such as a cookie. It is not possible to cut it, like a pencil. When students mention Heads or Tails, the teacher might move on by asking where they think it came from. If students did not bring up Heads or Tails, the teacher might want to say something like: last year, my students mentioned Heads or Tails. Do you use it too? After a short discussion, the teacher proposes students to play in teams of two: each team member should select Heads or Tails.

Using a coin, each team of two will perform 100 trials. Students have to record the whole sequence of their experimentation such as: Tails, Tails, Heads, Tails. ... Then each team of two will compare their results with another team of two.

The teacher will ask about the processes used to conduct the simulation and the results gotten. Then, the teacher will record on the blackboard all the results, on a table showing each side of the coin. The teacher will facilitate a discussion on the difference in the results and press on independence and uncertainty using the sequences gotten. The teacher will drag students' attention to contrast theoretical probability and the results gotten.

HOROSCOPE

Students will explore very low theoretical probabilities and magical thinking. They will develop critical thinking toward being wealthy by gambling: if it is worthy to buy lottery tickets and why.

The teacher will initiate a discussion on astrological signs according to students' birth dates. The teacher might ask students where we get information about astrological signs or what the purpose of those signs is. When a student mentions horoscope, it would be nice to ask students what do they know about them, if they use it or believe in it. The teacher will then propose to test the validity of the horoscope predictions using a popular lottery: Lottery 6/49. The teacher, with the assistance of students, will explain how this lottery works. They will decide together that four numbers out of six are needed to be considered as a winner. Then, the teacher will help students make teams of four and will give each team a printed horoscope.

In teams of four, students will first identify the prediction about luck according to their astrological sign. Then, they will select numbers and simulate a lottery.

The teacher will ask about processes used to conduct the simulation and the results gotten. Then, the teacher will record on the blackboard all the winners, i.e., students who had four numbers out of six. The discussion should highlight the real probability to win at Lottery 6/49, if it is a real mean to have wealth, and if the horoscope should be taken seriously.

DISCUSSION ABOUT THE LESSON PLANS

The contexts presented in the six learning situations played a major role when designing the lesson plans, but their role is equally important when enacting the lessons. Interpreting students' thinking in relation to the context is helpful in regard to pressing further on the ideas presented. Thus, the teacher might associate the ideas or the concepts discussed according to their context: gambling activities in a sociocultural context, risk in a financial context, probability in a mathematical context, ethical considerations such as addictions and weak chances to win in a citizenship context. Making decision using critical thinking in using the knowledge and values is also part of this context. Without mathematical knowledge, it is hard to have a proper picture of the risk involved in the gambling activities. Figure 9.2 shows the relationships among the contexts.

It is possible to support the development of mathematical knowledge in relation to critical thinking in regard to financial concepts and citizenship. Gambling activities are generally perceived as harmless entertaining pastimes; it is very important to help students to understand the risks associated with participation, such as losing money and getting addicted. These learning situations aim to provide some mathematical and financial background to students, because it is very hard to develop a critical stance without them. In order to do so, here are some examples of questions to be raised through discussions:

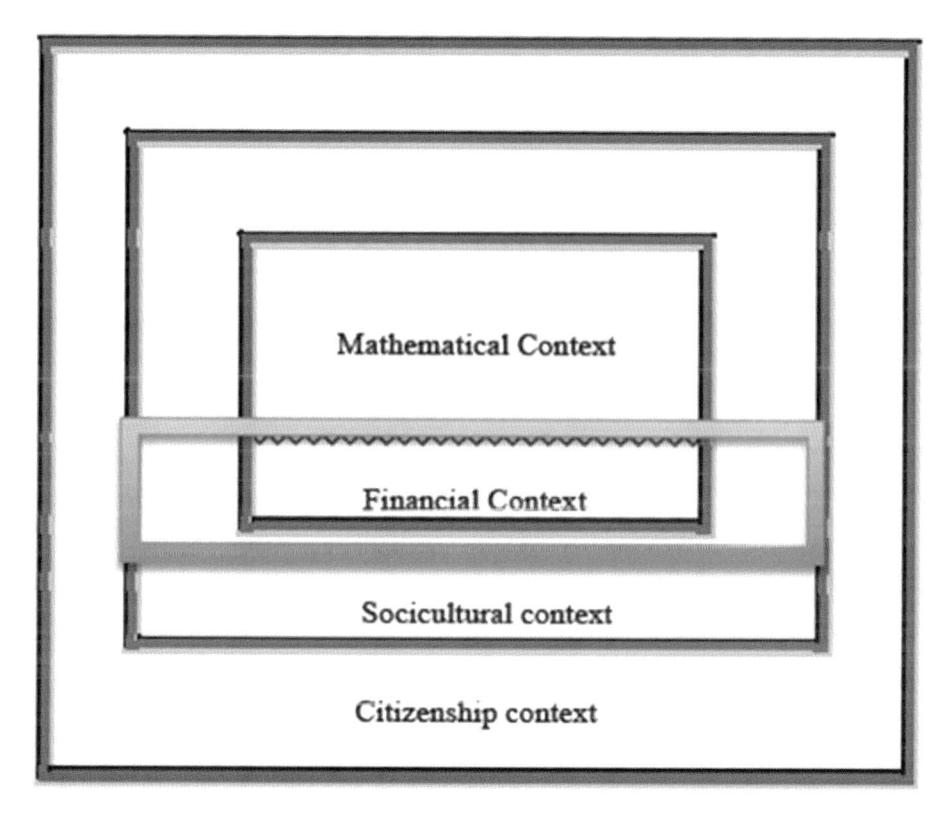

Figure 9.2: The Financial Context in Relation to the Other Contexts Present in the Classroom.

- How do you think your lucky charm might help you to win when you play soccer? When you have a scratch ticket?
- Why do you think that number 7 "is lucky" when playing dice? Do you think that it "is lucky" everywhere?
- Why do you think people want to wage or bet when playing with cards? Do you think that is an easy way to get money?
- If you know the probability to win, do you think it is helpful information in regard to participating in it or not?
- Why do you think it is fair to decide using Heads or Tails? Do you think someone might cheat?
- Horoscope provides information about your luck. What kind of information do you think it is relevant to look at before making a decision involving money?

The main financial concepts discussed here are risks and rewards, but it is possible to touch upon money and transactions, planning and managing finances, and financial landscape. Thus, students might raise the point to save money instead of buying lottery tickets as a means to get money. They might also say that the government manages casinos and national lotteries and uses the profits to finance hospitals. They might say that they received money on their birthday and they put this money in their bank account. Students will have a real opportunity not only to learn about probability and develop critical thinking toward gambling and risks; they will express their thoughts on money. Teachers should have a nonjudgmental stance and listen to students with an open mind: pressing on small and large outcomes of decisions made about money is a nice way to empower students in citizenship.

CONCLUDING REMARKS

The major aim of this chapter is to provide a framework on how teachers might use financial contexts to create complex and meaningful learning situations for students. Teaching in school should go beyond teaching the content to be tested on: it is about supporting people to live a better life in society, among their communities. As I pointed out, losing money and getting addicted to gambling are important issues to be considered in regard to supporting the development of financial literacy among the population. Being financially literate in respect of personal and community well-being is a concrete step toward a better world.

QUESTIONS FOR DISCUSSION

1. How do you define "gambling"? Does everyone gamble? How might knowledge of financial literacy practices influence a person's gambling?
2. Consider the different areas of finance presented in Savard's Table. To what extent do you perceive these areas as containing a form of gambling? What degrees of risk and reward accompany these areas?
3. What is luck? Do your choices influence the patterns of luck that you experience? To what extent are your choices influenced by your environments?
4. Consider the lucky object that Savard asks students to select in the first activity. How might other individuals perceive the object? For example, imagine that you found a lucky coin. Would the person who lost the coin feel lucky about the object? How do lucky objects enforce or counter egalitarian social ideology?
5. Figure 9.2 describes a system of social contexts. To what extent does fortune relate to a broader awareness of these contexts? Support your view.

NOTE

1. I translated this problem from French, created by a grade two teacher in Djibouti: *À la récréation, tu accompagnes ton petit frère de 1ère année chez la marchande pour lui acheter son goûter. Ton frère possède 150 F. Que pourrais-tu lui proposer?*

REFERENCES

Arseneault, L., Ladouceur, R., & Vitaro, F. (2001). Jeu de hasard et consommation de substances psychotropes: Prevalence, coexistence et conséquences. [Gambling and consumption of psychotropic drugs: Prevalence, coexistence and conséquences]. *Canadian Psychology, 42*(3), 173–184.

Arthur, C. (2012). Consumers or critical citizens? Financial literacy education and freedom. *Critical Education, 3*(6). Retrieved from http://ojs.library.ubc.ca/index.php/criticaled/article/view/182350

Bosshardt, W., & Walstad, W. B. (2014). National standards for financial literacy: Rationale and content. *The Journal of Economic Education, 45*(1), 63–70.

Briand, J. (2005). Une expérience statistique et une première approche des lois du hasard au lycée par une confrontation avec une machine simple. *Recherches en didactique des mathématiques, 25*(2), 247–281.

Campbell, C., Derevensky, J., Meerkamper, E., & Cutajar, J. (2011). Parents' perceptions of adolescent gambling: A Canadian national study. *Journal of Gambling Issues,* (25), 36–53.

Council for Economic Education. (2013). *National standards for financial literacy.* New York, NY: Council for Economic Education.

Crites, T. W. (2003). What are my chances? Using probability and number sense to educate teens about the mathematical risks of gambling. In H. J. Shaffer, M. N. Hall, J. Vander Bilt, & E. George (Eds.), *Futures at stake: Youth, gambling, and society* (pp. 63–83). Reno/Las Vegas, NV: University of Nevada Press.

Davies, P. (2015). Towards a framework for financial literacy in the context of democracy, *Journal of Curriculum Studies, 47*(2), 300–316.

Derevensky, J., & Gilbeau, L. (2015). Adolescent gambling: Twenty-five years of research. *Canadian Journal of Addiction/Le Journal Canadien d'Addiction, 6,* 4–12.

Halpern, D. F. (2003). *Thought and knowledge: An introduction to critical thinking* (4th ed.). Mahwah, NJ: Lawrence Erlbaum Associates.

Huston, S. J. (2010). Measuring financial literacy. *The Journal of Consumer Affairs, 44*(2), 296–316.

Konold, C. (1991). Understanding student's beliefs about probability. In E. V. Glasersfeld (Ed.), *Radical constructivism in mathematics education* (pp. 139–156). Dordrecht: Kluwer Academic Publishers.

Langer, E. J. (1975). The illusion of control. *Journal of Personality and Social Psychology, 32*(2), 311–328.

Lipman, M. (2003). *Thinking in education* (2nd ed.). New York, NY: Cambridge University Press.

Menchinskaya, N. A. (1969). Fifty years of soviet instructional psychology. *Soviet Studies in the Psychology of Learning and Teaching Mathematics, 1,* 5–35.

Mukhopadhyay, S., & Greer, B. (2001). Modeling with purpose: Mathematics as a critical tool. In B. Atweh, H. Forgasz, & B. Nebres (Eds.), *Sociocultural research on mathematics education: An international perspective* (pp. 295–311). Mahwah, NJ: Lawrence Erlbaum Associates.

OECD. (2016). PISA 2015 Financial Literacy Framework. In *Pisa 2015 Assessment and Analytical Framework: Science, Reading, Mathematic and Financial Literacy*. Paris: OECD Publishing.

Paul, R., & Elder, L. (2001). *Critical thinking: Tools for taking charge of your learning and your life*. Upper Saddle River, NJ: Prentice Hall.

Savard, A. (2008). *Le développement d'une pensée critique envers les jeux de hasard et d'argent par l'enseignement des probabilités à l'école primaire: Vers une prise de décision*. Thèse Inédite. Université Laval, Québec.

Savard, A. (2014). Developing probabilistic thinking: What about people's conceptions? In E. Chernoff & B. Sriraman (Eds.), *Probabilistic thinking: Presenting plural perspectives*. (Vol. 2, pp. 283–298). Berlin/Heidelberg: Springer.

Savard, A. (2015). Making decisions about gambling: The influence of risk on children's arguments. *The Mathematics Enthusiast, 12*(1, 2 & 3), 226–245.

Steffe, L. P., & D'Ambrosio, B. S. (1996). Using teaching experiments to understand students' mathematics. In D. D. Treagust, R. Duit, & B. Fraser (Eds.), *Improving teaching and learning in science and mathematics* (pp. 65–76). New York, NY: Teachers College Press.

Swartz, R. J., & Perkins, D. N. (1990). *Teaching thinking: Issues and approaches*. Pacific Groves, CA: Midwest Publications.

ten Dam, G., & Volman, M. (2004). Critical thinking as a citizenship competence: Teaching strategies. *Learning and Instruction, 14*(4), 359–379.

CHAPTER TEN

The Influence OF Teacher Attributes ON Financial Education Outcomes

J. MICHAEL COLLINS AND ELIZABETH ODDERS-WHITE
University of Wisconsin-Madison

NILTON PORTO
University of Rhode Island

INTRODUCTION

Relatively few young adults understand basic personal finance concepts. For example, Lusardi, Mitchell, and Curto's (2010) analysis of the financial literacy questions included in the 2007–2008 wave of the 1997 National Longitudinal Survey of Youth revealed that fewer than one-third of young adults ages 23 to 28 comprehend inflation, interest rates, and diversification. Similarly, De Bassa Scheresberg's (2013) analysis of data from the 2009 National Financial Capability Study found that young adults ages 25 to 34 lacked basic financial knowledge, and Mottola (2014) suggested that millennials displayed low levels of financial literacy using the 2012 wave of the same study. This low level of financial literacy knowledge early in life was associated with financial problems later in life, including lower savings levels and higher debt levels; the findings asserted that financial education has the potential to improve these outcomes (Lusardi & Mitchell, 2014).

Recognizing the potential benefits of beginning to build financial capability early, a number of state and local school authorities have added financial literacy requirements into their K–12 curriculum. According to the Council for Economic Education's Survey of the States (2007, 2016), the number of states mandating inclusion of personal finance content in their curricula through the enforcement of state standards increased from 28 in 2007 to 37 in 2016. Over the same period, the number of states requiring a course in personal finance for high school graduation jumped from seven to 17.

Such school-based programs show promise as a vehicle for delivering financial education. For example, Harter and Harter (2009) and Sherraden, Johnson, Guo, and Elliott (2011) found improvements in financial knowledge after financial education was delivered to older elementary school students. Go, Varcoe, Eng, Pho, and Choi (2012) found that financial education not only increased financial knowledge but also improved the self-reported financial behaviors of fourth and fifth graders.

One significant strength of school-based programs is their ability to reach all young people, regardless of socioeconomic status or personal/family circumstances. Accordingly, there is significant interest among educators and policy makers in developing financial education programs that are effective in delivering lasting financial knowledge that leads to positive financial behaviors in adulthood. The National Conference of State Legislatures reported that 28 states introduced, or had pending, legislation related to K–12 financial education in 2015 (http://www.ncsl.org/research/financial-services-and-commerce/financial-literacy-2015-legislation.aspx). At the national level, government agencies like the Consumer Financial Protection Bureau conduct research that supports their objective of guiding teachers, administrators, and policy makers in the development of effective K–12 financial education initiatives (http://www.consumerfinance.gov/youth-financial-education/).

At the same time, work by Way and Holden (2009) indicated that many teachers feel unprepared to teach financial education concepts. The authors surveyed over 500 K–12 teachers from eight U.S. states and found that while many teachers recognized the importance of teaching personal finance topics, few had been formally trained to do so. As a result, many teachers lacked confidence in this domain. In addition, results of a prior study had shown that women often have lower levels of comfort or familiarity with financial literacy topics (Lusardi & Mitchell, 2014), and according to the latest data available from the National Center for Education Statistics, over 75% of U.S. public school teachers are women (https://nces.ed.gov/programs/digest/d15/tables/dt15_209.10.asp?current=yes).

This lack of training is a potential cause for concern given the evidence that a wide range of teacher attributes—including preparedness and self-efficacy—impact student learning (e.g., Bacher-Hicks, 2015; Cho & Shim, 2013; Goldhaber & Anthony, 2007; Moore & Esselman, 1992; Stronge, Ward, & Grant, 2011). Teacher subject knowledge has also been found to contribute to student achievement (Metzler & Woessmann, 2012). In fact, a number of studies found that teacher academic achievement measured, for example, by test scores is one of the personal attributes most frequently found to be significantly correlated with student achievement (Eide, Goldhaber, & Brewer, 2004; Hanushek & Rivkin,

2006). Thus, it is perhaps unsurprising that Way and Holden (2009) concluded that "there is a great need to expand personal finance educational opportunities for pre-service and in-service teachers in order to meet both their personal and professional needs" (p. 76).

Not all research supports this view, however. For example, Henry et al. (2013) and Preston (2016) found little relation between a variety of measures of teacher preparation and student performance, and in fact, provided some evidence of a negative relation. Therefore, the impact of teacher attributes on student achievement remains an open question, particularly in subjects outside math and language arts, which are the focus of much of the existing literature.

We contributed to this body of work by studying the relation between teacher attributes and student outcomes in the context of an elementary school–based financial education program. In particular, we examined the connection between teachers' self-assessed preparedness and improvements in students' financial knowledge, attitudes, and behaviors using data from a field study conducted in fourth and fifth grade classrooms. We also studied the relation between teachers' self-efficacy and other attitudes about the lessons, as well as connections between teachers' attitudes and student outcomes. Our findings speak to the importance of equipping and supporting elementary school teachers to successfully teach personal finance content.

METHODS

The Intervention

Our data are drawn from a field study implemented in the 2011–2012 and 2012–2013 school years in a Midwestern school district that serves approximately 11,000 students in grades Pre-K through 12. The district is situated in a city of roughly 65,000 residents within a greater metropolitan area with a population of about 200,000. At the time of the study, just over 80% of students in the district were white and approximately 45% were eligible for free or reduced lunch, compared to a national average of just over 50% (according to the National Center for Education Statistics, 2012).

The study was structured as a randomized controlled trial in the district's 71 fourth and fifth grade classrooms (across 13 elementary schools). There were approximately 1,500 fourth and fifth graders total during the 2011–2012 school year. Half of the classrooms were randomly assigned to participate in the program during the study period (i.e., the educational "treatment" group), while the remaining "control" classrooms did not deliver the education until after the study's follow-up assessment had been completed. The same design was used during the second year of the study, but fifth graders did not receive the education because they had participated as fourth graders during the prior year.

Although all students participated in the program as part of their regular school day, we were only able to analyze data for students who signed an assent form and whose parent or guardian provided written consent. This halved our sample despite numerous attempts to inform parents about the project through fliers, letters, school newsletter articles, e-mails, and local media coverage. The final sample consisted of the 700 assenting students with parental consent who completed both the baseline and follow-up assessments, of whom 380 are in the educational treatment group that was the focus of our analysis here.

Students participated in weekly financial education lessons of approximately 45 minutes each for five weeks. Lessons were adapted from the Council for Economic Education's (CEE) *Financial Fitness for Life* (FFFL) curriculum for grades 3 to 5. FFFL is a carefully designed program that includes nationally normed assessments, aligns with state standards, and integrates well into other subjects. It has been employed in numerous academic studies, including Harter and Harter (2009) and Sherraden et al. (2011). Further, CCE is a long-standing, nationally recognized association of educators focused on economic and personal finance curricula.

The curriculum included concepts such as savings, financial decision-making, and money management, and students were able to practice applying these concepts using worksheets and other assignments. In one lesson, students considered tradeoffs between present and future consumption by studying an updated version of the fable "The Grasshopper and the Ant" in which the video-gaming grasshopper spends money and the hardworking ant saves (FFFL Lesson 4). Other lessons focused on developing and tracking savings goals and plans (adapted from FFFL Lesson 5) or introduced students to basic money management concepts like costs, benefits, and budgeting (FFFL Lesson 14). As noted above, all lessons were designed to integrate into existing math, social studies, or language arts curricula.

TEACHER TRAINING

Teachers attended a three-hour training session as part of a standard professional development day and were compensated $100 for spending time preparing the lessons outside of the normal workday. A recording of the training session was also made available for teachers to access online. Teachers also received a small financial incentive for completing surveys after every lesson ($25 total, provided at least four surveys were completed). We worked with the school district to distribute

THE INFLUENCE OF TEACHER ATTRIBUTES ON FINANCIAL EDUCATION OUTCOMES | 157

these payments to teachers after the study was completed. All materials needed to teach the lessons were printed and delivered to teachers before the beginning of the program. These included all handouts, visual aids, and a teacher's guide for each lesson. A website was also created containing timelines and information for teachers and parents. Teachers were able to use the website to find information pertinent to the program.

Teachers were given the opportunity to request that a local credit union educator deliver the lessons rather than teaching the content themselves. The local credit union also supported student-run bank branches in schools and is generally well known in the community. To ensure fidelity of treatment, the credit union educators attended the training session. Many also had experience delivering other financial education programs throughout the district. About 60% of teachers taught all of the lessons on their own; the remainder used staff from the credit union as instructors or co-instructors for one or more lessons. Teachers remained in the room even if they did not lead instruction and therefore were able to offer feedback on the lessons. Several teachers praised the ability of the credit union educators to engage students, providing anecdotal evidence of the quality of instruction. This model of local financial professionals engaging in school-based programs is considered common in the United States (Sukarieh & Tannock, 2009).

TEACHERS' ATTITUDES AND FEEDBACK

As mentioned above, all teachers were asked to complete a survey after each lesson, irrespective of whether they taught the lessons themselves or not. A total of 43 teachers responded to at least one post-lesson survey. Responses, which are scored on a 5-point scale with 1 being low, are summarized in Tables 10.1 and 10.2.

Table 10.1: Summary Teacher Survey Responses (Average of All Lessons Reported), N = 43.

	Mean	SD	Min	Max
How prepared did you feel to teach this lesson?*	4.09	0.87	1	5
Do you think the lesson was a valuable addition to the curriculum for your class?	4.24	0.67	1	5
Do you think the lesson material was appropriate for your students' learning level?	4.28	0.54	1	5
How interested in this lesson were your students?	3.78	0.51	1	5

*N = 26 teachers who delivered all the lessons.

Table 10.2: Summary Teacher Survey Responses (Average of All Lessons Reported), N = 43.

	Yes	No	Maybe
Has your classroom learned similar material at another point during the year?	11%	89%	N/A
Would you teach this lesson again in the future?	70%	25%	5%

Overall, teachers' feedback was very positive. Most teachers felt prepared to deliver the lessons (mean of 4.09, indicating "mostly" prepared) and found value in adding financial literacy to their curriculum (mean of 4.24). Teachers also scored the program highly in its appropriateness to their students' learning level (mean of 4.28 or "mostly" to "very"), although there was heterogeneity in teachers' responses across lessons. Despite this variation, teachers felt that their students were generally interested in the lessons (mean of 3.78, with 4 corresponding to "very" for this question). Only 11% of teachers answered that similar material had been taught at another point in the school year. When asked in the survey if they would teach this lesson again in the future, 70% of teachers answered yes and another 5% answered maybe. The remaining 25% of teachers responded that they would decline to teach the lesson in the future.

STUDENT OUTCOMES

Students' financial knowledge, attitudes, and behavior were all measured using a pre- and a post-survey, about 10 weeks apart. Teachers, who were provided paper copies of the surveys along with detailed instructions, administered the surveys to their students during 3-day windows before and after the treatment period. The baseline and follow-up surveys were identical, and the impact of the intervention was captured by the differences over time.

Financial knowledge was measured using 13 questions drawn from curriculum materials. Although there are other potential measures of financial and economic knowledge (see, for example, Huston, 2010), the intent here was to directly assess students' mastery of the FFFL learning outcomes. In addition, students answered a set of questions about their attitudes toward saving and another set of questions about their attitudes toward financial institutions, all of which were developed in consultation with experts in the field. These questions were then used to create composite scale measures for savings and banking attitudes. The composite scale of savings attitudes includes four survey questions drawn from prior studies. First, students were asked if they are saving for the future using a yes/no binary response. Next, the survey included three more questions using 5-point scales: "it is easy to save," "it is good to save," and "saving money is only for adults." Higher scores to any of these variables corresponded to a more positive financial attitude. The composite scale of banking attitudes scale was comprised of three variables, each also measured on a 5-point scale with a higher score corresponding to a more positive response: "banks are only for adults," "banks are useful," and "banks keep money safe." In both cases, the scales provided a sense of the variability of student responses. Cronbach's alpha, a measure of scale reliability, was approximately 0.6 for both scales; this score is considered statistically acceptable. In addition, responses for the control group were relatively stable from the pre-survey to the post-survey, offering an indication of test–retest reliability. Furthermore, recent work by Batty, Collins, and Odders-White (2016) provides additional evidence of the validity and reliability of some of our measures.

Finally, we assessed student responses to the following question: "If you have a savings account, about how much money do you think is currently in the account?" 1=$1 to $25, 2=$26 to $50, 3=$51 to $100, 4=$101 to $200, 5=$201 to $500, 6=more than $500. We recognized that students' self-reported savings levels are an imperfect measure of financial behavior that may reflect students' beliefs about the "right" answer as well as their socioeconomic status. As a result, we interpreted the results cautiously. Collectively, these questions reflected financial knowledge, attitudes, and behavior—all key components of financial literacy and capability.

RESULTS

We were interested in understanding whether teachers' attitudes and self-assessed preparedness impacted student outcomes in a financial education intervention. Table 10.3 below tests for differences in student outcomes based on teachers' self-efficacy for the 39 teachers who could be matched to student data in our sample. Teachers who felt "mostly" or "very" prepared were placed in the "well prepared" category, while those who felt "somewhat prepared" or worse were considered "less prepared." Teachers who opted not to teach the lessons themselves and to have a credit union educator deliver them instead were also classified as feeling "less prepared." The results in Table 10.3 confirm that there were no statistically significant differences in student scores at baseline based on teacher self-efficacy. In contrast, changes in scores between baseline and follow up—a measure of the success of the educational intervention—were greater for well-prepared teachers for three of the four outcome measures, although differences were only marginally statistically significant perhaps due to the small sample size. The statistical significance was strongest for changes in financial knowledge, where students taught by well-prepared teachers exhibit gains that were 56% greater than those whose teachers felt less prepared. The magnitude of differences in improvements in savings and banking attitudes across the two groups was even stronger (60% to 80% larger changes for students of well-prepared teachers), but the statistical significance of these differences approached only the 10% level. The overall sample size limits the power of this analysis. If we were willing to assume a one-sided alternative hypothesis in which student outcomes were positively associated with teacher self-efficacy, all but differences in the change in savings amount became statistically significant at conventional levels.

Table 10.3: Teacher Self-Efficacy and Student Outcomes (Means).

	Less Prepared		Well Prepared		
	μ	SD	μ	SD	p
N	22		17		39
Baseline knowledge	6.26	1.08	6.22	0.82	0.909
Change in knowledge	1.46	0.86	2.28	1.58	0.075
Baseline savings amount	4.48	0.67	4.54	0.72	0.777
Change in savings amount	0.05	0.58	0.03	0.45	0.899
Baseline savings attitude	0.86	0.26	0.93	0.22	0.405
Change in savings attitude	0.20	0.15	0.32	0.27	0.107
Baseline banking attitude	1.98	0.34	1.94	0.36	0.695
Change in banking attitude	0.25	0.36	0.45	0.37	0.104

While Table 10.3 suggests a weak connection between teacher self-efficacy and student outcomes, the results could be confounded by the influence of other factors. For example, whether the lesson was taught by the classroom teacher or a credit union educator could impact outcomes, as could differences in students' past exposure to financial topics in class. As noted in the introduction, gender could also impact teachers' level of comfort with the material, and therefore, student outcomes.

Table 10.4 examines the relation between student follow-up outcomes and teachers' self-assessed preparedness using ordinary least squares (OLS) regressions. (Correlations are reported in Table 10.5.) In each column of Table 10.4, the dependent variable was one of the student outcomes measured at follow-up. The regressions control directly for baseline levels as well as the other factors discussed above. Specifically, we include a "teacher taught" indicator that assumes a value of 1 if the teacher taught all of the lessons (and 0 if a credit union educator taught one or more). "Learned similar material before" equals 1 if the teacher reported

Table 10.4: Teacher Self-Efficacy and Student Outcomes (OLS).

	(1) Follow-up Knowledge	(2) Follow-up Savings Amount	(3) Follow-up Savings Attitude	(4) Follow-up Banking Attitude
N	37	36	36	36
Well prepared	0.565	0.187	0.0925	−0.0125
	(0.484)	(0.199)	(0.0684)	(0.0870)
Learned similar material before	−1.289	0.123	0.0520	−0.127
	(1.373)	(0.311)	(0.195)	(0.172)
Female	−0.228	−0.0724	0.0541	0.111
	(0.373)	(0.139)	(0.0722)	(0.0931)
Teacher taught	0.449	−0.255	0.0869	0.254**
	(0.368)	(0.203)	(0.0528)	(0.0822)

Controlling for baseline levels (data not shown). Robust standard errors are in parentheses. **$p<0.01$

Table 10.5: Correlations.

	Well Prepared	Valuable	Appropriate	Learned Before	Interested	Teach Again	Teacher Taught
Well prepared	1						
Valuable	0.447*	1					
Appropriate	0.411*	0.643***	1				
Learned before	−0.246	−0.100	−0.103	1			
Interested	0.517**	0.685***	0.655***	0.229	1		
Teach again	−0.006	0.546**	0.474*	−0.163	0.413*	1	
Teacher taught	0.410*	0.109	−0.094	0.011	0.085	−0.194	1

*$p<0.05$, **$p<0.01$, ***$p<0.001$.

that the class had learned similar material at another point. The estimates can be interpreted as the regression-adjusted marginal change in the classroom-level mean outcome related to the particular factor.

The results in Table 10.4 revealed a positive but statistically insignificant association between teachers' self-assessed level of preparation and changes in students' financial knowledge, savings amount, and savings attitudes. Teacher gender and students' prior learning experiences did not significantly relate to students' follow-up scores, and estimates were of mixed signs. Only the "teacher taught" indicator variable was significant (along with the baseline levels and constant term, which are not tabulated) in any of the regressions; the follow-up attitude about financial institutions showed greater improvements when lessons were fully teacher taught.

We were also interested in understanding the connection between teachers' sense of self-efficacy and their other attitudes about the lessons, as well as how these attitudes relate to student outcomes. Table 10.6 presents teachers' responses to three of the questions in Table 10.1 based on their perceived level of preparedness in delivering the lessons. We found that well-prepared teachers responded more favorably on average to all three questions, indicating that they were more likely to think the lessons were a valuable addition to their curriculum, appropriate for their students' level, and commanded students' interest.

Table 10.6: Teacher Self-Efficacy and Other Attitudes (N = 43).

	Less Prepared		Well Prepared		
N	25		18		43
	μ	SD	μ	SD	p
Do you think the lesson was a valuable addition to the curriculum for your class?	3.94	0.66	4.67	0.45	0.000
Do you think the lesson material was appropriate for your students' learning level?	4.02	0.52	4.63	0.33	0.000
How interested in this lesson were your students?	3.58	0.57	4.06	0.24	0.001

Finally, we examined the relation between teacher attitudes and student outcomes using regressions. We replaced the "well prepared" indicator variable with teachers' responses to the questions analyzed in Table 10.6, and also added an indicator of their willingness to teach the lesson again (equals 1 if teachers responded "yes" or "maybe"). Other control variables are as presented in Table 10.4.

The results are presented in Table 10.7. Students whose teachers felt that the lesson was appropriate for their class showed statistically significantly greater gains for three of the four outcome measures (all but banking attitudes). Similarly, gains were significantly larger for all but savings amount when teachers taught all of the lessons themselves rather than involving a volunteer credit union educator at least once. Coefficients on other variables were statistically insignificant (excluding baseline levels and the constant term, not tabulated) and of mixed sign.

Table 10.7: Teacher Attitudes and Student Outcomes (OLS).

	(1) Follow-up Knowledge	(2) Follow-up Savings Amount	(3) Follow-up Savings Attitude	(4) Follow-up Banking Attitude
Lesson was appropriate	0.860⁺	0.356*	0.124*	−0.0215
	(0.465)	(0.161)	(0.0567)	(0.108)
Lesson was valuable	0.0214	−0.106	−0.0458	−0.153
	(0.362)	(0.185)	(0.0617)	(0.0955)
Students were interested	−0.310	−0.0348	0.00319	0.199
	(0.773)	(0.155)	(0.0752)	(0.123)
Learned similar material before	1.183	0.154	0.0475	−0.101
	(1.374)	(0.302)	(0.205)	(0.234)
Willing to teach again	−0.263	−0.0957	0.0947	−0.0116
	(0.480)	(0.265)	(0.0937)	(0.153)
Female	−0.368	−0.101	0.0361	0.129
	(0.332)	(0.170)	(0.0844)	(0.0899)
Teacher taught	0.839*	−0.105	0.116⁺	0.291**
	(0.371)	(0.151)	(0.0570)	(0.0968)
N	37	36	36	36

Controlling for baseline levels (data not shown). Robust standard errors are in parentheses.
⁺$p<0.10$, *$p<0.05$, **$p<0.01$

DISCUSSION

We found some evidence of a positive connection between teachers' self-assessed preparedness and student outcomes. Although estimates often tended toward greater preparedness being associated with stronger student outcomes, the statistical significance of the relation was weak. While our analysis alone is certainly insufficient to draw broad conclusions—particularly given the relatively small sample size—it could suggest that teacher self-efficacy was not a critical driver of student achievement in the context of financial education. Comparability of student baseline scores across teachers who felt well prepared and those who felt less prepared suggested that the teachers in our sample did not feel more efficacious simply because their students were higher performing (an effect documented by Raudenbush, Rowan, & Cheong, 1992, among others).

Perhaps not surprisingly, we found a positive relation between teachers' sense of self-efficacy and their attitudes about the lessons. This could result from positive attitudes about the lessons fueling a sense of preparedness, a sense of preparedness leading to increased positive attitudes, or both. In contrast, we found little relation between teachers' attitudes and student outcomes. The one exception was teachers' responses to a question about the appropriateness of the content for their students' learning level. There were greater gains in financial knowledge, savings amount, and savings attitudes when teachers viewed the lesson as more appropriate. Because teachers responded to the surveys after completing the lessons, this result may simply reflect teachers' tendency to view content as appropriate if students appeared to have grasped the material. It is also important to note that in simple difference of means tests analogous to those in Table 10.3 (not reported) only one of the outcomes (change in savings attitude) was statistically significantly greater when teachers found the lessons more appropriate.

When the regular teacher taught all the lessons, rather than using a volunteer from a local financial institution, changes in students' financial knowledge and improvements in savings and banking attitudes were larger. We found no statistically significant relation between the "teacher taught" indicator and students' savings levels, maybe due to the limitations of this outcome measure discussed above. It was perhaps surprising that we observed greater improvements in attitudes about financial institutions when the lessons were taught entirely by a classroom teacher rather than a financial professional. One might have predicted that credit union educators would be more enthusiastic about, and familiar with, the financial services industry, potentially resulting in greater gains. That we found the opposite could reflect sensitivity on the part of credit union educators and a desire to remain "unbiased" in their delivery. Alternatively, the greater improvements in attitudes when classroom teachers taught the lessons could have stemmed from their stronger student relationships and pedagogical skills more than compensated for any lack of deep content expertise. The relative consistency with which lessons delivered entirely by classroom teachers corresponded to greater gains suggested that this second explanation was more likely.

Student outcomes showed no consistent or significant relation to teacher gender, perhaps suggesting that the teacher training was sufficient to counteract the lower levels of financial literacy and confidence documented for women in previous studies. Alternatively, the financial content covered in these lessons may have been basic enough that issues of financial literacy did not come into play, or perhaps less likely, teacher content knowledge and self-efficacy were simply not important determinants of student outcomes in this context.

IMPLICATIONS FOR TEACHER TRAINING AND POLICY

While we failed to document strong connections between teachers' self-assessed levels of preparedness and student outcomes, it would be a mistake to conclude that teacher training has no impact on student learning. The relatively weak association could reflect the complex relationship between self-efficacy and objective level of preparation or knowledge (see, for example, Raudenbush et al., 1992). It could also stem primarily from a lack of statistical power. In any case, all teachers and credit union educators in our sample were trained to deliver the lessons, and students demonstrated improvements in their financial knowledge, attitudes, and behaviors following the educational intervention (see Batty, Collins, & Odders-White, 2015, for a comparison of treatment-group to control-group outcomes). While we cannot observe what would have occurred had teachers received no training, anecdotal evidence in the form of teachers' written comments and evaluation of the training session suggested that it was an important component of the intervention. Moreover, our finding that student outcomes were stronger when classroom teachers (versus outside volunteers) taught lessons was consistent with the existing evidence on the importance of overall teaching skills and pedagogical knowledge for student outcomes (e.g., Baumert et al., 2010).

Teachers' assessment of the appropriateness of the content for their students' learning level also seemed to be important, including for non–knowledge-based outcomes like savings attitudes. If the goal of financial literacy is to influence not just understanding but also financial capability, then focusing on ways to deliver content that is well tailored and meaningful to students and teachers is especially important. The curriculum and delivery in this study, because it was part of a larger project, was highly standardized. In practice, teachers might benefit from more options to customize their approaches and content based on student needs and levels.

We recognize that teachers are under enormous pressure to show positive student outcomes in a variety of subjects, many of which are measured using standardized test scores. Adding another set of requirements can be challenging. The teachers in this study were formally trained, compensated for their time, and provided preprinted materials and student handouts—perhaps more support than many teachers would be provided in a standard implementation. Policy makers, school leaders, and curriculum developers must recognize these needs and actively support the implementation of any new standards. Simply mandating programs at the state or local level is unlikely to lead to positive results (see, for example, Brown, Collins, Schmeiser, & Urban, 2014). Of course, these efforts come at a cost. More work is needed to truly understand the impact of teacher training and other educational policies on students' financial education outcomes.

CONCLUSION

Financial education curricula and programs are increasingly being incorporated into K–12 education in the United States and globally. A key question when implementing these programs is whether teachers are sufficiently prepared and supported to confidently deliver financial content, and if not, how this may impact student outcomes. This small study of teachers' self-assessed preparedness and the associated changes in classroom-level knowledge, attitudes, and behaviors of students suggested weak positive associations between teacher self-efficacy and student outcomes. Given the structure and short intensity of this program, perhaps a wide variation in preparedness would not be expected. In a larger program, stronger associations could be observed.

It was interesting to note that using a local volunteer from a community financial institution, a strategy some schools might consider when implementing a new financial education program, resulted in smaller gains for students than when the material was taught by the regular classroom teacher. There were many possible explanations for this, including teachers' stronger pedagogical skills and greater familiarity with their students' ability, or students taking the content more seriously when it was delivered by their teacher. Importantly, it was likely that teachers who felt least comfortable with the material opted to use volunteers, and the counterfactual—in which these teachers implemented the curriculum—was not observed. Nonetheless, the results suggested that schools implementing approaches that rely on volunteers for teaching should take care to consider these potential influences and address them if possible.

QUESTIONS FOR DISCUSSION

1. What does teacher preparation mean to you? What are the characteristics of a prepared teacher?
2. The chapter describes lessons used to teach students about money. What values do these lessons convey? How do they shape student attitudes?
3. To what extent does classroom learning represent a dynamic between teacher and student? How does this dynamic shape interpretation of successful learning?
4. The community volunteer would supposedly have greater "content" knowledge than the teacher. This study would indicate that pedagogy could be more critical in learning outcome than content although suggesting that familiarity may be at play as well. What is your thinking?
5. How much can a school lesson or school lessons change behavior learned at home? How can a teacher use a student's personal context in learning financial skills/literacy?

REFERENCES

Bacher-Hicks, A. (2015). *Explaining teacher effects on achievement using measures from multiple research traditions* (Unpublished doctoral dissertation). Harvard University, Cambridge, MA.

Batty, M., Collins, J. M., & Odders-White, E. (2015). Experimental evidence on the effects of financial education on elementary school students' knowledge, behavior, and attitudes. *Journal of Consumer Affairs, 49*, 69–96.

Batty, M., Collins, J. M., & Odders-White, E. (2016). *Validity and reliability of elementary student financial education outcome measures*. Retrieved from https://centerforfinancialsecurity.files.wordpress.com/2016/09/validityreliabilitymeasures_final.pdf

Baumert, J., Kunter, M., Blum, W., Brunner, M., Voss, T., Jordan, A., ... Tsai, Y. M. (2010). Teachers' mathematical knowledge, cognitive activation in the classroom, and student progress. *American Educational Research Journal, 47*, 133–180.

Brown, A. M., Collins, J. M., Schmeiser, M. D., & Urban, C. (2014). *State mandated financial education and the credit behavior of young adults*. Divisions of Research & Statistics and Monetary Affairs Federal Reserve Board Working Paper 2014–68. Finance and Economics Discussion Series, Washington, DC.

Cho, Y., & Shim, S. S. (2013). Predicting teachers' achievement goals for teaching: The role of perceived school goal structure and teachers' sense of efficacy. *Teaching and Teacher Education, 32*, 12–21.

Council for Economic Education. (2007). *Survey of the states: Economic and personal finance education in our nation's schools*. Retrieved from http://councilforeconed.org/wp/wp-content/uploads/2011/11/2007-Survey-of-the-States.pdf

Council for Economic Education. (2016). *Survey of the states: Economic and personal finance education in our nation's schools*. Retrieved from http://councilforeconed.org/wp/wp-content/uploads/2016/02/sos-16-final.pdf

de Bassa Scheresberg, C. (2013). Financial literacy and financial behavior among young adults: Evidence and implications. *Numeracy, 6*(2), article 5.

Eide, E., Goldhaber, D., & Brewer, D. (2004). The teacher labour market and teacher quality. *Oxford Review of Economic Policy, 20*(2), 230–244.

Go, C. G., Varcoe, K., Eng, T., Pho, W., & Choi, L. (2012). *Money savvy youth: Evaluating the effectiveness of financial education for fourth and fifth graders*. Community Development Investment Center Working Paper 2012–02. Federal Reserve Bank of San Francisco. Retrieved from http://www.frbsf.org/community-development/files/wp2012-02.pdf

Goldhaber, D., & Anthony, E. (2007). Can teacher quality be effectively assessed? National board certification as a signal of effective teaching. *The Review of Economics and Statistics, 89*(1), 134–150.

Hanushek, E. A., & Rivkin, S. G. (2006). Teacher quality. In E. A. Hanushek & F. Welch (Eds.), *Handbook of the economics of education* (Vol. 2, pp. 1051–1078). Amsterdam: North-Holland.

Harter, C. L., & Harter, J. F. R. (2009). Assessing the effectiveness of financial fitness for life in eastern Kentucky. *Journal of Applied Economics & Policy, 28*(1), 20–33.

Henry, G. T., Campbell, S. L., Thompson, C. L., Patriarca, L. A., Luterbach, K. J., Lys, D. B., & Covington, V. M. (2013). The predictive validity of measures of teacher candidate programs and performance: Toward an evidence-based approach to teacher preparation. *Journal of Teacher Education, 64*(5), 439–453.

Huston, S. J. (2010). Measuring financial literacy. *Journal of Consumer Affairs, 44*, 296–316.

Lusardi, A., & Mitchell, O. S. (2014). The economic importance of financial literacy: Theory and evidence. *Journal of Economic Literature, 52*(1), 5–44.

Lusardi, A., Mitchell, O. S., & Curto, V. (2010). Financial literacy among the young. *Journal of Consumer Affairs, 44*(2), 358–380.

Metzler, J., & Woessmann, L. (2012). The impact of teacher subject knowledge on student achievement: Evidence from within-teacher within-student variation. *Journal of Development Economics, 99*(2), 486–496.

Moore, W. P., & Esselman, M. E. (1992, April). *Teacher efficacy, empowerment, and a focused instructional climate: Does student achievement benefit?* Paper presented at the annual meeting of the American Educational Research Association, San Francisco, CA.

Mottola, G. R. (2014). *The financial capability of young adults—A generational view.* Retrieved from http://www.usfinancialcapability.org/downloads/FinancialCapabilityofYoungAdults.pdf

National Center for Education Statistics, U.S. Department of Education. (2012). *Federal programs for education and related activities.* Digest of Education Statistics 2012 (Chapter 4). Retrieved December 20, 2016 from the National Center for Education Statistics Web site: http://nces.ed.gov/

Preston, C. (2016). University-based teacher preparation and middle grades teacher effectiveness. *Journal of Teacher Education, 68*(1), 1–15, doi:10.1177/0022487116660151

Raudenbush, S., Rowan, B., & Cheong, Y. (1992). Contextual effects on the self-perceived efficacy of high school teachers. *Sociology of Education, 65*, 150–167.

Sherraden, M. S., Johnson, L., Guo, B., & Elliott, W. (2011). Financial capability in children: Effects of participation in a school-based financial education and savings program. *Journal of Family & Economic Issues, 32*(3), 385–399.

Stronge, J. H., Ward, T. J., & Grant, L. W. (2011). What makes good teachers good? A cross-case analysis of the connection between teacher effectiveness and student achievement. *Journal of Teacher Education, 62*(4), 339–355.

Sukarieh, M., & Tannock, S. (2009). Putting school commercialism in context: A global history of junior achievement worldwide. *Journal of Education Policy, 24*(6), 769–786.

Way, W. L., & Holden, K. C. (2009). 2009 Outstanding AFCPE® Conference Paper Teachers' background and capacity to teach personal finance: Results of a national study. *Journal of Financial Counseling and Planning, 20*(2), 64–78.

CHAPTER ELEVEN

Economic Inequality AND Secondary Mathematics

ANDREW BRANTLINGER

The University of Maryland[1]

School reformers have long asserted that academic mathematics curriculum is elitist and wasteful so they call for teaching of only the most useful mathematics (see, for example, Thorndike, 1926). Early in the twentieth century, to address these concerns, administrative progressives developed vocational mathematics courses to meet the "needs" not met by the classical curriculum for the non-college-bound public school population (Cremin, 1964; National Council of Teachers of Mathematics (NCTM), 1970). These vocational classes were dead-end courses for working-class students and students of color and they existed alongside college preparatory mathematics courses for economically privileged white students (Kliebard & Franklin, 2003; NCTM, 1970; Oakes, 2005). Vocational mathematics courses ostensibly taught students the mathematics necessary for the "world of work." Consumer and business mathematics courses in such programs were designed to increase lower socioeconomic status (SES) students' financial literacy. For example, educators taught students to balance a checkbook and save in banks. Proponents of such courses claimed that they made students more rational and efficient in out of school contexts (Kliebard & Franklin, 2003). This narrow version of financial literacy left no space for a critique of consumerism and capitalism.

Advocates of vocational mathematics relied on unfounded assumptions about the applicability of school mathematics to out of school problem contexts. Proponents of standards-based reforms repeat many of the same unsubstantiated arguments about the general utility of school mathematics. For instance, the National

Council of Teachers of Mathematics (NCTM) (2000), an organization spearheading current standards-based reforms in mathematics education, states:

> Just as the level of mathematics needed for intelligent citizenship has increased dramatically, so too has the level of mathematical thinking and problem solving needed in the workplace, in professional areas ranging from health care to graphic design. (p. 5)

As this quote indicates, mathematics is assumed to play a crucial economic role in the modern, increasingly technological, world. Domain-specific mathematical problem-solving skills are assumed to transfer to real-world problems that might be encountered on the job or in one's everyday life. However, in the case of secondary education, there is little evidence to support claims of the benefits of teaching mathematics for practical purposes (Dowling, 1998; Steen, 2004). The utilitarian justification makes the subject of mathematics seem important and necessary. In a self-serving way, the utilitarian argument bolsters the historically contested position of secondary mathematics in the curriculum and obscures its important institutional and economic function as a gatekeeper discipline.

As the quote from the NCTM (2000) also shows, current standards-based reform rhetoric stresses the democratic role (e.g., "intelligent citizenship") that school mathematics might play. The idea that mathematics educators make democratic goals an explicit part of the curriculum resonates with many. Critical scholars such as Apple (1992) and Gutstein (2005) embrace the potential that school mathematics has as a political enlightenment tool while they analyze economic rationales for school mathematics espoused by mainstream groups and policy makers. Critical mathematics (CM) educators posit, again with little evidence, that people who understand mathematics can protect themselves from antidemocratic political and economic forces. For example, Niss (1983) claims that people who lack a meta-level understanding of how mathematics is used by corporations, financial institutions, and government agencies become "victims of social processes in which mathematics is a component" (p. 248).

CM has received attention in recent years as a politically and culturally relevant, though largely theoretical, curricular alternative to the more mainstream standards-based reform movement in mathematics. From the CM perspective, achieving equity in mathematics education does not mean teaching the required academic curriculum more effectively as standards-based reformers would have it, but rather radically altering the dominant learning goals, curricular content, and instructional methodologies. At the same time, CM educators such as Gutstein (2005) and Gutiérrez (2002) see CM as building on standards-based mathematics. For instance, CM educators advance the standards-based tenet that teachers should position students authoritatively to create and evaluate their own mathematical ideas.

CM educators aim to reconceive school mathematics as a critical literacy—a political tool subject designed to enable students to understand forces that shape their lives and to challenge the unjust socioeconomic order (Gutstein, 2005; Skovsmose, 1994). They extend Paulo Freire's (1971) ideas about critical language arts literacy pedagogy to mathematics instruction (Frankenstein, 1989, 1991, 1995; Gutiérrez, 2002; Gutstein, 2005) and adopt the Freirean ideals of critical consciousness raising, critical agency, and cultural relevance as pedagogical goals. Following Freire, CM educators discuss the need for students, particularly those from subordinated communities, to use school mathematics to reflect and act on the local problems they face in their lives (for examples, see Tate, 1995; Turner & Font Strawhun, 2005).

Similar to advocates of vocational and standards-based mathematics, CM educators ascribe a transformative power to mathematics to solve people's everyday and workplace problems. However, they also expect mathematics to address the political issues in students' lives. In the case of secondary mathematics, Dowling (1998) refers to this transformative power as a myth. He shows that the myth of real-world mathematical utility allows teachers and texts to present school mathematics as a set of use-values for students in remedial and lower track courses. It is not a coincidence that these students are disproportionately lower SES or of color. At the same time, texts designed for privileged students present mathematics as an esoteric discipline (which it is). This provides these students with "high status" exchange values that are valued in the educational and economic marketplace.

METHODS

The study of CM reported in this chapter was conducted in a night school program at Guevara (a pseudonym), a public high school in a large Midwestern metropolitan setting that served low SES Latino-American and African-American students. This was practitioner research; I was the teacher and researcher. At the time of the study, I had over nine years of experience as a mathematics instructor and had taught in urban schools for over four years. I was also an advocate of CM. My goal was to infuse my geometry curriculum with political themes and problem contexts that were relevant to my urban students' lives and social positionality. I wanted students to see that secondary mathematics could be politically useful and empowering. I did not see my critical-utilitarian goals as displacing college preparatory goals.

The geometry course was a remedial course designed to allow students to make up credit for past course failure. Most of the night school students were older (ages 18–19) than typical secondary students and many had a history of academic problems. When judged by middle-class standards, most also led difficult, stressful, and adult lives; some had children, some worked full-time jobs, several students told me they were in gangs, and one student told me he dealt drugs to make ends meet. The

Guevara night school students varied in achievement and future plans. Their plans included joining the military, or attending a postsecondary institution to study to be auto mechanics, engineers, nurses' aides, teachers, and lawyers.

The urban school system in which I taught includes a few elite schools designed primarily for middle-class students, but most schools in the district serve working-class students and students of color. Over the past decade, teachers have been increasingly pressured to teach to high stakes tests to improve the district's test scores. This pressure is particularly acute in neighborhood schools like Guevara that serve the urban poor (Lipman, 2004).

Security at Guevara is also highly visible and tightly enforced. In response to a CM assignment, Yasmín wrote:

> School to me is run like a jail. At least my school is. We have to wear uniforms. We can't even bring our own (see-through) book bags. We are given one and we all have ID numbers which is how we are known. Some school like mine run it like a jail because it's for our "protection." I think they go overboard. In my school we wear uniforms because too many people were wearing gang colors. (Student Work, November 19, 2003)

The night program did not possess much academic rigor. Jayla summed up her experiences at Guevara: "We don't really have to do anything in night school, but just be here, and *don't* talk, and just keep quiet." Jayla's observation resonates with Fine's (1991) observation that urban schools silence lower SES students of color. Indeed, many of the students in my night school course were taken aback that I expected them to work collaboratively and diligently in order to pass. In such an environment, it was not surprising that Guevara night school students seemed more concerned with getting through my course for accreditation than learning mathematics for its own sake.

DATA

The two primary data sources I draw on for this chapter are: (1) transcripts of videotaped lessons focused on classroom discourse and student participation in CM activities, and (2) transcripts of audiotaped interviews with night course students.

Discourse

Various assistants videotaped my Guevara lessons and, after completing the night course, I produced transcripts from eight hours (four from the beginning and four from the end) of tapes. Following the recommendations for discourse analysis of Duranti (1997) and Gee (2005), I not only transcribed the dialogue verbatim, but also represented such things as overlapping speech, rise in pitch and volume, and other evidence of enthusiasm or boredom. I noted eye contact, facial expressions, and gestures when they were visible on the tapes. These transcripts allowed me to analyze microlevel patterns in discourse and discursive student participation in the critical and standards-based mathematics lessons I taught.

Interviews

A graduate student (who had provided professional development for Guevara science teachers, an undergraduate majoring in anthropology) and I conducted approximately a dozen individual and focus group interviews with students before, during, and after the night course. In these interviews, students discussed their personal histories in school mathematics as well as their current experiences in the night course, and particularly their reactions to the CM component of my curriculum. Although not required to participate in the interviews, many night school students did so voluntarily. I used a mixed approach of personal and colleague interviews as well as individual and focus group interviews because I realized the benefits and drawbacks of researcher and outsider interviews as well as individual and focus group approaches (Merriam, 1998).

ANALYSIS

My approach to the discourse analysis was primarily deductive; I used analytical frameworks developed by others. I first broke up the lesson transcripts systematically into topically related sets (TRS) (Cazden, 2001; Mehan, 1979). As the name suggests, a TRS coheres around a topic or theme (e.g., economic inequality, solving a particular equation). When a considered topic changes, a new TRS begins. I next coded individual turns within TRS's as an *initiation, response,* or *feedback* (IRF) (Cazden, 2001; Mehan, 1979; Pruyn, 1999). Breaking up the discourse into TRSs and IRFs allowed me to separate salient participation structures in the classroom discourse to see, for example, whether classroom discourse was open to student contribution as well as who initiated new topics and the context in which they did so. I then used Pruyn's (1999) framework for critical classroom discourse analysis to further code individual utterances and discourse structures as they related to *subjectification* and *objectification* of students. Finally, I used Gee's (2005) constructs of *Discourse models* and *social languages* in order to capture student belief statements about themselves, mathematics, and politics. The social languages construct allowed me to examine student ownership of ideas via code switching (for details about the techniques and discourse analysis results, see Brantlinger, 2007). For the purposes of this chapter, I focus on students' ideas about the nature of school mathematics and politics, as well as their reflections on my course and CM projects.

FINDINGS

The Nature of Discourse in a Critical Financial Literacy Project

In the remainder of this chapter, I focus on a lesson from a three-day CM project on economic inequality or critical financial literacy. The critical goal of the CM project is to examine the distribution of income in the United States and other countries. The mathematical goal is to have students use their understandings of area to develop a statistical measure of the fairness of a country's distribution of income (Williams & Joseph, 1993). In the first component of the project, I ask students to write their reactions to two critical prompts, the first of which is the following:

> When President Bush claims that we're spreading democracy and freedom to Iraq and throughout the world he's talking about spreading political democracy ... Yet there is also economic democracy in which citizens receive a fair share of the economic output they help produce ... Do you think the U.S. economic system is fair to its citizens? Why or why not?

Student discussions of these critical prompts, and an activity where we modeled the U.S. distribution of income, are the focus of this chapter. I examine the more mathematical component of this project in more detail elsewhere (Brantlinger, 2007).

STUDENT RESISTANCE TO CRITICAL MATHEMATICS IN "SIBERIA"

The first two of the three excerpts of classroom discourse come when students are discussing this critical prompt in small groups. Shor (1996) refers to the back of the classroom as "Siberia" and to students who sit there as "Siberians." He notes these students tend to be the least engaged. During the first few weeks of night school, several of the Guevara Siberians came to class mildly drunk and high. By the time the lesson below occurs, my relationships with these students had improved markedly. The Siberians no longer come to class drunk and high. However, they continued to resist both CM and standards-based mathematics activities.

Typically, when students resist certain aspects of standards-based instruction such as communicating their mathematical ideas to peers, I rely on my position as teacher to get them to work. However, CM is different, in large part, because I cannot rely on my institutional authority when students resist it. The night school administration only gave wary consent to my critical instruction and research. If push came to shove, they would be unlikely to support critical pedagogy (hooks, 1994).

This first excerpt occurred with students in the Siberian corner of my classroom. It illustrates the nature of student resistance to the CM writing prompts about economic fairness. In this activity, student resistance takes the form of simply not writing, claiming excuses (e.g., need to sharpen pencils), and requesting further clarification even though the writing prompts are obvious. While the excerpt does not indicate how the delay tactics are overcome, I am able to get most students to begin writing by walking from group to group and making sure that they are on task.

Kampton, a Siberian who came to class drunk and threatened to fight me one night early in the night course, shows considerable engagement in *this* CM activity. He finishes writing a response to the first CM prompt before his groupmates begin. Kampton exhibits more engagement in the CM project than he does in most standards-based activities. He also appears quite eager to have me read his response (line 22).

Excerpt 11.1: Initial Student Response to the Initial CM Writing Prompt.[2]

1	In Siberia, Efrain and others around him had been talking about something other
2	than the CM project.
3	As I approach, they get quiet and begin looking at the CM handouts I had passed
4	out five minutes earlier.
5	Efrain (looks up from paper, to me): "Hey, can you say—can you tell me—what this
6	is asking?"
7	Me: "Basically, there are people who are janitors, there are people who are
8	teachers, there are people who are doctors, there are people who work at
9	McDonalds. Everybody gets paid something. Do you think what people get paid is
10	fair?"
11	Efrain: "Yeah, cause they went to school for it."
12	Me: "Okay. But then what about—there are a lot of people who didn't go to school
13	like jan[itors."
14	Efrain: "[exactly!"
15	Efrain leans forward waves hands for emphasis.
16	Efrain: "Just because they're janitors, they'd be getting paid (inaudible)."
17	Me: "Okay. So then write that down! It sounds like you think it's fair."
18	Efrain writes very little in response to the prompt in the next twenty minutes.
19	Kampton, meanwhile, has been patiently holding out his paper for me. Like several
20	students, and unlike others, he has had his head hunched over his paper and
21	began writing a response to the CM prompt with little hesitation.
22	Kampton (to me): "Can you read it and see if you understand it?"
23	Kampton had written the following initially: ""I would have to say yes & no.
24	Because the U. S. economic system sucks. I believe every one should be paid
25	equally. Because regardless of how much you make the Federal Government take
26	out the 15% amount of taxes so either way it goes, you working for less."

Once students begin to engage with CM activity, the hegemonic character of their discourse models for socioeconomic inequality becomes apparent. The emergence of hegemonic perspectives is also evident in prior CM activities; however, at the beginning of the night course, getting students to engage with CM could not be taken for granted, and they often did not express their views. In this lesson, Efrain begins the critical discussion in his small group when he argues that some people are paid more "because they went to school for [higher paying careers]." While there is some truth to this claim, it is also hegemonic in the sense that Efrain buys into the meritocratic and social mobility argument of neoliberals and neoconservatives (e.g., schools allow for equal opportunity, the disparate wage structure is fair) (see Apple, 2001).

CRITICAL STUDENT AGENCY IN ANOTHER CORNER OF THE CLASSROOM

In the opposite corner of the classroom, two groups of students exhibit critical agency similar to that shown by Kampton. In other words, I do not need to make my presence felt before these students engage with the CM activity. The students of Mexican heritage in this group use the CM writing prompt as an opportunity to discuss issues that were important to them as Mexican immigrants and Mexican-Americans. In drawing from their personal experiences, they breathe life into the CM activity and their enthusiasm seems to encourage potentially resistant students around them to take it seriously.

The exchanges reported in Excerpt 11.2 occur just after those included in Excerpt 11.1. The critical engagement and agency that Lupe, Amalia, and Eddie exhibit might be contrasted with the resistance I encounter from such students as Efrain who are seated on the other side of the classroom. These verbal exchanges point to the variability of impact that CM activities have. It is clear that these two groups of students have remarkably different initial reactions to the same activity. In addition, this range of reaction to CM is more pronounced, and difficult to predict, than it is in standards-based mathematics activities.

The conversation topic of immigration is sparked by Lupe's observation that immigrants are not included in the CM project questions and in the quintile data that we consider in the next component of the lesson.

The conversation leads to a small group discussion about the work that immigrants do and the low pay they receive. According to Lupe, Eddie has provoked her and his other groupmates by claiming, "that Mexicans are taking up all of the jobs" (line 9). She responds in defense of people of her ethnicity by stating that, "U.S. citizens are just lazy" (line 16). Note that Lupe and Juan are immigrants from Mexico, while Amalia's mother is a Mexican immigrant. I also note that

Excerpt 11.2: Critical Student Agency in Small Groups during CM.

1	I walk over near Eddie, Lupe, Juan, and Amalia at left front of classroom.
2	Amalia (smiles at me): "We're having a discussion and you're not included."
3	Lupe (to me): "Yeah, we're discussing I …"
4	Lupe waits a second, apparently, for my undivided attention as I survey the room.
5	Lupe: "This is important!"
6	Me (smiling): "Okay."
7	Lupe (points to Eddie): "He brought up a good thing—a good point."
8	Me (to Lupe): "What'd he say?"
9	Lupe: "He thinks that Mexicans are taking up all of th[e"
10	Amalia: "[Immigrants period!"
11	Lupe (points to Amalia): "Yeah!"
12	Lupe looks up and smiles at me.
13	Me: "Yeah. That's something we won't—I don't think we're gonna be able to get
14	quite with our mathematics. But we're going to be able to compare [Mexico to"
15	Lupe: "[And I was saying
16	that that's not true. It's just that U. S. citizens are just la-azy!"
17	Amalia, Lupe, Juan, and I laugh.
18	Eddie (a Puerto-Rican American): "You forgot to mention the work we do."
19	Lupe (looks at Eddie smiling): "Which is nothing! You don't do nothing!"
20	More laughs.

Juan generally opposes my inclusion of CM activities in the course and does not contribute much to this discussion even though he appears to listen to his groupmates. Eddie is Puerto-Rican American and does not see himself or his relatives as immigrants or, at least, he conveys that he does not put himself in the same ethnic category (or immigrant status) as Mexican-American students. In another CM conversation, Eddie provoked his Mexican heritage groupmates when he jokingly bragged that Puerto Ricans do not have to swim or take boats to mainland United States because they have U.S. citizenship.

As a critical educator, I want the CM project on economic inequality to be relevant to the lived experiences of all of my students; however, the economic data (i.e., income inequality as measured by quintiles of documented wage earners) I collected for the class to work with over the next few days do not include data on immigrants. While I encourage students such as Lupe to discuss the work that immigrants do and the low pay that many earn, my curriculum design work suggested that making the mathematical component of the CM project more culturally relevant to all students by matching the data with their ethnic background was not easy. To my knowledge, the extant distribution of income data—readily available online—simply does not include data on immigrants. More generally, my experiences with CM curriculum design lead me to conclude that it is difficult, if not impossible, to find real-world examples that are both mathematically appropriate and culturally relevant to all students in a diverse classroom (Brantlinger, 2007). I believe I would not feel as constrained by the required curriculum and the fear of content irrelevancy if I were a sociology or history teacher. As a secondary mathematics teacher, however, I am concerned that the political questions, and the discussions they elicit, divert students' attention from the mathematical-learning goals of the course.

My apologetic response to Lupe: "That's something I don't think we'll be able to get to quite with our mathematics" (lines 13 and 14), shows that I feel inhibited as a critical teacher by the required secondary mathematics curriculum. At the same time, I encourage students to discuss political issues that are important to them even if the connection to secondary mathematics is weak. As might be noted, despite my apologies about the rigidity of secondary mathematics, Lupe and her groupmates seem unfazed. Lupe gets my attention by stating, "this is important!" (line 5). Shortly thereafter, Lupe asserts her opinion that, "U.S. citizens are just lazy!" (line 16). Lupe is clearly enthusiastic about the chance to discuss immigration and does not seem to care if the mathematics content that she is required to learn is included in the CM lesson that day. Her enthusiasm indicates the degree of ownership over the critical discussion that many Guevara students have in such CM activities. Although her tone was joking and friendly, Amalia challenges my institutional authority to make classroom decisions during politicized discussions by playfully stating: "We're having a discussion and you're not included" (line 2). These actions indicate the ownership that some students feel over some critical topics.

As Amalia indicates, mathematical conversations never seem to be "theirs" while some critical activities, though certainly not all, could be. Additionally, though it is not apparent from these excerpts, Guevara students also often use a vernacular register during CM activities that signal a degree of ownership that they do not exhibit during standards-based activities (Brantlinger, 2007). The differences in student engagement may be the result of my students' exposure to years of traditional mathematics instruction that positions them as passive mathematics learners. Standards-based mathematics signal school as a way that CM activities do not. In interviews and through classroom participation, Guevara students assert that mathematical knowledge should flow through me, the teacher, despite my attempts to reposition them more authoritatively with respect to the creation and evaluation of mathematical ideas (Brantlinger, 2007). I also believe tracking has diminished my students' self-efficacy about, and engagement in, school mathematics (Oakes, 2005).

SIMULATING THE DISTRIBUTION OF U.S. INCOME

The transcript reported in Excerpt 11.3 covers a discussion that came approximately 30 minutes later in the same CM lesson. After the initial discussions presented in Excerpts 11.1 and 11.2, I sorted students into five quintile groups and distribute candy to these groups in a way that models the inequities in the 2001 U.S. distribution of income (what I call a "modeling activity"). This activity provokes both enthusiastic and critical reactions from students (see Brantlinger, 2007). Following the modeling activity, I request that students discuss why and how wealthy people support and justify this level of economic inequality. Excerpt 11.3 comes several minutes into this discussion.

Excerpt 11.3: Critical Whole Class Discussion of Economic Fairness.

1	Lucee: "I think that it's not fair because—that if we—they give us like—okay, cause
2	some people don't have higher educations than other people because most people
3	they simply just don't have enough money. And they have either a large family or a
4	real small family that they gotta help out. Either you got someone at home that can't
5	work or whatever, or there's issues whatever and you gotta work so you can't go to
6	school."
7	Me: "Yeah."
8	Lucee: "So, all that stuff. But if someone gives like someone else like the
9	opportunity, and they develop the skills, they can just be as smart as anybody else
10	who went to school. They just didn't have all the time to do all that stuff that they
11	did."
12	Me: "Yeah."
13	Lucee (scrunches body and face up and looks at desk): "Yeah."
14	Me: "So, if you have less money, then you gotta spend more time working, and then
15	you can't go to school and stuff like that."
16	Lucee: "Yeah."
17	Stephie raises hand in back of room.
18	Me: "Okay, go ahead, Stephie."
19	Stephie: "Okay, I don't think that—(she points to Lucee) like she was saying that—if
20	you don't go to school you can't work. Because, like I'm going to use myself as an
21	example. Like I work, and I go to school, and even though I don't have my high
22	school diploma, I moved up little by little and I became manager. So, it's not that.
23	You just gotta push yourself forward, and you'll do it."

24	Me: "I think both you guys agree that you have to work harder than pe[[ople."
25	Stephie: "[[It's not that
26	hard. I don't think it's that much harder."
27	Kampton: "But, for a person with strong willpower [that person …"
28	Efrain: "[I believe that everything you get –
29	everything you want, you need to work hard for it."
30	Robi (has hand raised): "Yeah."
31	Kampton: "Or, kiss a lot of ass."
32	Efrain: "Yep."
33	Me: "Next, huh ah. I mean I'll be honest—well, I'll take that up another time (to
34	Efrain). Remember you said that."
35	Lupe: "What [[comes easy, goes easy."
36	Robi: "[[Mister B. I think, in a way, it is fair, that like rich people get more.
37	Because if you went that extra step, to be [like a higher education or something."
38	Princess: "[But some people get it from their
39	parents!"
40	Shannon: "Right!"
41	Robi: "You deserve more than somebody who didn't take that extra step or use it."
42	Princess: "Okay, but [[some people inherit."
43	Shannon: "[[if you're born rich you …"
44	Me: "Yeah, did you take—I mean so—if you're born to be rich did you [take an extra
45	step?"
46	Amalia:
47	going to stay rich."
48	Robi: "But, if you're already born to, then what's the point of working hard any
49	more?"
50	A number of students talk over each other at this point.
51	Lucee: "If any—well you know what he's talking about. If you took that extra
52	step. There's people who wanna take that extra step!"
53	Shannon: "Right!"
54	Lucee: "But they don't really have the opportunity. They can't [it's not really
55	their decision [[they have to go."
56	Efrain:
57	[[it's really their way of life."

58	Lucee (turns towards Efrain): "**You just, <u>fucked</u> up!** saying that."
59	Lucee then covers her mouth, turns back towards me at front, and smiles.
60	Many students laugh.
61	Me: "Nah, I mean. I definitely hear what you're saying—besides the f-word there –
62	the rest of what you're saying."

The discussion reported in Excerpt 11.3 illustrates the three results of CM outlined earlier. First, though the changes are not transparent in this short discussion, Excerpt 11.3 illustrates a shift of the students who now participate and their engagement in critical activities. Lucee, Kampton, and Efrain regularly resist participating fully in standards-based activities; however, they exhibit considerable critical agency in this whole class discussion. Not only do they participate voluntarily, but their contributions are also far more elaborate than they have been in whole class discussions of standards-based mathematics tasks to date. Moreover, this excerpt points to a shift in the orientation of some students toward CM. In week 2, Lucee called a CM lesson "goofy" while Efrain asserted that, "it's not what we're here for." Both students refused to participate meaningfully in earlier CM activities, whereas they both are engaged in this CM discussion.

Second, in terms of students' discourse models for social inequality, Lucee takes up a counter-hegemonic position when she argues that there are structural factors that limit the life chances of students from low SES backgrounds, and includes herself in this category. Stephie disagrees with Lucee when she invokes a more hegemonic model stating; "If you push yourself forward, you can do it" (line 23). Stephie's argument recreates the hegemonic, status quo argument "that anyone who works hard will make it." Perhaps because Stephie's message is more hopeful, many of the Guevara students support it. For them, any degree of mobility requires a positive attitude and a good work ethic. They were not born rich and would not have things handed to them. Perhaps their contributions reflect that social reality rather than the lack of critical consciousness of the unfairness of their circumstances when they compare themselves to their affluent suburban counterparts. In the discussion that ensues, a smaller number of students (e.g., Lucee, Shannon, and Princess) and I support the counter-hegemonic position, while Stephie and the majority of the participants argue from the hegemonic position.

STUDENT INTERVIEWS: MIXED STUDENT REACTION TO CRITICAL MATHEMATICS

Interviews with students confirm what I had observed while teaching: Guevara student reaction to CM was mixed, with some supporting it, some actively resisting it. The most resistant students told me that they did not see CM as school mathematics. Many Guevara students were in the middle, a more subtle but powerful form of student resistance that I faced as a CM teacher. A similar situation surfaced when I taught CM at another Chicago secondary school in the summer of 2004. In this class, a handful of students shared their appreciation of my critical themes and asked me, "Why don't we study [critical themes] in school?" Other students at this second school told me, "You should have become a history teacher" rather than a mathematics teacher given my desire to discuss politicized content in schools.

Interviews with Guevara students also indicate that the inclusion of CM activities changed—or at least reinforced—student opinions about the real-world relevance and utility of school mathematics. Consider this post-interview with two Guevara students conducted by the researcher who worked with Guevara science teachers:

Jaime: "And what I like about Mr. B. (the author) is that he did not only use math, well, he **did** use math in every subject."
Ana: "He used, like, charts and stuff."
Jaime: "He used charts, statistics, and all that—of how income works. And how it is in the United States, and how it is in Mexico. He would compare stuff like that."
Ana: "Yeah, the value of the money that you use."
... [a bit later in the interview] ...
Interviewer: "So what is math and where does it come from?"
Jaime: "Well, like I said, math is a tool. Basically it came back, I think it comes from way back. I think it's ancient. It's, I think that it's a way of how they survived in the past. You know. Cause they used math in real survival because of the fact that like how I told you before Mr. B. always used like, this income tax of how to divide things in categories. Like low-income high-income. And I think that it was their source of planning how, how much food you're gonna get individually. And I think that's how they used the math, in the back, in ancient times."

Hence, my CM activities apparently reinforced the idea that secondary mathematics is a "tool" subject that is broadly relevant to important economic and political issues. To be clear, while this was one of my goals as a CM educator, I have come to question whether such utilitarianism is wholly beneficial or appropriate. While some mathematics may be practical, the academic mathematics that colleges value was developed for intellectual, as opposed to manual, disciplinary reasons (D'Ambrosio, 1997). As discussed at the outset of this chapter, vocational mathematics works to instill similar practical beliefs about school mathematics. I return to this theme in the discussion section at the end of this chapter.

While students such as Jaime and Ana discussed CM activities in a positive light, a handful of Guevara students never seemed to approve of CM. Two high achieving students, Juan and Sonny, stated such things as, "this is not mathematics" about CM toward the end of the course as they and others had earlier. Juan wrote the following in response to the CM activity presented here:

> I don't think you should teach these because we're wasting time studying things that it doesn't belong in this class. Instead of doing these you should teach us math equations that we have never studied. That's my point of view. I hope you don't take offense and lower my grade because that would be unfair. I'm just being honest. By the way, yes, I like the [standards-based] work that you give us but I don't like this [CM] kind of work. I told you before. (January 21, 2003)

While I am sympathetic to Juan's perspective—actually tend to mostly agree with him after conducting my study—it also might be that critical activities posed a threat to the students, such as Juan and Sonny, who enjoyed comparatively high academic status in the night course classroom. Regardless of the motives behind such criticism of CM content, relatively strong opposition of this kind from the academically strongest students made teaching CM stressful and difficult too for me to manage—something I was not used to as an experienced urban secondary math teacher.

DISCUSSION: THE PROBLEMATIC PROMISE OF CRITICAL MATHEMATICS

In this chapter, I have attempted to show the promise of CM to prompt critical financial literacy among students, while raising awareness of dilemmas with the idea that secondary mathematics be reconceived as a critical literacy. Though imperfect, there were many positive outcomes to CM at Guevara. Issues of economic fairness and racism resonated with several students who previously had been disengaged in standards-based activities. Elaborated student contributions and the use of vernacular social language suggest that many students felt ownership over CM topics in ways that they did not in standards-based mathematics activities.

However, despite some encouraging results related to CM instruction, it is unclear whether teachers can simultaneously meet critical and mathematical goals in secondary mathematics. Although I designed the featured activities to motivate the need for subsequent mathematical analyses, the critical activities featured here were nonmathematical.

After conducting my study, I have come to believe that teachers can parse CM activities into politically oriented activities that are essentially independent from the mathematics components. While political discussions may serve to motivate subsequent mathematical analyses, critical discussions do little to further understandings of secondary mathematics. Nor did the activities featured here serve as a bridge into mathematics involvement. On the other hand, the mathematical components of CM projects did not do much to raise my students' critical consciousness of economic unfairness. Computing a mathematical measure of economic inequality (i.e., the Gini coefficient) tells very little about how people experience economic inequality. My low SES students lived economic inequality and, for the most part, using school mathematics to deepen their understandings of historic inequities seemed unconvincing to them.

An analysis of my planned CM curriculum further supports my claim that critical content displaces mathematics content (Brantlinger, 2007). The displacement of mathematics was not my intention as a critical curriculum designer and teacher. I was disappointed with this result, in large part, because it ran counter to theoretical discussions of CM that imply much more critical and mathematical cohesion. For instance, the CM advocate Gutstein (2003) describes the symbiotic relationship between critical and mathematical goals this way:

> Reading the world with mathematics means to use mathematics to understand relations of power, resource inequities, and disparate opportunities between different social groups and to understand explicit discrimination based on race, class, gender, language, and other differences. ... I tried to help my students learn how to do this by having them complete real-world projects in which mathematics was the primary analytical tool. (p. 45)

After conducting my own study, I have become wary of claims that CM can be mathematically and politically powerful at the same time. Gutstein (2005) is more concerned with middle school mathematics where academic displacement may pose less of a problem than it does in more advanced mathematics programs.

Finally, in focusing on use-values for subordinated students, CM shares problematic assumptions with vocational mathematics courses described at the outset of this paper. Both stress the utility of school mathematics in maximizing the quality of people's everyday activities. However, just as the focus on use-values in the vocational curriculum translates into a loss of mathematical exchange-value (e.g., credentials), CM advocates have similarly ignored (or glossed over) the credentialing role of nonutilitarian school mathematics content. Colleges require students to learn mathematics that, put simply, is not particularly useful outside of the discipline of mathematics (e.g., angle sums of polygons). In ignoring the gatekeeper role of school mathematics, CM advocates run the risk of creating dead-end courses similar to vocational courses. This is particularly problematic given the fact that CM is theorized with low SES students of color in mind.

CONCLUSION

Rather than attack the related practices of tracking and curriculum differentiation that exacerbate school inequality (Oakes, 2005), advocates of critical and vocational mathematics create a real-world useful, and markedly distinctive, mathematics curriculum for students who are largely lower SES students or of color. They cite the irrelevance and elitism inherent in college preparatory mathematics as justification and proceed to read considerable differences (e.g., in learning styles, in future social, political, and economic positions) onto students from subordinated communities.

For these reasons, I cannot support Gutstein's (2005) goal of reconceptualizing school mathematics as a critical literacy. However, I do support the inclusion of critical pedagogy in the general school curriculum for *all* students. For reasons that are beyond the scope of this paper (see Dowling, 1998; Steen, 2004), the inclusion of critical real-world relevant material in subjects such as history and literature does not come at the same price that it does in mathematics. One important reason, however, is that Neo-Marxist and postmodern (critical) perspectives are valued in such disciplines.

While I voice concerns with CM, I generally support critical pedagogy. I believe it can disrupt harmful hegemonic curricular messages and practices promoted in many U.S. schools. It should be clear from this chapter that many of my students appreciated the opportunity to think critically about political issues that affected them. For some Guevara students, though certainly not all, political topics and discussions appeared more meaningful to them than school mathematics. Unfortunately, many students, low track students in particular, do not feel they are learning much of value in secondary mathematics (Brantlinger, 2007; Chazan, 2000; Romagnano, 1994). If we want students to learn material that is more relevant to their lives, we should rethink what secondary mathematics and how much of it we require all students to learn. However, as Steen (2004) notes, the power to change the mathematics curriculum is largely in the hands of university mathematics departments who require college freshman to have precalculus knowledge. Secondary mathematics teachers have little influence over college requirements. Individual activist mathematics teachers who stray far from the college preparatory curriculum put students at risk.

CHAPTER UPDATE

In 2016, the premise of this article—that secondary school mathematics as currently presented in schools is apart from the lives of students—is very much alive and well in the popular press and among scholars. Andrew Hacker is a professor emeritus of political science at Queens College, City University of New York and a prolific author. His latest best seller is called *The Math Myth: And Other STEM Delusions*. The central theme of the book is that advanced mathematics requirements, like algebra, trigonometry and calculus, are "a harsh and senseless hurdle" (p. 13) keeping far too many Americans from completing their basic education and achieving personal goals and productive lives. Hacker rejects the Common Core standards arguing instead for numeracy knowledge. This book has created a literal firestorm of the meaning, utility, and overall value of advanced mathematics in the lives of students.

QUESTIONS FOR DISCUSSION

1. Brantlinger states that he disagrees with critical mathematics, yet agrees with critical theory. To what extent do you consider numbers as representing absolute or relative concepts? How may your response relate to your interpretation of Brantlinger's position?
2. Students express mixed reactions to critical mathematics. How does the context of the learner account for the different views that they take?
3. Brantlinger's work describes discussions with students in a secondary classroom. To what extent may conversations, such as those that Brantlinger has with his students, be relevant in middle level classrooms? In elementary classrooms?
4. This book concerns the financial literacy of children and youth. How may a critical perspective of mathematics relate to understandings of personal finance?
5. Literature that concerns culturally responsive teaching describes the patterns of social judgment that develop based on patterns of language use. To what extent may differences in mathematics perspectives prompt social judgments? What examples can you think of?

NOTES

1. Dr. Brantlinger conducted his research for this study while affiliated with MetroMath at The CUNY Graduate Center.
2. Please note that in all of the excerpts the symbols "["and"[["indicate overlapping speech. For example, the exchange below would be interpreted as Tom beginning the "Hi Andrew" after Andy had started the "how" but before it ended. Andy: Hi Tom, ho[w
Tom: [Hi Andrew.

REFERENCES

Apple, M. (1992). Do the standards go far enough? Power, policy, and practice in mathematics education. *Journal for Research in Mathematics Education, 23*, 412–431.
Apple, M. (2001). *Educating the "right" way: Markets, standards, god, and inequality.* New York, NY: RoutledgeFalmer.
Brantlinger, A. (2007). *Geometries of inequality: Teaching and researching critical mathematics in a low-income urban high school* (Unpublished doctoral dissertation). Northwestern University, Evanston, IL.
Cazden, C. (2001). *Classroom discourse.* Portsmouth, NH: Heinemann.
Chazan, D. (2000). *Beyond formulas in mathematics and teaching: Dynamics of the high school algebra classroom.* New York, NY: Teachers College Press.
Cremin, L. (1964). *The transformation of the school.* New York, NY: Vintage Books.
D'Ambrosio, U. (1997). Ethnomathematics and its place in the history and pedagogy of mathematics. In A. B. Powell & M. Frankenstein (Eds.), *Ethnomathematics: Challenging Eurocentrism in mathematics education* (pp. 13–24). New York, NY: State University of New York Press.
Dowling, P. (1998). *The sociology of mathematics education: Mathematical myths/pedagogic texts.* London: Falmer Press.
Duranti, A. (1997). *Linguistic anthropology.* Cambridge, UK: Cambridge University Press.
Fine, M. (1991). *Framing dropouts: Notes on the politics of an urban high school.* Albany, NY: State University of New York Press.
Frankenstein, M. (1989). *Relearning mathematics: A different third R-radical maths.* London, UK: Free Association Books.
Frankenstein, M. (1991). Incorporating race, gender, and class issues into a critical mathematical literacy curriculum. *Journal of Negro Education, 59*, 336–359.
Frankenstein, M. (1995). Equity in mathematics education: Class in the world outside the class. In W. G. Secada, E. Fennema, & L. B. Adajian (Eds.), *New directions for equity in mathematics education* (pp. 165–190). Cambridge, UK: Cambridge University Press.
Freire, P. (1971). *Pedagogy of the oppressed* (M. B. Ramos, Trans.) New York, NY: Seabury Press.
Gee, J. P. (2005). *An introduction to discourse analysis: Theory and method.* London, UK: Routledge.
Gutiérrez, R. (2002). Enabling the practice of mathematics teachers in context: Towards a new equity research agenda. *Mathematical Thinking and Learning, 4*(2 and 3), 145–187.
Gutstein, E. (2003). Teaching and learning mathematics for social justice in an urban, Latino school. *Journal for Research in Mathematics Education, 34*(1), 37–73.
Gutstein, E. (2005). *Reading and writing the world with mathematics: Toward a pedagogy for social justice.* New York, NY: Routledge.
Hacker, A. (2016). *The math myth: And other STEM delusions.* New York, NY: New Press.
hooks, B. (1994). *Teaching to transgress: Education as the practice of freedom.* New York, NY: Routledge.
Kliebard, H. M., & Franklin, B. M. (2003). The ascendance of practical and vocational mathematics, 1893–1945: Academic mathematics under siege. In G. Stanic & J. Kilpatrick (Eds.), *A history of school mathematics* (Vol. 1, pp. 399–440). Reston, VA: National Council of Teachers of Mathematics.
Lipman, P. (2004). *High stakes education: Inequality, globalization, and urban school reform.* New York, NY: Routledge Falmer.
Mehan, H. (1979). *Learning lessons: Social organization in the classroom.* Cambridge, MA: Harvard University Press.

Merriam, S. B. (1998). *Qualitative research and case study applications in education.* San Francisco, CA: Jossey-Bass.
National Council of Teachers of Mathematics. (1970). *A history of mathematics education in the United States and Canada.* Washington, DC: National Council of Teachers of Mathematics.
National Council of Teachers of Mathematics. (2000). *Principles and standards for school mathematics.* Reston, VA: National Council of Teachers of Mathematics.
Niss, M. (1983). Considerations and experiences concerning integrated courses in mathematics and other subjects. In M. Zweng, T. Green, J. Kilpatrick, H. Pollack, & M. Suydam (Eds.), *Proceedings of the Fourth International Congress on Mathematical Education* (pp. 247–249). Boston, MA: Birkhäuser.
Oakes, J. (2005). *Keeping track: How schools structure inequality* (2nd ed.). New Haven, CT: Yale University Press.
Pruyn, M. (1999). *Discourse wars in Gotham-west: A Latino immigrant urban tale of resistance and agency.* Boulder, CO: Westview.
Romagnano, L. (1994). *Wrestling with change: The dilemmas of teaching real mathematics.* Portsmouth, NH: Heinemann.
Shor, I. (1996). *When students have power: Negotiating authority in a critical pedagogy.* Chicago, IL: The University of Chicago Press.
Skovsmose, O. (1994). *Towards a philosophy of critical mathematical education.* Dordrecht: Kluwer Academic Press.
Steen, L. A. (2004). *Achieving quantitative literacy: An urgent challenge for higher education.* Princeton, NJ: Mathematical Association of America.
Tate, W. F. (1995). Returning to the root: A culturally relevant approach to mathematics pedagogy. *Theory into Practice, 34*, 166–173.
Thorndike, E. L. (1926). *The psychology of algebra.* New York, NY: The Macmillan Company.
Turner, E., & Font Strawhun, B. T. (2005). With math, it's like you have more defense. In E. Gutstein & B. Peterson (Eds.), *Rethinking mathematics* (pp. 81–87). Milwaukee, WI: Rethinking Schools.
Williams, J., & Joseph, G. G. (1993). Statistics and inequality: A global perspective. In D. Newlson, G. G. Joseph, & J. Williams (Eds.), *Multicultural mathematics: Teaching mathematics from a global perspective* (pp. 175–204). New York, NY: Oxford Press.

CHAPTER TWELVE

Personal Finance Education FOR Young Children

Why Isn't It Happening? What Needs to Be Done?

BONNIE T. MESZAROS
University of Delaware

MARY C. SUITER[1]
Federal Reserve Bank of St. Louis

CASE FOR PERSONAL FINANCE EDUCATION

In 2013, the Financial Industry Regulatory Authority (FINRA) Investor Education Foundation in cooperation with the U.S. Department of the Treasury and the President's Advisory Council on Financial Capability conducted the second national study of American adults' financial capability. The study updated the benchmark key indicators from the 2009 study, evaluated how these financial capabilities vary with demographic, behavioral, attitudinal, and financial literacy characteristics, and explored other topics, such as student loans and medical debt. The results of the 2012 study indicated that more Americans have "rainy day funds" and that the ability of Americans to make ends meet has improved since 2009. The results also indicate that the majority of Americans do not have money set aside for emergencies and are not planning for life events such as retirement. In addition, in 2012, more than two out of five of those surveyed paid only minimum balances on credit cards. Nearly one-third of those surveyed indicated that they borrowed from nonbank organizations, such as payday loan companies or pawn shops. And, although less than 14% of those surveyed were able to answer all five questions on the FINRA Investor Education Foundation financial literacy quiz correctly, nearly 75% of those surveyed had positive perceptions about their financial knowledge and their math skills, indicating possible overconfidence in their financial acumen.

The study also found that in general, measures of financial capability are much lower among: (1) younger Americans, (2) those with household incomes below $25,000 per year, and (3) those with no postsecondary education. In addition, the study results showed that African-Americans and Hispanics are more likely to be financially vulnerable and that women tend to have somewhat lower levels of financial capability than men.

Results such as these imply that Americans need help understanding personal finance content and issues and with making informed financial decisions. The financial decisions that individuals must make today are far more complex than simply opening a bank account and writing checks to pay bills. According to Eric Heckman (2015), in a society where pensions no longer exist, employees are on their own regarding their financial futures, and yet they have little education, training, or experience in the basics, much less the more sophisticated personal finance topics. Most high school and most college graduates graduate with little or no personal finance education. As a result, they are not equipped to make informed personal finance decisions.

Policy makers and academicians continue to draw attention to the benefits of financial education to individuals as well as to the economy as a whole. Two former Federal Reserve Chairs, Alan Greenspan (2001) and Ben Bernanke (2006a, 2006b), have emphasized the need for financial education to improve outcomes for individuals and for the economy overall. In a 2012 speech, then Federal Reserve Chair Bernanke stated, "As the recent financial crisis illustrates, consumers who can make informed decisions about financial products and services not only serve their own best interests, but collectively, they also help promote broader economic stability."

The idea that positive individual financial behavior benefits society as a whole was reinforced by the former Governor of the Federal Reserve System, Elizabeth Duke. She stated in a 2011 speech:

> Well-informed, financially educated consumers are in a better position to improve their economic security and well-being. In turn, these financially secure families are also better able to contribute to thriving communities and thereby further foster community economic development. And, as these communities thrive, the marketplace as a whole becomes more effective and efficient. Clearly, life-long financial education and the ready availability of decision-making tools and assistance are essential to this process. (2011)

Both President George W. Bush and President Barrack Obama drew attention to the importance of financial literacy by establishing advisory councils on the topic. In their 2014 study, Anna Maria Lusardi and Olivia Mitchell (2014) provide evidence through their research that these policy makers are correct—individuals' personal financial decision-making has an impact on the overall economy. Personal finance education is critical for the future of individuals and the economy as a whole; thus it requires the efforts of schools and parents.

STATUS OF K–12 FINANCIAL LITERACY EDUCATION

Since the 2007–2009 financial crisis, policy makers, politicians, business owners, and advocacy groups have stressed the importance of a more financially literate society. To reach the goal of a financially literate society, these groups have advocated for inclusion of personal finance in the K–12 curriculum believing that students well-grounded in personal finance when they leave high school will make better decisions as consumers, borrowers, and savers. The Consumer Financial Protection Bureau's Director, Richard Cordray, agrees. He stated, "Financial education in our schools is critical to the financial well-being of future generations" (2015a, 2015b).

Yet, the growth of financial education in America's schools and the impact of financial education over the past decade have not been promising. The Council for Economic Education conducts a survey of economic and personal finance education every two years. The current Survey of the States (Council for Economic Education, 2016) shows that growth of personal finance education in America's schools has stalled. In 2016, 45 states have K–12 standards for personal finance but only 37 of these states require that the standards be implemented. This is only a slight increase over the 2014 survey. Twenty-two states require that a personal finance class be offered but only 17 states require that a high school course in personal finance be taken and even fewer, seven states, have a standardized test for personal finance. Having standards and requiring courses be offered does not necessarily lead to a change in student knowledge or their capabilities. To ensure that personal finance courses are taught, cover meaningful content, and use quality instructional materials may require that students are tested at the state level.

Champlain College's Center for Financial Literacy's 2015 National Report Card on State Efforts to Improve Financial Literacy in High Schools analyzed data from a variety of sources and gave states a financial literacy grade based on graduation requirements, educational standards, state mandates, and assessment policies. The most recent report showed a growth in states that received a "B," going from 13 states in 2013 to 20 in 2015. These states required that personal finance topics be taught to all students as a graduation requirement but left the implementation to the local districts. In spite of an increasing number of states receiving a "B" grade, 26 states still received a "C" or lower (Center for Financial

Literacy, 2015). It is clear that more needs to be done to ensure that all students graduating from high school are educated in personal finance.

The impact of this lack of knowledge on adult personal finance behaviors continues to be discouraging. A recent survey of 140 economies found that the United States ranked 14th, tied with Switzerland, with 57% of the adult population considered to be financially literate (Klapper, Lusardi, & Van Oudheusden, 2015). Two areas of concern frequently in the news are student loan debt and savings for retirement. The Consumer Financial Protection Bureau released a finding that federal student loan debt had surpassed $1 trillion and that 7 million borrowers were in default on a federal or private student loan (Chopra, 2013). The Government Accountability Office's 2013 Survey of Consumer Finances found that in households age 55 and older, about half had no retirement savings (Government Accountability Office, 2016). With the increase in complexity of financial products and the increased responsibility of individuals for their own financial security, financial education is vital.

SUCCESS OF FINANCIAL EDUCATION IN THE K–12 CLASSROOMS

The Organization for Economic Cooperation and Development (OECD, 2014) conducted its first assessment on personal finance in 2012. The PISA (Programme for International Student Assessment) was designed to determine the proficiency of 15-year-old students in demonstrating and applying personal finance knowledge and skills, learned in and out of school. Eighteen countries participated and the United States did not fare well. It ranked ninth.

However, several studies have shown the positive impact of financial education on student learning when certain factors are in place. Asarta, Hill, and Meszaros (2014) looked at students who took the high school personal finance course, Keys to Financial Success. They concluded that teacher training combined with the use of a well-designed curriculum significantly improved the average personal finance knowledge of students. Other studies showed increases in student knowledge if they are taught by trained teachers using a particular curriculum package or program (Harter & Harter, 2012; Walstad, Rebeck, & MacDonald, 2010). Swinton, DeBerry, Scafidi, and Woodard (2007) found that in Georgia, high school students whose teachers attended personal finance workshops did better on a statewide assessment than students of teachers who did not attend. Furthermore, the more workshops teachers took the greater gains their students made on statewide assessments.

Fewer studies have been conducted with younger children and many are smaller in scope. However, they all show positive results. Larry Senesh was a leader in developing instructional materials for young children, grades 1–6. Using Senesh's first grade materials, *Our Working World: Families at Work* (1963), Larkins and Shaver (1969) found that students who were exposed to economics using these materials performed better on economics tests than first graders not exposed to economic instruction. Other studies drew similar conclusions. Students taught by trained teachers using quality materials demonstrate statistically significant gains in economic knowledge (Kourilsky, 1977; Laney, 1989; Morgan, 1991). More recently, studies have been conducted specifically looking at the impact of the use of personal finance curriculum in the elementary classroom on student knowledge gains. Berti and Monaci (1998), using interviews, found that young students who received 20 hours of instruction about banks not only learned more than students in the control group but also retained that knowledge when interviewed four months later. Other studies that used personal finance lessons also concluded that young children can and do learn personal finance concepts in the early grades through middle school (Butt, Haessler, & Schug, 2008; Grody, Grody, Kromann, & Sutliff, 2008; Harter & Harter, 2009; Sherraden, Johnson, Guo, & Elliott, 2011; Suiter, 2006). More recently, Hagedorn, Schug, and Suiter (2016) found that participation in a six-hour Money Savvy Kids program taught by teacher-librarians who were given access to a self-study training program and online training session positively affected third graders' attitudes and knowledge about spending, saving and investing money.

Studies focusing on financial capabilities at the K–12 level are limited. Bernheim, Garrett, and Maki (2001) found that states with mandates for financial education saw an increase in the rate at which the students from these states saved and accumulated wealth as adults. In a 2015 FINRA-sponsored study (Urban, Schmeiser, Collins, & Brown, 2015), researchers selected three states, Georgia, Idaho and Texas, that had implemented financial education mandates after 2000. They compared the credit behaviors of young adults in these states with credit behaviors of young adults in a bordering state that did not have mandated personal finance requirements. Three years after personal finance education was implemented, young adults had improved credit scores and lower credit delinquency rates than young adults in the adjacent states. After further analysis, the researchers concluded that Georgia, Idaho, and Texas had well-planned, rigorous financial education courses that were carefully implemented and that assessed students. This indicates that the type of mandate matters and has possible implications for state educational policies. This study offers promising guidelines for states striving to not only improve student knowledge but also student capabilities.

Not everyone agrees that personal finance education in the schools is necessary. Willis (2008, 2011) argues that mandated personal finance education does not work. However, the authors of this chapter would argue that few, if any, states have implemented a K–12 spiraling curriculum with a capstone course and analyzed the results in terms of both financial knowledge gained and financial capabilities. A study of undergraduate freshmen at the University of Arizona followed students from first year of college to young adulthood. Soyeon and Serido (2011) found that the more financial education the students had before college and received in college along with repeated exposure to financial concepts, both formal and informal, resulted in the most powerful contributions to financial capability. This approach lends support to establishing a scope and sequence beginning in the early grades and continuing with increased sophistication through the grades much as other school subjects do.

THE CASE FOR STARTING EARLY

Personal finance, like other subjects, should be taught beginning in the early grades and expanded upon as students move through the grades, for a variety of reasons. Young children make economic decisions on a daily basis, including consumer choices involving spending, saving, and even borrowing (Suiter & Meszaros, 2005). In fact, children between the ages of 6 and 12 have more than a trillion dollars in buying power (Robinson, 2012).

Children recognize at an early age that they can't have everything they want but don't understand why. When asked why they must make choices, they often respond that someone else is prohibiting them from getting everything they want or that when they become adults choices will no longer be a problem (Meszaros & Suiter, 1998). Further, recent research indicates that children form their ideas about spending and saving as early as seven (Whitebeard & Bingham, 2013). In a 1991 study, Walstad and Schug found that students' economic ideas are often based on misconceptions. As a result, these misconceptions are difficult to change later in the students' careers and their misperceptions persist even if economics is taught. These results combined with those of Whitebeard and Bingham (2013) indicate that our students need knowledge and skills at an early age to help them make informed decisions about managing their money and to help them develop healthy financial habits.

When asked if personal finance is something every student should know, the response of elementary teachers and administrators is overwhelmingly positive (Way & Holden, 2010). Way and Holden (2010) found that teachers believe that understanding basic concepts of spending and saving, setting savings goals, earning income, and making choices is important and helps young children to navigate and make sense of their daily lives. Yet, most elementary schools devote limited time to social studies which includes economics and personal finance. When asked why, the primary reason is lack of time in the school day (Fitchett, Heafner, & VanFossen, 2014). There just isn't enough time to teach all that is currently required due to high-stakes testing that places greater emphasis on math, English/language arts, and science (Heafner & Fitchett, 2012; VanFossen, 2005). Since social studies at the K–5 level is under-tested (Fitchett & Heafner, 2010), many teachers integrate social studies into the English language arts (ELA) curriculum (Heafner & Fitchett, 2012). The effectiveness of the integration approach varies ranging from effective curricula (Field, Bauml, & Ledbetter, 2011) to curricula lacking substantive content and skills (Pace, 2011). This raises concerns about the effectiveness of relying on the integration approach for social studies instruction (Thornton & Houser, 1996; VanFossen, 2005). It is not unusual for elementary students to receive social studies instruction for fewer than 20 minutes per day (Thornton & Houser, 1996; VanFossen 2005). The result is little time for any one social studies content area let alone the addition of personal finance. The demands on the elementary classroom teacher are many and fitting personal finance into an already overcrowded curriculum seems daunting.

But, a scarcity of time in the elementary school day is not the only reason that personal finance is neglected. Teachers admit they feel uncomfortable teaching personal finance (Way & Holden, 2010). They lack an understanding of the content and therefore tend not to teach what they do not know. This is true across the grades. Loibl (2008) found that high school teachers are not prepared to teach a full range of personal finance topics and the content taught varied by the discipline. Loibl's survey included a short quiz given to teachers who taught in a variety of disciplines, such as business, family and consumer science, and social studies. Most teachers struggled. In a later study, Loibl and Fisher (2013) found that teachers who took a number of college level personal finance courses faced fewer challenges in teaching personal finance. These studies reinforce the need for topic-specific training for personal finance, business, and social studies teachers for topic-specific teachers. For the most part, social studies teachers do not receive training in personal finance. Elementary teachers may shy away from teaching personal finance because they feel unprepared. Yon and Passe (1990) found that during student teaching, preservice teachers received less social studies instruction than in other areas. This resulted in preservice teachers feeling inadequate. In some cases, cooperating teachers encouraged the preservice teachers to avoid teaching social studies in order to have more time to spend on teaching other subjects (Bolick, Adams, & Willox, 2010).

Way and Holden (2010) found similar results in their two-year study. They addressed the extent teachers felt competent and confident to teach personal finance. They found that in states that had adopted personal finance standards or guidelines, 63.8% of the teachers indicated they did not feel qualified to use their state's financial literacy standards and less than 20% felt very competent to teach personal finance. Only 37% of K–12 teachers had taken a college course in personal finance and even fewer, 11.6%, had taken a workshop on teaching personal finance.

When schools do decide to teach personal finance in the elementary grades, there are few financial resources to support these efforts. Unfortunately, even with personal finance mandates, states provide few, if any, funds to support the implementation. Therefore, schools and teachers search for free or inexpensive materials. There is a wide array of options. For example, the Jump$tart Coalition Clearing House lists nearly 1,000 financial education resources. These resources range from lesson plans, teacher guides, and books to videos, games, online materials, and other resources. Additional products are available from financial institutions, government agencies, and nonprofits.

Unfortunately, not all instructional materials are of equal quality. Many focus on insignificant or inaccurate content, such as needs and wants or writing a check. Some are not pedagogically sound because they include content at inappropriate grade levels or focus on lecture style content delivery. And still others promote a particular product from a financial institution or present a biased approach. Evaluating instructional materials is time consuming and a step that the individual classroom teacher may skip. This results in teachers relying on materials that may not be the most effective in teaching personal finance.

Most think that achieving the goal of a financially literate society rests in large part with the schools. In a study of teacher preparedness to teach personal finance, 89% of K–12 teachers agree that students should either take a financial education course or pass a competency test for high school graduation (Way & Holden, 2010). However, some think that financial literacy education belongs in the home. According to a New York Daily news article by Meredith Engel (2015), Bill Hardekopf, chief executive officer at lowcards.com, thinks that school-based financial education is important but that financial education is the responsibility of parents. Unfortunately, not all parents provide the necessary financial education. And, many parents do not demonstrate sound financial habits. The Charles Schwab 2011 Teen and Money Survey found that parent discussions about money didn't necessarily translate into knowledge of financial tools for children. And, when asked about topics that their parents discuss with them, children report that money management fell near the bottom along with conversations about sex, drugs, and alcohol.

These results were confirmed by the T. Rowe Price's 2016 Parents, Kid, and Money Survey. Only 15% of the 1,000 parents surveyed indicated they set aside a specific time to discuss financial topics with their kids. The remaining 85% talk with their kids for a few minutes as things come up. When the children were surveyed the results were almost identical to that of the parents. The survey also found that 71% of the parents were reluctant to discuss financial matters with their kids and 58% let kids make bad financial decisions so they can learn from their mistakes. Given these results, financial education cannot be left to parents or schools alone. Research shows that collaboration of parents, schools, and community leads to student success (Epstein, Coates, Salinas, Sanders, & Simon, 1997;

Jeynes, 2005, 2007; Shannon & Bylsmna, 2003). A similar cooperative effort may be a viable path to achieving a financially literate society.

Because so little time is available for teaching personal finance in the elementary grades, the infusion approach is seen by teachers, school administrators, and financial educators as the means for ensuring that young children receive social studies instruction that includes economics and personal financial (Good et al., 2010). Integrating personal finance into the curriculum seems like a reasonable solution. It provides a context for learning math and language arts. If this is the case, why is it so difficult for teachers to teach personal finance in a meaningful ways using integration? Good et al. (2010) found that 60% of teachers used integration to cover social studies content. Yet, the success of this approach is mixed (Field et al., 2011; Pace, 2011). The authors of this chapter often hear teachers rave about the professional development programs that use children's literature that incorporate language arts skills and math to teach personal finance. However, those teachers also say they can't implement these materials because they don't teach social studies—specifically economics and personal finance. They fail to see the connections.

Many free and inexpensive materials are available but most are stand-alone lessons or units and fail to show teachers how to integrate the lessons into other areas they are required to teach. Making connections across disciplines is difficult, especially for elementary teachers who have limited content knowledge in personal finance and limited time to plan or rewrite instructional materials. Therefore, as much as they might recognize the value of the personal finance materials presented during professional development opportunities or their professional learning communities, these lessons will not be taught unless teachers are provided instructional materials for math and language arts that use personal finance as the context for teaching these disciplines and spell out specifically how these help them address the standards their state or district expects them to teach.

Overcoming the Stumbling Blocks

Using quality instructional materials that provide rich instruction for students and that are accurate and unbiased is critical. Whether materials are free, inexpensive, or require a financial investment on the part of a school district, materials selected for classroom use need to be vetted before being put in the hands of teachers. One tool for selecting appropriate materials is a set of rubrics designed for use by school district teachers, or parents. These rubrics provide guidance for the selection process. Some questions these rubrics address are:

- Do the instructional tools employ sound pedagogical techniques?
- Is the economic and personal finance content accurate?
- Are the materials standards-based?

- Are they developmentally appropriate?
- Are they impartial in the treatment of concepts and areas of debate?
- Do they avoid the use of, or reference to, any particular financial product?

There are four rubrics, one each, for instructional packages, textbooks, stand-alone lessons, and an additional category which includes podcasts, videos, computer games, online courses, and workbooks. These are available on the National Association of Economic Educators website (http://www.naee.net/curriculum_info.shtml). The site also includes a glossary of personal finance and economic terms for judging content accuracy. The glossary is helpful to teachers, administrators, or parents who may not be familiar with some of the concepts.

Another evaluation tool, Youth Financial Education Curriculum Review Tool, was developed by the Consumer Financial Protection Bureau. The Curriculum Review Tool is designed to help evaluators review and compare financial education curricula across four key dimensions—content: knowledge and skills covered in the curriculum and how well they align with national standards; utility: guidance for using curriculum; quality: accuracy and presentation of materials and efficacy: impact of the curriculum on students. It can be accessed at http://www.consumerfinance.gov/reports/youth-financial-education-curriculum-review-tool/.

Districts and schools often struggle to determine what personal finance content is appropriate to teach at various grade levels. The *National Standards for Financial Literacy* (Council for Economic Education (CEE), 2013) can provide guidance when developing a spiraling curriculum. The document has six standards: Earning Income, Buying Goods and Services, Saving, Using Credit, Financial Investing, and Protecting and Insuring. They are purposely written using nontechnical language so they can be taught by teachers who are not trained in personal finance or economics. A copy of the standards can be downloaded at http://councilforeconed.org/wp/wp-content/uploads/2013/02/national-standards-for-financial-literacy.pdf.

The reality is that parents and schools need to work together to achieve the goal of a financially literate society. There is a body of education research that supports the connection between parents and schools in achieving education goals. Research shows that parental involvement in their children's learning positively affects their children's performance in both primary and secondary schools (Jeynes, 2005, 2007; Jordan, Snow, & Porsche, 2000). Although this research isn't specific to personal finance, it has implications for engaging parents in helping students understand their finances. The current classroom environment places many demands on teachers' time, and creating a meaningful program for parents and their children may seem an overwhelming task (Ingram, Wolfe, & Lieberman, 2007). However, there is much evidence that establishing home and school connections reaps benefits for students. And, we need to begin early—we do not wait until high school to teach students other challenging content, such as mathematics and science. Yet, we wait to teach them personal finance—content that they need in their daily lives.

Critical to the success of parent/teacher partnerships is helping parents determine what to teach, how to teach it, and where to access materials either from the school or online. The Federal Reserve Bank of St. Louis has parent pages linked to a number of children's books. These activities and questions are designed specifically for parents to use when reading popular children's books with their children. As teachers use the personal finance lessons linked to these books, they can send home the parent pages and encourage parents to use the questions and answers to reinforce what is being covered in the classroom. These lessons and parent questions are available at https://stlouisfed.org/education.

To help parents and teachers identify personal finance and economic concepts in popular children's books, Hopkins and Gallagher (2003), authors of *Spotting Economics: From Africa to Ice Cream (http://www.econ-fun.com/)* developed a set of questions that can be used to initiate discussions on a particular concept. We have provided a list of revised sample questions that parents and teachers can use to identify and teach personal finance concepts. Each concept is underlined.

Did anyone experience <u>scarcity</u> (when wants exceed resources available)?

- Did anyone/is anyone making a <u>choice</u>?
- What is the <u>opportunity cost</u> (the highest-valued alternative given up) of the choice made?
- Were any <u>tradeoffs</u> made (someone gave up a little of something to get a little more of something else)?
- Was <u>money</u> used to make exchanges?
- Were people <u>saving</u> (not spending)?
- Did anyone have a <u>savings goal</u>?
- Did people earn <u>income</u> for work they performed?
- Were <u>investments in human capital</u> made (efforts to improve the education, experience or skills a person has)?
- Did someone <u>borrow and/or lend</u> money?

Several websites offer parents insights into teaching their children about personal finance and provide materials. Teachers can encourage parents to check out these sites as they are teaching specific personal finance concepts with their students. These sites offer material that satisfied the criteria in the rubrics previously mentioned.

The Federal Deposit Insurance Corporation's *Money-Smart—A Financial Education Program* (https://www.fdic.gov/consumers/consumer/moneysmart/young/html) includes Parent/Caregiver Guides in English and Spanish for grade clusters from Pre-K to 12. These include conversation starters and depending on the grade level, activities to do at home, family activities, children's books, articles, and links to online resources, tools, games and apps. The Consumer Financial Protection Bureau also offers links to materials and activities for Pre-K through young adulthood (http://www.consumerfinance.gove/parents/). Parents will find the site useful for ideas to develop a dialogue with their children about money and for lessons on savings, making choices, and debt.

The Mint provides parent information, ways to initiate parent/child conversations about money, and suggestions on how to model financially responsible behaviors for children (www.themint.org). Two ebooks, *Financial Fitness for Life Parent Guides*, one for K–5 and one for 6–12 (Whaley, 2011), are available on the EconEdLink website (http://www.econedlink.or/afterschool/parent-resource.php). These are companions to the *Financial Fitness for Life* curriculum packages for grades K–2 (Wright, 2010) and 3–5 (Reiser, 2010). The parent guides offer teachers suggestions, activities, and reading lists to send home so parents can reinforce what is taught in the classroom.

The infusion approach seems to be the answer to weaving personal finance into the elementary school day. Fitchett et al. (2014) found that teachers spent more time on social studies when it was integrated into ELA instruction. To do this, teachers need instructional materials that clearly point out how spending class time on a particular personal finance concept is also helping students master a Common Core, state or district ELA standard in a meaningful way. Reviewing materials to insure they meet this goal is critical. Too often, publishers and authors say a lesson addresses a Common Core standard but on further inspection it is really a word match. There are several good sources for lessons that incorporate language arts or math, teach personal finance, and satisfy the criteria of the rubrics of the National Association of Economic Educators and the Consumer Financial Protection Bureau. A few of these are highlighted here.

The Federal Reserve Bank of St. Louis (www.stlouisfed.org/education) has an extensive list of children's books with lessons that teach personal finance and address Common Core State Standards and most have question and answers for parents, and whiteboard applications. The lessons described here all have connections to ELA or math as well as the *National Standards for Financial Literacy* (CEE, 2013).

Alexander Who Used to be Rich Last Sunday by Judith Viorst—Alexander receives a dollar from his grandparents and he plans to save it for a walkie-talkie. Unfortunately, he spends it all, a little at a time on gum, a snake rental, fines, and other small items. The lesson teaches about saving, savings goals, and spending. The students practice counting to 100 by 2s, learn that 100 pennies equals a dollar, and create and analyze bar graphs. They discuss Alexander's choices and give advice on how he could save his money to reach his goal.

Less than Zero by Stuart Murphy—Perry the penguin is trying to save nine claims to buy a scooter. His friends entice him to borrow money for a ticket for the ice circus. Perry borrows, finds, earns, and loses clams, and learns valuable lessons about money. In the lesson students use a line graph to track Perry's spending and borrowing. They also write a paragraph describing the advice Perry should give to other penguins who are thinking of borrowing clams to buy something they want.

Uncle Jed's Barbershop by Margaree King Mitchell—the story is about an African-American barber who is saving to buy his own barbershop. Along the way he uses his savings to pay for his niece's operation and suffers further loss when his bank closes during the Great Depression. Ultimately, much later in life he reaches his goal. The lesson teaches about saving, savings goals, opportunity cost, and segregation. Students play a card game and solve problems using multiplication.

Just Saving My Money by Mercer Meyer—Little Critter wants a skateboard. His father tells him he must save his money. Little Critter earns income and saves his money. Eventually he reaches his goal only to change his mind and buys a robot dinosaur. Students learn about saving, savings goals, and income. They use clues from the text and pictures to answer questions. They play a game that requires writing math sentences to determine if they have met their savings goals. They also draw a picture and write a sentence about a personal savings goal and how they can earn income to achieve their goals.

Something from Nothing by Phoebe Gilman—Joseph's grandfather makes him a blanket. Eventually the blanket becomes a coat, then a vest, tie, handkerchief, and a button. Each time the grandfather makes a new item students identify the opportunity cost, what was given up, and cut out the item. In a supplemental math lesson they make a tangram of the jacket. Students deconstruct the tangram as each item grandfather makes is identified in the story. They identify the number of sides, three, four or five, each piece has to create a bar graph and interpret their findings.

$martPath (http://www.smartpath.online/) is an online resource for teachers of grades 1–6. The units have lessons that teach about financial responsibility covering such concepts as saving, spending, financial decision-making, and budgeting. All lessons are mapped to the core standards for math, the Ohio Learning Standards and Jump$tart National Standards in K-12 Personal Finance Education. Units include multiple lessons each with interactives, pre and post assessments, review and homework assignments.

Money as You Learn (http://www.moneyasyoulearn.org/) is an online resource that provides educators with tools to infuse personal finance into their teaching of Common Core State Standards. Teachers can search by grade clusters, K–2, 3–5, 6–8, and 9–12, and then refine their search to view by grade appropriate tasks and lessons for ELA or math. The lessons and tasks are designed to teach personal finance using real-world contexts and applications that are required by the Common Core. They also enhance problem-solving and research skills.

Kiddynomics, An Economics Curriculum for Young Learners (https://www.stlouisfed.org/education/kiddynomics-an-economics-curriculum-for-young-learners) is a series of six lessons designed for PreK/K students. The lessons are designed to teach personal finance/economics using children's books and integrate kindergarten readiness skills such as categorizing objects, counting, and letter recognition. Active learning strategies encourage students to ask and answer questions, participate in group discussions and build vocabulary. Lessons also include songs, dramatic play, and art.

CONCLUSION

The Great Recession served as a wake-up call regarding the need for a financially literate society. Policy makers and academic researchers point out that financial education benefits individuals and society as a whole. This has focused attention on the need for personal finance education in the schools—particularly in secondary schools—to achieve the goal of financial literacy or capability. However, successful implementation of personal finance in K–12 schools has been limited for a number of reasons: in general, teachers lack personal finance background, the quality of materials used to teach personal finance in K–12 classrooms varies, and not all states have adopted standards or guidelines in personal finance. In addition, when personal finance is required, it is often only in the high school. Yet, there's evidence that young children form their money habits early in their lives. So, it is important that we start early and build personal finance knowledge as we do with other disciplines in the school curriculum. Although educators and parents tend to agree that we should start early, we have not had great success in integrating personal finance into the K–8 grades, and a required high school course is not the norm throughout the country.

If we want to achieve the goal of a financial literate and financially capable society, there are several steps we must take. First, we must use the personal finance standards and benchmarks that have been developed to provide clear curriculum guidelines, and student assessment. Further, we need to provide teachers with training both during their preservice education and in subsequent professional development, so that they are comfortable teaching the content and prepared to use tools for evaluating personal finance curriculum materials for their classrooms. Research shows that students learn the content, when their teachers know the content and use high-quality classroom resources (Watts, 2005).

Using children's literature as a vehicle for blending economics and personal finance into language arts and math classes is one sensible way to address the overcrowded curriculum. Students have the opportunity to learn the content and make connections among disciplines, and it relieves the pressure teachers feel to carve time out for teaching one more discipline. In addition to integrating instruction into elementary classrooms, we need to continue instruction in middle school and complete personal finance instruction with a high school course.

However, we cannot rely solely on the schools if we want to ensure that students are financially literate. Involving parents can help achieve this goal. Research shows that parent involvement leads to student success at school (Jeynes, 2005, 2007; Jordan et al., 2000). Not only can parents reinforce the content taught at school, they can expand on it and provide students with opportunities to apply what they learn—opportunities that aren't available at school.

This chapter suggests some resources that are available to help teachers and parents address the urgent need for personal finance education that can help our citizens of the future make sound financial decisions that contribute to their well-being and the well-being of society as a whole.

QUESTIONS FOR DISCUSSION

1. Observe that personal financial habits appear to be established by age seven. To what extent are schools responsible for the habits of young children? To what extent are parents responsible? To what extent are the children responsible? How do your responses inform about the nature of appropriate classroom instruction?
2. The authors convey that there is a need for quality curricula materials. How do you define quality in terms of instruction? In terms of content?
3. Teaching and learning represent reciprocal learning processes. How do you view this notion as applying to preparation of teachers to teach financial literacy?
4. Knowing the critical importance of parent modeling and influence, how would you begin to involve parents in school-based financial literacy instruction?
5. The scarcity of time and teacher discomfort with the subject matter are noted as two barriers to curricular inclusion of financial literacy, which do you feel will be the most difficult to overcome? Why?

NOTE

1. The views expressed in this article are those of the author and not those of the Federal Reserve Bank of St. Louis or the Federal Reserve System.

REFERENCES

Asarta, C. J., Hill, A. T., & Meszaros, B. T. (2014). The features and effectiveness of the keys to financial success curriculum. *International Review of Economics Education, 16*, 39–50.
Bernanke, B. S. (2006a). *Conversation with the Chairman: A Teacher Town Hall Meeting.* Federal Reserve Board of Governors, Washington, DC. Retrieved from http://www.federalreserve.gov/newsevents/speech/bernanke20120807a.htm
Bernanke, B. S. (2006b). *Financial Literacy: Testimony before the Committee on Banking, Housing, and Urban Affairs of the United States Senate.* Retrieved from http://www.federalreserve.gv/newsevents/testimony/Bernanke20060523a.htm
Bernheim, B. D., Garrett, D. M., & Maki, D. M. (2001). Education and saving: The long-term effects of high school financial curriculum mandates. *Journal of Public Economics, 80*(3), 435–465.
Berti, A. E., & Monaci, M. G. (1998). Third graders' acquisition of knowledge of banking: Restructuring or accretion? *British Journal of Educational Psychology, 68*(3), 357–371.
Bolick, C., Adams, R., & Willox, L. (2010). The marginalization of elementary social studies in teacher education. *Social Studies Research and Practice, 5*(1), 1–22. Retrieved from http://www.socstrpr.org/files/Vol%205/Issue%202%20-%20Summer,%202010/Research/5.2.3.pdf
Butt, N. M., Haessler, S. J., & Schug, M. C. (2008). An incentives-based approach to implementing Financial Fitness for Life in the Milwaukee public schools. *Journal of Private Enterprise, 24*(1), 165–173.
Center for Financial Literacy. (2015). *Is your state making the grade? 2015 National report card on state efforts to improve financial literacy in high schools.* Champlain College Center for Financial Literacy. Burlington, Vermont. Retrieved from file:///C:/Users/h1mcs01/Downloads/2015_National_Report_Card%20(1).pdf
Charles Schwab Corporation. (2011). *Teen and money survey.* Retrieved from http://www.schwabmoneywise.cm/public/moneywise/calculators_tools/families_mone_surves/teens_mone_survey
Chopra, R. (2013, August 5). *A closer look at the trillion* [Blog post]. Retrieved from http://www.consumerfinance.gov/about-us/blog/a-closer-look-at-the-trillion/
Consumer Financial Protection Bureau. (2015a). *Advancing K-12 financial education: A guide for policymakers* [Press release]. Retrieved from http://www.consumerfinance.gov/reports/advancing-k-12-financial-education-a-guide-for-policymakers/
Consumer Financial Protection Bureau. (2015b). *Resources for parents and caregivers.* Retrieved from http://www.consumerfinance.gov/money-as-you-grow/
Consumer Financial Protection Bureau. (2016). *Youth financial education curriculum review tool.* Retrieved from http://www.consumerfinance.gov/youth-financial-education/
Council for Economic Education. (2013). *National standards for financial literacy.* New York, NY: Council for Economic Education. Retrieved from http://www.councilforeconed.org/wp/wp-content/uploads/2013/02/national-standards-for-financial-literacy.pdf
Council for Economic Education. (2016). *Survey of the states: Economic and personal finance education in our nation's schools.* New York, NY: Council for Economic Education. Retrieved from http://councilforeconed.org/wp/wp-content/uploads/2016/02/sos-16-final.pdf
Duke, E. (2011). *The Federal Reserve System and Individual Financial Planning.* Speech given at the 2011 Virginia Beach Financial Planning Day, Virginia Beach, Virginia, 22 Oct 2011. Retrieved from http://www.federalreserve.gov/newsevents/speech/duke20111022a.htm
Engel, M. (2015). Students taking financial education courses have better credit. *New York Daily News.* Retrieved from http://www.nydailynews.com/life-style/students-financial-education-better-credit-stud-article-1.2106166?cid=bitly

Epstein, J., Coates, L., Salinas, K. C., Sanders, M., & Simon, B. S. (1997). *School, family and community partnership: Your handbook for action.* Thousand Oaks, CA: Corwin Press.

Fan, X., & Chen, M. (2001). Parental involvement and students' academic achievement: A meta-analysis. *Educational Psychology Review, 13*(1), 1–22.

Federal Deposit Insurance Corporation. (2017). *Money smart—A financial education program.* Retrieved from https://www.fdic.gov/consumers/consumer/moneysmart/

Federal Reserve Bank of St. Louis. (2015). *Parent Q&As.* Retrieved from https://www.stlouisfed.org/education/parent-resources

Feinstein, L., & Symons, J. (1999). Attainment in secondary school. *Oxford Economic Papers, 51*(2), 300–321.

Field, S., Bauml, M., & Ledbetter, M. (2011). Every day success: Powerful integration of social studies content and English-language arts. *Social Studies and the Young Learner, 23*(3), 22–25. Retrieved from https://d3jc3ahdjad7x7.cloudfront.net/Ha6YEXIerx41RdtwHWiI2kALtO-JPLA1IgKVnnflakzJey79P.pdf

FINRA Investor Education Foundation. (2013). *National financial capability study.* Retrieved from http://www.usfinancialcapability.org/downloads/NFCS_2012_Report_Natl_Finading.pdf

Fitchett, P., & Heafner, T. (2010). A national perspective on the effects of high-stakes testing and standardization on elementary social studies marginalization. *Theory and Research in Social Education, 38*(1), 114–130. Retrieved from https://www.researchgate.net/publication/254336543_A_National_Perspective_on_the_Effects_of_High-Stakes_Testing_and_Standardization_on_Elementary_Social_Studies_Marginalization

Fitchett, P., Heafner, T., & VanFossen, P. (2014). An analysis of time prioritization for social studies in elementary school classrooms. *Journal of Curriculum and Instruction, 8*(2), 7–35. Retrieved from http://www.joci.ecu.edu/index.php/JoCI/article/viewFile/v8n2p7/pdf

Good, A., Heafner, T., Rock, T., O'Connor, K., Passe, J., Waring, S., & Byrd, S. (2010). The de-emphasis on social studies in elementary schools: Teacher candidate perspective. *Current Issues in Education, 13*(4), 1–22. Retrieved from https://cie.asu.edu/ojs/index.php/cieatasu/article/viewFile/620/98

Governments Accountability Office. (2016). *Survey of consumer finances.* Retrieved from http://www.gao.gov/assets/680/670153.pdf

Greenspan, A. (2001). *The importance of education in today's economy.* Speech presented at the Community Affairs Research Conference of the Federal Reserve System. Retrieved from http://www.federalresreve.gove/boarddocs/speeches/2001/20011026/default.htm

Grody, A. D., Grody, D., Kromann, E., & Sutliff, J. (2008). *A financial literacy and financial services program for elementary school grades—Results of a pilot study.* Retrieved from http://ssrn.com/abstract=1132388 or http://dx.doi.org/10.2139/ssrn.1132388

Hagedorn, E., Schug, M., & Suiter, M. (2016). A collaborative approach to financial literacy in the Chicago public schools. *Journal of Private Enterprise, 31*(1), 79–90.

Harter, C. L., & Harter, J. F. R. (2009). Assessing the effectiveness of financial fitness for life in eastern Kentucky. *Journal of Applied Economics and Policy, 28*(1), 20–33.

Harter, C. L., & Harter, J. F. R. (2012). Does a graduate course in personal finance for teachers lead to higher student financial literacy than a teacher workshop? *Journal of Consumer Education, 29,* 35–46. Retrieved from http://www.cefe.illinois.edu/JCE/archives/vol29.html

Heafner, T., & Fitchett, P. (2012) National trends in elementary instruction: Exploring the role of social studies curricula. *The Social Studies, 103*(2), 67–72. Retrieved from http://www.tandfonline.com/doi/full/10.1080/00377996.2011.592165?scroll=top&needAccess=true

Heckman, E. R. (2015). Financial literacy in the workplace. In J. Liebowitz (Ed.), *Financial literacy education: Addressing student, business, and government needs* (pp. 179-196). Boca Raton, FL: CRC Press, Taylor & Francis Group.

Hopkins, M., & Gallagher, S. (2003). *Econ-fun master questions list for spotting basic economic concepts.* Retrieved from http://www.econ-fun.com/

Ingram, M., Wolfe, R., & Lieberman, J. (2007). The role of parents in high-achieving, schools serving low-income, high risk-populations. *Education and Urban Society, 29*(4), 479–497.

Jeynes, W. H. (2005). A meta-analysis of the relation of parental involvement to urban elementary school student academic achievement. *Urban Education, 40*(3), 237–269.

Jeynes, W. H. (2007). The relationship between parental involvement and urban secondary school student academic achievement: A meta-analysis. *Urban Education, 42*(1), 82–110.

Jordan, G., Snow, C., & Porsche, M. (2000). Project EASE: The effect of a family literacy project on kindergarten students' early literacy skills. *Reading Research Quarterly, 35*(4), 524–546.

Klapper, L., Lusardi, A., & van Oudheusden, P. (2015). *Insights from the Standards & Poor's ratings services global financial literacy survey.* Retrieved from http://gflec.org/wp-content/uploads/2015/11/3313-Finlit_Report_FINAL-5.11.16.pdf

Kourilsky, M. (1977). The kinder-economy: A case study of kindergarten pupils' acquisition of economic concepts. *The Elementary School Journal, 77*(3), 182–191.

Laney, J. (1989). Experience and concept label type effects on first graders' learning, retention of economic concepts. *Journal of Educational Research, 82*(4), 231–236.

Larkins, A. G., & Shaver, J. P. (1969). Economics learning in grade one: The USU assessment studies. *Social Education, 33*(8), 958–963.

Loibl, C. (2008). *Survey of financial education in Ohio's schools: Assessment of teachers, programs, and legislative efforts.* Ohio State University P-12 Projects. Retrieved from https://education.ohio.gov/getattachment/Topics/Academic-Content-Standards/Financial-Literacy-and-Business/Financial-Literacy/Loibl_ExecutiveSummary_print-1.pdf.aspx

Loibl, C., & Fisher, P. (2013). Academic discipline and personal finance instruction in high school. *Journal of Financial Counseling and Planning, 24*(1), 15–33.

Lusardi, A., & Mitchell, O. S. (2014). The economic importance of financial literacy: Theory and evidence. *Journal of Economic Literature, American Economic Association, 52*(1), 5–44.

Meszaros, B., & Suiter, M. (1998). The case for economics in the elementary classroom. *The Region, 12*(4), 39–43.

Morgan, J. C. (1991). Using *Econ and Me* to teach economics to children in primary grades. *Social Studies, 82*(5), 195–197.

National Association of Economic Educators. (2015). *Curriculum Review Rubrics.* Retrieved from http://www.naee.net/curriculum_info.shtml

OECD. (2014). *PISA 2012 Results: Students and money: Financial literacy skills for the 21st century* (Vol. VI). Paris: PISA, OECD Publishing. Retrieved from http://dx.doi.org/10.1787/9789264208094-en

Pace, J. (2011). Teaching literacy through social studies under No Child Left Behind. *The Journal of Social Studies Research, 36*(4), 329–358. Retrieved from http://www.education.ucf.edu/jssr/docs/ArticlePace.pdf

Reiser, M. L. (2010). *Financial fitness for life 3–5.* New York, NY: Council for Economic Education.

Robinson, J. (2012). The next generation of consumers. *Bostino.* Retrieved from http://bostino.streetwise.co/channels/the-next-generation-of-consumers/

Senesh, L. (1963). *Our working world: Families at work.* Chicago, IL: Science Research Associates.

Shannon, G. S., & Bylsmna, P. (2003). *Nine characteristics of high-performing schools: A research-based resource for school leadership teams to assist with the school improvement process.* Office of the Superintendent of Public Instruction, Olympia, WA.

Sherraden, M. S., Johnson, L., Guo, B., & Elliott, W. (2011). Financial capability in children: Effects of participation in a school-based financial education and savings program. *Journal of Family & Economic Issues, 32*(3), 385–399.

Soyeon, S., & Serido, J. (2011). *Young adults' financial capabilities Wave 2: Arizona pathways to success for university students.* Retrieved from http://tcainstitute.org/APLUS-Wave-2-Report.pdf

Suiter, M. (2006). *Effectiveness of an interdisciplinary approach to teaching mathematics and economics in middle school mathematics classrooms* (Unpublished dissertation research). University of Missouri, St. Louis, MO.

Suiter, M., & Meszaros, B. (2005). Teaching about saving and investing in the elementary and middle school grades. *Social Education, 69*(2), 92–95.

Swinton, J., DeBerry, T. W., Scafidi, B., & Woodard, H. C. (2007). The impact of financial education workshops for teachers on students' economics achievement. *The Journal of Consumer Education, 27*, 63–77.

Thornton, S., & Houser, N. (1996). *The status of elementary social studies in Delaware: Views from the field.* Retrieved from http://files.eric.ed.gov/fulltext/ED404239.pdf

T. Rowe Price. (2016). *8th Annual Parents, Kids, and Money Survey.* Retrieved from https://corporate.troweprice.com/Money-Confident-Kids/images/emk/2016pkmresultsdeckfinal-160322181149.pdf

Urban, C., Schmeiser, M., Collins, M. J., & Brown, A. (2015). State of financial education mandates: It's all in the implementation. *Insights: Financial Capability.* Washington, DC: FINRA Investor Education Fund. Retrieved from https://www.finra.org/sites/default/files/investoreducation-foundation.pdf

VanFossen, P. (2005). "Reading and math take so much time …": An overview of social studies instruction in Indiana. *Theory and Research in Social Education, 33*(3), 376–403. Retrieved from http://www.tandfonline.com/doi/pdf/10.1080/00933104.2005.10473287?needAccess=true

Walstad, W. B., Rebeck, K., & MacDonald, R. A. (2010). The effects of financial education on the financial knowledge of high school students. *Journal of Consumer Affairs, Special Issue: Financial Literacy, 44*(2), 336–357.

Walstad, W. B., & Schug, M. (1991). Teaching and learning economics. In J. Shaver (Ed.), *Handbook of research on social studies teaching and learning* (pp. 311–449). New York, NY: Macmillan.

Watts, M. (2005). *What works: A review of research on outcomes and effective program delivery in precollege economic education.* New York, NY: Council on Economic Education (formerly the National Council on Economic Education). Retrieved from http://www.councilforeconed.org/wp/wp-content/uploads/2011/11/What-Works-Michael-Watts.pdf

Way, W., & Holden, K. (2010). *Teachers' background & capacity to teach personal finance.* National Endowment for Financial Education. Retrieved from http://www.nefe.org/what-we-provide/primary-research/grant-studeis-teachers-preparedness-and-mone-man.aspx

Whaley, P. (2011). *Financial fitness for life parent guide.* New York, NY: Council for Economic Education.

Whitebeard, D., & Bingham, S. (2013). Habit formation & learning in young children. *Money Advice Services.* London: Money Advice Services.

Willis, L. E. (2008). Against financial literacy education. *Iowa Law Review, 94*, 8–10.

Willis, L. E. (2011). The financial education fallacy. *The American Economic Review, 101*(3), 429–434.

Wright, D. (2010). *Financial fitness for life, K-2.* New York, NY: Council for Economic Education.

Yon, M., & Passe, J. (1990). The relationship between the elementary social studies methods course and student teachers' beliefs and practices. *Journal of Social Studies Research, 14*(1), 13–24.

PART THREE
Socio-Historic Moral Issues

CHAPTER THIRTEEN

A Representation OF Vulnerability IN National Strategies

Targeting the Needs of Disadvantaged Consumers with Financial Education and Inclusion Efforts

FLOOR E. KNOOTE AND SOFIA L. ORTEGA TINEO

Dimes Consultancy

Evidence is growing to support the idea that financial education needs to be relevant and applied to be effective. When populations are given the opportunity to participate in the formal financial system, their experiences may vary drastically, as often products and services are not offered in equal terms across the board. Low-income households and other vulnerable populations, which face a lack of financial capabilities and institutional barriers to participation in the financial system, require initiatives that equally target ability and opportunity in reaping the fruits from participation in the financial system. In spite of national efforts to take these realities into account, there is often disconnect between decision makers' approach and the real needs of vulnerable populations, which can lead to programs, curricula, or strategy priorities being inappropriate and ineffective. This paper analyzes how vulnerability is incorporated in financial literacy and financial inclusion policy formulation, outreach, and implementation to explore where this disconnect occurs. The second part describes the methodology used. The third part provides definitions and a conceptual framework. The fourth part describes the details of national strategies for financial education (NSFE) and inclusion. The fifth part offers comparison between case study countries to identify best practices, challenges, and opportunities in reaching vulnerable populations. Finally, conclusion and recommendations are offered.

METHODOLOGY

Two complementary levels of data collection were used in this study, consisting of secondary data analysis and key stakeholder interviews. Secondary data analysis, in this study, was used to sketch both the context of the international and national policy environments and will provide the academic background for concepts used in the chapter (vulnerability, financial inclusion, financial capability, financial education, and national strategies). This method of data collection provides a cost-effective way of gaining a broad understanding of the research questions. Secondary data are, in this study, additionally helpful in designing subsequent primary research questions and can provide a baseline with which to compare primary data collection results.

Key stakeholder interviews, along with focus groups and surveys, are one of the primary methods of gathering qualitative data. Insights gleaned from stakeholder interviews provide the basis for stakeholder analysis. The main objective of the stakeholder interview is to elicit detailed information and opinions on an issue through wide-ranging discussion rather than specific questioning. The desired outcome of the interview is to gain a broad overview of the interviewees' opinions about a specific topic that may reveal hidden concerns or ideas that would not be expressed in response to a set number of specific questions. A consideration of the interview is that it can be time consuming and therefore expensive and it requires skilled interviewers.

1. Analysis of secondary data was used to explore the definition of vulnerability, the evidence of and to identify best practices in financial capability interventions, and international guidelines and national experiences of strategy development. Sources of information included academic journals, public policy documents as well as national strategy documents.
2. Key stakeholder interviews were used to collect key data points on implementation of national strategies and to validate the information collected by the national strategy documents. Case study selection was based on the stage of implementation of the national strategies and the level of existing relationship between authors and the implementing bodies.

The interviews took place for about approximately 90 minutes and involved several key informants from field teams of the implementing institutions. The questions of the interview were, in some cases, translated to Spanish for the convenience of the interviewees. Additionally, several of the key stakeholders chose to complement the interview with written information.

Limitations of the study include (1) the data collected through interviews was self-reported and generally involved the perception of the interviewee, and

(2) the institutions interviewed were a sample of the many institutions involved in the strategy implementation. The analysis is based on perceptions of individuals involved in the process.

CONCEPTUAL FRAMEWORK: RELATIONSHIPS BETWEEN VULNERABILITY, CONSUMER PROTECTION, FINANCIAL CAPABILITY, AND FINANCIAL INCLUSION

Consumer vulnerability is fundamentally linked to the concepts of financial inclusion, consumer protection, and financial capabilities. This section describes those underlying relationships.

THE VULNERABLE CONSUMER

It is often stated that many people in vulnerable situations would not describe themselves as "vulnerable." These discussions imply an "us and them" mind-set, which categorizes vulnerable consumers into specific minority groups and demonstrates vulnerability as "purely related to the individual's characteristics" (Financial Conduct Authority, 2015, p. 17). Literature, however, suggests that the definition of vulnerability may actually be more fluid and complex than is suggested above, especially taking into account individual's environments and their reactions toward them. For example, indebtedness often causes feelings of shame, which not only causes personal psychological strain but also goes hand in hand with social exclusion and isolation (Hayes, 2000).

Both the personal characteristic and societal exclusion appear in commonly used definitions of vulnerable consumers, For example, the European Commission defines a vulnerable consumer as "A consumer, who, as a result of socio-demographic characteristics, behavioural characteristics, personal situation, or market environment … and at higher risk of experiencing negative outcomes in the market" (European Commission, 2016a, 2016b, p. 2). The G20 and Organisation for Economic Cooperation and Development (OECD) (2014) mention that "vulnerability can also be a broad term relating to a particular susceptibility of consumers to detriment based on their personal characteristics" (p. 29).

The United Kingdom Financial Conduct Authority (FCA, 2015) defines accordingly that "A vulnerable consumer is, due to their personal circumstances … especially susceptible to detriment, particularly when a firm is not acting with appropriate levels of care" (p. 7), implying specifically the role of external actors in exacerbating vulnerability. In most of these definitions, consumers are additionally described as a heterogeneous rather than a homogeneous group. Clearly, protecting such a wide, varied group of people who experience vulnerability on both a personal and societal level, "presents the authorities with a range of challenges" (Cartwright, 2011, p. 1) and leads to "no uniform definition of consumer vulnerability across, or even within, jurisdictions" (G20/OECD, 2014, p. 29).

Causes of Vulnerability

Researchers have attempted to set out a list of elements that help to identify where vulnerability is prone to exist. Burden (1998) sets out seven vulnerable groups being the elderly, the young, the unemployed, those with a limiting, long-standing illness, those in low-income households, members of ethnic minorities, and those with no formal educational qualifications (Burden, 1998, p. 10). Cartwright (2011) uses five vulnerability elements in a "taxonomy of vulnerability" (Cartwright, 2011, p. 2). Three of these relate to situations where the consumer faces choices in accessing financial services—information vulnerability, pressure vulnerability, and redress. A fourth and fifth relate to lack of choice faced by certain consumers—supply vulnerability and impact vulnerability—which concerns the greater impact of loss, or harm, on particular consumers. It has been contended that poverty is one of the most significant factors in vulnerability, as well as a constant justification for consumer law (p. 47).

Disadvantage and Vulnerability

Where characteristics of vulnerability persist, the consumer is often described as "disadvantaged." It is key to make the distinction between vulnerability and disadvantage, which in policy documents is not always clarified. Andreasen (1975) highlights that "consumer vulnerability is *not* the same thing as disadvantage." "Disadvantaged consumers" are those "who are particularly handicapped in achieving adequate value for their consumer dollar in the urban marketplace because of their severely restricted incomes … or their minority racial status" (p. 6); in this sense, consumer vulnerability *can* mean belonging to a socioeconomic group likely to be less empowered, or lacking full capacity to operate as consumer (European Consumer Consultative Group, 2013).

LINKING VULNERABILITY TO FINANCIAL INCLUSION, CONSUMER PROTECTION, AND FINANCIAL CAPABILITY

Financial Inclusion

"In order to impact people at the base of the pyramid, consumer protection must be grounded in an understanding of the realities of low income consumers' financial experience" (CGAP, 2016). Vulnerability can be considerably exacerbated by the conduct and policies of financial institutions. The way financial institutions design their products can impact the ease with which a consumer interacts with them. Unease could create additional stress for the customer, or "withdraw from the market altogether" (FCA, 2015, p. 18), bringing about other vulnerabilities. This is why consumer protection policies are a sine qua non instrument to achieve greater level of equality within the financial system.

Financial Exclusion

"Financial exclusion refers to a process whereby people encounter difficulties accessing and/or using financial services in the mainstream market that are appropriate to their needs" (EC, 2008, p. 9). Overall, the literature shows that similar types of people are disproportionately affected by lack of financial services in spite of the level of exclusion in their country, categorized by those living on low incomes (EC, 2008, p. 38). Financial exclusion has been shown to link closely to social exclusion in several studies and policy makers should therefore consider financial exclusion issues "in all courses of action regarding social exclusion or poverty" (Smyczek, 2009, p. 223).

Financial Capability

Although the evidence of the "financial capability" concept is still in the nascent stages of development, research indicates that the important benefits of greater financial capability could contribute to decreasing the vulnerability of the consumer (Lusardi & Mitchell, 2014). Teaching financial capability in a "learning while doing" approach could generate benefits over teaching financial knowledge in classroom settings (Johnson, & Sherraden, 2007). However, there has been no "carefully-crafted cost-benefit analysis indicating which sorts of financial education programs are most appropriate … for which kinds of people" (Lusardi & Mitchell, 2014, p. 34), as a range of situation-specific features could be related to the impact of financial education, and include location and delivery method (O'Prey & Shephard, 2014). There is a need to design capability interventions that address the knowing–doing gap and additionally take psychological and cultural factors into account (CFI, 2016, p. 3). Some promising practices have been identified and relate to the components listed below.

Applicability

A wide variety of delivery methods have been developed to deliver financial education, specifically to young populations (OECD, 2013). However, these curricula are not specifically tailored to the specific needs of vulnerable populations. Scholarship increasingly highlights that financial education needs to be relevant and applied to be effective. For example, schoolchildren find financial education programs, which are relevant to their lives, more engaging and, in addition, programs have been more successful when they are "based on what consumers will in practice engage with (not what the authorities would like them to engage with)" (Mundy, 2013). As the literature suggests that materials need to be immediately engaging to be effective, some programs incorporate curricula created for teenagers to address what they *want* to learn about using money in order to truly appeal to teenagers (Varcoe, Martin, Devitto, & Go, 2005). These need to clearly include financial decisions, which the student is able to make in real life.

Teachable Moments

Reaching consumers at the right time is key in building financial capability. Information that is provided just in time is more likely to resonate and to influence behavior. This approach emphasizes targeting people in situations that have specific financial consequences and includes vulnerable consumers like migrants and the poor (CFI, 2016).

Messenger

The messenger of financial capability interventions is key in behavior change. Popular television has been found to have a positive impact on knowledge. For example, "Viva Seguro," a radio-based financial education program in Colombia and the use of soap operas in Latin America have shown to generate positive results on retention of knowledge. Results showed to be context specific as those who identified more closely with the characters in the soap opera were more likely to change their behavior (World Bank, 2014a). The utilization of the individual's own social networks to relate information is effective in the creation of positive financial habits (Di Giannatale, 2012).

CONCLUSION: LINKING VULNERABILITY TO NATIONAL POLICIES

The context-specific nature of successful financial capability building, depending on personal as well as circumstantial factors, highlights and amplifies the challenge to design policies which take appropriate account of the interests of consumers described as disadvantaged or vulnerable. It is not surprising that, to the extent that we can identify broader classes of people who are likely to be vulnerable, public policy makers are more likely to help level the playing field for whole groups of consumers (Baker, Gentry, & Rittenburg, 2005, p. 10), and "streamline" consumers. This is often related to the fact that the development of policies for financial inclusion involves multiple stakeholders from various public and private sector institutions. Public–private partnerships have become critically important to achieving financial inclusion goals (AFI, 2015, p. 12). Literature on financial inclusion underscores the importance of effective coordination mechanisms for the successful implementation of strategies for different consumer segments as well as the costs involved in these processes (AFI, 2015, p. 12).

In this sense, products are often not designed to meet needs of "nonstandard" consumers who do not fit into brackets (FCA, 2014, p. 38). Even though policy makers worldwide have recognized the diversity of the consumer and most have identified more than one target audience, "almost all of them use the same tools and methodologies indiscriminately, with the same format for delivery and content for audiences" (Organisation for Economic Co-operation and Development [OECD], 2013, p. 28). International and national parties have come up with their own definitions in developing a national strategy with a vulnerability focus. The characteristics of the individual, their circumstances, static and transitory states, and the practices of providers, all appear in these definitions in various ways (FCA, 2014, p. 19).

When talking of financial capability infrastructures, these distinctions are key, as solutions for the issues that consumers face lie in the nuances of the operationalization of policy. The next part examines how regulators take account of the particular interests of vulnerable consumers in implementation.

NATIONAL STRATEGIES FOR FINANCIAL EDUCATION AND INCLUSION

The incorporation of NSFE into the policy agendas of the developed countries gained relevance in the beginning of the 2000s (OECD, 2013), becoming a powerful trend in the rest of the world after the financial crisis in 2007 (OECD/INFE, 2009). A few years later, the interest in Financial Inclusion Strategies (NFIS) increased, as a result of the Maya declaration of 2011 (AFI, 2015). NSFE are regarded as one of the tools financial regulatory authorities can utilize to further financial literacy at the national level. These tools are often seen as a companion to consumer protection and inclusion policies. As part of NFIS or as complementary to consumer protection policies, financial education aims to build financial capabilities and helps people recognize their rights and duties as financial consumers (OECD/INFE, 2014). The OECD (2013) has issued a series of high-level principles[1] with the aim to support governments defining the scope, governance mechanism, and the role of main stakeholders in the different stages of implementation of the national strategy, key priorities, target groups, and delivery mechanism. Particularly relevant to the aim of this study is the mapping and consultation phase suggested by both the OECD (ibid) and the Association for Financial Inclusion (AFI) in regard to financial inclusion and education policies. Strategies are to be developed through a broad consultative process (AFI, 2013, p. 2). According to AFI, 31 countries have approved an NSFI, while OECD (2013) indicates the existence of 45 NSFE worldwide.

VULNERABILITY IN NATIONAL STRATEGIES

In both NSFE and NSFI, the attention to vulnerable populations is prominent. Taking a closer look at the 20 national strategy documents selected for this study, 16 documents state to have an intention to establish specific outreach procedures to (what is described depending on the context) as "vulnerable groups." The definition of what vulnerability entails or which groups are to be tended to is as varied as the focus and content of the strategy documents themselves. We identified a tendency toward defining vulnerable populations in socioeconomic terms and often characterized as "excluded" or "marginalized." However, even though in a majority of the sample, a specific definition of vulnerability is not included in the strategy document, the link between vulnerability and poverty is confirmed, and the terms disadvantaged and vulnerable are used interchangeably. Rural population, especially rural women, urban low-income households, minorities, youth, and the extremely poor are indicated as vulnerable groups in all 20 strategy documents that were consulted for this study.

INTERNATIONAL POLICY GUIDANCE FOR TARGETING VULNERABLE GROUPS

International organizations such as the World Bank and OECD have devoted efforts to help national authorities determine the best course of action to include vulnerable populations in NSFE and NSFI. Although a set of established guidelines does not yet exist, international actors have identified a series of best practices for different stages of the strategy formulation process in regard to the inclusion of vulnerable populations and their specific needs.

FINANCIAL EDUCATION VS. FINANCIAL INCLUSION

The OECD highlights in its recommendations that when targeting vulnerable groups "additional efforts are needed" to reach these populations, as these groups may be easily the victims of fraud, tend to be less resilient, risk a downward spiral of poverty, and often lack confidence, literacy, and access to resources. This description again indicates how heavily the socioeconomic component is emphasized in defining vulnerability. In addition, the OECD's financial consumer protection principles highlight targeting those with "low income" and those "less experienced" (OECD, 2011).

Involving different institutions already targeting vulnerable groups is a key recommendation (OECD/INFE, 2014, 2015; World Bank, 2014), as well as identifying sociodemographic groups that are financially at risk through baseline studies of the population's financial capabilities and demand-side surveys. These instruments are often mentioned as sufficient to identify specific target groups, and to assess their vulnerabilities (OECD/INFE, 2014).

Comparing the NFIS documents with NFES documents, it appears that, in NFIS, it has been more feasible to provide detailed action plans on how vulnerable (especially the poor) can be reached and how to subsegment more specific categories of vulnerabilities. This may be due to the fact that NSFI have been able to somewhat successfully integrate actions within already existing mechanisms and infrastructures to serve the underserved such as conditional cash transfers, rural banks, and mobile money, while at the same time creating a new array of products and services tailored to these groups.

CONCLUSION

Although vulnerability is addressed in NSFE and NSFI, a clear definition of what defines these vulnerable groups is often not provided in the strategy documents or is rather vague. However, there seems to be a consensus in which groups are included as such, which may have been reached through the common denominators of developing economies, such as high level of poverty, rural or young population, or simply through the guidance of international organizations. Whether this is due to more effort dedicated to conducting detailed assessments of these needs (often supported by the World Bank), or whether it is due to a clear consensus on what kind of financial capability interventions vulnerable (and especially disadvantaged) populations require, remains to be determined. The following section will provide an in-depth exploration of this question.

TARGETING VULNERABILITY THROUGH STRATEGY IMPLEMENTATION

This section looks into the implementation processes of several NFIS and NFES in Latin America to discern how they are reaching vulnerable populations.

COUNTRY BACKGROUNDS

National Strategies for Financial Inclusion—Peru

According to the Global Findex (2014), 29% of the population in the country owns a bank account in the formal financial system, around 27% of the population is between 15 and 29 years of age (INEI, 2015), 21% lives in rural or remote areas, 22% of the population lives in poverty (World Bank, 2015), and close to 13% belongs to an ethnic minority[2] (INDEPA, 2010). The National Strategy for Financial Inclusion, launched in July 2015, materialized Peru's resolution to promote financial development with aims to expand financial products and services to more Peruvians, focusing on payments, savings, finance, insurance, consumer protection, financial education, and vulnerable groups (ASBANC, 2015; Comisión Multisectorial de Inclusión Financiera, 2016). This strategy recognizes citizens living in peri-urban or rural areas, the unemployed or sub-employed, youth, seniors, illiterate or semi-illiterate, ethnic minorities, people with mental or physical disabilities, migrants and displaced people as vulnerable. The Peruvian NSFI (Comisión Multisectorial de Inclusión Financiera, 2016) features a working group for vulnerable populations. This working group may breach the gap usage and also decrease social exclusion and vulnerabilities (p. 46).

Mexico's National Policy for Financial Inclusion

Of Mexico's population, 24.9% are between 15 and 29 years of age (INEGI, 2015a), 51% are women (INEGI, 2015b), and around 21% are considered rural. Of the total population of Mexico, only 39% have a formal account (Global Findex, 2014). Mexico focused on developing a more inclusive financial system in recent years through a National Council for Financial Inclusion in 2011 and the financial reform in 2013–2014 (CNBV, 2016) as well as adaptations to generate simplified accounts and the creation of a National Policy for Financial Inclusion (Politica Nacional de Inclusión Financiera, 2016). The policy delineates six axes to serve as guidelines for public policy, all of which include elements pertinent to vulnerable populations, but only two that make specific mention to them. These two are "The development of financial infrastructures in unattended areas" and "Increased supply and use of formal financial services to underserved and exclude populations." (ibid.). Both of these axes are seeking to address the need to create innovative partnerships to allow for the penetration of financial services to remote areas, as well as encourage new business models to tend to the needs of rural populations.

Brazil's National Strategy for Financial Education

In Brazil, 68% of the adult population (over 15 years of age) owns an account at a formal financial institution (Global Findex, 2014), 14% of the population lives in rural areas (World Bank, 2015), and poverty rate was about 8.9% in 2013 (IFAD, 2016). As part of the country's effort to foster economic growth and decrease inequalities, a National Strategy for Financial Education (NSFE) was developed in 2013. The NSFE includes efforts to reach women beneficiaries of "Bolsa Família" selected on the basis of their role as head of household, and low-income retirees due to pervasive indebtedness in this segment (OECD, 2013). The Financial Education Programs are realized with partnership of the Ministries responsible for each of the target populations. The local agents of the Governmental Social Assistance network are fundamental pieces in the puzzle, especially to convene large numbers of beneficiaries.

COLOMBIA' NATIONAL STRATEGY FOR ECONOMIC AND FINANCIAL EDUCATION

Colombia's NFES is supported by a series of studies (Garcia, Grifoni, Lopez, & Mejía, 2013; Mejía et al., 2016; Reddy, Bruhn, & Tan, 2013) indicating low levels of financial capabilities among the population. In order to coordinate existing efforts on financial education at the national level, the government created the "Administrative System for Economic and Financial Education" as well as decreed the creation of a multi-sectoral committee to develop NFES (Comisión Intersectorial de Inclusión Financiera, 2016). Although the final strategy document has not yet been released, efforts to reach vulnerable populations are being undertaken by the Department for Social Prosperity and Banca de las Oportunidades. Life experience and life strategies are used to relate financial education content to rural and conflict-affected populations. Colombia's rural population is 24% (World Bank, 2015) and some estimates calculate at least 250 000 youth are affected by the armed conflict in the country (UNICEF, 2016).

COMPARATIVE ANALYSIS

The Key Stakeholder Interviews were employed following a couple of steps. First, interviewees were selected according to designated criteria (areas of expertise, representation of groups and ministries). Based on these, a total of 12 individuals participated in the interviews. Interviewees of all four countries underwent the interview as a group; Brazil complemented their interview with written answers.

Interviews were conducted over Skype and phone using a recording device. Third, the interviews were transcripted and in the case of Colombia and Mexico, were translated into English. Last, the transcripts were compared per question. Comparison between case study countries was made to identify best practices, challenges, and opportunities in reaching vulnerable populations. The questions covered topics on Segmentation of Vulnerable Groups and Degree of Inclusive Processes as well as the tailoring of programs, Communication, and the Challenges faced in rolling out the programs and products (aka the interventions).

Segmentation Methods and Needs Assessed

Assessments of the needs of the population in terms of financial literacy and products should be conducted before a policy is developed. The assessment can draw information from various surveys and national data sources and should enable a better definition of the NS main targets, priorities and short- and long-term objectives (OECD, 2012). First, definitions of vulnerable groups ranged between "people living in areas with no financial infrastructure or without any access to financial services" (L. Fabre, CONDUSEF, personal communication, July 17, 2016), "showing people's inability to earn a [sustainable] income" (J. Álvarez Gallego, personal communication, July 8, 2016) and "those in a situation of exclusion and poverty" (R. Buendia, personal communication, July 18, 2016). In addition, diverse segmentation methods were used. Peru used several demand and supply surveys on access and usage and held interviews with key stakeholders to segment Peru's population considering age, location, and income level; indigenous, young, and rural populations were established as most vulnerable. The strategy goals include: there is outreach to adults and youth with financial education (out of the school system and in the school system); increased points of access for excluded communities while promoting a culture of savings in rural communities, building resilience of small business owners.

In contrast, in Mexico, CONDUSEF used statistics from their own complaint mechanism to establish needs, cross-referencing complaints, and the current offer of products as well as information from the National Institute of Statistics to see where problems occurred, segmenting by product need as well as by geographic location.

Colombia commenced a different and more integrated approach by basing segments on existing definitions of those groups historically marginalized; socially, politically, and culturally, classified as those living in extreme poverty, living in poverty, or identified as the victims of armed conflict. Colombia is also working with an existing program that is considered best practice. This program is currently being tested per target segment, and will later be adapted to the selected target segments.

Brazil's relevant target segments were identified through an in-depth analysis in this sample, resulting in segmentation by age groups, by education level: by income level, by economic activity, and by region. The approaches of design thinking and behavior design were used. Extensive field research (interviews, focus groups) was conducted in three Brazilian regions, leading to the identification of four main personas for each target population. Personas are characters that represent the patterns of behavior that were observed. Field research inputs and persona analysis were then used as a basis for the development of 10 potential solutions.

In conclusion, methods and the level of assessments differ considerably per country, depending on the objectives of the strategy. It seems plausible that the more detail is available about the different categories of people per vulnerable segment, the more tailored the intervention can be. However, it is yet to be determined whether level of needs assessment will have an impact on the eventual reach and impact of the national strategy on vulnerable populations. As financial and social vulnerabilities appear to be strongly interlinked, using existing definitions (J. Álvarez Gallego, personal communication, July 8, 2016) may additionally help align financial capability efforts with other efforts related to social exclusion, potentially having a broader impact in the long term.

Consultation Process

International guidelines indicate that consultations with target segments are a key component of the national strategy development process reference. Participatory approaches are considered key to the successful implementation of a strategy. This means broad and in-depth consultations with relevant stakeholders in the public and private sectors, as well as civil society. Consultations are sometimes carried out with financially excluded groups, but information on the extent of these consultations is scant, and the representation of the poorest such as low-income rural women is not clear (AFI, 2015, p. 5). This section explores whether representatives of vulnerable groups were in fact included in the consultation process on content and delivery of the national policy.

Brazil implemented an inclusive strategy in developing the NFES based on the fact that "it would be impossible to design an effective financial education solution from the offices in the middle of Sao Paulo, and essential to immerse ourselves in different Brazilian realities and co-create with beneficiaries, in their realities" (AEF Brazil, personal communication, July 23, 2016). In-depth field research, with 100 beneficiaries of each target population, was used which involved ethnographic tools such as visiting homes, and joining in daily routines. The solutions were refined with the participation of 1500 people of each target population, in all five Brazilian regions. During the experimentation phase, prototype test sessions, observation of the use of the tool; workshops; round tables; in-depth conversations as well as demand-side surveys were used, clearly indicating that to establish financial capability needs of vulnerable populations, demand surveys alone were insufficient. Colombia indicated that collaboration with the Department for Social Prosperity including organizations leading the issue of victims occurred. Instead of a consultation process with the vulnerable populations, they discussed with the organizations representing the groups. In the institution's other work with vulnerable populations, however, several instruments were used, including a demand-side survey on financial inclusion. Similarly, in Peru, meetings were held with different organizations that represent vulnerable groups from public, private, and civil society organizations. In addition, a vulnerable population group, with the aim of adjusting all relevant policies issued by the national strategy to the needs of the vulnerable groups—and with the broader objective of improving quality of life in these populations—was created.

Mexico indicated that consultations would have been very valuable in defining needs of vulnerable populations; however, it did not do so in a formal or full scale due to limited resources. A survey was conducted on how vulnerable [especially rural] population use, understand, and perceive financial services. Mexico indicated a clear desire to follow-up [on the instruments they had used] in order to explore if the products are really working for vulnerable people and for the families.

In conclusion, these cases indicate a diverse range of steps and levels of intensity that were used to make the process inclusive with vulnerable groups. All parties indicated that in designing interventions for vulnerable populations, personal involvement is key in developing and evaluating the pilot interventions, and that survey use does not always suffice. However, often, difficulties faced in evaluation processes as well as lack of resources appear to obstruct the inclusiveness of the process. The development of economical methods to conduct consultations and focus groups that include vulnerable groups may present itself a clear opportunity in the creation of effective financial capability interventions for the vulnerable that match their needs.

Tailoring of Programs and Coordination of Content

Where tailoring financial capability programs to the needs of each population appears key to keep them relevant and have impact, this section explores what processes implementing institutions use to tailor interventions and whether the content that was delivered to beneficiaries was coordinated in any way. Brazil indicates that education interventions were completely tailored to their users, as they were revealed and formed in the process of development. "This openness allowed that consultants could build on feedback of beneficiaries and adapt programs accordingly" (AEF Brazil, personal communication, July 23, 2016). The biggest concerns in the tailoring process were to ensure that solutions fit populations' daily life and local organizations' capabilities. In Colombia, specific approaches to reach different populations are the goal. To ensure that the content is focused on the needs of the population, utilization of a coordination mechanism through the different subcommittees of the strategy is suggested.

Peru conversely indicated that the most useful way to tailor the financial education programs for their work has been to train the trainers in financial capability (R. Buendia, personal communication, July 18, 2016). Coordination of financial education materials differs from being on a general basis with one set for each target population, with differentiating levels of knowledge (AEF Brazil, personal communication, July 23, 2016) to nonexistent as parties choose their own content and materials (R. Buendia, personal communication, July 18, 2016). Mexico indicated that one of the most common approaches to tailor financial products for vulnerable populations is to simplify the product, such as restricting some functionalities, not charging certain fee, or promote them in a different way. Tailoring national curricula often requires much planning and design.

In conclusion, all countries indicate attempting to tailor the delivery of the interventions to vulnerable target segments. These case studies do make clear that tailoring financial products may involve a more manageable process than tailoring financial education programs to the needs of vulnerable populations. The complexities arising from the fact that messaging and language are key components in making financial education relevant. Processes related to tailoring materials for financial education for the development and implementation of programs is therefore costly, as mentioned by all interviewees. In this sense, some of the interviewees have pointed out to training teachers (and training of trainers) as being a cost-effective way to ensure effective delivery of financial education to vulnerable segments.

Communication Methods/Delivery

Appropriate communication can help further raise awareness on the importance of financial education and financial inclusion. It may also reinforce buy-in from the population at large (OECD, 2012). This section explores how, in the case study countries, communication to vulnerable groups was established.

In Peru, communication action plans have been created for each product and general information is delivered through awareness campaigns with rural areas targeted specifically. Digital and graphic materials have been produced, soap operas are used, and some materials are translated in local languages (R. Buendia, personal communication, July 18, 2016). In Brazil, the communication/dissemination channels were defined in partnership with local government agencies. Similarly, the most appropriate channel for each location was used including radio, pamphlets, and calls. Consultants of the project, local instructors from governmental agencies, and local agency teams were the ones delivering the financial education content (AEF Brazil, personal communication, July 23, 2016). In Colombia, geography is a main impediment in delivery and communication so local radio or regional television was also used. Additionally, the implementing institutions took advantage of the existing social programs such as the Department of Social Prosperity. People of the regions, municipalities, who were community leaders delivered financial education materials (J. Álvarez Gallego, personal communication, July 8, 2016). Mexico has established a partnership with businesses at the national level to deliver financial education materials; users can request a financial education workshops or material, and CONDUSEF provides necessary and relevant information, while making use of already existing infrastructures for delivery (L. Fabre, CONDUSEF, personal communication, July 17, 2016).

In conclusion, the use of "simple" communication and awareness techniques such as radio and television are seen as effective ways to deliver information on financial capability and inclusion. This is in line with the findings. In addition, the involvement of local individuals, who speak the local languages or come from similar background as program participants, is stated as key in delivering effective financial education messages. Local governance institutions can therefore be considered key partners in the implementation of national financial education projects to vulnerable groups.

Implementation

A strategy is only as effective as its implementation. Implementation practices therefore deserve a great deal of attention. This section explores the biggest implementation challenges that the country cases faced in reaching vulnerable groups.

As noted in the previous section, Colombia indicated that the main challenge they face is finding the delivery channels to do so, to ensure that they are applicable "in spite of the little income they receive" (J. Álvarez Gallego, personal communication, July 8, 2016). In addition, in order for the coordinating body to ensure that all entities that serve vulnerable populations can reach the same objectives and content in terms of financial education, they indicate that creating synergies to avoid duplication of effort is key but challenging. In line with this, for Mexico, the greatest challenge is aligning all collaborating institutions similarly assuring that financial inclusion efforts are undertaken in a responsible manner providing not only the products, but also encouraging all sectors to focus additionally on financial education while developing consumer protection regulation at the same pace. Peru also indicates coordination of activities to be difficult, especially in "how to develop strategic alliances between sectors" (R. Buendia, personal communication, July 18, 2016).

For all three countries, determining what works and what does not work for each population takes time and resources not always available. They indicate that mapping what is available and what has been proven to be effective is important in order to access best practices available at the local level. In Brazil, the most challenging implementation issue in reaching vulnerable groups is the impossibility of reaching them directly on a large scale; thus, it is necessary to use intermediaries, for example local government institutions.

In conclusion, all cases indicate the challenge of creating alliances and synergies between implementing institutions, and ensuring that local governance is a partner. Investing in a strong coordination and interparty communication structure could be a significant opportunity to grow the efficiency in the implementation phase, as indicated by recommendations of international organisations working on the development of a national strategy for both FE and FI (AFI, 2015; OECD, 2013). In addition, there appears to be different implementation challenges for financial education and for financial inclusion efforts.

CONCLUSION

Determining applicability of content for diverse populations appears to be more difficult to establish for financial capability than for financial products. As the managerial process to adapt curricula is more complicated and time consuming than adapting product features in financial inclusion efforts, raising the same level of interest in financial education efforts remains a challenge. For financial inclusion efforts, it is challenging to develop consumer protection interventions and regulations in line with the speed of development of financial products specifically to meet the needs of vulnerable consumers. These observations suggest that there is a need to develop effective and efficient methods to determine the needs of populations. Involvement of the target populations in this process leads to the most detailed assessment and evaluation of solutions for these needs, and effective tailoring of financial capability interventions can build on existing structures, whether it is networks or programs.

CONCLUDING REMARKS AND RECOMMENDATIONS

NSFE and inclusion have been a powerful policy trend in recent years. The policies associated promise to not only help develop more stable and inclusive financial systems, but also improve the quality of lives of the involved populations, especially those living in poverty or at risk. However, defining these groups and designing and developing policies that respond to their most immediate needs can present a big policy challenge. The challenges associated with this endeavor start in the process of defining vulnerable populations and being knowledgeable of related and existing national definitions of disadvantage. Although this muddling of concepts and definitions does not seem to affect the objectives and message of national strategies, it could represent a challenge for the further segmentation, tailoring, and implementation of programs.

Tailoring interventions not only to needs, but also to the realities and routines of the population, may be the second biggest challenge when targeting vulnerable groups. The case studies indicate that the heterogeneity of "the vulnerable segment" requires diverse implementation approaches, and the availability of ample human and financial resources. These elements also affect the likelihood of performing thorough needs assessments and evaluation of pilot interventions. Cases indicate that policy makers have opted for using already existing tools (e.g., national statistics, population census, and baseline studies) to feed into tailoring process, which in their judgment seems a more efficient use of resources. Although there seems to be ample recognition of the fact that inclusive consultation processes could be beneficial to offer a deeper understanding of these groups, these methods are not widely used among policy makers. In this sense, more often than not, interest groups and representing government organizations are the ones able to advocate for the needs and expectations of these segments, when drafting policies that will affect them.

The cases also point out different implementation challenges in financial education than in financial inclusion interventions. The need to provide individuals with relevant, relatable, and accurate information makes finding the right delivery methods for financial education a sometimes seemingly unsurmountable task. Participants in this study expressed their beliefs that coordination of local actors, and the dissemination of responsibility and resources are key to successful implementation. However, it still seems necessary "to examine whether countries have a tendency to embark on over-ambitious strategies and are not paying adequate attention to aligning the scope of their strategies with its available resources and institutional capacity to implement them." "Implementation can no longer be considered separately from formulation—if they are, countries risk their strategies failing" (AFI, 2015, p. 16). Based on these cases and conclusions, the authors propose the following recommendations for policy makers as well as for further research:

— Determining different levels of vulnerability, based on behavior, across target segments, like *personas*, as seen in the Brazil case, seems to render a better understanding of vulnerability than by determining general target groups. We recommend investing in detailed needs assessments that allows defining vulnerability in terms of needs and not in homogenous categories.
— Inclusive consultations are key in needs assessments as well as in pilot testing. Investing in consultation processes with the identified segments

directly is therefore key. This challenge could, in the view of the authors, be interesting since it would allow policy makers, consultants, and research to develop economical ways to conduct inclusive consultations and cost-effective inclusive pilot evaluations.
— Knowing what works and what is available is essential to develop a cost-effective strategy. Linking existing initiatives that already target vulnerable groups, as for example the case in Colombia, will not only build on interventions and safe considerable resources, but also encourage collaboration with key stakeholders at different levels. Stocktaking exercises in the initial phases of the strategy development is crucial for knowledge building but will also allow sustainable partnerships across sectors, as well as allowing for all institutions involved to acquire ownership and therefore responsibility over the impact of the national strategy.
— Coordination and effective outreach have shown to be big challenges. Alliances with local governance structures, the utilization of an existing social infrastructure, and investing in a solid coordination mechanism is crucial to effectively reach vulnerable populations.
— Continuous linking with researchers to collaborate on assessments of teacher training, to conduct inclusive needs assessments, and to learn more about alternative evaluation is key.

DISCUSSION QUESTIONS

1. How do you define legitimate financial needs? How does your social context relate to your definition?
2. The chapter indicates that government efforts employ resources for purposes of efficiency or conversation. What similarities and differences do you observe between government efforts and community perceptions?
3. BankOn is a commercial effort in several cities across the United States to serve underbanked and unbanked vulnerable populations; San Francisco is the most notable site. How might the information in this chapter inform that effort?
4. Community Reinvestment Act (CRA) is a government effort in the United States to encourage depository institutions to help meet the credit needs of their communities. Research three or four local banks and locate their CRA efforts on their websites.
5. How might the definition of "vulnerability" vary across contexts in our country/your state? How would you define a vulnerable population? What metric would you use?

NOTES

1. The high-level principles provide a definition and policy framework for national strategies for financial education. They sketch out the different steps or components of these national strategies which include: a preparatory phase aimed at defining the concepts, scope, and purpose of the strategy, as well as assessing and mapping the current situation; the establishment of adequate governance mechanisms and the identification of key stakeholders' roles; the development of a dedicated roadmap including key priorities, target audience, impact assessment, and resources to be used; the promotion of appropriate and efficient delivery mechanisms as well as the evaluation of individual programs.
2. There are 51 indigenous peoples in Peru. Main ethnolinguistic groups are Arawak, Aru, Cahuapana, Romance, Harakmbut, Huitoto, Jíbaro, Pano, Peba-Yagua, Quechua, Tacana, Tucano, Tupi-Guarani, Uro-Chipaya, and Zaparo.

REFERENCES

Alliance for Financial Inclusion (AFI). (2013). *Putting financial inclusion on the global map. The 2013 Maya Declaration Progress Report.* Kuala Lumpur: AFI.

Alliance for Financial Inclusion (AFI). (2015). *National Financial Inclusion Strategy: Current State of Practice.* AFI Financial Inclusion Strategy Peer Learning Group (FISPLG). Kuala Lumpur: AFI

Andreasen, A. R. (1975). *The disadvantaged consumer.* New York, NY: Free Press.

Asociación de Bancos del Perú – ASBANC. (2015). Por 8 años consecutivos, Perú líder en Microfinanzas. *ASBANC Semana, 5*(178), 6. Retrieved from http://goo.gl/1X4Ceg

Baker, S. M., Gentry, J. W., & Rittenburg, T. L. (2005). Building understanding of the domain of consumer vulnerability. *Journal of Macromarketing, 25*(2), 126–139.

Burden, R. (1998, April). Vulnerable consumer groups: Quantification and analysis. *OFT Research Paper 15.* London, UK: OFT.

Cartwright, P. (2011). The vulnerable consumer of financial services: Law, policy and regulation. *Financial Services Research Forum.* Retrieved from https://www.nottingham.ac.uk/business/businesscentres/crbfs/documents/researchreports/paper78.pdf

Center for Financial Inclusion. (2016). *A change in behavior: Innovations in financial capability.* Report 2016 April. Retrieved from https://centerforfinancialinclusionblog.files.wordpress.com/2016/04/a-change-in-behavior-abridged-version.pdf

CGAP. (2016). Protecting Consumers. *CGAP Website.* Retrieved from https://www.cgap.org/topics/protecting-customers

Comisión Intersectorial de Inclusión Financiera. (2016). *Estrategia Nacional de Inclusión Financiera en Colombia (Borrador para comentarios del público).* Retrieved from http://goo.gl/wsGGmu

Comisión Multisectorial de Inclusión Financiera. (2016). *Estrategia Nacional de Inclusión Financiera,* Perú. Retrieved from http://goo.gl/uP5RMr

Comisión Nacional Bancaria y de Valores—CNBV. (2016). *Consejo Nacional de Inclusión Financiera.* Retrieved from http://goo.gl/nXCwTZ

Consejo Nacional de Inclusión Financiera. (2016). *Politica Nacional de Inclusion Financiera. (2016).* Junio 2016, Cd. De Mexico Retrieved from: https://www.gob.mx/cms/uploads/attachment/file/110408/PNIF_ver_1jul2016CONAIF_vfinal.pdf

Demirguc-Kunt, A., Klapper, L., Singer, D., & Van Oudheusden P. (2015). *The Global Findex Database 2014: Measuring financial inclusion around the world.* Policy Research Working Paper 7255, World Bank, Washington, DC. Type. Time series.

Di Giannatale, Sonia; Elbittar, Alexander; Maya, Lucy; Ramírez, Alfredo and Roa, Mari Jose. (2012). *Redes sociales, confianza y hábitos financieros: un análisis empírico.* Documentos de Investigación - Research Papers 3, Centro de Estudios Monetarios Latinoamericanos, CEMLA.

European Commission. (2016a). *Understanding consumer vulnerability in the EU's key markets.* Retrieved from http://ec.europa.eu/consumers/consumer_evidence/market_studies/docs/consumer_vulnerability-factsheet_web_final_en.pdf

European Commission. (2016b). *Guidelines. Tool #28: Impacts on consumers.* Retrieved from http://ec.europa.eu/smart-regulation/guidelines/tool_28_en.htm

European Commission. (2008). *Financial services provision and prevention of financial inclusion.* Retrieved from http://www.fininc.eu/gallery/documents/final-report-2007-and-summary/financial-services-provision-and-prevention-of-financial-exclusion-final-report.pdf

European Consumer Consultative Group. (2013). *European Consumer Consultative Group Opinion on consumers and vulnerability.* Retrieved from: http://ec.europa.eu/consumers/archive/empowerment/docs/eccg_opinion_consumers_vulnerability_022013_en.pdf

Financial Conduct Authority. (2014). *Consumer credit and consumers in vulnerable circumstances.* Retrieved from: https://www.fca.org.uk/publications/research/consumer-credit-and-consumers-vulnerable-circumstances

Financial Conduct Authority. (2015). Consumer vulnerability in financial services. *Occasional Paper 8*, 2015 February, FCA.

G20/OECD. (2014). *Effective approaches to support the implementation of the remaining G20/OECD high level principles on consumer protection.* Task Force on Financial Consumer Protection, September 9, 2014, OECD.

Garcia, N., Grifoni, A., Lopez, J. C., & Mejía, D. (2013). *Financial Education in Latin America and the Caribbean: Rationale, overview and way forward.* OECD Working Papers on Finance, Insurance and Private Pensions, No. 33, Paris: OECD.

Hayes, T. (2000). Stigmatizing indebtedness: Implications for Labeling Theory. *Symbolic Interaction, 23*(1), 29–46.

Instituto Nacional de Estadistica e Informatica (INEI). (2015). *En el Día Internacional de la Juventud. El 27% de la población peruana son jóvenes.* [Press release]. Retrieved from https://goo.gl/s87oEl

Instituto Nacional de Estadistica y Geografia (INEGI). (2015a). *Mujeres y hombres en México ¿Cuántos somos?* [Data Bank]. Retrieved from http://goo.gl/Ps7eDQ

Instituto Nacional de Estadistica y Geografia (INEGI). (2015b). *Estadisticas a proposito del Día Internacional de la juventud (12 de Agosto)* [Press release]. Retrieved from http://www.inegi.org.mx/saladeprensa/aproposito/2015/juventud0.pdf

Instituto Nacional de los pueblos Andinos, Amazónicos y Afroperuanos – INDEPA. (2010). Mapa etnolingüístico del Perú. *Rev Peru Med Exp Salud Publica, 27*(2), 288–291. Retrieved from http://www.scielosp.org/pdf/rpmesp/v27n2/a19v27n2.pdf

International Fund for Agricultural Development (IFAD). (2016). *Investing in rural people in Brazil.* Retrieved from https://goo.gl/2D4dNe

Johnson, E., & Sherraden, M. S. (2007). From financial literacy to financial capability among youth. *Journal of Sociology and Social Welfare, 34*(3), 119–145.

Lusardi, A., & Mitchell, O. (2014). The economic importance of financial literacy. Theory and evidence. *Journal of Economic Literature, 52*(1), 5–44.

Mejía Anzola, D., & Rodríguez Guzmán, G. (2016) *Socio-economic determinants of financial education: Evidence for Bolivia, Colombia, Ecuador and Peru*. Caracas: CAF. Retrieved from http://goo.gl/s05I2A

Mundy, S. (2013). *Emerging Insights*. Recommendations on Developing National Financial Literacy Strategies. PowerPoint presentation at USAID/FINREPII, March 2013.

OECD. (2011). *G20 High-level Principles on Financial Consumer Protection*. October 2011, OECD, Paris. Retrieved from; https://www.oecd.org/g20/topics/financial-sector-reform/48892010.pdf

OECD. (2012). *OECD/INFE high level principles on national strategies for financial education*, August 2012, OECD, Paris.

OECD. (2013) *Advancing national strategies for financial education*. Retrieved from https://goo.gl/NPmL9w

OECD/INFE. (2009). *Recommendation of the council on good practices on financial education and awareness relating to credit*. Retrieved from http://goo.gl/6GJcnq

OECD/INFE. (2014). *Progress report on Financial Education*. Retrieved from: http://www.oecd.org/finance/financial-education/OECD-INFE-Fin-Ed-G20-2014-Progress-Report.pdf

OECD/INFE. (2015). *National strategies for financial education OECD/INFE policy handbook*. Paris: OECD.

O'Prey, L., & Shephard, D. (2014). *Financial education for children and youth: A systematic review and meta-analysis*. Aflatoun Working Paper 2014.1C.

Reddy, R., Bruhn, M., & Tan, C. (2013). *Financial capability in Colombia: Results from a national survey on financial behaviors, attitudes and knowledge*. Washington, DC: The World Bank. Retrieved from http://goo.gl/jwx6Ly

Smyczek, S. (2009). *Financial Exclusion as Barrier to Socio-Economic Development*. Baltic Business and Socio-Economic Development 2009. Gunnar Prause (ed.). 5th International Conference Kalmar Sweden Sept 2009

UNICEF. (2016). *Childhood in the Time of War: Will the Children of Colombia know peace at last?* UNICEF Child Alert, 2016. Retrieved from: https://www.unicef.org/media/files/UNICEF_Colombia_Child_Alert2(2).pdf

Varcoe, K. B., Martin, A., Devitto, Z., & Go, C. (2005). Using a financial education curriculum for teens. *Financial Counseling and Planning*, 16(1), 63–71.

World Bank. (2014a). *Mucho Corazón: Using a soap opera as a vehicle for financial education in Mexico*, September 4, 2014. Retrieved from http://www.worldbank.org/en/results/2014/09/04/using-a-soap-opera-as-a-vehicle-for-financial-education-in-mexico

World Bank. (2014b). *Global Financial Development report 2014: Financial inclusion*. Washington, DC: World Bank.

World Bank. (2015). *World Bank Open Data* [Data bank]. Retrieved from http://data.worldbank.org

CHAPTER FOURTEEN

Grasping the Foundational Roots of Economic Perceptions

Precolonial West Africa and the Bantu

THOMAS A. LUCEY
Illinois State University

DARRELL P. KRUGER
Appalachian State University[1]

JEFFREY M. HAWKINS
University of Wisconsin, Milwaukee[2]

INTRODUCTION

The early 21st-century global society experiences economically related humanitarian challenges. While the symptoms of these problems (e.g., military conflicts, employee abuse, unethical marketing, and environmental degradation) tend to receive media headlines, the substance of these challenges lies in psychological patterns that may be traceable back to societal foundations. A substantial interpretation of economic influences on societal behavior and judgment patterns requires understanding of such relationships within basic cultures: those that lacked development of complex social networks and institutions. After understanding such principles, one may extend these ideas to advanced models.

This chapter offers an interpretation of the origins of the precolonial West African culture by considering its prehistory, economic history, societal theory, religious ideals, and moral teachings. Drawing from this information, a literature review interpreting precolonial Bantu societies, associated economic perspectives, and societal patterns ensues.

WEST AFRICA

Prehistory

Not surprisingly, our review of literature concerning precolonial sub-Saharan West Africa found little information about early West African society. This finding lends itself to some conjecture about the details of events. Lentz and Sturm (2001) point out that, lacking written records, interpretations of African history relate to the training and context of the writer. As social studies educators, we interpret the archeology literature through the bias of our training in finance and ethics, South African archeology, and multicultural relationships.

We begin with Shaw (1981) who describes archeological evidence of populations during the middle stone age (30,000 Before the Common Era (BCE)) as being local and specialized, with regional differences. While Brooks (1985) explains that the Sahara experiences a series of alternating rainy and arid periods, Mauny (1978) and Stock (1995) note that, though the area sustained some prehistoric life, early Saharan populations' overgrazing, trampling, burning, and cutting of plant growth caused the Sahara to dry out around 5,000 BCE. As the desert expanded, populations moved south, invading the southern cultures (Mauny, 1978), although forest dwellers nearest to the Ivory Coast might have interacted only with members of their own society (Phillipson, 1982). These societies provided evidence that specialized primitive population centers prompted environmental destruction and forced migration.

Archeologists perceive different stages (and forms) of societal development from north to south. Technological development apparently related to environmental suitability (Hopkins, 1973; Posnansky, 1981). While Hill (1978) writes "there ought to be no escaping the plain fact of 'backwardness' in precolonial West Africa, in terms of lack of ploughs" (p. 131). Diamond (1999) points out that a myriad of environmental factors affected personal and cultural processes. The following sections explore relationships of these environments to economic patterns in societies.

ECONOMIC PROCESSES

An interpretation of precolonial West African social structures and the economic conditions prompting them begins with Horton's (1971) argument that five important features (low food production with a poorly developed trade or currency, overexploitation of fixed tracts of land, overpopulation of land, decentralized decision-making, low communication technology development) characterized West Africa at the start of the colonial era.

The authors recognize that much literature revises Horton's ideas; however, his work provides a basis for beginning these conversations. Horton (1971) interprets these factors as characterizing an agricultural population that quickly outgrew its resources, but lacked the communication (and possibly knowledge) to facilitate organizational networks for meaningful responses.

However, Hopkins (1973) posits a simultaneous presence of various organizational systems, and technological development prompted by environmental unsuitability, rather than incapable populations. According to Hopkins (1973), the number of people was small for a large volume of inferior land. This imbalance, along with prohibitive climatic conditions, prompted low agricultural productivity. Since farmers could not survive full days of activity, they had time for nonagricultural pursuits; thus, some environments allowed for development of specialized crafts while others fostered agricultural pursuits.

In contrast to agricultural populations, forest cultures experienced limited or no extra-societal contact, and a lack of large centralized societies. Fage (1977) observes that the indigenous West Atlantic coast forest peoples developed village societies, but without extensive political-economic structures or social stratification. These peoples did not have much trans-Saharan trade experience until contact with Muslims (Fage, 1977).

SOCIETAL THEORY

Interpretations of social structures may offer connections to economic influences. Horton (1971) recognizes that the various environments prompted diverse societal structures, prompting three lineage systems (the segmentary lineage system [see Haviland, Prins, Walrath, & McBride 2004]; the dispersed, territorially defined communities, and the large compact village) within precolonial West African society. His description of these systems clarifies the contextual relationship of societal processes and behaviors.

Segmentary Lineage System

Horton (1971) perceives this system as organized in a "top to bottom" (oldest to youngest ages) genealogical hierarchy. This lineage system only occurred when three conditions existed: steady birth-based population increase, readily accessible land supply, and a dispersed (rural) settlement pattern with scattered homesteads (Haviland et al., 2004).

The system provided for autonomy of each unit except in the event of conflict, with the communities resolving internal conflicts. In this setting, individuals were concerned only with extended family issues; thus, all lineage segments were considered equal (Horton, 1971). This system was certainly different from "developed" societies where wealth ownership determined the importance of lineage.

Leadership prevailed over authority in this system, although the lower levels of the structures may have experienced authority, with elders deliberating over matters of justice, disputes, and communal activities (Horton, 1971). When intra-societal disputes occurred, the disputes persisted until either compromise or war occurred. This structure prompted compromise, as a segment that did not win a conflict would be absorbed into a lower order of grouping.

However, Horton (1971) observes a paradoxical order to this system. On one level, it discouraged societal differences and authority internally, unless threatened externally. In such instances, the system encouraged powerful leaders for large segment groups. We see the systemic structures as prompting leadership based on contextual needs. Strong leadership was called upon to repel external threats. As communities become larger, formal decision-making structures became perceived as necessary for societal organization. The size of the community needing such structure apparently depended on a combination of factors such as the environment, technology, and community.

Dispersed Territorially Based Communities and Large Compact Village

Horton (1971) theorizes that limitations of the segmentary lineage community prompted development of territorially based communities. In these settings, the highest organizational level either forgot (through diminished communication) or abandoned (through behavioralist justification) genealogical concepts and lineages became divided between "landowners" and "latecomers." This division became the complementary basis for division of labor where new community members needed work and established members provided employment. While compensation for labor occurred, alliance with the community may have provided an element of accountability. Without a complementary relationship, the community lacked cohesiveness necessary for firm loyalties.

Horton (1971) theorizes that community need requirements prompted large compact village formation. In such communities, as in rural areas, spatial distances determined societal distance (Horton, 1971). These settings involved no genealogical scheme, as institutions obliterated lineage structures and prompted societal divisions. While Horton (1971) interprets such processes as more effective than lineages, we believe these processes seeded the comparative patterns that fostered communal discord and individual ambition. These societies developed as economic responses to their environments (Hopkins, 1973). Members may have adjusted their bases for decision-making in conformance with popular sentiments.

Davidson (1998) consolidates Horton's (1971) communities into three societal divisions. First, vertical divisions occurred among senior chiefs, free farmers, and "unfree" servants or slaves. Second, horizontal divisions occurred among people of different clans, villages, or neighbors. Finally, similar to the formation of guilds in late medieval Europe, divisions occurred through trade groups, although Hill (1978) writes, "while rural craftsmen such as weavers and dyers, often preferred to work alongside each other in groups ... each man usually operated on his own account, being subject to no constraint from his fellow" (p. 132). Davidson writes that these class divisions did not entail harsh class distinctions of contemporary European societies, possibly, because the European scarcity of land prompted a concept of land ownership (not fully attained in West Africa). Davidson's conceptualization appears to express the simultaneous cohesion of Horton's (1971) three societal systems. Iliffe (2005) claims that this "growing stratification" (p. 15) was one of three factors (the other two being establishment of Islam and adaptation of warhorses) from 1000 to 1500 CE that fostered the development of West African aristocracies.

It is possible that the nature of the environment related to the established social system. Hopkins (1973) comments that slavery occurred in areas when local free-market labor was inadequate; needs for slaves occurred in Ashanti and Dehomati, although Hill (1978) writes that "slave holding, though widespread, probably always involved a minority of farmers" (p. 130). Such evidence suggests the existence of long established trade markets, precolonial societal inequities, and conflicts of interest between labor and the employer (Hopkins, 1973), Darling's bi-protective earthworks (as cited in Ben-Amos Girshick & Thornton, 2001) indicate the presence of orderliness among social classes in a system of restrictive economic control.

Hopkins (1973) indicates that earthworks may have been barriers to prevent slaves from escaping communities. Hill (1978) asserts that, "All the evidence in that rural economies in contemporary West Africa are innately inequalitarian at any point in time ... there are always powerful forces ... which tend ... to enhance the living standards of the rich and to depress those of the poor" (p. 130). Yet Iliffe (2005) argues that slavery originated in West Africa during the early 700s, and intensified with social stratification. Whether or not slavery practice developed or was imported, human values readily become secondary to economic pursuits at any stage of societal development.

This society embodied elements of respect among economic classes. Hopkins' (1973) observation that reciprocity and redistribution occurred in both private and public sectors indicated that in the rural communal system, as modeled by the lineage segment, there was not any distinction among these sectors. The communities' focus required reciprocity and redistribution for success. However, as society became centralized and structured, private and public sectors became distinct. Individual pursuits coexisted with communal processes.

It is possible that as different systems developed, different ideas concerning citizenship and community arose. While individual variations may have existed and precise features of societies remain to be determined, we believe a competitive focused society may model processes that prompt an individual to experience ethical dilemmas between individual pursuits and communal expectations. A cooperative setting may model processes where this dilemma does not occur; however, a specialization system that lacks individual choice necessarily prompts elements of individual disenchantment. Whereas a system based on mutual support allows for harmony, but requires elements of accountability to limit acts of selfishness and abuse.

Several theories interpret patterns of economic development in precolonial Africa. Perinbam (1977) describes the ideas of the substantivists, traditionalists, and the structural neo-Marxists. Austin (2004) verifies the discrediting of substantivist theories and argued for a connection between economic behaviors and interpretations of values. Societies did not evolve independently; however, their patterns of organization and communication related to patterns of contact with other cultures.

ROLE OF RELIGION AND FOLKLORE

The communities' religious practices and folklore provide some insight into West African community interpretations of itself and its world. Early West African religious conceptualizations of the earth spirit may have reflected this cooperative nature. The earth spirit provided laws that priests interpreted and enforced for all men, though changes depended on interpretation and cultural dominance (Lentz & Sturm, 2001). Ezi, Nri, and Igbo societal rituals provided evidence for such earth-based concepts (Isichei, 1997). Political community developed because of these complementary economic needs. Achebe's description of the egwugwu—a masquerader who impersonates village ancestral spirits—in his much acclaimed *Things Fall Apart* (1959) emphasizes the relationship between the spiritual and physical needs of Igbo society.

Horton (1971) recognizes that religion in West Africa represented "a theoretical interpretation to the prediction of worldly events" (p. 106). Man was interpreted as occupying an environment controlled by an invisible order of personal beings where sickness and misfortune were consequences for misbehavior (Achebe, 1959; Horton, 1971). Early societies used religion as an incentive to coerce behavioral expectations of their members.

The communal authority figures had special relationships with these forces. The antitheses of this system involved cults of communal gods or of lineage ancestors who challenged the social order (Horton, 1971). The crucial feature of this religion involved both the social relationship of people to the other people and to the gods. Because of this situation, a man's entrance into a new group prompted a new spiritual relationship as well, associated with the new community dependency. The gods also represented community "outsiders," and therefore could objectively reconcile community conflicts (Horton, 1971).

Social conditions affected interpretations of religious schema. Greene (1996) concludes, "all concerned have failed to recognize the extent to which African religious conceptions were deeply influenced by the power dynamics within a given polity or region" (p. 136). Ellis and Harr (1998) write "In all known pre-colonial African political systems and states, religious performance played an important role ... rulers were endowed with sacred duties, such as causing rain to fall and crops to grow, and charged with upholding the cosmic order generally" (p. 187). Social structures, order, and prosperity were the measures of religious favor. "Even in the so-called stateless societies of old Africa, real public authority actually lay with ritual experts who mediated between the visible and invisible worlds" (Ellis & Harr, 1998, p. 187).

Iliffe (2005) observes that differences in perceptions of honor occur among cultures, with interpretations economically related. Writing "In both Europe and China, the primary criterion of honor shifted over time from rank and behavior to moral character, from what a person had or did to what a person was" (p. 5). Iliffe observes that different interpretations of honor occur among social classes and, hence, different precolonial West African societies. These interpretations also depended on the observer. For example, in the West African Savanna, the word ola (honor) meant recognition of authority whereas according to the oriki (indigenous "praise songs") esteem, courage, decency, and moderation were honorable traits. In environments having strong state structures, honor related to rank or status. Stateless structures interpreted honor as respect of one's peers. When a culture became economically centralized and stratified, honor became a matter of social class, level, or achievement.

Thus, a transition in religion occurred as societies changed economically. Early communities recognized a sense of environmental dependency and peer-based honor with outsiders interpreted by earth-based priests. Societies experiencing economic prosperity employed religion as a vehicle for preserving social order. In an age of economic excess, Kerekous' modern religiously fundamental political processes in Benin (Strandsbjerg, 2000) employed a dualistic "good and evil" theme, identifying the leader's personal experience with that of society, and prompting messianic imagery. Such modern political processes encouraged a comparison-based setting that prompted assimilative rather than cooperative processes.

As society becomes economically polarized, it wrestles with religious challenges in a "for or against" climate that threatens acceptance and cooperation.

Honor transitions from a horizontal concept to a vertical concept. In precolonial Africa hierarchical power structures, honor lost a community focus. The setting involved community based on the needs determined by political leadership, rather than the needs of all members.

FOLKLORE

West African folklore provides clues about expectations for societal conduct in this framework. By personifying the animal kingdom, West Africans developed and adopted folk tales that paralleled those of other cultures. The northern Nigerian (Hausen) tale of the Spider, the Guinea Fowl, and Francolin (Lee, 1946) paralleled that of the Benga tale of the Leopard's marriage journey (Nassau, 1970). In both tales, the main characters (or tricksters) repeated deceptive practices for personal gain, prompting their demise for community betterment. Such stories provided lessons discouraging individual ambitions in community-based settings. Other stories contained important community lessons as well. The Tale of the Quarcoo Bah-Boni (Lee, 1946) provided a lesson about the importance of cooperation into a new community; the tale of Anasi and Nothing (Nassau, 1970) offered a lesson about the ill consequences for obsessions of wealth and competitiveness. From a societal perspective, the tricksters may represent lower economic members who employ cunning and deception to outwit the directness and force of upper-classed members trying to preserve social order. Further research into economic patterned origins of West African folktales could shed light on such patterns in these stories.

Precolonial West Africa witnessed a setting of diverse cultural groups stemming from its abundant land and climatic variation. These societies ranged from rural community based to village competitive based, with the nature of this community or competition clearly economic. In subsistence agricultural settings, familial relationships allowed for intragroup conflict and resolution, while prompting intergroup unity in times of need. These settings contrasted with village contexts, where institutions fostered individual anonymity to de-emphasize individual accountability and prompt a competitive-based societal hierarchy.

We see formal political structures as developing from communal economic needs, even as the society focused more on competition and institutional development, obscuring perceptions of the extended lineages. The abbreviated family took precedence in a specialized village environment. Finally, the government became a symbolic representation of community ideals. Ellis and Harr (1998) comment, "Religion and politics are both systems of ordering the power inherent in human society, in the process of which elements of hierarchy and authority tend to emerge" (p. 195). A wealthy competitive and individualist North American society needs to consider the benefits (both within and outside society) of cooperative processes and the values of shared leadership.

BANTU

The Bantu represent a pertinent society for study because of the success in their cultural expansion and dominance of all sub-Saharan African regions (Stock, 1995). Although we interpret the Bantu with a broad perspective, we acknowledge that variances occurred among different Bantu communities. The discussion begins with conventional understandings of Bantu migrations, and then presents recent accounts.

TRADITIONAL INTERPRETATIONS

While archeologists historically interpreted the Bantu-speaking people as originating from the Lower Niger River and Cameroon, researchers have theorized that migration occurred through various processes. Challenging popular theories of organized migration, Lwanga-Lunyiigo and Vansina (1988) attributed the growth to a combination of famine, epidemics, and wars that forced small groups into new geographic areas. Vansina (1990) expanded on this conceptualization by interpreting these processes as unintentional: various factors (food production, nutrition, diseased environments, barriers between habitats, density of encountered populations, intercultural relationships, and changes in social dynamics) caused populations to develop at various rates in different environments.

Just as different environmental and societal inducements and deterrents prompted expansion from the Fertile Crescent to Europe and the New World, Bantu culture developed from a balance of environmental and societal influences. This theory is pivotal to understanding the economic challenges that modern society faces. The argument that economic achievement results solely from individual (or societal) effort fails to account for various environmental determinants.

One's conceptualization of the Bantu movement depends on his or her interpretation of their adaptation to rainforest environments. While the reader might interpret our argument as shifting from economics to environment as a cornerstone of societal change, we point out that economics is not simply a matter of resource availability, but of resource awareness and management. For example, the Bantu's presence in the rainforests was not an economic advantage; their patterns of adaptation and use of resources prompted their development.

Ehret and Posnansky (1982) write that the expansion gradually extended into the rainforest, with the Bantu following natural transportation paths, such as rivers. Vansina (1990) affirms that the Bantu encountered pygmy guides who taught them how to adapt to various rainforest settings and held that the migrating peoples possessed favorable perceptions of indigenous rainforest inhabitants. Eventually, the pygmy influence diminished because the pygmies lacked the communal continuity necessary to offset the dominance of the expanding Bantu. Within the rainforest, the pygmy had not developed the social structures necessary for responding to the organized Bantu.

Over time, the Bantu gained control of the new environments and developed their settlements. Vansina (1990) reasons that as the Bantu expanded and became less dependent on the pygmy, their perceptions of the Pygmy changed. At first, the Bantu considered the pygmy "first of land, inventors of fire, teacher of habitats, wise healers, with medicinal plants, first metallurgists, and first farmers" (p. 56). However, as the Bantu settled and overcame dependence on the pygmy, they downgraded their former hosts as human surplus, eventually deploring the pygmies as "despised, uncivilized, a sub-human race, and unfit for (sex) with farming women" (p. 56). During the 19th century, colonists reinforced these attitudes, as "all surviving bands of pygmies ... were serfs for the villagers, who held ambivalent views of them" (p. 56). It appears that economic contexts affected interpersonal interpretation. The Bantu apparently appreciated pygmy assistance provided upon their initial encounters in the rainforest, yet as Bantu gained more control of the environment, successive generations belittled the pygmy populations.

To rationalize the Bantu's attitudinal change as being based purely on perceptions of cultural economic differences ignores the lack of an opposite effect in the pygmy. The economically (defined as contextually meaningful resources and knowledge) advantaged pygmy assisted the early Bantu: they shared their resources and knowledge to those in need. In a situation of economic control, the Bantu did not share with the pygmy. This situation raises a question concerning the conditions prompting elements of community versus competition between economically inferior groups.

Two immediate responses present themselves. First, Diamond (1999) provides some clues in his widely acclaimed work. As illustrated in the encounters between the colonizing Europeans and the indigenous American populations, it is possible that the Bantu culture developed in environments having superior nutritional and environmental resources. As the population developed beyond their areas' supportive capacities, they spread to outlying environments. In their contact with the pygmy, the interfacing may have begun amicably on a small scale; however, it became divisive as contact occurred on larger scales. We think that perceptions of economic need or advantage provided an incomplete attitudinal difference; they resulted from cultural perceptions of superiority. The Bantu rationalized their economic superiority because the nature of their society had changed to an economically based organization. Within Bantu society, economics, rather than community, provided the socialization bases. Members communicated with those having similar societal roles, thus prompting ideas of technical expertise.

Second, we note that prior to the Bantu contact; the pygmy society lacked cohesive community within the rainforest. As Diamond (1999) points out that limited archeological evidence from the African rainforests exists, the nature of the rainforest environment and the dispersed natures of the pygmy societies not only had limited community development, but also prompted few large settlements. Thus, the environment supported fewer large settlements and greater amounts of isolation. Because the pygmy societies experienced geographic sprawl rather than compact settlement, they lacked an element of community bond. Consider the parallel of the indigenous Americans who exercised a widely disbursed existence, and who generally did not build large monuments. The Bantu interaction with the pygmy may have involved different value systems. By applying Iliffe's (2005) interpretations, one might conceptualize the Bantu as employing a more hierarchical interpretation of honor than the pygmy did. Each society employed different patterns of rainforest use. Just as corporate executives from International Paper might interpret the Amazon rainforest differently than the indigenous populations, so did the Bantu interpret the knowledge of the African rainforest differently from the pygmy.

WAVE EXPANSION THEORY

Vansina's (1995) wave expansion model depicted three phases of Bantu dispersal. According to Vansina's theory, the original Bantu language changed first through contact with the Moam-Nkam, expanded east toward the Great Lakes, as a secondary, seagoing, movement toward lower Oggoue. Second, as the extreme dialects became increasingly distant, they became their own languages: the East and West Bantu. Third, the proto-west Bantu expanded south as the proto-east Bantu expanded toward southeast Africa. This wave expansion theory explained a pattern of language changes more efficiently than an idea of migration along specific paths.

Vansina (1995) held that many language dispersions occurred at different times, but not sequentially, and interpreted them as many Bantu scatterings indicating at least nine "diffusions" over 2,000 years. Each possessed different characteristics and had its own history. As the Bantu faced different economic and environmental choices, there was bound to be some dissent among groups.

We think that Vansina's diffusions may have resulted from irreconcilable differences within the group. History witnesses similar patterns within expanding and branching cultures, such as the founding of the United States and Australia as distinct countries from British Colonies. Yet limitations to these patterns also occur. The U.S. Civil War represented an effort at cultural separation related to many issues, including political representation. Conflicts occur among, between, and within societies. On a foundational level, it appears that resource access represents a critical element to cultural expansion. However, such expansions do not occur without conflict. As societies grow past a critical mass, they develop a complexity requiring cohesive networks of internal structures.

PROTO-BANTU SOCIETIES

We now consider the structure of Bantu societies. Vansina (1990, 1995) conceptualized the basic units of early Bantu as large households: groups of which formed a village. These households and villages were tied together in a district. All of these units chose their own memberships (Vansina, 1990). While achievement, not inheritance, was the basis for identifying leaders of houses and villages, leadership brought wealth and wives for those who obtained it (Vansina, 1990).

Districts involved clusters of villages and houses within "deserts or dead areas." While districts had no chief and no principal village, their importance lay in the provisions for defense, common security, matrimonial alliances, and trading processes. The village represented the foundation of Bantu society (Vansina, 1990). However, the village represented a social image more than a physical reality. As groups migrated, social roles and relationships were maintained.

The house was established by a "big man" and lasted beyond his death. It was the basic food production unit involving 10–40 people: family, friends, and dependents. This arrangement prompted inequitable social structures, as linguistic evidence exists for the several terms reflecting economically based personal relationships (Vansina, 1990).

SOUTHEAST AFRICA BANTU

Building upon Vansina's (1995) wave theory, Ehret (1998) provided evidence for the diversity of culture in southeast Africa, and observed several themes to the Bantu social history from 300 BCE to 400 CE. First, Kaskazi and Kusi peoples combined agricultural traditions with food gathering, hunting, and fishing elements (Ehret, 1998), forcing assimilation of established hunter-gathering peoples into a new social system (Ehret, 1998). Second, the Kusi made thatch roofed round houses while the Kaskazi developed conical roofed or rectangular flat roofed houses, depending on their setting (Ehret, 1998). The Kaskazi villages also varied with setting. For example, the Kusi started an established pattern along a single street, but this changed to irregular patterns of "constituent households" (p. 248). Such patterns may have indicated economically derived perceptual differences within the communities. These differences among households occurred when sedentary populations observed intra-cultural differences.

Ehret (1998) suggested that the kin chiefship generally changed into a less structured authority figure. However, patterns of different authority bases were evident. For example, the Nyasa retained only a lineal form of kin chiefship; yet, the pre-Makua associated the word "owner" with their word for chief or king (Ehret, 1998). In the Sala Shona communities, the higher positions of kin authority disappeared without causal evidence and the manner of how the following institutions come about is uncertain (Ehret, 1998).

The early southeast Bantu of the first century CE linguistically connected the words "to rule" and the root of the word "chief," but this relationship differed in successive southeast Bantu society (Ehret, 1998). Among the Kosi peoples, leadership involved a term for hereditary-based authority, and expanded the scope to be a wealth-based leader of a larger local grouping of people. The word "Kûm" changed in meaning, "to be honored" to "to be rich." However, in the 3rd or 4th century CE, new larger social units occurred. The chiefship was based on tracing legitimacy back to family heads.

Ehret (1998) supported Vansina's (1995) belief of a multifaceted Bantu history that varied among groups, and observed that changes occurred with different scales and organizational processes. Traditions would have been difficult to maintain over long distances and time, forgetting ancestral histories and recreating and kin authority.

The Zulu of South Africa serve to illustrate how economic influences shaped societal patterns in the Phongolo-Mzimkhulu region during the late 18th century into the early 19th century among the Bantu of southeast Africa (Wright & Hamilton, 1989). The dominant process during this period was the political expansion and centralization of the Zulu chiefdom into the powerful kingdom that Shaka (reigned 1816–1828) founded and shaped.

Academics offer at least three explanations as to why the Zulu chiefdom, one of about a dozen between the Phongolo and Mzimkhulu rivers at this time, became dominant, incorporating other chiefdoms to form the Zulu Kingdom. First, growth in population led to an intensification of conflict over resources. A variation on this demographic argument is the ecological explanation that provides a second rationale for the changed political structure among the Bantu in southeast Africa. More specifically, conflict over grazing and water resources were at the core of the conflict rooted in unscientific farming practices (Wright & Hamilton, 1989). Finally, the impact of international trade with the arrival of the Portuguese and the ivory trade with natives precipitated internal conflicts within the geographically circumscribed area of southeast Africa. These explanations strike more deeply than the "great man" theory posited by Bryant (Wright & Hamilton, 1989). Irrespective of which of the three explanations holds more weight, it is beyond dispute that modification of the prevailing Bantu economic system had a profound impact on the settlement system of the Zulu and surrounding chiefdoms in southeast Africa under the leadership of Shaka and subsequent Zulu Kings concluding with Cetshwayo in 1879.

Although Shaka is credited with centralizing the political system in southeast Africa during the first two decades of the 19th century, the dominance of this settlement pattern is evident in his successor, Dingane's royal kraal at Mgungundlovu on the White Mfolozi River (Colenbrander, 1989). Prior to the creation of a large centralized royal kraal where the Zulu King resided together with a large standing army, the settlement system consisted of scattered family kraals paying tribute to a chief. Sedentary agriculture coupled with seminomadic pastoralism characterized a dispersed settlement pattern. The large centralized royal Zulu kraal meant that the Zulu King was dependent on his subjects through tribute (food and young men and women) from chiefs to keep the army and settlement fed and functioning. This changed economic system clearly had a tangible impact on the settlement pattern of the Zulu chiefdoms. The royal Zulu kraal was clearly engaged in a parasitic relationship with the dispersed chiefdoms in the outlying hinterland.

CONCLUSIONS

As they became more sedentary and wealth focused, Bantu societies changed from horizontally respectful and cooperative coexistence to vertically competitive postures. These changes were evident among villages and cultures. As competition became more acute, societal conflict intensified to the point of eradication.

The world community experiences a similar circumstance, as economically successful cultures expand their spheres of global influence. These cultures have developed a global plantation system that exploits the third world of precious natural resources, such as petroleum. Emphasizing a horizontal interpretation of honor that fosters respectful dialogues may initiate mutually amicable resolutions of these challenges.

CHAPTER UPDATE

In 2014, Elizabeth Kolbert published "The Sixth Extinction," which provided scientific evidence for human kind's diminishing of the earth's habitability. Her work describes archeological research that supports the interbreeding theory for Neanderthal extinction; however, there are also claims that Neanderthals lacked the immunity system to support encounters with humans (http://phys.org/news/2016-04-neanderthals-infected-diseases-africa-humans.html).

Kolbert's (2014) "insanity gene," which motivates human exploration of the unknown—or undemonstrated may serve to take a risk in an unproven theory and/or have faith in something unseen. It represents a form of confidence. This confidence yields benefits when founded on solid principles; however, it portends catastrophes when resting on flimsy evidence.

Research (Narvaez, 2014; Panksepp & Biven, 2012) that documents the environmental effects on behavioral development conveys the fallacy of attributing resource control to individual merit. The history of precolonial Africa demonstrates how economic comparisons shape populations' dispositions. Narcissism represents an associate of resource control and manipulation. It also has the potential to represent a symptom of a society's demise.

DISCUSSION QUESTIONS

1. What are some examples in your life where you encountered someone who controlled different amount of resources than you?
2. The authors describe a relationship between religion and social views. How your views of religion changed with your social experiences? How or why?
3. The authors describe different social views among society in relation to their geographic dispersions. How may your past or present sense of place influence your social visions?

NOTES

1. Dr. Kruger was affiliated with Illinois State University at the time of this chapter's original publication.
2. Dr. Hawkins was affiliated with Oklahoma State University at the time of this chapter's original publication.

REFERENCES

Achebe, C. (1959). *Things fall apart.* New York, NY: Anchor Books.
Austin, G. (2004). *The problem of "embeddedness" and global economic history.* Retrieved from http://www.lse.ac.uk/collections/economicHistory/GEHN/GEHN%20PDF/The%20Problem%20of%20Embeddedness%20-%20Gareth%20Austin.pdf
Ben-Amos Girshick, P., & Thornton, J. (2001). Civil war in the Kingdom of Benin, 1689–1721: Community or political change? *Journal of African History, 42*(5). 353–376.
Brooks, G. E. (1985). *Western Africa to c/1860 A.D. A provisional historical schema based on climatic periods.* Indiana University African Studies Program Working Paper Series No. 1.

Colenbrander, P. (1989). The Zulu kingdom. In A. Duminy & B. Guest (Eds.), *Natal and Zululand from earliest times to 1910: A New History* (pp. 83–115). Pietermaritzburg, KwaZulu-Natal: University of Natal Press.
Davidson, B. (1998). *West Africa before the colonial era: A history to 1850*. New York, NY: Addison Wesley Longman.
Diamond, J. (1999). *Guns, germs, and steel: The fates of human societies*. New York, NY: W.W. Norton and Company.
Ehret, C. (1998). *An African classical age: Eastern and Southern Africa in world history 1000 B.C. to A.D. 400*. Charlottesville, VA: University of Virginia.
Ehret, C., & Posnansky, M. (1982). *The archeological and linguistic reconstruction of African history*. Berkeley, CA: University of California.
Ellis, T., & Harr, G. T. (1998). Religion and politics in sub-Saharan Africa. *The Journal of Modern African Studies, 36*(2), 175–201.
Fage, J. D. (1977). Upper and Lower Guinea. In R. Oliver (Ed.), *The Cambridge History of Africa, Volume 3: c. 1050–c. 1600* (pp. 463–518). London, UK: Cambridge University.
Greene, S. E. (1996). Religion, history, and the supreme gods of Africa: A contribution to the debate. *Journal of Religion in Africa, 26*(2), 122–138.
Haviland, W. A., Prins, H. E. L., Walrath, D., & McBride, B. (2004). *Cultural anthropology: The human challenge*. New York, NY: Wadsworth Publishing.
Hill, P. (1978). Problems with A. G. Hopkins' Economic History of West Africa. *African Economic History*, (6), 127–133.
Hopkins, A. G. (1973). *An economic history of West Africa*. London, UK: Longman Group.
Horton, R. (1971). Stateless societies in the history of West Africa. In J. F. Ade Ajayi & M. Crowder (Eds.), *History of West Africa* (Vol. 1, pp. 78–119). London, UK: Longman Group.
Iliffe, J. (2005). *Honour in African History*. Cambridge, UK: Cambridge University Press.
Isichei, E. (1997). *A history of African societies to 1870*. Cambridge, UK: Cambridge University Press.
Kolbert, E. (2014). *The sixth extinction: An unnatural history*. New York, NY: Henry Holt.
Lee, F. H. (1946). *Folk tales of all nations*. New York, NY: Tutor Publishing.
Lentz, C., & Sturm, H.-J. (2001). Of trees and earth shrines: An interdisciplinary approach to settlement histories in the West African savanna. *History of Africa, 28*, 139–168.
Lwanga-Lunyiigo, S., & Vansina, J. (1988). The Bantu-speaking peoples and their expansion. In M. Elfasi (Ed.), *UNESCO General History of Africa – III, Africa from the seventh to the eleventh century* (pp. 140–162). London, UK: Heinemann Educational Books.
Mauny, R. (1978). Transaharan contacts and the Iron Age in West Africa. In J. D. Fage (Ed.), *The Cambridge History of Africa, Volume 2: c. 500 BC–A.D. 1050* (pp. 272–341). Cambridge, UK: Cambridge University Press.
Narvaez, D. (2014). *Neurobiology and the development of human morality*. New York, NY: W.W. Norton.
Nassau, R. H. (1970). *Where animals talk: West African folklore tales*. New York, NY: Negro Universities.
Panksepp, J., & Biven, L. (2012). *The archeology of the mind: Neuroevolutionary origins of human emotions*. New York, NY: W.W. Norton.
Perinbam, B. M. (1977). Homo Africanus: Antiquus or Oeconomicus? Some interpretations of African Economic History. *Comparative Studies in Society and History, 19*(2), 156–178.
Phillipson, D. W. (1982). The later stone age in sub-Saharan Africa. In J. D. Clark (Ed.), *The Cambridge History of Africa, Volume 1: From the Earliest Times to c. 500 B.C.* (pp. 410–477). Cambridge, UK: Cambridge University Press.

Posnansky, M. (1981). Introduction to the later prehistory of Subsaharan Africa. In G. Mokhtar (Ed.), *UNESCO General History of Africa II, Ancient Civilizations*. (pp. 533–551). London, UK: Heinemann Educational Books.

Shaw, C. T. (1981). The prehistory of West Africa. In J. Ki-Zerbo (Ed.), *UNESCO General History of Africa I, Methodology and African Prehistory* (pp. 611–633). London, UK: Heinemann Educational Books.

Stock, R. (1995). *Africa south of the Sahara: A geographical interpretation*. New York, NY: The Guilford Press.

Strandsbjerg, C. (2000). Kérékou, God and the ancestors: Religion and the conception of political power in Benin. *African Affairs, 99*, 395–414.

Vansina, J. (1990). *Paths in the Rainforests: Toward a history of political tradition in Equatorial Africa*. Madison, WI: The University of Wisconsin.

Vansina, J. (1995). New linguistic evidence and 'The Bantu Expansion'. *Journal of African History, 36*(2), 173–195.

Wright, J., & Hamilton, C. (1989). Traditions and transformations: The Phongolo-Mzimkhulu region in the late eighteenth and early nineteenth centuries. In A. Duminy & B. Guest (Eds.), *Natal and Zululand from earliest times to 1910: A new history* (pp. 49–82). Pietermaritzburg, Kwa-Zulu-Natal: University of Natal Press.

CHAPTER FIFTEEN

Using Stories to Teach Complex Moral Concepts to Young Children

CHIARA BACIGALUPA
Sonoma State University

INTRODUCTION

Stories are a potentially important component of a curriculum designed to help young children develop sophisticated understandings of the moral aspects of economic decisions. Some books introduce moral concepts directly related to economics and social justice, such as sharing, delayed gratification, resourcefulness, giving to others, and the value of community. Stories provide role models, offer advice on moral questions, and raise provocative issues related to specific moral themes.

In addition to raising economic and social justice themes, books portray skills and dispositions that children need to develop before they can make sound moral decisions. In order to act morally, children need to be able to consider the perspectives of other people, develop and act upon empathetic feelings, understand the consequences of particular actions on others, recognize and think critically about the specific factors relevant to a particular issue, and put moral issues above other concerns (Rest, 1983). These skills and dispositions are prerequisites for consideration of and acting upon complex moral questions. Stories portray characters who model these skills and dispositions, and they provide opportunities for the reader to practice moral skills and explore moral dispositions. For example, many stories ask the reader to consider a perspective that may be new to them, thus encouraging the development of perspective-taking abilities.

Because stories raise specific moral themes, portray positive moral actions, and encourage the practice of moral skills and dispositions, educators often recommend them as a valuable way to enhance moral education programs for children. However, it is not clear that children interpret stories in the same ways that adults do. According to Rosenblatt's (1938/1995) transactional theory of reading, a reader understands a story in light of the reader's previous experiences and existing knowledge. The text of a story guides the interpretation, but each reader constructs a unique understanding of the story according to the particular memories and ideas he or she uses to make sense of the text. Thus, it is possible for different readers to construct different understanding of a given story.

The potential to interpret a single text in multiple ways has important implications for the practice of using stories to teach moral messages. If it is possible for different readers to build different understandings of a text, then readers might construct understandings of a particular story that are different from the message that the author intended or different from the message that is generally recognized as inherent in the story. When the readers are children, with limited experiences and knowledge, it seems even more likely that their understandings will differ from those of the adults who hope the stories will teach specific moral lessons.

This chapter discusses partial findings of a qualitative study that investigated the understandings of a group of kindergarten children constructed in response to a story about sharing. I explain how children's story interpretations differed from those of adults, and I argue that those differences were likely due to factors in their social environment. I end with a discussion of implications for moral education.

THEORIES/RESEARCH INFORMING THIS STUDY

The belief that children can learn moral and social concepts from stories is widespread. Many different authors have suggested that both parents (e.g., Bennett, 1995; Coles, 1989; Kilpatrick, Wolfe, & Wolfe, 1994) and teachers (e.g., DeVries & Zan, 1994; Koc & Buzzelli, 2004; Lamme, Krogh, & Yachmetz, 1992) should use stories to teach moral concepts. Because there is widespread agreement that educators can use stories to teach children moral concepts, it is surprising that so little research exists on what children seem to learn from stories with moral themes.

Lehr (1991) read different kinds of stories to preschool and kindergarten-age children individually, and then asked the students questions such as, "What do you think this story is trying to teach you or tell you? What is the most important idea in this story?" (p. 38). Lehr found that preschoolers and kindergartners did have an understanding of literary themes, but that they tended to focus on different aspects of the story than did adults. For example, when the children in her study heard *The Three Little Pigs*, they were more concerned with the pigs' safety than they were with the pigs' ability to make wise decisions. Perhaps because the children did not view themselves as needing to leave home and start making their own decisions, they ignored that aspect of the story and focused instead on aspects that were more relevant to concerns they had themselves experienced—matters of safety.

Lehr's (1991) study suggests that although children do respond to the themes in stories, they might also ignore themes that they perceive as uninteresting or irrelevant. This finding raises the question of whether children are interested in the moral themes in stories. Junker (1998) investigated whether children in a multiage first to third grade classroom explored moral subject matter when they participated in literature study groups. Junker did not choose the books specifically as moral texts, although many of them did contain moral themes. Junker found that the children in her study spontaneously made statements about moral events or issues in the text; they offered interpretive moral commentary in response to texts; and they shared moral stories from other contexts in response to texts. Thus, the children did show interest in moral themes.

Narvacz, Gleason, Mitchell, and Bentley (1999) asked third, fifth, and eighth grade students to identify moral themes in several stories written by the researchers. They found that third grade children who were asked to match statements reflecting the themes of the stories consistently identified statements that reflected the plot rather than the theme. In this study, then, the moral themes did not seem to be what captured younger children's attention, and the study casts doubt on the ability of young children to extract moral themes from stories.

Clare, Gallimore, and Patthey-Chavez (1996) analyzed the conversations between fourth grade students and their teacher on moral themes found in stories the class read together. The teacher in this study used instructional conversations (IC)—a model in which the teacher relies more heavily on joint exploration of issues—rather than on teacher-directed conversations where the teacher attempts to direct students toward predetermined answers. These researchers found that students in the IC groups expressed more sophisticated understandings of the encountered moral issues than did children in a control group. They concluded that simply reading stories does not necessarily lead to moral growth. Instead, stories are more likely to enhance moral development when teachers facilitate discussions about relevant issues at an appropriate developmental level. This study suggests that the discussions that surround a story may be a more important catalyst for moral growth than are the stories themselves.

These research studies offer evidence that, despite apparent difficulties with recognizing moral themes in stories, young children are interested in and able to discuss moral themes, that the aspects of stories that capture children's attention may be different from the themes that interest adults, and that discussion of story themes may be an important catalyst for moral growth. However, none of these studies focused on how children understood and interpreted specific moral themes in the stories. If we do not know how children understand stories with moral themes, then we cannot be sure that the stories are conveying the moral instruction intended. The study described here explored the question, "How do young children understand stories with moral themes?"

METHODS

My focus in this study was on the meanings that younger children might create in response to hearing stories with moral themes. I read and discussed twenty-three stories with moral themes with a group of kindergarten children in an after-school childcare program. I visited the program three days a week for two-and-a-half hours per visit, for approximately sixteen weeks. The kindergarten group included nine children and their teacher, Lacey (all names are pseudonyms).

Children's discussions of the stories played two roles in this study. On the one hand, they were intended to heighten children's understandings of the stories. At the same time, the discussions were a source of data—children's verbal responses to the stories were an important source of information about the meanings they were constructing.

The reading/discussion sessions were videotaped with a camera that faced the children in order to capture their gestures and facial expressions. I also recorded daily field notes as I observed the children during the rest of their regular activities. In these observations, I focused on children's interactions with one another. After each session, I created more detailed field notes from those hastily recorded in the field. Each night I also wrote my own impressions in a journal, and transcribed the day's videotapes.

The descriptions presented here come from my daily field notes, journal entries, and videotapes of the story readings. To make sense of the data, I followed the ethnographic tradition, as described by Creswell (1998). I read all of the data at least twice and then coded it with Nvivo® software. After coding the data, I looked for themes, patterns, and relationships in the categories that seemed most interesting, and then wrote interpretive narratives (Wolcott, 1994) based on those themes, patterns, and relationships. In order to check my interpretations, I (1) compared different data sources for the same event (e.g., videotape and field notes of a particular story reading); (2) asked the children's teacher to evaluate my initial narratives for consistency with her understanding of the events I described; and (3) rechecked my sources for data that might contradict my interpretations.

RESULTS

When I analyzed the data, I found that the children in this study consistently identified general moral themes and made prescriptive statements consistent with those themes. For the most part, the children and I agreed that a particular story might be about "honesty" or "lying," and we also agreed that the author probably intended to convey the message "You should tell the truth," or "Lying is bad." However, when we discussed the reasons why a particular action might be wrong, the children's comments were often quite different from my thinking. In some cases, the children's different interpretations seemed consistent with their developmental levels. As the children gained more experience and knowledge, they would likely grow closer to adult interpretations. For example, the children often gave punishment-oriented reasons when asked why a particular action (such as lying) was bad, even when the books suggested alternative reasons. A punishment-oriented response is consistent with the kinds of thinking Kohlberg (1976) documented among younger children. One may find more information about some of the developmental factors that affected children's interpretations in Bacigalupa (2007).

However, the children's levels of development did not completely explain unexpected interpretations. One story in particular elicited quite sophisticated arguments from the children. In this case, the differences between their interpretations and mine seemed to be rooted in the kinds of messages they regularly received from their social environments. We will examine this case more closely.

A Story about Sharing

This section describes children's responses to the story *This Is Our House* (Rosen & Graham, 1998)—a story about a young boy on a busy playground who refuses to share a large cardboard box converted to a playhouse. Before we discuss the story and the children's reactions to it, let us first consider the social context—especially as it relates to sharing—that these children experienced as part of their regular classroom activities. In this classroom, as in most early childhood classrooms, children were expected to share school materials. They took turns with popular toys and passed the markers around the art table. Generally, the children did well with sharing classroom materials, and when conflicts arose, those conflicts were quickly resolved with reminders about the obligation to share school items.

Sharing became a more difficult problem, however, when the children needed to share items they had brought from home. Items from home were generally more popular than school materials, and the potential for conflicts over sharing was great. Presumably, to avoid such conflicts, I observed the teacher enforce three rules about the use of toys from home. First, children could only use toys from home at certain times, with teacher permission. Second, children were expected to share toys from home with all children who wanted to play with those toys. Third, the child who owned the toy made most of the rules about what happened with the toy. In most cases, this meant that the child who had brought in the toy was in charge of making sure that everyone who wanted a turn did receive a turn with it, and that the toy was used in a manner acceptable to the owner. In some cases, these rules led to conflict-free play episodes.

In other cases, however, conflicts arose. For example, Claudia brought a sled to school for the children's winter music program. One day, Matthew found the sled in the gym and began to play with it.

> … Matthew sits in the sled. Claudia tells him it is her sled and says she wants it. Matthew (who by now has climbed out of the sled and is holding it), lets go of the sled, but Kris picks it up. Claudia whines, "Give me my sled. Give me my sled." Lacey says, "Let her have it. It's her sled from home." (Field Notes, 17 December 2004)

In this case, Claudia wanted her sled back and she did not want the other two children to play with it. When Lacey said, "Let her have it. It's her sled from home," Lacey used an appeal to property rights to justify Claudia's position. The message sent by Lacey was that Claudia could choose whether to let Matthew and Kris play with the sled because it belonged to Claudia.

The response Lacey made to the situation seems to be a reasonable way to mediate the conflict. It was clear that Claudia owned the sled and that she did not want anyone else to use it. If we accept the premise that the person who owns a piece of property should decide what happens to that property, then allowing Claudia to take the sled away from Matthew and Kris makes sense.

Letting Claudia keep the sled from Matthew and Kris, however, was contradictory to one of the classroom rules—the rule that children were to share items from home. In this case, when Claudia exercised her right to decide what happened with her sled, she chose not to share the sled. I did not realize the importance of this point until after we read the story *This Is Our House* (Rosen & Graham, 1998).

I had chosen to read *This Is Our House* (Rosen & Graham, 1998) because I had noticed that items from home often led to conflicts. I hoped that reading and discussing this story (and others like it) would shed light on how the children viewed sharing. In *This Is Our House*, the protagonist is George, a young boy who is playing in a large cardboard box painted to look like a house. As the other children on the playground come by and ask to enter the box, George refuses to let them in. Eventually, though, George has to go inside to use the restroom, and when he leaves, the other children take over the box. When George returns, the children deny him access to the box, and he realizes that sharing is the better option.

The following discussion took place during our second reading of the story, just after we reached the point in the story when George leaves the box in order to use the restroom. George tells the other children they must stay out of the box while he is gone.

Chiara: George went in to the bathroom, so what are they going to do? Matthew, Claudia, Anna, Kris, Sean: Go in!

USING STORIES TO TEACH COMPLEX MORAL CONCEPTS TO YOUNG CHILDREN | 257

Chiara: Do you think it's okay for them to do that? Matthew, Kris, Anna, Claudia: No!
Sean: No, because they have to listen to what he says. Chiara: Why do they have to listen to what he says?
Sean: Because it's his house. Claudia: Because it's his house.
Chiara: It's his house?
Kris: No it isn't. It's the playground's house.
Sean: No, it's not.
Claudia: No. Kristie, he made it. He made it so it's his house. And what those other …
Kris: He didn't make it, did he, Chiara?
Chiara: I don't think he made it. Claudia: He did make it. I know he did. Anna: Yeah, he did.
Matthew: No, he didn't. Anna: Yes he did. So that's …
Matthew: No he didn't!
Claudia: (in an angry voice) No, he didn't, Matthew! Chiara: Well, we don't know …
Matthew: You don't know! Claudia: Yeah! Yeah, I do! Matthew pushes Claudia.
Claudia: Don't! Lacey: Claudia!
Chiara: Wow, you guys! We don't know. We don't know if he did make it or he didn't make it.
Claudia: Maybe his dad maked it. Gosh, Matthew! Matthew: Well, you don't know!

(Video Transcript, 18 February 2004)

The high levels of emotion expressed in this argument suggest that the questions raised here were significantly meaningful to the children. Let us take a closer look at what the children said.

Sean suggested that the children should not enter George's box when he leaves because they have to listen to what George says. Further, Sean says the children have to listen to what George said because he owns the box. The book is actually inconclusive on the question of whether or not the box belongs to George. Although two girls in the story suggest that George does not own the box, it is not clear where the box came from or whether the girls are correct.

Claudia appeared to agree with Sean that the box belonged to George, and she added a new consideration. Claudia stated that George owned the house because he made it. Matthew argued that George did not make the house. Again, the text does not say who made the box, and the children continued to debate the point back and forth.

The text does not directly consider the question of whether or not George owns the box, yet the children's behaviors suggested that they felt the question was crucial. In fact, these children were struggling with the philosophical issue of property rights. When Claudia suggested that George owned the house because he made it, she was calling upon the idea that a person who makes something has specific rights related to that object. John Locke (1690/1966) argued the idea that a person has a property right in something if he/she has mixed in his or her own labor, and this belief is prevalent in American capitalist society.

The question of whether or not George made the box is important, then, because according to Locke's principle, if he made it, he owns it. Why is it important to establish that he owns it? It is important because of Sean's statement that the children are obligated to comply with George's request that they stay out because he owns the box. With that statement, Sean calls upon a second important principle. The idea that people have the right to decide the use of their property for themselves (as long as they do not unduly harm others) is a principle advocated by Robert Nozick (1974) and widely accepted in our society.

I was interested in returning to the discussion, but as the transcript shows, the children's emotions were running high. I made one last attempt to return to the topic of property rights.

Chiara: So, maybe his dad made it [the house]. If his dad did make it, and it belongs to him, is that a good reason to keep everybody out?
Kris: No! I share my stuff. Anna: I share.
Claudia: I share my stuff with my friends.
Kris: You don't share stuff with Anna or Emily.
Claudia: Because they're mean. Or, well, Anna bothers me, so I don't do it. (Video Transcript, 18 February 2004)

At this point, it was clear to me that we were heading into another explosive argument, and I decided to abandon our discussion and return to reading the book. I include this last part of the discussion, though, to make three points: (1) the children cared very deeply about the question of whether one is obligated to share one's personal property—so deeply, that emotion and passion fill their discussion; (2) Claudia maintained that she was not obligated to share personal possessions; and (3) Kris actively took up the possibility that one might be obligated to share personal possessions. We will return to this last point shortly.

Two opposing viewpoints dominated the conversation above. One viewpoint, expressed by Sean and Claudia, was that George was justified in excluding children from the box if he owned the box. The other viewpoint, expressed by Matthew and Kris, was that George should share the box. When I read over the transcript of this conversation, I considered and reconsidered these two different viewpoints. Even though it seemed clear to me that the author felt George should share the box, Sean's position was nonetheless logically sound.

As I thought about the children's experiences with this issue, I realized that these children regularly heard ideas and experienced situations that could lead them to adopt either position. That is, their classroom used both rules about property rights and rules about sharing. For example, when the teacher was called upon to resolve conflicts over toys from home, she often had to invoke both sharing and property rules. The teacher usually allowed children from home to make rules about the use of toys, but at the same time, expected children to share their personal possessions. Children who refused to share items from home often were asked to put the item away.

An analysis of the data depicting conflicts over toys from home revealed there were many instances in which children succeeded in not sharing their toys from home (even though the official rule was that they must share). First, many children did not share toys from home and got away with it because the excluded child did not solicit adult help. That is, among themselves, children did not necessarily expect that, or insist upon sharing of items from home. This fact is significant if you consider that some researchers (Corsaro, 1985; Davies, 2003) believe peer expectations have at least as much influence as do adult expectations on how children perceive and order their worlds. Thus, Sean and Claudia had many experiences in the world of their peers where children did not feel compelled to share toys they owned.

Second, Lacey inconsistently enforced the rule that children had to share toys from home. Earlier, I described an incident in which Lacey told Kris and Matthew to give Claudia back her sled because the sled belonged to Claudia. In this case, Lacey did not tell Claudia she had to share the sled. Although the times when Lacey insisted a child share toys from home outnumbered the times when she did not, there were numerous instances such as this one when Lacey did not require children to share toys they owned. Thus, it is likely that the children received mixed messages in regard to adult expectations about sharing personal property.

Finally, children who insisted on not sharing a toy could choose to put the toy away. While this outcome appears to be a logical consequence intended to help children learn to share, it really had another consequence as well. Because the classroom usually applied the prescription to put the toy away if it caused conflict when infractions were called to the attention of the teacher, children who did not want to share did not have to confront their own or their peers' feelings about the matter. They were able, instead, to choose not to share. Although such situations offered opportunities to discuss the value of sharing, the teacher rarely acted upon those opportunities.

Given this disregard for the rule that children should share toys from home and the lack of attention that they paid to reasons for why they should share toys, it is reasonable that Sean and Claudia might conclude from their experiences that people who own an item can choose not to share it. Outside this particular classroom, there is additional support for this position. In the dominant culture these middle class European-American children experienced, rights concerning property ownership are often elevated over other considerations. Our laws and social customs usually stop short of infringing on property rights, even when doing so might be in the common interest. For example, we do not force the wealthy to make charitable donations (although we do encourage them to do so) because we believe they have a right to accumulate and spend their wealth as they please. Bowles and Gintis (1987) argue that this tension between property rights and community considerations is one of the main impediments to true democracy in the United States today. Although children do not consciously think about property rights and democracy at this level, they regularly experience a culture that upholds property rights at the expense of community and interpersonal considerations.

Thus, even though the official rule in this classroom was that toys must be shared, there was also plenty of evidence in the classroom and in the larger environment to suggest that sharing personal property is not required. The position that George does not have to share the box if he owns it is thus an understandable way of looking at the story, even though most adults interpret the story very differently.

A MORAL ANALYSIS OF THE STORY

Sean can answer the question of whether George is justified in excluding children from his playhouse differently than the story suggests because two different kinds of moral reasoning can be applied to the story's central problem. Blum (1994) describes these two ways of reasoning about moral dilemmas as a choice between universality and particularity.[1]

Universalism is the idea that moral principles can be decided upon ahead of time, using logic and reason to decide what is right. Universal principles are fair and just because they are decided without regard to who is involved and without regard to particular features of the situation. The principles apply to anyone who finds himself or herself in a given situation.

The rule that a child who owns a toy gets to make the rules governing the use of that toy (including decisions about whether or not to share it) would be a universal rule. Suppose the parents in the homes that surround the playground decide they need a rule about whether or not children who play on the playground have to share their personal property. Perhaps there have been many conflicts over personal property, and they want a simple rule the children can use to resolve those conflicts. They come to a decision that any child who brings a toy to the playground does not have to share that toy. The decision is made before any conflicts have occurred, and the rule will be applied fairly in any situation that might arise in the future. This rule is a universal prescription, which from a justice perspective is logically consistent and fair. Just as adults are not required to share their wealth, children in this scenario are not required to share their private property.

In the discussion of *This Is Our House* (Rosen & Graham, 1998) above, Sean and Claudia applied this universal principle to the problem that George does not wish to share the house with his peers. They assumed there is a rule or principle governing this situation that says George gets to make decisions about the house if he owns it. If George owns the house, he is not breaking any rules when he excludes the other children from playing in it. Likewise, the other story characters would have the right to exclude George from playing with toys that they owned.

It is also interesting that Matthew, who argued that George did not own the house, seems to be arguing from the same universal principle. Matthew argued that George did not own the house. If George did not own the house, then the rule that says one does not have to share one's personal property did not protect him. Thus, the universal principle that someone who owns their property gets to decide what to do with it could be used to argue both that George must share the house (because he does not own it and thus has no property right in it) and that he need not share the house (because he does own it).

However, there is another way to look at this problem. Recall my attempt to return to the discussion after the argument became heated:

Chiara: So, maybe his dad made it [the house]. If his dad did make it, and it belongs to him, is that a good reason to keep everybody out?
Kris: No! I share my stuff. (Video Transcript, 18 February 2004)

Here, I raised the possibility that even if George did own the house, maybe he should share it. Kris seemed to agree. Unfortunately, the children and I did not pursue this line of thought because I felt that group tension was too high for further productive talk.[2] However, it is a position that deserves further consideration. It is possible to argue that even though George might be justified in excluding children from his box, he isn't being very "nice" when he does so. Benhabib (1992) argues that universal, justice-oriented conceptions of morality often fail to produce solutions that encompass this concept of "being nice." Benhabib (1992) gives an example of three brothers—two of them are doing well through their own hard work and effort, but one of them is struggling financially. Benhabib (1992) argues that, although it would be just of the first two brothers to refuse to help the third, helping him would be morally preferable. She says, "There would be nothing 'unjust' in the decision of the two elder brothers not to help the younger one, but there would be something morally 'callous,' lacking in generosity and concern in their actions" (p. 186). Thus, some issues seem to demand considerations beyond justice-oriented rationales.[3]

Blum (1994) says these kinds of considerations belong to the category he calls particularity. Particularity recognizes that making moral decisions often requires knowledge of the particular people and circumstances that are involved in a moral situation. According to this view, a moral agent makes decisions by considering all of the available information about a situation, including information about emotional states. Decisions made in a particular case cannot necessarily be generalized to other situations, precisely because other people and other concerns are involved in those other situations. In the case of George's box, an approach using principles of particularity might consider how George's behavior affects individual children or the impact it has on this playground community. Perhaps there are particular children who do not have access to personal playhouses who should receive special consideration, or perhaps sharing is valued because it is likely to lead to a more enjoyable playground community for everyone. A reader who includes these kinds of caring considerations in his/her thinking is likely to conclude that it would be morally preferable for George to share the box, regardless of whether he is obligated to do so from a justice perspective.

This philosophical analysis shows that there are at least two defensible ways to analyze George's behavior in the story *This Is Our House* (Rosen & Graham, 1998). Sean and Claudia have applied to George's situation a universal, justice-based rule. This rule is one they have experienced in their social environment. Most adults, however, interpret the story to say that George should share the box with his peers, and they rely on care-based considerations (what Blum (1994) refers to as particularity) to justify that interpretation. Although the adult interpretation of the story does seem to be more consistent with the intentions of the story author, we must acknowledge that Sean and Claudia have adopted a valid position that is supported by logical, justice-based principles. Furthermore, some of the children's experiences reinforce this validity of their position.

This analysis of the children's responses to *This Is Our House* (Rosen & Graham, 1998) shows that the messages children receive from their real-life contexts may conflict with the ideas presented in stories. In this instance, we uncovered tension between the principles of sharing and property rights. Similar tension may exist between other principles teachers might expect children to learn from books. For example, many stories seek to illustrate the benefits of cooperation, yet teachers read those stories in classrooms where many learning activities are quite competitive. Other stories seek to help children understand the principles of tolerance and diversity, yet popular culture bombards children with messages that conformity is good. Children read stories in particular contexts that may reinforce or undermine the moral ideas adults hope children will learn from those stories.

IMPLICATIONS

While this qualitative research cannot be used to generalize about how all young children understand stories with moral themes, it does suggest that adults who wish to use stories as part of a moral education curriculum should consider the following points. First, children live in environments that send multiple messages about how to make moral decisions. Sometimes, those messages may be inconsistent with the ideas found in stories, and those inconsistencies may lead children to conclusions different from those we intend. Adults may need to scrutinize the environment for inconsistencies between children's experiences and the moral ideas to be learned. Adults who are aware of those inconsistencies can work to eliminate some of them, and they can help children to think carefully about those that cannot be eliminated.

Second, the moral messages in stories may be complex—even in stories about issues that seem quite simple. On the surface, *This Is Our House* (Rosen & Graham, 1998) seems to be a simple story about sharing. Yet, the reader can interpret the story in different ways, and it takes quite a bit of analytical thought in order to sort out different ways of thinking about the story as well as positive appropriate responses to the different interpretations.

Furthermore, the kind of complexity represented by this example is crucial to moral growth. The power of a story such as *This Is Our House* (Rosen & Graham, 1998) lies not in its ability to get children to restate rules that they have already heard (e.g., "you should share") but in its potential for sparking discussions in which children are encouraged to think about the reasons why some behaviors are preferred. It is the discussions the stories engender, rather than the stories themselves, which will help children to advance the sophistication of their thinking to higher levels. In order to take full advantage of the opportunities for growth presented by the discussions, adults must be able to analyze both the arguments implied by the stories, and the arguments of the children who discuss the stories. As the discussion of *This Is Our House* presented here shows, the arguments suggested by the text and voiced by the children can be quite sophisticated. To work with such material effectively, adults must be willing to wrestle with complexity.

Finally, although there is some evidence to suggest that even younger children can engage in sophisticated philosophical discussions (Matthews, 1980; Pritchard, 1996), we must remember that very young children often learn best through hands-on experience. According to both Piaget (1929/1998) and Vygotsky (1934/2002), children construct understandings of concepts because of multiple real-world encounters with objects and people. According to these theories, children construct initial understandings of moral concepts through repeated exposure to the rules and reasons people give as children negotiate interpersonal relationships. Children's real-life, context-rich experiences are the basis for their moral learning.

When children read stories with moral themes, they use their existing understanding of concepts—an understanding based on experiences—to make sense of the ideas they hear in the stories and attendant discussions. At the same time, the ideas children hear in stories and discussions can contribute to the further development of those concepts. However, in this chapter and elsewhere (Bacigalupa, 2007), I have presented evidence that the new information children hear from stories does not necessarily change their existing understandings, and the question of whether discussions would be more effective than stories were in causing changes in the conceptual understandings of very young children remains unresolved. However, if it is true that many of the concepts children learn are ultimately based on their real-life experiences, it would be logical to focus at least some of our educational efforts on their real-life experiences.

In focusing on real-life experiences as important teaching tools for young children, I am not denying that stories and discussions do potentially contribute to children's understandings. The data I have presented here do not preclude that possibility. My conclusion is simply that story readings and discussions occur in particular contexts, and we need to recognize that the kinds of experiences that are available in any particular context shape the understandings that children construct in response to stories and discussions.

CONCLUSION

Stories have a potentially valuable place in a curriculum designed to help children develop a solid understanding of the moral implications of financial and economic decisions. Some stories directly introduce specific moral concepts related to economic issues. *This Is Our House* (Rosen & Graham, 1998) is an example of a book that can promote discussions about sharing. A book such as *This Is Our House* also has the potential to support the development of more general moral skills and dispositions, such as perspective taking. However, children do not always respond to stories in the ways adults expect them to respond. Further research is needed to determine the effectiveness of story discussions in changing children's existing moral perceptions. In addition, because children often rely on their day-to-day experiences to make sense of stories and discussions, children's real-life experiences are of primary importance when planning moral curriculum for young children.

CHAPTER UPDATE

Bacigalupa's chapter speaks to the intersection of storytelling, psychology, and moral development. Since its publication, work in all three areas provides additional information about these relationships. While Lee et al. (2014) find that the manner in which stories present morals relates to patterns of student receptivity, Bacigalupa's work conveys the importance of recognizing all children stories differently.

These interpretations may involve innate and contextual influences. Narvaez and Bock (2014) explain in the multi-ethics theory how the brain develops into various states as influenced by one's environment. This framework identifies three (safety, engagement, and imagination) factors that shape moral processing and explain the different patterns of right and wrong that individuals may perceive.

Narvaez and Bock's (2014) findings underscore the importance of facilitating classroom learning founded on openness and acceptance to build communities of compassion. Studies such as Rabin and Smith (2013) and Hawkins, Agnello, and Lucey (2015) affirm the importance of dialogue and dramas to initiate such conversations.

QUESTIONS FOR DISCUSSION

1. What was your favorite book as a child? If possible, locate the book and reread it. What lessons in the book surprised you upon rereading? Do you think that the book affected your moral growth in any fashion? Why or why not?
2. Write a story retelling the book in the last item from the perspective of a supporting character. What lessons does your story emphasize? How are these lessons similar or different to those in the original? How does the context of the new main character affect the lesson focus?
3. The Harry Potter series had tremendous impact on modern young readers. Discuss the moral lessons inherent in the stories. How does the book represent and construct moral dilemmas? What are the objections to the Harry Potter series? Compare and contrast the moral focuses of those supporting the series and those opposed to it. What values does each side espouse?
4. What are your definitions of particularity and universality? Give an example of each in your own experience. Compare your definitions with your classmates or colleagues.
5. Research the availability of children's books specifically designed to teach values; The Value Tales, children's religious texts, etc. Think about Bacigalupa's comment:

"I have presented evidence that the new information children hear from stories does not necessarily change their existing understandings, and the question of whether discussions would be more effective than stories were in causing changes in the conceptual understandings of very young children remains unresolved."

What are some recommendations you would make to parents or teachers about the use of these texts?

NOTES

1. Blum's distinction between universality and particularity is based on the ongoing philosophical discussion about the distinctions between justice-based reasoning (Kohlberg, 1976) and care-based reasoning (Gilligan, 1982).
2. The fact that the children's discussion can become so heated is another aspect of using stories to teach moral lessons that should be explored further. I chose not to pursue this issue here.
3. For another discussion on the differences between and limits of justice-based reasoning (universality) and care-based reasoning (particularity), see the discussion of micromorality and macromorality in Rest, Narvaez, Bebeau, and Thoma (1999).

REFERENCES

Bacigalupa, C. (2007). *Why children's interpretations of stories with moral themes often differ from adult interpretations*. Paper presented at the annual conference of the American Educational Research Association. Chicago, IL.
Benhabib, S. (1992). *Situating the self: Gender, community, and postmodernism in contemporary ethics*. New York, NY: Routledge.
Bennett, W. J. (Ed.). (1995). *The moral compass*. New York, NY: Simon and Schuster.
Blum, L. A. (1994). *Moral perception and particularity*. New York, NY: Cambridge University Press.
Bowles, S., & Gintis, H. (1987). *Democracy and capitalism: Property, community, and the contradictions of modern social thought*. New York, NY: Basic Books.
Clare, L., Gallimore, R., & Patthey-Chavez, G. G. (1996). Using moral dilemmas in children's literature as a vehicle for moral education and teaching reading comprehension, *Journal of Moral Education, 25*(3), 325–341.
Coles, R. (1989). *The call of stories: Teaching and the moral imagination*. Boston, MA: Houghton Mifflin Company.
Corsaro, W. (1985). *Friendship and peer culture in the early years*. Westport, CT: Greenwood Publishing Group.
Creswell, J. W. (1998). *Qualitative inquiry and research design: Choosing among five traditions*. Thousand Oaks, CA: Sage Publications.
Davies, B. (2003). *Shards of glass: Children reading and writing beyond gendered identities*. Cresskill, NJ: Hampton Press.
DeVries, R., & Zan, B. (1994). *Moral classrooms, moral children: Creating a constructivist atmosphere in early education*. New York, NY: Teachers College Press.
Gilligan, C. (1982). *In a different voice: Psychological theory and women's development*. Cambridge, MA: Harvard University Press.
Hawkins, J. M., Agnello, M. F., & Lucey, T. A. (2015). Villain or hero: Student interpretations of African trickster tales. *Multicultural Education, 22*(3/4), 21–26.
Junker, M. S. C. (1998). *Searching for the moral: Moral talk in children's literature study groups* (Doctoral dissertation, Arizona State University). Retrieved from Dissertation Abstracts International, 59, 11A.
Kilpatrick, W., Wolfe, G., & Wolfe, S. M. (1994). *Books that build character: A guide to teaching your child moral values through stories*. New York, NY: Simon & Schuster.

Koc, K., & Buzzelli, C. A. (2004). The moral of the story is ... Using children's literature in moral education. *Young Children, 59*(1), 92–97.

Kohlberg, L. (1976). Moral stages and moralizations: The cognitive developmental approach. In T. Lickona (Ed.), *Moral development and behavior* (pp. 299–316). New York, NY: Holt, Rinehart, & Winston.

Lamme, L. L., Krogh, S. L., & Yachmetz, K. A. (1992). *Literature-based moral education: Children's books and activities for teaching values, responsibility, and good judgment in the elementary school.* Phoenix, AZ: Oryx Press.

Lee, K., Talwar, V., McCarthy, A., Ross, I., Evans, A., & Arruda, C. (2014). Can classic moral stories produce honesty in children? *Psychological Science, 25*(8), 1630–1636.

Lehr, S. (1991). *The child's developing sense of theme: Responses to literature.* New York, NY: Teachers College Press.

Locke, J. (1690/1966). *Second treatise of government.* New York, NY: Barnes and Noble.

Matthews, G. (1980). *Philosophy and the young child.* Cambridge, MA: Harvard University Press.

Narvaez, D., & Bock, T. (2014). Developing ethical expertise and moral personalities. In L. Nucci, T. Krettaneuer, & D. Narvaez (Eds.), *Handbook of moral and character education* (2nd ed., pp. 140–158). New York, NY: Routledge.

Narvaez, D., Gleason, T., Mitchell, C., & Bentley, J. (1999). Moral theme comprehension in children, *Journal of Educational Psychology, 91*(3), 477–487.

Nozick, R. (1974). *Anarchy, state, and utopia.* New York, NY: Basic Books.

Piaget, J. (1929/1998). *The child's conception of the world.* London, UK: Routledge.

Pritchard, M. S. (1996). *Reasonable children: Moral education and moral learning.* Lawrence, KS: University Press of Kansas.

Rabin, C., & Smith, G. (2013). Teaching care ethics: Conceptual understandings and stories for learning. *Journal of Moral Education, 42*(2), 164–176.

Rest, J., Narvaez, D., Bebeau, M. J., & Thoma, J. (1999). *Postconventional moral thinking: A Neo-Kohlbergian approach.* Mahwah, NJ: Lawrence Erlbaum Associates.

Rest, J. R. (1983). Morality. In P. Mussen (Ed.), *Handbook of child psychology: Cognitive development* (4th ed., Vol. 3, pp. 556–628). New York, NY: Wiley.

Rosen, M., & Graham, B. (1998). *This is our house.* Cambridge, MA: Candlewick Press.

Rosenblatt, L. M. (1938/1995). *Literature as exploration.* New York, NY: The Modern Language Association of America.

Vygotsky, L. S. (1934/2002). *Thought and language.* Cambridge, MA: The MIT Press.

Wolcott, H. F. (1994). *Transforming qualitative data: Description, analysis, and interpretation.* Thousand Oaks, CA: Sage Publications.

CHAPTER SIXTEEN

Economics, Religion, Spirituality, AND Education

Encouraging Understandings of Compassionate Dimensions[1]

THOMAS A. LUCEY
Illinois State University

INTRODUCTION

The word economics derives from the dialogue *Oeconomicus*, written by the ancient Greek philosopher Xenophon. The discourse portrays economics as a cooperative household relationship that is necessary for successful farming (Pomeroy, 1994). This relationship's success depends on each member performing and valuing the other's expectations. Financial management represents part of this process, but not its focus.

Xenophon's dialogue means much for today's diverse society. Oeconomicus must value the necessity of various household members' contributions, regardless how much money each brings in. Spouses or partners should share their combined financial resources. Regardless of pay, each spouse contributes to the unit's economic welfare. Members distracted by vices hamper the family's economic pursuits through the reduced amount and/or quality of their contributions. Although members of the household have different economic roles, each should value the importance of others' contributions. Thus, Xenophon views the family as a cooperative economic unit that values individual differences and sacrifices individual ambitions that can occur at the cost to the whole. Pursuit of personal vices results in adverse consequences to both the individual and the family unit.

People have made economic-based personal judgments for a long time. The earliest societies in precolonial Africa (Berntsen, 1976) and ancient Egypt (Hayes, 1965) judged their members on patterns of food gathering. Adults (Hira & Mugenda, 1999) and adolescents (Trzcinski, 2002) continue to judge others on economic differences, while college students attribute traits to others based on economic class (Cozzarelli, Wilkinson, & Tagler, 2001). Within and among societies, financial status determines opportunities for quality housing, healthcare, education, and governance.

It also relates to patterns of legal services and (for the convicted) sentencing. According to the Bureau of Justice Statistics and the Sentencing Project (http://www.sentencingproject.org/criminal-justice-facts/) the United States owns the highest rate of incarceration of any country. The situation results from an exponential increase since the middle 1970s owning to more frequent and lengthier prison sentences. These conditions have a devastating effect on people of color and the poor who the government elite target and who lack the resources to effectively defend against corporate prosecutors that take liberty with their evidence (Alexander, 2012; Hedges, 2015).

The environmental influences on individual development represent important aspects of multicultural theory. To appreciate Banks' (2006) higher-level stages of multicultural practice, a society should both know and embrace these influences to foster respectful conversations that bring economic equality. Understanding the connections among morality, religion, spirituality, and economics offers information about the influences on students' beliefs and behaviors.

One aspect of spiritual development involves the nature of religious traditions. Traditions provide important reminders of cultural foundations. MacIntyre (1988) explains that conflicting traditions prompt moral conflict. He observes that modern society distorts the ancient Greek understanding of personal virtues by failing to consider their original environments (1984). He also recognizes that these challenges impair moral conversations, and calls for a reassessment of ethical foundations (1988). MacIntyre's historical review models a method for considering religious, spiritual, and economic relationships. The traditions that MacIntyre chronicles begin with the stories of heroic societies. By going beyond these traditions and interpreting ideals of other cultures, we might discover other spiritual ideas.

I argue that patterns of religious interpretations relate to patterns of economic-based structuring and environments. Although not in the depth of MacIntyre's (1984, 1988) efforts, this endeavor offers a historical interpretation that connects Egyptian processes with patterns of precolonial African societies, before considering the economic messages in preaching by Jesus of Nazareth. Finally, it explores economic influences on postmodern moral and spiritual interpretations before discussing liberation theology and its role in financial learning.

ANCIENT EGYPT AND PRECOLONIAL EAST AFRICA

This section relates patterns of ancient Egyptian society with those in precolonial East Africa. Each part provides a summary of conditions in ancient Egypt before explaining the East African parallels.

Developmental Environments

Early Egyptian society developed from settlements organized for subsistence. With tribal chiefs perceived as possessing magical/religious powers (Trigger, 1982; Vercoutter, 1981), southern kings unified competing tribal societies, dividing the aggregate into providences or nomes (Trigger, 1982). The structure created economic efficiency that "exploited the country ... more effectively" (Vercoutter, 1981, p. 719). Early in Egypt's history, a small group of powerful organizers managed the resources for larger groups of peoples.

As in Egypt, the interior precolonial East African cultures developed authority structures to suit their needs. These structures developed nearly two thousand years after Egypt's, however. For example, in the Sog and southern Rub cultures, patrilineal clans extended back to 1,000 BCE and functioned well without political authority positions (Ehret, 1998).

Schoenbrun (1998) observes that until the middle of the first century CE, people could choose between mothers and fathers' people to decide how to pass on property to emphasize linearity. Members excluded outsiders from this inheritance system because they could not get into the family sequence. Ehret (1998) provides linguistic archeological evidence that the word for "lineage" derived from "line of objects." Thus, an inheritance becomes an economic tool for demonstrating familial superiority through operant conditioning, bestowing wealth to those who fit the standards to receive the standard of gain admission to a family (e.g., through marriage) and to those family members who preserve or teach family values to their descendants. Wealth becomes a tool for social manipulation.

Economics represents a discipline involving choices. As the interior East African societies grew wealthier, inheritance changed from a process of choice to a vehicle for control and exclusion.

Pharaonic Egypt

Society in the Old Kingdom appeared to be a cooperative system based on social role. The society used no money, as everyone belonged to organizations that supplied their needs (Vercoutter, 1981). Yoyotte (1981) points out that the economic system contained no bourgeoisie and experienced rare "middlemen" aside from commercial agents of the pharaoh or temples. The cooperative social structure did not last, as power struggles among the wealthy upper class increased the power of great nomal chiefs during the last dynasties of the Old Kingdom (Kemp, 1982; Yoyotte, 1981). The upper class competed for power and unifying image of the divine king failed (Aldred, 1961).

Economics also played a role in the early belief systems of precolonial interior East African systems. Within the Southern Cushite system, the clan head held an important position in community religious observances, allotting cultivable land to those in need (Ehret, 1998). The Sudanic religion modeled this societal structure, conceptualizing one spiritual force for sky and rain. Ehret (1998) mentions that the Western Rift people's understanding of spirit changed from "sky" to "sun" during the last millennium BCE, but it is unclear why this change occurred.

Perhaps this change evolved with the understandings of function. Sky, sun, and rain are all weather elements that primitive cultures depended on for survival, because these processes nourished plants and animals. These also replenish water sources that lacked source springs. Similarly, the clan head had a religious power to grant land to those needing it. The natural elements of the sky represented natural tools for economic decision-making. Just as the sky covers, protects, and nourishes the earth, so, in a self-dependent community, did the clan head cover, protect, and nourish the clan through religious duties, military processes, and goods distribution. The sun differentiates the sky into night and day and in the process, defines and clarifies the activities and processes of the earth and its creatures. Within classical East African society, cultures began to interpret the clan head's role as both religious and as political. That differentiation established spheres of duties and obligations and privileges.

Societies employed myths to rationalize natural phenomena and to provide for social order. For example, from the 1000 to 500 BCE, the Great Lake communities experienced a change in kinship group leader to a "diviner-doctor." Schoenbrun (1998) points out the societal connections between wellness and material betterment, observing that these key societal figures "possessed a great variety of powers, among them the power of healing …" (the word for their societal role) derives from … "to be honored" (p. 108). The *mufÛmÛ* was originally a rainmaker of sorts; however, as society became more structured, it recognized his connections with "ancestral knowledge, that spiritual knowledge that controls over life, death, and nature" (p. 108).

The languages of the Bantu embraced many social areas, such as the political, healing, and spirituality. Healers endeavored to respect all societal members, possibly challenging their resistance to ambitious leaders. The Great Lakes Bantu considered ethics as "the set of judgments passed on human or national actions, not on intention alone, moral power and its effect were inherently and ultimately social" (Schoenbrun, 1998, pp. 111–112).

Both Pharaonic Egypt and precolonial East Africa witnessed transformations of religious understanding. Wealth accumulation distracted the upper class from their obligations to other societal members, yet precolonial cultures modified their religious and spiritual understandings to maintain community health. To optimize individual economic opportunity, the Egyptians' upper class obsessed over their financial gains, losing genuine understandings of societal welfare.

Middle and New Kingdoms

The Middle Kingdom witnessed efforts to reorganize the administration processes, but lacked the peaceful security experienced by the Old Kingdom (Aldred, 1961). Once again, a pattern emerged where economic control provided the basis for human judgment, weakening society through failed community.

The New Kingdom witnessed pharaohs' efforts to address political corruption and national security (Bakr, 1981). During this period, government maintained and enhanced the agricultural economy, while preserving societal attitudes and needs. According to O'Connor (1982), while a middle class developed, the society's hierarchical structure prompted divisions based on occupation. The middle and lower class possessed little political influence except when this order was disrupted (O'Connor, 1982).

Although respect theoretically occurred between classes, this situation did not prompt opportunities for social advancement. The education system reinforced social immobility as the elite perpetuated class distinctions through their education systems (Aldred, 1961). Civil service recruits had a moral code that involved a "scorn for commonality" that also called for a respect for social order (Yoyotte, 1981). Evidence of compassion for the lower classes existed, as the code prescribed that "… If poor cultivator is in arrears with his taxes, remit 2/3rds of them" (Aldred, p. 180). Through associated codes, the lower classes received enough support to provide subsistence, but insufficient amounts for societal advancement.

It would be helpful at this point to distinguish between compassion and empathy. Compassion represents a sense of awareness or understanding of another. According to Noddings (2008), it represents less of a warm and fuzzy emotion than rather a comprehension or knowledge of another's experience. Empathy represents a much stronger connection, involving an emotional sense of the other. It relates to being within another person's mind such that one appreciates the feelings associated with the other's perspective. The Egyptians experienced compassion for those in need because of their recognizing the plight of those in needs and the importance of modifying customs to accommodate them.

In summary, Pharaonic Egypt experienced the development and decline of a storage and redistribution system where the upper class traded the surplus to increase personal power and wealth (Trigger, Kemp, O'Connor, & Lloyd, 1983). As the upper class grew wealthier and the middle class developed, the society experienced internal and external challenges, in part prompted by climate changes. Simultaneously, within the leadership, religion became a process for material advancement, rather than spiritual development. The Egyptians "understood tensions and conflicts threatening their social stability" (O'Connor, 1982, p. 844); however, the elite's obsession with material preservation prompted spiritual commoditization.

RURAL AND URBAN IDEALS

To provide more information of how contexts related to patterns of social expectation, I transition to the writings of philosophers from ancient Greece. The socioeconomic contexts of the ancient Greek philosophers affected the nature of their moral interpretations. These largely upper class philosophers limited their interpretations of ethical behavior to what they considered as appropriate for them. For the Athenian Aristotle (trans. 1954), economic character represented a virtue to be attained through sound community relationships, through reflection on the merits of others as means for acquiring income and disbursing expenditures. The basis for judgment concerned personal introspection and extension of virtues to personal relationships. Xenophon's ethical model stemmed from a rural, agrarian foundation. Where Aristotle interpreted moral behavior through a *polis* lens, Xenophon employed a rural foundation, stressing the interdependence of economic role-players.

It is important to recognize the differences in moral understandings prompted by urban and rural contexts. Studies (e.g., Bulach & Peddle, 2001; Gándara, Gutiérrez, & O'Hara, 2001) illustrate different patterns of rural and urban values that occur. Within these different environments, religion and spirituality involve different emphases: individualist/competitive ideals in polis/city/urban contexts and group/community ideals in rural settings.

An illustration of rural and urban ethical differences lies within the social justice efforts of Jesus of Nazareth. According to Hoppe (2004), Jesus interpreted the Jewish tradition as in relationship with a god who was a proponent of social justice, and advocated the rights of the poor. Hoppe (2004) points out that the history of the Jewish culture, as described in the Torah and successive texts, depicts a culture's ongoing spiritual struggle with economic conditions. On one side of the coin, the struggle was one of oppression and poverty, and asking for divine intervention to alleviate oppression. Examples of heroes in these stories were Moses and Esther (Costas, 1989). Yet, the other side depicts the personal and societal struggles of employing corrupt processes to become rich and preserve wealth. For example, Hoppe (2004) describes the transition of the young impoverished David, who overcame the challenges of the wealthy King Saul, became king, and grew in royalty, and immorality—forgetting his poverty roots.

Yet one needs to practice care with literal accounts of religious scripture. For example, Armstrong (1993), Borg (2006), and Crossan (2015) argue that biblical scriptures do not always present authentic historical accounts and that triangulation with artifacts from other cultures informs about the purposes and intentions of their meanings. For example, Jesus's remark to give to Caesar what is Caesar's criticized the Jewish temple authority for abandoning the basis for their faith for collusion with Roman leadership; it was not advocacy for the separation of Church and State (Borg & Crossan, 2006). Crossan (2015) observes within the Bible a patterned assertion of justice followed by a response of injustice. Thus, for example, when considering the letters of the New Testament attributed to the Apostle Paul, one may notice some letters were genuinely written by Paul while others were written in his name but inconsistently with his beliefs (Borg & Crossan, 2009).

Through history, this conflict between disciples of violent structure and equality recurs. For example, MacIntyre (1990) argues that Augustine's beliefs of a theological hierarchy involve challenges that do not adequately address the relationships between "particulars and universals," the nature of divine influence on human understandings, and the interpretation of human intelligence. Hooker (1593, 1648/2002) describes the efforts of Calvinists to prompt governmental reform inconsistently with Jesus' model. Both of these conflicts involve hierarchical frameworks for interpreting spirituality that lack legitimate justification bases. These flawed processes persisted into American colonization and afterward. Christian rhetoric became the rationale for European colonization. Loewen (2007) explains that the purpose of Columbus' voyage was exploitation of the indigenous peoples, not a quest for a path to the Far East, and that Ponce De Leon's search for a fountain of youth represented a myth that drew attention away from efforts to capture slaves. Mixon (2000) describes the economic motives associated with prosecutors in the Salem Witch Trials.

Economics provided the justification for hierarchical societal structures with racist overtones. Anderson (1988) describes the systemic efforts in the 1800s and early 1900s of white northern industrialists to develop an education system designed to perpetuate subservience of African Americans. The United States experiences patterns of resegregation and material inequities in its schools brought about through a series of legal decisions (Kozol, 2005; Orfield, 2001). These decisions continue a human struggle with institution structured decision-making that prompts inequitable living conditions.

Through history, a pattern of economically founded arguments to justify hierarchical societal structures recurs. As patterns of economic control dominate patterns of thinking, dominant minded individuals pervert sound bites of religious scripture out of context by the upper class to perpetuate hierarchical power structures rationalized through merit and economic efficiency (see, for example, Phillips, 2006). In these processes, religion often becomes an occupational "trade" that spins material fulfillment as the consequence of spiritual faithfulness.

In a smaller society that experiences less pronounced differences, as illustrated in precolonial East Africa (Schoenbrun, 1998), religion represents a societal vehicle to preserve a balance that is respectful for all members. Likewise, the books of the Old and New Testaments describe a Judeo-Christian god who is an advocate for the poor and oppressed and a messiah who resisted the economic-based definition of worldly success and challenged the collusion between Jewish and Roman authorities (Crossan, 2015; Hoppe, 2004).

PROSPERITY THEOLOGY

A society that becomes increasingly urban and materialistic should recognize how Christian tradition underlies the nature of modern North American history, and how early 21st-century society shapes Christian dogma in a manner suited to its ideals. "Prosperity theology" represents a pattern of thinking through which one interprets material wealth as the reward for living as instructed in scripture. Several problems exist with this approach to scripture interpretation. First, this approach reduces the acceptable interpretations of religious literature to one literal meaning. Scripture involves four dimensioned interpretations: historical, moral, allegorical, and anagogical (spiritual) (MacIntyre, 1990). Literal scripture interpretation is like considering one side of a pyramid, or taking one witness's account of an event: it may be accurate on the face, but the meaning changes with depth.

Second, literal interpretation ignores the meanings of words that are lost in translation between languages. Different ancient Greek words provided acceptable bases for the modern English word "love" depending on the type of love involved (e.g., *philos* and *eros*). The commandment to love one's neighbor has peculiar meanings if one translates the incorrect type of love into that passage. Prosperity theology provides a one-dimensional interpretation of scripture that ignores the original contexts of the languages in which the scriptural writers composed.

Finally, prosperity theology rests upon a behaviorist framework that materially rewards those who follow scripture-based lifestyles. The contradiction with this belief system involves the counterexample of the poor who do God's will, but are not materially rewarded.

Taking a particular passage from any of the biblical scripture and using it to support a life decision, without understanding the contexts of the passage, would be inappropriate. A literal interpretation requires an awareness of the context for the writing. Just as one must understand the Christian influences on C. S. Lewis and J. K. Rowling to realize the meanings of Narnia and Hogwarts, one recognize the sociohistorical contexts of the stories from the Bible to interpret them properly (Crossan, 2015).

Such literal scriptural interpretations occur, in part, because of efforts to pursue a social agenda. For example, Tickle and Sweeney (2014) observe how political maneuvering shaped the working of the Nicean creed, which governs Christian faith. Other arguments for a contextual interpretation of scripture are not difficult to find. As Costas (1989) points out in his discussion of biblical interpretation,

> The biblical text is, still a human word ... that the words of the prophets and apostles are used ... does not exempt Scripture from historical conditioning ... The truth of faith is mediated by our respective sociohistorical contexts. (p. 17)

Efforts to literally apply isolated scripture passages to modern settings without considering the sociopolitical contexts of their writing risks oversimplify and distort their intended meanings. This situation poses a difficulty for an early 21st-century North American capitalist context in that it equates salvation with wealth acquisition.

LIBERATION THEOLOGY

Liberation theology provides a basis for focusing on the needs of the socio-economically disadvantaged. According to Gayarre (1994), liberation theology represents an approach to faith founded on the views of the material and spiritual poor. It focuses on religion within historical, social, and economic contexts to provide a religious justification for social justice. This framework provides the religious foundation for promoting societal diversity through education. Kirylo (2003) claims that liberation theology provides a way of life that develops awareness of inequities and injustices, offers transformation, and applies solutions.

Liberation theology provides a theological basis for supporting curriculum reform because it relates to societal injustices that have occurred for some time, thus providing direction for the future. Financial educators could deepen students' understandings of the inequitable resource distributions and the unjust processes through reflection and problem-solving.

MODERN CONTEXT

Adopting this theological perspective represents critical considering in the development of financial education curricula. Reframing early 21st-century America's—perhaps the most materially wealthy society in history—financial education curricula within the context of liberation theology represents a daunting task. It is very difficult for early 21st century's guilt- and innocent-oriented society to accept Jesus' message of compassion. This punishment and reward system manifests in financial literacy education efforts, which emphasizes development of personal financial net worth.

There are at least two counterarguments to liberation theology. The first, as described by Pinar, Reynolds, Slattery, and Taubman (1995), claims that liberation theology represents a materialist framework at core; however, liberation theology advocates a process of community building, by fostering awareness of the material addictions that obscure perceptions of society's common humanity. Within this conceptualization, financial education is at risk of perpetuating material addictions and promoting possession-based human interpretations. The preceding literature summary illustrates this process in society.

A second counterargument involves a perception of limited universality. Schubeck (1995) affirms that liberation theologies influence moral thinking, but notes that they also provide another form of morality, rather than providing an alternative moral posture for society. Schubeck (1995) employs the analogy of a mother providing her children with different, but individually appropriate, responses to their behaviors to illustrate the different moral needs of social groups. This analogy illustrates how different people require different means of spiritual support, based on their socioeconomic contexts. Schubeck's analogy undermines his argument. While the mother's particular responses to her children's behaviors are different, the nature of her responses is the same. Liberation theology advocates support of the poor, not just the materially disadvantaged. As Jesus practiced a ministry of compassion to those who sincerely sought it, liberation theology espouses a philosophy of empathy, to those who are poor materially, spiritually, and/or professionally.

APPLICABILITY TO FINANCIAL EDUCATION

The counterargument to Schubeck (1995) provides the grounds for connecting financial education with liberation theology. In its current condition, financial education processes do not do enough to address the needs of all learners because they do not consider the variety of contexts from which they derive. Consider that Moschis (1985) describes ten ways that home environments affect consumer socialization development. Varcoe et al. (2001) find that different patterns of financial priorities occur among high school students. Children develop in a variety of contexts, prompting different patterns of financial education needs. As it exists, financial education tends to represent a process for developing understandings of wealth accumulation. To promote compassionate spirituality, financial education should address the human consequences of financial decisions and respond to the needs of the poor. Educators should guide discussions about financial inequities among students.

Postmodern first world societies are so complex that unbalanced wealth distribution and economically driven judgments permeate conventional thinking. Financial education curricula tend not to address these topics. Recent literature (e.g., Arthur, 2012; Lucey, Agnello, & Laney, 2015; Pinto & Coulson, 2011) points to the ideological fallacies and biases associated with conventional approaches to financial literacy. These authors raise concerns that the many layers of social structures create for an environment that defines financial practice in terms of the wellness of those who wield economic power. This contrasts with the development or reinforcement of the practicing individual's personal identity and self-worth.

The richest country in the early 21st century has a spiritual challenge of shedding a rose-colored glass view of a behavioral approach to morality. Hoppe (2004) provides biblical evidence that poverty represents a man-created phenomenon brought about by oppressive rules (or standards) designed to preserve societal structures that benefit the elite. If or how financial education addresses the human consequences associated with financial decision-making informs about the core values that guide societal decisions.

An alternative approach to financial education involves both spiritual and material reconceptualizations. In prescribing existing standardized curricular and instruction agendas, decision makers impair students' holistic wellness. While one could argue that standards prompt equal achievement patterns, the processes for developing the standards and the methods of their measure compromise such possibilities. Methods for measuring student achievement should interpret student understanding and application of financial principles within their social contexts.

What might spiritually aware financial education processes be like? Lucey and Lorsbach (2013) have posited a framework for interpreting patterns of fulfillment engendered by different curricula motivations (see Table 16.1). Applying this framework to financial education, one might observe that existing processes could arguably fulfill learners' intellectual and aesthetic curiosities, but not their moral and spiritual needs. As they exist, financial education curricula foster technical and practical interest, but lack emancipatory elements for all students to succeed based on a holistic sense of identity.

Table 16.1: Framework for a Fulfilling Curriculum.

Nature of Fulfillment (Morris, 1997)	Curricular Interests (Grundy, 1987)	Nature of Text Interpretation (MacIntyre, 1990)
Intellectual	Technical/Practical	Historical
Aesthetic	Practical/Emancipatory	Allegorical
Moral	Emancipatory	Moral

---Spirituality---

One may argue against this framework by claiming that society tends to premise personal finance on mutually acceptable financial transactions. For example, the employer is obligated to pay the employee for his or her labor and the consumer is obligated to pay the merchant for goods and or services. Likewise, the borrower is obligated to pay the creditor for the use of money over time; banks and investment firms are obligated to pay depositors and investors for the use of their funds. While this author does not argue that credit represents an underlying tenet of personal finance, Nucci (2001) distinguishes between moral behavior and social convention (or law). Thus, one should consider under which categories financial obligations fall.

In a capitalist-intensive society, financial exchanges represent matters of social convention, not moral behavior. The nature of the financial relationships determines the terms of the agreement. While negotiations may occur, the party controlling resources possess more advantage than does the party seeking resources. If social justice represents a procedural, rather than a distributive matter, the conditions under which credit require scrutiny.

How may financial educators implement a morally and spiritually fulfilling curriculum? While a complete theory remains to be developed, McLaughlin (2003/2013) observes that spirituality contains five strands: (1) search for meaning, (2) inner space, (3) spirit in life, (4) response to natural/human world, and (5) collective aspects. Such a spiritual approach may prompt reconsideration of humankind's relationship with nature to foster much needed reconsideration of Christian disregard for indigenous American worldview (Four Arrows, 2014). The use of art-based learning processes offers potential for stimulating awareness, conversation, and action with regard to these injustices (Lucey & Laney, 2012).

CONCLUSIONS

It is acknowledged that this chapter does not fully discuss the various forms of spirituality that exist and their relationships to social phenomena. The increasing frequency of religiously justified terrorist activities and the creation of a similarly founded political state may be interpreted as a deep-rooted religiously founded response of anger to secular society founded on behavioral capitalism (Armstrong, 1991; Bobbitt, 2002). A spiritually compassionate approach to financial literacy offers potential for educating young citizens about their social responsibility to care for others as an element of their financial practice.

Research (e.g., Cozzarelli et al., 2001; Hira & Mugenda, 1999; Taylor & Overbey, 1999; Trzcinski, 2002) indicates that financial status relates to interpretations of self and to perspectives of, and relationships with, others. Because economic patterns relate to personal interpretations at many age levels, research should continue to examine how or if financial education may shape these relationships at different stages of human development.

Economic pressures hamper humankind's ability to fulfill its spiritual needs. Precolonial East African societies modified their religious ideas to suit societal structures and the Egyptian bureaucrats reinterpreted their roles in periods of societal success.

Now, as then, early 21st-century civilization faces the challenge of realizing that its views of personal finance distort understandings of spirituality and, therefore, understandings of itself. The concept of a judgmental god who punishes the sinful by making bad things happen contradicts the biblical accounts of a god who listens and responds to those in need (Hoppe, 2004).

Scientific reasoning and materialism put economic blinders on society, preventing its peripheral vision of a multidimensional reality. In its present state, financial education perpetuates such views, espousing ideas of financial acquisition and growth, rather than financial parity and community. A curriculum of financial compassion and empathy may cultivate community values of cooperation and selflessness to balance the finite nature of wealth-based ideologies. Conversations and experiences of financial and economic cooperation should empower students to critically explore the spiritual depths of material fascinations. Absent realization of the full meanings of its individual and cultural identities, society faces a shallow future—and there can certainly be no long-term economic benefit from that.

QUESTIONS FOR DISCUSSION

1. What do you feel represents the current societal basis for interpreting people? How does it compare to the ideas of Xenophon, as described in the chapter?
2. The chapter argues that civilization distorts Christianity to serve its own economic agenda. How would you respond to this argument? Support your position using social context and contextualized interpretation of scripture sources.
3. What are the similarities and differences between prosperity theology and liberation theology? Upon what premises does each depend?
4. Look closely at Table 16.1. What curricular interest do you view as a priority? Describe your background and its influence on your preference.
5. Lucey observes a pattern with regard to societies and their views of money. Do you consider his observations plausible/reasonable? What are some indicators in the current United States that support your thinking?

NOTE

1. Portions of this chapter were originally published in the first edition of *Financial Literacy for Children and Youth*. The author appreciates the comments, conversations, and suggestions of Alan Bates, Reverend Howard Bowlin, Jeffery Hawkins, Jin-Ah Kim, Anthony W. Lorsbach, and Reverend Andrew McBeth toward the development of the original work.

REFERENCES

Aldred, C. (1961). *The Egyptians*. London, UK: Thames and Hudson.
Alexander, M. (2012). *The new Jim Crow: Mass incarceration in the age of colorblindness*. New York, NY: The New Press.
Anderson, J. D. (1988). *The education of Blacks in the South, 1860–1935*. Chapel Hill, NC: University of North Carolina Press.
Aristotle. (1954). *The Nichomachean ethics* (Trans.). Oxford, UK: Oxford University Press.
Armstrong, K. (1991). *Holy war: The crusades and their impact on today's world*. New York, NY: Anchor Books.
Armstrong, K. (1993). *A history of God: The 4000-year quest of Judaism, Christianity, and Islam*. New York, NY: Knopf Publishing.
Arthur, C. (2012). *Neoliberalism, the consumer, and the citizen*. Rotterdam, The Netherlands: Sense Publishers.
Bakr, A. A. (1981). Pharaonic Egypt. In G. Mokhtart (Ed.), *UNESCO General History of Africa II, Ancient Civilizations* (pp. 84–111). London, UK: Heinemann Educational Books.
Banks, J. A. (2006). *Cultural diversity and education: Foundations, curriculum & teaching* (5th ed.). Boston, MA: Allyn & Bacon.
Berntsen, J. L. (1976). The Massai and their neighbors: Variables of interaction. *African Economic History, 1*(2), 1–11.
Bobbitt, P. (2002). *The shield of Achilles: War, peace, and the course of history*. New York, NY: Knopf.
Borg, M. J. (2006). *Jesus. Uncovering the life, teachings and relevance of a religious revolutionary*. New York, NY: Harper Collins.
Borg, M. J., & Crossan, J. D. (2006). *The last week. What the Gospels really teach about Jesus's final days in Jerusalem*. New York, NY: Harper Collins.
Borg, M. J., & Crossan, J. D. (2009). *The first Paul: Reclaiming the radical visionary behind the Church's conservative icon*. New York, NY: Harper Collins.
Bulach, C. R., & Peddle, J. (2001, October). *A comparison of character traits for rural, suburban, and urban students*. Paper presented at the Character Education Partnership Conference, Denver, CO.
Costas, O. E. (1989). *Liberating news: A theology of contextual evangelization*. Grand Rapids, MI: William B. Eerdmans Publishing.
Cozzarelli, C., Wilkinson, A. V., & Tagler, M. J. (2001). Attitudes toward the poor and attributions for poverty. *Journal of Social Issues, 57*(2), 207–227.
Crossan, J. D. (2015). *How to read the Bible and still be a Christian. Struggling with divine violence from Genesis through Revelation*. New York, NY: Harper Collins Publishers.
Ehret, C. (1998). *An African classical age: Eastern and Southern Africa in world history 1000 B.C. to A.D. 400*. Charlottesville, VA: University of Virginia.
Four Arrows. (2014). "False doctrine" and the stifling of indigenous political will. *Critical Education, 5*(13). Retrieved from http://ojs.library.ubc.ca/index.php/criticaled/article/view/184496
Gándara, P., Gutiérrez, D., & O'Hara, S. (2001). Planning for the future in rural and urban high schools. *Journal of Education for Students Placed at Risk, 6*(1 and 2), 73–93.
Gayarre, J. L. (1994). The challenges of liberation theology to neoliberal economic policies. *Social Justice, 21*(4), 34–45.
Grundy, S. (1987). *Curriculum: Product or praxis*. London, UK: Falmer Press.
Hayes, W. C. (1965). *Most ancient Egypt*. Chicago, IL: University of Chicago Press.
Hedges, C. (2015). *Wages of rebellion. The moral imperative of revolt*. New York, NY: Nation Books.

Hira, T. K., & Mugenda, O. M. (1999). The relationships between self-worth and financial beliefs, behavior, and satisfaction. *Journal of Family and Consumer Sciences, 91*(4), 76–82.

Hooker, R. (1593, 1648/2002). *On the laws of ecclesiastical polity* (A. McGrade, Ed.). Cambridge, MA: Cambridge University Press.

Hoppe, L. J. (2004). *There shall be no poor among you: Poverty in the Bible*. Nashville, TN: Abingdon Press.

Kemp, B. J. (1982). Old kingdom, middle kingdom, and second intermediate period in Egypt. In J. D. Clark (Ed.), *The Cambridge History of Africa, Volume 1: From the Earliest Times to c. 500 B.C.* (pp. 658–761). Cambridge, UK: Cambridge University Press.

Kozol, J. (2005). *The shame of the nation: The restoration of apartheid schooling in America.* New York, NY: Crown Publishers.

Loewen, J. (2007). *Lies my teacher told me: Everything your American History textbook got wrong* (Revised Ed.). New York, NY: Touchstone.

Lucey, T. A., Agnello, M. F., & Laney, J. D. (2015). *A critically compassionate approach to financial literacy.* Rotterdam: Sense Publishers.

Lucey, T. A., & Laney, J. D. (2012). From classroom to community: Preparing preservice teachers in the art of teaching about social justice. In A. Honigsfeld & A. Cohan (Eds.), *Breaking the mold of education for culturally and linguistically diverse students: Innovative and successful practices for 21st century schools* (Vol. 3, pp. 53–60). Lanham, MD: Rowman and Littlefield.

Lucey, T. A., & Lorsbach, A. W. (2013). Beyond the technical: Interpreting dimensions of curriculum. *The Educational Forum, 77*(2), 176–191.

MacIntyre, A. (1984). *After virtue* (2nd ed.). Notre Dame, IN: Notre Dame Press.

MacIntyre, A. (1988). *Whose justice, which rationality?* Notre Dame, IN: Notre Dame Press.

MacIntyre, A. (1990). *Three rival versions of moral enquiry: Encyclopaedia, genealogy, and tradition.* Notre Dame, IN. Notre Dame Press.

McLaughlin, T. (2003/2013). Education, spirituality and the public school. In D. Carr & J. Haldane (Eds.), *Spirituality, philosophy, and education* (pp. 185–199). New York, NY: Routledge.

Mixon, F. J., Jr. (2000). Homo economicus and the Salem Witch trials. *The Journal of Economic Education, 31*(2), 179–184.

Morris, T. (1997). *If Aristotle ran General Motors. The new soul of business.* New York, NY: Owl Books.

Moschis, G. P. (1985). The role of family communication in consumer socialization of children and adolescents. *Journal of Consumer Research, 11*(4), 898–913.

Noddings, N. (2008). Caring and moral education. In L. P. Nucci & D. Narvaez (Eds.), *Handbook of moral and character education* (pp. 161–174). New York, NY: Routledge.

Nucci, L. P. (2001). *Education in the moral domain.* Cambridge, UK: Cambridge University Press.

O'Connor, D. (1982). Egypt, 1552–664 B.C. In J. D. Clark (Ed.), *The Cambridge history of Africa, Volume 1: From the earliest times to c. 500 B.C.* (pp. 830–940). Cambridge, UK: Cambridge University Press.

Orfield, G. (2001). *Schools more separate: Consequences of a decade of resegregation.* Retrieved from the UCLA Civil Rights Project: https://civilrightsproject.ucla.edu/research/k-12-education/integration-and-diversity/schools-more-separate-consequences-of-a-decade-of-resegregation/orfield-schools-more-separate-2001.pdf

Phillips, K. (2006). *American theocracy. The peril and politics of radical religion, oil, and borrowed money in the 21st century.* New York, NY: Penguin Books.

Pinar, W. F., Reynolds, W. M., Slattery, P., & Taubman, P. M. (1995). *Understanding curriculum: An introduction to the study of historical and contemporary curriculum discourse.* New York, NY: Peter Lang.

Pinto, L. E., & Coulson, E. (2011). Social justice and the gender politics of financial literacy education. *Journal of the Canadian Association for Curricular Studies, 9*(2), 54–85.
Pomeroy, S. B. (1994). *Xenophon: Oeconomicus*. Oxford, UK: Clarendon Press.
Schoenbrun, D. L. (1998). *A green place a good place: Agrarian changes, gender, and social identity in the Great Lakes region to the 15th century*. Portsmouth, NH: Heinemann.
Schubeck, T. L. (1995). Ethics and liberation theology. *Theological Studies, 56*(1), 107–122.
Taylor, D. S., & Overbey, G. (1999). Financial practices and expectations of student and non-student consumers. *Journal of Family and Consumer Science, 91*(4), 39–42.
Tickle, P., & Sweeney, J. M. (2014). *The age of the spirit. How the ghost of an ancient controversy is shaping the church*. Grand Rapids, MI: Baker Books.
Trigger, B. G. (1982). The rise of civilization in Egypt. In J. D. Clark (Ed.), *The Cambridge History of Africa, Volume 1: from the Earliest Times to c. 500 B.C.* (pp. 478–547). Cambridge, UK: Cambridge University Press.
Trigger, B. G., Kemp, B. J., O'Connor, D., & Lloyd, A. B. (1983). *Ancient Egypt: A social history*. Cambridge, MA: Cambridge University Press.
Trzcinski, E. (2002). Middle school children's perceptions of welfare and poverty: An exploratory, qualitative study. *Journal of Family and Economic Issues, 23*(4), 339–359.
Varcoe, K. P., Peterson, S., Garrett, C., Martin A., René, P., & Costello, C. (2001). What teens want to know about financial management. *Journal of Family and Consumer Sciences, 93*(2), 30–34.
Vercoutter, J. (1981). Discovery and diffusion of metals and development of social systems up to the fifth century before our era. In J. Ki-Zerbo (Ed.), *General History of Africa I, Methodology and African Prehistory* (pp. 706–729). London, UK: Heinemann Educational Books.
Yoyotte, J. (1981). Pharaonic Egypt. In G. Mokhtar (Ed.), *General History of Africa II, Ancient Civilizations* (pp. 112–135). London, UK: Heinemann Educational Books.

CHAPTER SEVENTEEN

Behavioral Economics

Making High School Economics Personal

KATHLEEN S. COOTER
Bellarmine University

As a former high school economics teacher, I found it quite a challenge to make mandated economics content relevant to adolescents. The state standards to be addressed in the class reflected the political leanings of the state; a textbook committee at the state level also decided upon the approved textbook list from which a school district could choose was also decided by.

Teaching to the standards was the expectation. Many economics teachers feel the same. As Schug et al. (2003) suggest in their work, *Is Economics Your Worst Nightmare?*, teachers feel

1. The content of economics seems dense and abstract. It is difficult to make economics relevant to teachers, never mind students.
2. Economics is sometimes thought to be politically conservative. Some social studies teachers do not wish to be associated with such thinking.
3. Economics is sometimes thought to be all about money, greed, and selfishness. Many teachers don't like to see social concerns get reduced to such issues.
4. Many social studies teachers have had little or no coursework in economics. Even those who have had one or two introductory courses may think they know too little to plan and teach courses of their own. (p. 73)

If it is our nightmare as teachers, what about students? At semester start, many of my students shuddered while looking at the text and clearly considered economics as graphs, charts, dense text, or closely typed pages in the back of the business section of the newspaper—much of which was indecipherable to them. To many, it was simply a mandatory class that was, in the most part, unrelated to their personal or economic lives. There was an attitude among them that it would be enough to just get through the course to graduate—truly an utterly forgettable and somewhat painful content for most. Schug et al. (2003) agree stating

> ... Economics does strike many students and social studies teachers today as remote and difficult. As the discipline has matured, economists have sought to be ever more precise in their work, and their search for precision has led them increasingly to the use of rigorous, abstract language, including the language of mathematical operations and models. As a result, even students in Econ 101 now are apt to encounter technical analyses, expressed in compressed, quantitative terms, where they may have expected to find advice about personal finance or general discussions about wealth and poverty. (p. 73)

Economic theory and content are historically built on patterns, inputs, outputs, models, and predictions or as Cardell et al. (1996), state "Economics is characterized by well-developed predictive theories of human behavior. A wide variety of empirical tests of models based on those theories have been developed, as well as extensive and reliable data bases to test the theories" (p. 454). This consideration of economics is typical of what is taught in the Economics high school course in 20 states. Usually it is a semester course of study offered to upperclassmen in high school and successful completion is often mandatory for graduation (Council for Economic Education, 2016). Jabbar (2011) suggests that most economic theories currently taught are divorced from the daily experiences of students (p. 446). How to make this mandatory course of study matter or have relevance to the teenager is a dilemma. I suggest meeting them where they are—as consumers.

TEENAGERS AS CONSUMERS: WELCOME TO GENERATION Z AND BEYOND

Cyberanthropologist Amber Case states,

> The human brain is wired to adapt to what the environment around it requires for survival. Today and in the future it will not be as important to internalize information but to elastically be able to take multiple sources of information in, synthesize them, and make rapid decisions (as quoted in Anderson & Rainie, 2012, p. 9).

"From their earliest years, they (GEN Z) have been shaped by social media, e-commerce, and on-demand services, using technology to customize the information they receive, the products they buy, and the interactions they have", said Ian Cross, director at the Bentley University Center for Marketing Technology as quoted in the Boston Globe (Geller, 2015). The entire Gen Z population or "Gen

Zers" has known nothing but an Internet-connected world. Kowalska (2012) states:

> Present trends of young consumers' behavior are strongly conditioned by development of new technologies and opportunities offered by the Internet's availability. Nowadays young people use new technologies in order to assist in the process of consumption, identification of needs, search for information and purchase of products and services. All those transformations had impact on formation of new trends in young consumers behavior, among which may be mentioned: spread of technology consumption, granting mass consumption, homogenization of consumption and phenomenon called "crowdsourcing." (p. 101)

According to the Hampton Roads marketing group (2015), teenagers control an annual purchasing power of $208.7 billion dollars. The NPD Group, Inc., a leading market research company that tracks consumer-spending habits, cites some interesting data about teen consumerism. Their 2012 study on shopping behaviors of teens revealed that teens are persuaded by multiple factors when deciding what to purchase with word-of-mouth and brand significance topping the list. "In true adolescent fashion, teens continue to be influenced by their friends when it comes to trends," said Marshal Cohen, chief industry analyst, The NPD Group, Inc. "Teenagers also care 20 percent more than the average adult shopper about brands, most likely due to peer pressure." Even though shopping for brand names is more important to teenagers than it is to the average shopper, teens still search for bargains while relying on adult income and approval of purchase. "This generation of teens has grown up in a tough economic climate, so they appreciate value," said Cohen. "With a sluggish teen job market, teens depend more than usual on their parents to buy the products they want." Results indicate that brand-savvy teens find more labels they desire for less at off-price retailers and outlets than at department stores and specialty retailers. If given the choice to purchase a technology or fashion item, technology will make the sale with this group (NPD, 2012).

The preceding content points to a shifting consumer psychology as indicated by environmental conditions. For more than a century, it has been known that marketers can shape consumers' patterns of reasoning.

An 1884 editorial in Scientific American discussed "the curious processes of reasoning" that women used in deciding to buy a sewing machine on an installment plan. The author discovered the "psychological fact, possibly new," that women "will rather pay $50 for a machine in monthly installments of five dollars rather than $25 outright, although able to do so" (Munn & Beach, 1884).

Thus, knowing how environments shape economic reasoning affect potential for financially literature consumer to resist efforts influence their surroundings. In 1925, Viner lamented that

> Human behavior, in general, and presumably, therefore, also in the market place, is not under the constant and detailed guidance of careful and accurate hedonic calculations, but

is the product of an unstable and unrational complex of reflex actions, impulses, instincts, habits, customs, fashions and hysteria. (pp. 373–374)

Viner's view certainly seemed to bemoan the lack of predictability and instability in human actions in and out of the marketplace. Thus, try as we may, the human population cannot escape its membership in the animal kingdom.

John Maynard Keynes (1936) used the term "animal spirit."

Most, probably, of our decisions to do something positive, the full consequences of which will be drawn out over many days to come, can only be taken as the result of animal spirits—a spontaneous urge to action rather than inaction, and not as the outcome of a weighted average of quantitative benefits multiplied by quantitative probabilities. (pp. 161–162)

In the late 1940s, Nobel Prize winner Simon created the term "bounded rationality" which provided the modern starting point for behavioral economics as a field within traditional economics. This became the start of what can be labeled as an interdisciplinary approach to economics—melding and utilizing psychology, sociology, and economics. This broadening of perspective rejects simplistic rational modeling of economic agents as a sole indicator of economic measure and embraces Simon's "bounded rationality" (1947).

For Simon, economists are primarily social scientists and as thus must be prepared to name the key attributes of human actors (Simon, 1985, p. 303). "Behavioral economics is the name we give to the research enterprise that seeks to meet these needs," states Simon (1986, p. xvi).

Louis Uchitelle of the New York Times (2001) wrote, "In the histories of Economics still to be written, the Spring of 1994 will almost certainly be flagged as momentous. Behavioral economics had finally arrived" (p. 1).

During that "momentous" spring, Uchitelle notes that the Department of Economics at Harvard University had decided to hire a behavioral economist (i.e., David Laibson), whose Ph.D. dissertation "drew as much on psychology and quirky behavior as on standard economics." Other doctoral programs at other leading universities soon followed with graduate-level behavioral economics offerings.

CURRENT STATUS OF BEHAVIORAL ECONOMICS: A BOOM IN POPULARITY

Clearly economists have considered the human aspect of economic decision-making and the role of the unstable human decision maker worthy of study for centuries. But this human element is given short shrift in high school texts or omitted completely. Yet certainly the topic itself is compelling, well documented and researched; most importantly to the students of today, it is germane to daily decisions in an era of rapid-fire information and consumer overload.

Behavioral economics is seeing a popular interest as it becomes more mainstream and accessible to the general public. Works like Ariely's readable and friendly book "Predictably Irrational" (2008) has ignited public awareness and interest. Game theorist Herbert Gintis (University of Massachusetts, Amherst) sums it up well:

> Disciplinary boundaries in the behavioral sciences were set up many decades ago and do not reflect contemporary insights into the nature human sociality. We behavioral game theorists have simply followed questions concerning human behavior and strategic interaction wherever they take us in terms of disciplinary specialties. Rather than being "muscling in" or "imperialism," our demeanor is a rather exemplary exercise of the scientific method. Moreover, we are just as insistent on bringing ideas from psychology, sociology, and the other social sciences into economics, as we are to use economic theory to enrich psychology, sociology, anthropology, and the other behavior disciplines. (2011, p. 1)

Behavioral economics is becoming a widespread area of study in economics as well as in the wider behavioral science. There have been special issues published by international scholarly journals indicating a growing interest between disciplines. In 2013, the journal *Health Psychology* published an issue on the intersection between health psychology and behavioral economics, while the *Review of Income and Wealth* published a special issue in 2014 on poverty, development, and behavioral economics (Samson, 2015).

WHY TEACH TEENAGERS ABOUT THE DECISION-MAKING ASPECTS OF BEHAVIORAL ECONOMICS?

High school teachers would argue that the motivation of adolescents is a central problem. The question of "Why do I need to know this?" is often heard from teenagers who live in what behavioral economists labeled "present-biased preferences" in that they value immediate rewards more highly than future payoffs. Lavecchia Liu, and Oreopoulos (2014) point out that this bias changes over time, but it is particularly strong in younger years peaking in adolescence. This inability to see past current realities when making decisions may have drastic and dramatic long-term effects.

Frankly, behavioral economics is essentially acknowledging the fact that all humans of all ages make poor decisions. Certainly we can assert this is true in daily decision-making but considering the factors influencing a decision could also have serious long-term life consequences.

An important but depressing study by Keeney (2008) explored the impact of bad decision-making on our lives and deaths. Keeney estimated that about half of all deaths among adults 15–64 years old in the United States are caused or aided by bad personal decisions, particularly those relating to smoking, not exercising, criminality, drug and alcohol use, and unsafe sexual behavior.

Using Centers for Disease Control and Prevention data, Kenney carefully defined the decision itself as well as how it was linked to premature death. For instance, if someone died after being broadsided by a drunk driver, it was not considered premature because the deceased did not make the decision that led to their death. However, if the drunk driver died then it was considered as a premature death because the decision to drive drunk, and dying as a result, are clearly connected. Certainly there are a variety of instances where multiple decision paths are available (the drunk driver also has the option to take a cab, ride with a designated driver, or call a friend), and where these other decision paths are not chosen despite the fact that they are less likely to result in the same negative outcome (i.e., fatality). These results suggest that more effort directed toward improving personal choices regarding life risks may be an effective and economical way to save lives (2008).

WHAT DO TEACHERS NEED TO KNOW OR CONSIDER ...

Adding topics to an already rigorous content is a daunting challenge. It takes time to learn a new topic and feel comfortable with sharing it with students. The aspect of behavioral economics that is appealing and, I suggest applicable to people of all ages, is that decision-making without regard to age is often affected by the same somewhat predictable behavioral patterns. I suggest you begin with some very basic patterns and terms of the field and apply them first to your own decisions.

Think first about your own personally most regretted economic or personal decision and a decision that was significantly positive in outcome as well. What were the circumstances in place at the time that influenced you? How can we help students understand the "behind the curtain" of their economic and personal decisions?

BUILDING ON SEMINAL RESEARCH: "BOUNDED RATIONALITY"

According to Simon (1947), the limited attentional capability of humans results in their bounded capacity to be rational. Many of our decisions are not fully thought through and we can only be rational within the limits of time and cognitive capability. Herbert Simon indicated that there were two major causes of bounded rationality: Limitations of the human mind—general cognitive ability and the structures within which the mind operates—time, place, habit, culture, situation, etc. In other words, people often make decisions in less than optimal conditions with less than complete information. We are very much influenced by perceptions and passions in our decision-making. Slovic, Peters, Finucane, and MacGregor (2005) studied the role of affect in decision-making—how does the emotional state affect risk behaviors and often the decisions we make. The current affective and conative status of the person making the decision is an important aspect of choice and decision; thus the emotional state of the individual can be a determining factor particularly when stress burdens the decision landscape.

While considering the impact of the affective state of the individual in the process, behavioral economists have researched and enumerated repeated patterns of behavior that affect personal decisions. The following is a list of patterns to consider as we teach students to understand and analyze the Why of their personal and economic decisions.

Tunneling: Intense focus with loss of more comprehensive perspectives

Research documents how worry and distraction—what Mullainathan and Shafir (2013) refer to as "tunneling"—cause intense focus on decisions made in a crisis mode ultimately, affect our ability to make good decisions. You may well ignore tasks or issues that appear less urgent because of your single-minded focus on another goal/problem. Basically, this growing body of research illustrates that when people are in a situation where they are so focused on one outcome and do not have or take the time to consider a wider perspective, they are not smart decision makers. This selective inattention was dramatically and humorously illustrated by Simon and Chabris's gorilla experiment in 1999. This experiment asked the subjects to watch a game of basketball and count passes between players wearing white jerseys. As subjects focused on the action on the court, a gorilla walked through the scene quite clearly. Half the viewers never saw the gorilla despite the fact that it clearly walks centrally through the action on the court. Iterations of this experiment are readily available on YouTube.

ANTS: Automatic negative thoughts—"That will never work." "I always make that mistake."

These are automatic negative thoughts that paralyze actions, both social and economic, in our lives. It is often the failure to believe that there is a positive outcome that stops actions. "I could never save enough to go to college." ANTS stop further investigation and risk but also diminish future rewards.

TTWWADI: That is the way we have always done it

TTWADI is otherwise known as status quo bias and default power. Status quo bias is evident when people prefer things to stay the same by doing nothing or by sticking with a decision made previously; individuals have a strong tendency to remain at the status quo, because the disadvantages of leaving it loom larger than advantages (Samuelson & Zeckhauser, 1988). This is probably evident already in your spending if despite new information, you consistently stay with the same products. This is typical in automobile purchasing—labeled owner "loyalty."

Ease: "Just not worth hassling about"

This is what is labeled "fluency bias." People have a tendency to do what is easiest for them and heavily rely on past experiences to make choices, often without considering new data.

Consider the Amazon website. When you purchase something on Amazon, prior to final checkout you are often asked if, based on this purchase, would you like to buy another product as well. The additional product may be by the same manufacturer or have some likenesses to what you have already decided to purchase. Amazon offers this because clearly you have established a preference and the likelihood that you will demonstrate fluency bias and purchase more of a similar product is high.

Novemsky, Dhar, Schwarz, and Simonson (2007) manipulated the fluency of a product by listing its features in either an easy or hard to read font. Easy to read fonts doubled the number of people willing to purchase the product. People want to repeat a comfortable pattern of behavior or choose the easiest way possible at times; whether or not this is the "best" choice is the question.

Self-serving Bias: Good for me or not my fault

This is known as the self-serving bias—the tendency to attribute positive outcomes to our internal, or personal factors, and negative outcomes to situational, or external factors allowing us to maintain a positive self-concept. If the decision turns out well, we are pleased and take credit. If the decision turns out poorly, it is the fault of outside influences not our personal failings. We tend to avoid blame for poor decisions by blaming others or outside influences. Stewart (2005) researched how people placed blame after a traffic accident. Subjects demonstrated the overwhelming tendency to blame factors such as inclement weather, road conditions, vehicle malfunctions, or other drivers for the accident despite factual evidence that many of the accidents were caused mainly by their own behaviors—alcohol, fatigue, poor judgment, or simple bad driving. This behavior is also labeled and researched as the "Myth of Merit"—the "I deserve this" or "It is not my fault because …" (Grantham, 2013).

Emotional Reaction: Just makes me feel better …

People often consume goods to appease their emotional needs. Atalay and Meloy (2011) found that 62% of consumers admitted that they purchase goods to cheer themselves up and another 28% purchased goods as a form of celebration. There is an uptick in emotional purchasing at times of life stressors—marriage, divorce, having a child. Psychologists assert that this purchasing wise or unwise serves to at least temporarily relieve anxiety or feel more in control of a changing situation (Atalay & Meloy, 2011).

Scarcity: Filling an immediate need

Scarcity is a driving force in human behavior. Scarcity is demanding of attention—this attention is both intentional and automatic. We most often consider scarcity when a basic need is unmet—such as hunger. Mullainathan and Shafir (2013) offer many examples of how scarcity changes thinking and decisions. One example cited is the rapidity of word recognition based on the thirst. Thirsty subjects read the word **Water** faster than they read Water when not thirsty. Identical results occurred when very hungry subjects were asked to read the word **Cake** (p. 9). When we have an intense physical or emotional need, we react differently and more rapidly to fill that need. An example for most of us is considering how much more you spend at a grocery store when you walk in hungry.

THERE ARE NO NEUTRAL DECISIONS

Behavioral economics is an interesting topic that crosses into the social sciences in a personal and useful manner. It is intriguing to have the tools, really the labels—to consider personal economic decisions and analyze the behaviors, the situation and context, and the influence of personal habits and culture.

Possibly the lesson that behavioral economics can best interest and inform an adolescent student is that there is no neutral decision. Every decision, be it economic or otherwise, impacts others. All of us affect one another by our actions; when we act as a group, those actions can send the price of shoes soaring or bring down a society.

Economics is personal. The economic decisions of youth are significant not simply due to what their spending does for the larger economy, but rather because those decision processes become learned and habitual. Learning to consider the patterns or rationale behind those decisions at an early age may yield powerful behavioral change with significant life outcomes.

Additionally, it is important to know that these behavioral patterns are not confined to any one socioeconomic group or age—we are all influenced by these behavioral economic patterns. The difference in decision impacts most often has to do with the safety net of family or available assistance. People who live in poverty are dramatically affected by scarcity and typically have little wealth or few family resources on which to rely in times of distress. It might help us understand why people in economic distress act in ways that we deem or judge as inappropriate due to their circumstances; those same actions are regarded as commonplace in higher income families. An example would be a family in poverty purchasing costly and popular gym shoes for their children; many of us judge this purchase as improper ignoring the cultural forces that drive the action.

Where to begin? Certainly some of the authors and works in the text above will be helpful. It may be best for teachers to begin by visiting the website https://www.behavioraleconomics.com/introduction-to-be/

One valuable book resource is *Teaching for Democracy in an Age of Economic Disparity* (2016) edited by Maley and Davis. Certainly the Ted Ariely and Karen Armstrong TED talks (https://www.ted.com/) are a valuable introduction into the basic concepts of the field as well as how to understand the decisions of others by acknowledging our human commonalities in a compassionate, nonjudgmental manner.

Motivating students to appreciate and understand the complexities and the human daily connections to traditional economics is difficult—certainly in my experience. The addition of the personal and more immediately relevant topic of behavioral economics may assist students to why individual decisions matter. As we consider the need to teach students to be more reflective and inquisitive about not only about their experiences as economic and personal decision makers, but also about decision makers in our world, it may lead to a more compassionate understanding of others. As Armstrong wrote in her book *Twelve Steps to a Compassionate Life*, "As we seek to create a more compassionate world, we too must think outside the box, reconsider the major categories of our time, and find new ways of dealing with today's challenges" (2011, p. 66).

This awakening to behavioral economics may help to create a pathway to a meaningful study of traditional economics as well as a personal awareness of our shared behaviors and humanity.

DISCUSSION QUESTIONS

1. Reread Cooter's background information that concerns the history leading to the establishment of the term Behavioral Economics. To what extent may this summary support the notion that people are rational dependent animals (MacIntyre, 1999)?
2. Think of the poor financial decisions that you made. To what extent were they habitual? Impulsive? Are you responsible for your choices or should you blame someone else? What is the basis for your justification?
3. Think of five adverse situations that you face. How might the expected outcomes differ from if you addressed them in a positive light?

4. Cooter states that it is difficult to engage students in the appreciation of microsystems and their complexities. Yet politicians and economists are two groups of professionals that recognize the microsystems that comprise a society. What ways of motivating student learning about this topic can you think of?
5. This chapter concerns the economic learning needs of secondary education. To what extent, if any, is personal economics a topic of learning importance for elementary and middle level environments? Justify your response.

REFERENCES

Anderson, J., & Rainie, L. (2012). *Main findings: Teens, technology, and human potential in 2020*. Retrieved from http://www.pewinternet.org/2012/02/29/main findings-teens-technology-and-human-potential-in-2020/

Ariely, D. (2008). *Predictably irrational: The hidden forces that shape our decisions*. New York, NY: Harper.

Armstrong, K. (2011). *Twelve steps to a compassionate life*. New York, NY: Knopf.

Atalay, A. S., & Meloy, M. G. (2011). Retail therapy: A strategic effort to improve mood. *Psychology of Marketing, 28*, 638–659. doi:10.1002/mar.20404

Cardell, N. S., Fort, R., Joerding, W., Inaba, F., Lamoureaux, D., Rosenman, R., ... Bartlett, R. (1996). Laboratory-based experimental and demonstration initiatives in teaching undergraduate economics. *American Economic Review, 86*(2), 454–459.

Council for Economic Education. (2016). *Survey of the states*. Retrieved from http://councilforeconed.org/policy-and-advocacy/survey-of-the-states/

Geller, J. (2015). Move over millennials. Gen Z is the new audience. *Boston Globe*, September 1, 2015. Retrieved from https://www.bostonglobe.com/business/2015/08/31/brands-turn-attention-towards-gen/wV99rNryDEEEhd06UjioFN/story.html

Gintis, H. (2011). Reply to Binmore: Social Norms or Social Preferences? Retrieved from http://www.umass.edu/preferen/gintis/ReplyToBinmore.pdf

Grantham, D. G. (2013). The myth of merit. *Behavioral Healthcare, 33*(6), 4.

Hampton Roads Marketing. (2015). *Buying power and influence of teenagers*. Retrieved August 11, 2016 from http://www.hamptonroadsmarketingnow.com/blog/buying-power-

Jabbar, H. (2011). The behavioral economics of education: New directions for research. *Educational Researcher, 40*(9), 446–453.

Keeney, R. (1982). Decision analysis: An overview. *Operations Research, 30*(5), 803–838.

Keynes, J. M. (1936). *The general theory of employment, interest and money*. London: Macmillan Cambridge University Press.

Kowalska, M. (2012). The internet impact on market behavior of young consumers. *Journal of International Studies, 5*(1), 101–106.

Lavecchia, A. M., Liu, H., & Oreopoulos, P. (2014). *Behavioral economics of education: Progress and possibilities*. NBER Working Paper 20609. Retrieved from http://www.nber.org/papers/w20609

MacIntyre, A. (1999). *Dependent rational animals*. Peru, IL: Open Court Publishing.

Mullainathan, S., & Shafir, E. (2013). *Scarcity: Why having too little means so much*. Times Books. New York, NY: Henry Holt & Company, LLC.

Munn, O. D., & Beach, A. B. (Eds.). (1884, August). Anomalies of the sewing machine business. *Scientific American, 51*(6), 80.

Novemsky, N., Dhar, R., Schwarz, N., & Simonson, I. (2007). Preference fluency in choice. *Journal of Marketing Research, 44*(3), 347–356. doi:10.1509/jmkr.44.3.347

NPD Group, Inc. (2012). *The NPD Group reports teen credit word-of-mouth most reliable shopping source.* Retrieved from https://www.npd.com/wps/portal/npd/us/news/press-releases/pr_120813b/

Samson, A. (Ed.). (2015). *The behavioral economics guide 2015*. Retrieved from http://www.behavioraleconomics.com

Samuelson, W., & Zeckhauser, R. (1988). Status quo bias in decision making. *Journal of Risk and Uncertainty, 1*(1), 7–59. doi:10.1007/BF00055564

Schug, M., Lopus, J., Morton, J., Reinke, R., Wentworth, D., & Western, R. (2003). Is economics your worst nightmare? *Social Education, 67*(2), 73–78.

Simon, H. (1947). Administrative behavior: A behavioral model of rational choice. *Quarterly Journal of Economics, 9*, 99–118.

Simon, H. (1978). Rationality as process and as product of thought. *American Economic Review, 68*(1), 1–16.

Simon, H. (1985). Human nature in politics: A dialogue of psychology with political science. *American Political Science Review, 79*, 293–304.

Simon, H. (1986). Preface. In B. Gilad & S. Kaish (Eds.), *Handbook of behavioral economics* (pp. xvii–xxii). London: JAI Press.

Simons, D. J., & Chabris, C. F. (1999), Gorillas in our midst: Sustained inattentional blindness for dynamic events. *Perception, 28*, 1059–1074.

Slovic, P., Peters, E., Finucane, M. L., & MacGregor, D. G. (2005). Affect, risk, and decision making. *Health Psychology, 24*(4 Suppl), S35–S40. doi:10.1037/0278-6133.24.4.S35

Stewart, A. E. (2005). Attributions of responsibility for motor vehicle crashes. *Accident Analysis & Prevention, 37*, 681–688.

Uchitelle, L. (2001, February 11). Personal decisions are the leading cause of death. *New York Times*, Section 3, p. 1.

Viner, J. (1925). The utility concept in value theory and its critics. *Journal of Political Economy, 33*, 369–387.

Contributors

Carmela Aprea is Full Professor and Head of the Chair of Business and Economics Education at the Friedrich Schiller University Jena (Germany). She holds a Diploma Degree in Business and Economics Education from the Goethe University Frankfurt (Germany) and a PhD in the same field from the University of Mannheim (Germany).

Chiara Bacigalupa is a Professor in the Department of Early Childhood Studies at Sonoma State University.

Andrew Brantlinger is an Associate Professor in the College of Education at the University of Maryland.

Mary E. Brenner is a Professor in the Department of Education at the University of California, Santa Barbara.

Jaime Christensen is Director of Academics at Spectrum Charter School, Pleasant Grove, Utah.

J. Michael Collins is Faculty Director of the Center for Financial Security at the University of Wisconsin, Madison. He is an Associate Professor at the La Follette School of Public Affairs and at the School of Human Ecology. He is also a family economics specialist for UW-Extension, Cooperative Extension, and an affiliate of the Institute for Research on Poverty and Center for Demography and Ecology. Collins studies consumer decision-making in the financial marketplace, including the role of public policy in influencing credit, savings, and investment choices. His work includes the study of financial capability with a focus on low-income families. He is involved in studies of household finance and well-being supported by leading foundations and federal agencies. In 2015, Palgrave Macmillan released a book Collins edited called *A Fragile Balance: Emergency Savings and Liquid Resources for Low-Income Consumers.*

Kathleen S. Cooter is Professor of Early Childhood/Special Education, Bellarmine University, Louisville, Kentucky.

Bettina Greimel-Fuhrmann (née Greimel) is a Professor of Business Education at Vienna University of Economics and Business (Wirtschaftsuniversität Wien, short WU), and Head of the Institute for Business Education as well as of the academic program Social Skills at WU. Her main areas of research are economic education with special emphasis on financial education, the development of skills and educational quality. Her work is dedicated to promoting economic literacy, mainly by educating her students to become effective business teachers who have acquired the competencies of planning, implementing, and reflecting teaching and learning processes in both educational and business contexts. She is also co-editor and author of textbooks of business studies that are used at business colleges and schools all over Austria. She is coordinator of various research projects on economic literacy as well as financial literacy. She is co-editor of the recently published International Handbook of Financial Literacy (2016, Springer) and represents WU as an affiliate member of the OECD International Network on Financial Education (INFE) and therefore established contacts with educational initiatives in financial education all over the world.

Jeffrey M. Hawkins is Associate Professor—Social Studies Education in the Department of Curriculum and Instruction, University of Wisconsin, Milwaukee.

Mary Beth Henning is the Co-Director of the Northern Illinois University Center for Economic Education and an Associate Professor of Social Studies Education in the Department of Literacy and Elementary Education at Northern Illinois University. Her research interests focus on K–12 social studies education and studying elementary teacher education. She currently serves as the Vice President for the Illinois Council for Social Studies and was on the writing team for the 2016 Illinois Social Science Learning Standards.

Sarah Johnston-Rodriguez is an Associate Professor of Special Education in the Department of Special and Early Education at Northern Illinois University. Currently, her research addresses transition from school to adulthood for students with disabilities, specifically focusing on career planning and self-determination for at-risk adolescents from culturally diverse backgrounds.

She is a founding and current board member of the Illinois Chapter of APSE (Association for Persons Supporting Employment First).

Floor E. Knoote has managed multiple international research projects around youth economic development as well as on peace-building in Latin America, Europe, and Africa, and has supported national authorities in evidence-based policy development and evaluation. She has co-founded Dimes, which supports institutions in developing programs and policies in social and economic inclusion. She holds a BSc in Youth Forensic Psychology, an MA in International Relations, and an MSc in International Criminology.

Darrell P. Kruger is Provost and Executive Vice Chancellor at Appalachian State University, Boone, North Carolina.

James D. Laney is Professor and Chair of Teacher Education and Administration, University of North Texas, Denton, Texas.

Thomas A. Lucey is a Professor of Elementary Education at Illinois State University, Normal, Illinois.

Anand R. Marri is an Associate Professor of Social Studies and Education at Teachers College, Columbia University. He also serves as vice president and Head of Outreach & Education at the Federal Reserve Bank of New York. A former high school social studies teacher, his research focuses on economics education, civic education, multicultural education, and teacher education. He is principal investigator for *Understanding Fiscal Responsibility* and *Loot, Inc.*, which aim to improve the economic literacy of K–12 students. In addition to authoring several book chapters, his work has appeared in journals such as *Action in Teacher Education, Journal of Social Studies Research, Multicultural Perspectives, New Educator, Social Education, Social Science Docket, Political Science Quarterly, The Social Studies, Theory & Research in Social Education, Teacher Education & Practice, Teachers College Record, Urban Education,* and *Urban Review*. He has also contributed articles to *CNN* and the *New York Times*. He serves on the editorial board of several leading journals.

Bonnie T. Meszaros is Assistant Professor of Economics and Associate Director of the Center for Economic Education and Entrepreneurship at the University of Delaware. She holds a BA in history from Ohio Wesleyan University, an MA in social studies education, and a PhD in curriculum from the University of Delaware. She is a past president of the National Association of Economic Educators and recipient of its Bessie B. Moore Service Award, John C. Schramm Leadership Award, Patricia Elder International Award, and James B. O'Neill Multiplier Award. She was project director and served on the writing committee for the Voluntary National Content Standards in Economics, was a member of the writing team for the National Standards for Financial Literacy, and has authored and co-authored numerous economic and personal finance curricula, journal articles, and book chapters.

Elizabeth Odders-White is the Kuechenmeister Bascom Associate Professor in Business and Senior Associate Dean for academic programs at the Wisconsin School of Business at the University of Wisconsin–Madison. She is also an affiliate of the UW-Madison Center for Financial Security. Her long-standing interest in financial capability among youth has grown to become the primary focus of her research. Odders-White holds a PhD in finance from Northwestern University, as well as a bachelor of science in applied mathematics and a bachelor of fine arts in vocal performance, both from Tulane University.

Nilton Porto is Assistant Professor of Personal Finance in the Department of Human Development and Family Studies at the University of Rhode Island. Prior to returning to academia, he spent over a decade in various management positions in the banking industry after obtaining an MBA in finance from Case Western Reserve University. His research applies behavioral economics tools to personal finance and consumer behavior issues. He is a board member of the Rhode Island Jump$tart Financial Coalition for Personal Finance Literacy. He received his PhD in household economics from the University of Wisconsin–Madison.

Annie Savard is an Associate Professor in Mathematics Education in the Department of Integrated Studies in Education at McGill University. Her research interests concern the contribution of mathematics in primary school to the development of citizenship skills such as decision-making and critical thinking in relation to financial literacy, according to an ethnomathematics perspective. Her interests include the conceptual field of probabilities in the teaching and learning of mathematics, inquiry-based learning, as well as the use of robotics for the development of scientific and mathematical skills in a multidisciplinary context. She studied professional development of teachers in initial training and through professional learning communities. She is a member of the Center for the Study of Learning and Performance (CSLP/CEAP). She taught 15 years in elementary school and she is an international consultant in Mathematics Education. For more information, visit anniesavard.com.

Julia Schultheis holds a master's degree in Business and Economics Education from the Friedrich Schiller University Jena (Germany). In her master thesis she conducted a comprehensive literature review on how lay people represent the economic and financial crisis. She is a graduate research assistant and PhD student at the Chair of Business and Economics Education of the Friedrich Schiller University Jena (Germany).

Debbie Sonu is an Associate Professor at Hunter College and doctoral faculty in the Urban Education Program at the Graduate Center, City University of New York. Her research interests include curriculum theory and practice as it relates to urban schooling and social justice pedagogies in the United States. Her work has been published in *Curriculum Inquiry, Journal of Teacher Education,* and the *Journal of Curriculum Theorizing,* among others. She is the co-author of *Education for the Nation?: Teaching and Learning Within and Across Nations in a Global Age* (Palgrave Macmillan, 2015) and co-editor of *Pedagogical Matters: New Materialisms and Curriculum Studies* (Peter Lang, 2016). Currently, she is studying the perspectives of youth and children as they engage difficult knowledge, violence, and injustice.

Kathleen Stolle is an undergraduate student research assistant at the Chair of Business and Economics Education of the Friedrich Schiller University Jena (Germany).

Mary C. Suiter is Assistant Vice President at the Federal Reserve Bank of St. Louis, where she is responsible for the St. Louis Fed's economic and personal finance education outreach. Dr. Suiter received her BS in economics from the University of Missouri–St. Louis, her MS in economic education from the University of Delaware, and her PhD in Teaching and Learning from the University of Missouri–St. Louis. She served on the writing committees for the Voluntary National Content Standards in Economics and the National Standards for Financial Literacy, and has authored and co-authored numerous social studies and personal finance curricula, journal articles, and book chapters. She served as president of the National Association of Economic Educators and has received its Bessie B. Moore Service Award, Patricia K. Elder International Award, and Technology Award. In 2013, she received the University of Delaware Alfred Lerner College of Business and Economics Alumni Association Award of Excellence.

Sofia L. Ortega Tineo has worked hand in hand with financial regulatory authorities, diverse ministries, and financial institutions in building policies to increase financial access and improve levels of financial capability across Latin America and the Caribbean. She holds a BA in International Studies, an MA in Tourism and Sustainable Development, and an MSc in International Development. She is a co-founder of Dimes.